NorthStar 4

READING & WRITING

FOURTH EDITION

Authors	ANDREW K. ENGLISH
	LAURA MONAHON ENGLISH
Series Editors	FRANCES BOYD
	CAROL NUMRICH

Dedication

To my lovely wife, Laura, without whose
support and guidance none of this would
have been possible.

Andrew K. English

NorthStar: Reading & Writing Level 4, Fourth Edition

Copyright © 2015, 2009, 2004, 1998 by Pearson Education, Inc.
All rights reserved.

No part of this publication may be reproduced, stored in a retrieval system, or transmitted in any
form or by any means, electronic, mechanical, photocopying, recording, or otherwise, without the
prior permission of the publisher.

Pearson Education, 10 Bank Street, White Plains, NY 10606

Staff credits: The people who made up the **NorthStar: Reading & Writing Level 4, Fourth Edition** team,
  representing editorial, production, design, and manufacturing, are Kimberly Casey, Tracey Cataldo,
  Rosa Chapinal, Aerin Csigay, Mindy DePalma, Dave Dickey, Nancy Flaggman, Niki Lee, François Leffler,
  Amy McCormick, Mary Perrotta Rich, Robert Ruvo, Christopher Siley, and Debbie Sistino.

Text composition: ElectraGraphics, Inc.
Editorial: Lakeview Editing Services, LLC

Library of Congress Cataloging-in-Publication Data

Haugnes, Natasha, 1965–
  Northstar 2 : Reading and writing / Authors: Natasha Haugnes, Beth Maher. — Fourth Edition.
     pages cm
  ISBN-13: 978-0-13-338216-7 (Level 2) – ISBN 978-0-13-294039-9 (Level 3) – ISBN 978-0-13-338223-5
(Level 4) – ISBN 978-0-13-338224-2 (Level 5)
1. English language—Textbooks for foreign speakers. 2. Reading comprehension—Problems,
exercises, etc. 3. Report writing—Problems, exercises, etc. I. Maher, Beth, 1965- II. Title. III.
Title: Northstar two. IV. Title: Reading and writing.
  PE1128.H394 2015
  428.2'4—dc23

                                                                                    2013050584

Printed in the United States of America

ISBN 10: 0-13-338223-0
ISBN 13: 978-0-13-338223-5

3 4 5 6 7 8 9 10—V057—20 19 18 17 16 15

ISBN 10: 0-13-404977-2 (International Edition)
ISBN 13: 978-0-13-404977-9 (International Edition)

1 2 3 4 5 6 7 8 9 10—V057—20 19 18 17 16 15 14

CONTENTS

WELCOME TO

NORTHSTAR

A BLENDED-LEARNING COURSE FOR THE 21ST CENTURY

Building on the success of previous editions, *NorthStar* continues to engage and motivate students through new and updated contemporary, authentic topics in a seamless integration of print and online content. Students will achieve their academic as well as language and personal goals in order to meet the challenges of the 21st century.

New for the FOURTH EDITION

★ Fully Blended MyEnglishLab

NorthStar aims to prepare students for academic success and digital literacy with its fully blended online lab. The innovative new MyEnglishLab: *NorthStar* gives learners immediate feedback—anytime, anywhere—as they complete auto-graded language activities online.

★ NEW and UPDATED THEMES

Current and thought-provoking topics presented in a variety of genres promote intellectual stimulation. The authentic content engages students, links them to language use outside of the classroom, and encourages personal expression and critical thinking.

★ EXPLICIT SKILL INSTRUCTION and PRACTICE

Language skills are highlighted in each unit, providing students with systematic and multiple exposures to language forms and structures in a variety of contexts. Concise presentations and targeted practice in print and online prepare students for academic success.

★ LEARNING OUTCOMES and ASSESSMENT

A variety of assessment tools, including online diagnostic, formative and summative assessments, and a flexible gradebook, aligned with clearly identified unit learning outcomes, allow teachers to individualize instruction and track student progress.

THE NORTHSTAR APPROACH TO CRITICAL THINKING

What is critical thinking?

Most textbooks include interesting questions for students to discuss and tasks for students to engage in to develop language skills. Often these questions and tasks are labeled critical thinking. Look at this question as an example:

When you buy fruits and vegetables, do you usually look for the cheapest price? Explain.

The question may inspire a lively discussion with students exploring a variety of viewpoints—but it doesn't necessarily develop critical thinking. Now look at another example:

When people in your neighborhood buy fruits and vegetables, what factors are the most important: the price, the freshness, locally grown, organic (without chemicals)? Make a prediction and explain. How can you find out if your prediction is correct? This question does develop critical thinking. It asks students to make predictions, formulate a hypothesis, and draw a conclusion—all higher-level critical thinking skills. Critical thinking, as philosophers and psychologists suggest, is a sharpening and a broadening of the mind. A critical thinker engages in true problem solving, connects information in novel ways, and challenges assumptions. A critical thinker is a skillful, responsible thinker who is open-minded and has the ability to evaluate information based on evidence. Ultimately, through this process of critical thinking, students are better able to decide what to think, what to say, or what to do.

How do we teach critical thinking?

It is not enough to teach "about" critical thinking. Teaching the theory of critical thinking will not produce critical thinkers. Additionally, it is not enough to simply expose students to good examples of critical thinking without explanation or explicit practice and hope our students will learn by imitation.

Students need to engage in specially designed exercises that aim to improve critical thinking skills. This approach practices skills both implicitly and explicitly and is embedded in thought-provoking content. Some strategies include:

- subject matter that is carefully selected and exploited so that students learn new concepts and encounter new perspectives.
- students identifying their own assumptions about the world and later challenging them.
- activities that are designed in a way that students answer questions and complete language-learning tasks that may not have black-and-white answers. (Finding THE answer is often less valuable than the process by which answers are derived.)
- activities that engage students in logical thinking, where they support their reasoning and resolve differences with their peers.

Infused throughout each unit of each book, *NorthStar* uses the principles and strategies outlined above, including:

- Make Inferences: inference comprehension questions in every unit
- Vocabulary and Comprehension: categorization activities
- Vocabulary and Synthesize: relationship analyses (analogies); comparisons (Venn diagrams)
- Synthesize: synthesis of information from two texts teaches a "multiplicity" approach rather than a "duality" approach to learning; ideas that seem to be in opposition on the surface may actually intersect and reinforce each other
- Focus on the Topic and Preview: identifying assumptions, recognizing attitudes and values, and then re-evaluating them
- Focus on Writing/Speaking: reasoning and argumentation
- Unit Project: judgment; choosing factual, unbiased information for research projects
- Focus on Writing/Speaking and Express Opinions: decision making; proposing solutions

THE NORTHSTAR UNIT

1 FOCUS ON THE TOPIC

*CT Each unit begins with a photo that draws students into the topic. Focus questions motivate students and encourage them to make personal connections. Students make inferences about and predict the content of the unit.

UNIT 1

GENIUS: NATURE OR Nurture?

1 FOCUS ON THE TOPIC

1. Why are some people geniuses and others are not? Does the environment a person is raised in (nurture) create a genius, or is it because the person was simply born that way (nature)? Which part do you think each of these plays in being a genius?

2. What is one special talent or ability that you have? When did you first become aware of it? Did it come naturally, or did you have to practice a long time to perfect it? Explain. (You may instead answer these questions about someone you know who has a talent or

MyEnglishLab

CT A short self-assessment based on each unit's learning outcomes helps students check what they know and allows teachers to target instruction.

Home | Help | Test student, reallylongname@emailaddress.com | Sign out

NORTHSTAR 4 READING & WRITING

1 Unit 1

Check What You Know

Look at the list of skills. You may already know how to do some of these. Don't worry if you don't know how to do some or all of these skills. You will learn and practice them in Unit 1.
Check the skills that you already know. Put an X by the number.

Vocabulary

1. Infer word meaning from context
2. Recognize word roots to create and use related nouns, verbs, adjectives, and adverbs

Reading

3. Identify the main idea of each paragraph in a reading
4. Identify and categorize details and examples
5. Scan a text to locate specific information
6. Infer a writer's assumptions
7. Distinguish voice in quotations

Writing

8. Identify and write the topic sentence and controlling idea of a summary paragraph
9. Write a summary paragraph

Vocabulary
1.
2.
Reading
3.
4.
5.
6.
7.
Writing
8.
9.
10.
11.
12.
Grammar
13.

*indicates Critical Thinking

Two contrasting, thought-provoking readings, from a variety of authentic genres, stimulate students intellectually.

A GENIUS EXPLAINS
By Richard Johnson
The Guardian

1   Daniel Tammet is talking. As he talks, he studies my shirt and counts the stitches. Ever since the age of three, when he suffered an epileptic fit, Tammet has been obsessed with counting. Now he is 26, and a mathematical genius who can figure out cube roots quicker than a calculator and recall pi to 22,514 decimal places. He also happens to be autistic, which is why he can't drive a car, wire a plug, or tell right from left. He lives with extraordinary ability and disability.

2   Tammet is calculating 377 multiplied by 795. Actually, he isn't "calculating": there is nothing conscious about w[...] the answer instan[...] has been able to s[...] and textures. The [...] a motion, and five [...] I multiply numbe[...] The **image** starts [...] a third shape em[...]

3   Tammet is a "**savant**," an individual with an astonishing, extraordinary mental ability. An **estimated** 10% of the autistic population—and an estimated 1% of the non-autistic population—have savant abilities, but no one knows exactly why.

4   Scans of the brains of autistic savants suggest that the right hemisphere might be **compensating** for damage in the left hemisphere. While many savants struggle with language and comprehension (skills associated primarily with the left hemisphere), they often have amazing skills in mathematics and memory (primarily right hemisphere skills). Typically, savants have a limited vocabulary, but there is nothing limited about Tammet's vocabulary.

5   Tammet is creating his own language[...]

CT Students predict content, verify their predictions, and follow up with a variety of tasks that ensure comprehension.

4. He remembers being given a Ladybird book called *Counting* when he was four. When I looked at the numbers, I 'saw' images. It felt like a place I could go where I really belonged. *(paragraph 14)*

············ GO TO MyEnglishLab *FOR MORE SKILL PRACTICE.*

CONNECT THE READINGS

STEP 1: Organize

Reading One (R1) and Reading Two (R2) both talk about genius. A Venn diagram can show where the ideas about genius are found. Read the statements in the box. Write the number of the statement in the correct part of the diagram. Include the paragraph number where the information is found.

1. "Genius" may be the result of brain chemistry.	2. A person can be a genius and also be disabled.	3. People at the top (experts) work harder than other people.
4. Genius = talent + hard work.	5. "Genius" is being studied by scientists.	6. Expertise requires a lot of practice.
7. Special talents can also cause problems.		

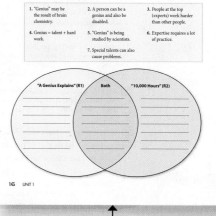

"A Genius Explains" (R1)   Both   "10,000 Hours" (R2)

16   UNIT 1

10,000 HOURS TO MASTERY
by **Harvey Mackay**

1   For years, I have preached the importance of hard work, determination, **persistence**, and practice—that perfect practice—as key ingredients of success. A nifty new book seems to support my theory.

2   Malcolm Gladwell has written a fascinating study, *Outliers: The Story of Success* (Little, Brown & Co.), which should make a lot of people feel much better about not achieving instant success. In fact, he says it takes about 10 years, or 10,000 hours, of practice to attain true **expertise**.

3   "The people at the very top don't just work harder or even much harder than everyone else," Gladwell writes. "They work much, much harder." Achievement, he says, is talent plus preparation. Preparation seems to play a bigger role.

4   For example, he describes the Beatles: They had been together seven years before their famous arrival in America. They spent a lot of time playing in strip clubs in Hamburg, Germany, sometimes for as long as eight hours a night. Overnight sensation? Not exactly. Estimates are the band performed 1,200 times before their big success in 1964. By comparison, most bands don't perform 1,200 times in their careers.

The Beatles

5   Neurologist Daniel Levitin has studied the formula for success extensively and shares this finding: "The **emerging** picture from such studies is that 10,000 hours of practice is required to achieve the level of mastery associated with being a world-

CT Students are challenged to take what they have learned and organize, integrate, and synthesize the information in a meaningful way.

MyEnglishLab
Home | Help | Test student, reallylongname@emailaddress.com | Sign out
NORTHSTAR 4   READING & WRITING

1   Unit 1

Vocabulary Practice

Match each vocabulary item with its definition. Click on the items to make a match.

Compensate	To keep facts in your memory.
Retain	The total when you add two or more numbers together.
Estimate	A genius, or very intelligent in one or more areas.
Flexible	Very worried about something, or showing you are very worried.
Predictable	Able to change easily.
Disabled	To judge the value or size of something.
Anxious	Unable to use a part of your mind/body in a way that others can.
Interaction	A picture that you have in your mind.
Image	
Benefit	The money or other advantages that you get from something such as insurance or the government, or as part of your job.
Savant	
Sum	

MyEnglishLab

Auto-graded vocabulary practice activities reinforce meaning and pronunciation.

EXPLICIT SKILL INSTRUCTION AND PRACTICE

CT Step-by-step instructions and practice guide students to exercise critical thinking and to dig deeper by asking questions that move beyond the literal meaning of the text.

MAKE INFERENCES

UNDERSTANDING ASSUMPTIONS

An inference is an educated guess about something that is not directly stated. In "A Genius Explains," there are quotes from Daniel Tammet and Kim Peek that show what others might assume about the two men's disabilities. What assumptions can you infer from these quotations?

Look at the example and read the explanation.

Daniel (*paragraph 6*): "I just wanted to show people that disability needn't get in the way."

People think that <u>someone with a disability cannot do as much as someone without a disability</u>.

When other people realized that Daniel had a disability, they assumed that he would have problems in other areas of his life. By showing people that he could achieve remarkable things, even though he was "technically disabled," he wanted to show that their assumptions were wrong. His disability wasn't going to hold him back.

Work with a partner. Read the following quotes from Daniel and Kim. What assumptions do the quotes show that people have made about them? Complete the sentences.

1. Daniel (*paragraph 18*): "It was also the first time I was introduced as 'Daniel' rather than 'the guy who can do weird stuff in his head.'"

   Others didn't think that Daniel was _____

   _____: "You don't have to be handicapped to be different—everybody's

   _____

   _____

   9): "It sounds silly, but numbers are my friends."

   bly think that numbers _____

   _____

   9): "It isn't only an intellectual or aloof thing that I do. I really feel
   tional attachment, a caring for numbers."

   bly assume that Daniel's relationship to numbers _____

   _____

   ): " I like to do things in my own time and in my own style, so an
   nd bureaucracy just wouldn't work."

   expect Daniel to _____

DISTINGUISHING VOICE IN QUOTATIONS

Distinguishing voice is an important reading skill as it can sometimes be confusing whether we are reading the author's words or someone else's words. One indication of a change in voice is quotation marks. Another indication is a change in pronouns, for example, from third person (*he, she,* or *they*) to first person (*I* or *we*). In order to fully comprehend the text, you need to notice when a shift in voice takes place to know who is speaking.

Authors often shift the voice in their writing by using quoted speech. Quotations can:

- add first-hand validity to a point the author has made.
- provide details or examples of what the author has been talking about.
- continue the story in another voice for added interest.

In paragraph 3 of Reading Two, Mackay includes two quotations from Gladwell's book. This adds validity to what Mackay says, as the words are Gladwell's. In paragraph 5, the author includes an extended quotation from Daniel Levitin. This quotation gives several details and examples of how much time it takes for true mastery to occur.

2 Read the following excerpts from Reading One. All double quotation marks have been removed. Underline the sections where the voice changes from the author's to someone else's. Add quotation marks where necessary. Then discuss the following questions with a partner:

- How do you know where the change in voice occurs?
- Who is speaking where you added quotation marks?
- Why might the author have chosen to use quotations in the examples?

1. To [Tammet], pi isn't an abstract set of digits; it's a visual story, a film projected in front of his eyes. He learnt the number forwards and backwards and, last year, spent five hours recalling it in front of an adjudicator. He wanted to prove a point. I memorised pi to 22,514 decimal places, and I am technically disabled. I just wanted to show people that disability needn't get in the way. (*paragraph 6*)

2. [Tammet] lives on the Kent coast, but never goes near the beach—there are too many pebbles to count. The thought of a mathematical problem with no solution makes him feel uncomfortable. Trips to the supermarket are always a chore. There's too much mental stimulus. I have to look at every shape and texture. Every price, and every arrangement of fruit and vegetables. So instead of thin... week?', I'm just really uncomfortable. (*paragraph 7*)

3. Peek was shy and introspective, but he sat and held Ta... so much—our love of key dates from history, for instan...

Explicit skill presentation and practice lead to student mastery and success in an academic environment.

MyEnglishLab

Key reading skills are reinforced and practiced in new contexts. Meaningful and instant feedback provide students and teachers with essential information to monitor progress.

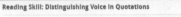

Home | Help | Test student, reallylongname@emailaddress.com | Sign out

MyEnglishLab   NORTHSTAR 4 READING & WRITING

1   Unit 1

Reading Skill: Distinguishing Voice in Quotations

Read the news article below about savant Stephen Wiltshire. The quotations are missing. Put the numbers corresponding to the quotations where they belong to add validity, to provide details or examples, or to continue the story in another voice for interest.

1. "I'm going to live in New York [some day]. I've designed my penthouse on Park Avenue."
2. "He is possibly the best child artist in Britain."
3. "These drawings testify to an assured draughtsmanship and an ability to convey complex perspective with consummate ease. But more importantly, they reveal his mysterious creative ability to capture the sensibility of a building and that which determines its character and its voice. It is this genius which sets him apart and confers upon him the status of artist. For a child who was once locked within the prison house of his own private world, unable to speak, incapable of responding to others, this thrilling development of language, laughter and art is a miracle."
4. "I noticed early on that Stephen wasn't speaking other than random sounds. At the playground he would sit in the dirt while the other toddlers ran around."
5. "Young Stephen was an exceptional drawer even at 5 years old. He was able to accurately sketch animals, cars and architectural drawings of imaginary cityscapes."

3 FOCUS ON WRITING

Productive vocabulary targeted in the unit is reviewed, expanded upon, and used creatively in this section and in the final writing task. Grammar structures useful for the final writing task are presented and practiced. A concise grammar skills box serves as an excellent reference.

STEP 2: Synthesize

Work with a partner. Imagine that one of you is Daniel Tammet and the other is Malcolm Gladwell. On a separate piece of paper, write three questions that you would like to ask each other. Use information from Step 1. Exchange your questions with your partner and write answers.

················· GO TO MyEnglishLab TO CHECK WHAT YOU LEARNED.

3 FOCUS ON WRITING

VOCABULARY

REVIEW

Complete the word scramble puzzle. By rearranging the letters, you will be able to form vocabulary words used in the unit. Use the circled letter from each word to find the bonus word.

1. e a i t c t r n o n i	i n t e r a c t i o n	Communication or collaboration
2. l i a a m s i t s i e	_ _ _ _ _ _ _ _ _ _	This is what takes the brain so long to do, according to Dr. Levitin.
3. v a n t a s	_ _ _ _ _	A person with extraordinary mental skills might be this.
4. f r o a m t r n s	_ _ _ _ _ _ _ _	To change
5. e p i r d b t e a l c	_ _ _ _ _ _ _ _ _ _	Because of his need for structure, Daniel Tammet's life is this.
6. p e i e e x s t r	_ _ _ _ _ _ _ _	What you may acquire after thousands of hours of practice
7. f n i t b e o	_ _ _ _ _ _	An advantage
8. n m z i e g g e	_ _ _ _ _ _ _ _	Starting to appear
9. u n x a o i s	_ _ _ _ _ _ _	Nervous or eager
10. m p n o e s a t e c	_ _ _ _ _ _ _ _ _ _	To make up for a weakness
11. b l d s i e d a	_ _ _ _ _ _ _ _	Unable to perform certain activities

Bonus Word (This is the quality you might need to have to complete this puzzle!)

_ _ _ _ _ _ _ _ _ _

Genius: Nature or Nurture? 17

GRAMMAR

1 Read the sentences based on the two readings. Look at the boldfaced verbs. Notice how they change the meaning of the underlined verbs that follow them. What added information do they provide?

a. Malcolm Gladwell has written a fascinating study, *Outliers: The Story of Success,* which **should** make a lot of people feel much better about not achieving instant success.

b. Scans of the brains of autistic savants suggest that the right hemisphere **might** compensate for damage in the left hemisphere.

c. For instance, Tammet **has to** drink his cups of tea at exactly the same time every day.

1. In sentence *a,* does **should** indicate advice or does it express likelihood?

2. In sentence *b,* does **might** indicate speculation or a conclusion?

3. In sentence *c,* does **has to** indicate a conclusion or necessity?

Modals and semi-modals are auxiliary ("helping") verbs. They are always followed by the base form of the verb.

MODALS AND SEMI-MODALS:
ADVICE, LIKELIHOOD, NECESSITY, SPECULATION, AND CONCLUSIONS

Advice: *should, ought to,* and *had better*

SUBJECT	MODAL	VERB (BASE FORM)	THE REST OF THE SENTENCE
You	should (not)	practice	10 hours a day.
	ought (not) to*		
	had better		

Likelihood: *should* and *ought to*

SUBJECT	MODAL	VERB (BASE FORM)	THE REST OF THE SENTENCE
Gladwell	should (not)	explain	his theory.
	ought (not) to		

Ought to, like *have (got) to,* is considered a semi-modal because the word *to* is placed between it and the verb that it is modifying. *Had better* is also considered a semi-modal because it is two words. The meanings of these semi-modals are similar to their modal counterparts except that *had better* often implies a threat. "You had better listen to me (or else you are going to have a problem)." When asking a question, speakers generally use *should* instead of *ought to* or *had better.*

(continued on next page)

Genius: Nature or Nurture? 21

MyEnglishLab

Auto-graded vocabulary and grammar practice activities with feedback reinforce meaning, form, and function.

MyEnglishLab

Home | Help | Test student, reallylongname@emailaddress.com | Sign out

NORTHSTAR 4 READING & WRITING

1 Unit 1

Vocabulary Review 2

Look at the bolded word in each sentence. What part of speech is it? Drag the sentences to the categories.

It is amazing how much information we have to **retain** in this class.

Some immigrant groups have **assimilated** better to life in the United States than ot

He **persistently** denies his involvement in the crime.

The **estimated** number of savants is the world is probably far below the actual num

The **sum** of that is 24. She **expertly** prepares the holiday meal. You would think she w

Robert is very **predictable**. You know exactly what he is going to do next.

This class requires a lot of **interaction** between the students.

Nouns

MyEnglishLab

Home | Help | Test student, reallylongname@emailaddress.com | Sign out

NORTHSTAR 4 READING & WRITING

1 Unit 1

Grammar 1: Modals and Semi-Modals

Choose the best modal or semi-modal to complete the sentence.

1 We [ ] study if we want to do well on the exam.

2 She [ ] be really exhausted after working a 14-hour day.

3 Marta and Sam [ ] complete this assignment by Thursday. If not, they will get a zero.

4 Savants [ ] have difficulties interacting with large groups because they are often shy.

5 If everything goes fine, we [ ] be finished with this chapter next week.

A TASK-BASED APPROACH TO PROCESS WRITING

FINAL WRITING TASK

In this unit, you read about different geniuses and how they achieved their expertise.

You are going to **write a summary paragraph about a current or past genius. Be sure to include why this person is considered a genius and how he or she achieved expertise.** Use the vocabulary and grammar from the unit.*

PREPARE TO WRITE: Group Brainstorming

Group brainstorming is a good way to get ideas for writing. In brainstorming, you think of as many ideas as you can. Don't think about whether the ideas are good or bad; just write down all ideas.

1 Work with a small group. Brainstorm a list of geniuses, past or present, that you know about. The person can be from any time period or culture. Don't stop to discuss the genius. Just concentrate on thinking of as many examples as possible.

Geniuses

1. _____   6. _____
2. _____   7. _____
3. _____   8. _____
4. _____   9. _____
5. _____   10. _____

2 Individually, choose one genius that you find interesting and want to write about. Research this person to find information about his or her life and achievements. Be sure to include why this person is considered a genius and how he or she achieved expertise. Take notes about what you find out. Make sure the notes are in your own words and not copied word-for-word.

_____
* For Alternative Writing Topics, see page 33. These topics can be used in place of the writing topic for this unit or as homework. The alternative topics relate to the theme of the unit but may not target the same grammar or rhetorical structures taught in the unit.

Genius: Nature or Nurture? 25

CT A final writing task gives students an opportunity to integrate ideas, vocabulary, and grammar presented in the unit.

---

1 Examine the paragraph and discuss the questions with the class.

Autistic savants have specific abilities or skills, but they are not without certain limitations in other areas of life. An autistic savant is a person with an unusual ability, skill, or knowledge that is much more developed than that of an average person. In fact, many savants have highly developed mathematical skills. Others are able to retain large amounts of information in their memory. For example, some autistic savants can recite entire dictionaries or telephone books word for word. Still others are able to draw detailed maps of an area after flying over it once in a helicopter. Despite the fact that the autistic savant has these specific abilities or skills, he or she may have difficulties with other types of mental or physical tasks and social interactions. For instance, some savants may have trouble doing simple tasks, such as tying their shoes or driving a car. Additionally, an autistic savant may have problems talking to people or even making eye contact. So, despite their advanced skills and abilities in certain areas, savants may encounter difficulty with seemingly simple tasks.

1. What is the topic of this paragraph?
   _____

2. The first sentence is the topic sentence. What two ideas are presented in this sentence?
   _____
   _____

3. How does the content of the rest of the paragraph relate to the topic sentence?
   _____
   _____

Genius: Nature or Nurture? 27

CT Students organize their ideas for writing using a particular structural or rhetorical pattern.

Home | Help | Test student, reallylongname@emailaddress.com | Sign out

MyEnglishLab   NORTHSTAR 4 READING & WRITING

1 Unit 1

Writing Skill: Topic Sentences and Controlling Ideas

Choose the best correction of the fragmented sentence.

1 Because many Savants have extraordinary skills.
   ○ Because many Savants have extraordinary skills they achieve success.
   ○ Because many Savants have extraordinary skills, they achieve success.
   ○ They achieve success because have extraordinary skills.

2 She was preparing for the exam they visited.
   ○ She was preparing for the exam when they visited.
   ○ When she was preparing for the exam they visited.
   ○ She was preparing for the exam and they visited.

3 The day before the big competition they practicing for five hours.
   ○ The day before the big competition, they practicing for five hours.
   ○ When the day before the big competition they practicing for five hours.
   ○ The day before the big competition, they practiced for five hours.

4 After Malcom Gladwell's book was published it became a number one best seller.
   ○ After Malcom Gladwell's book was published, it became a number one best seller.
   ○ Malcom Gladwell's book was published after it became a number one best seller.
   ○ After, Malcom Gladwell's book was published it became a number one best seller.

MyEnglishLab

Key writing skills and strategies are reinforced and practiced in new contexts. Immediate feedback allows students and teachers to monitor progress and identify areas that need improvement.

---

separated twins had developed in a remarkably similar manner. Nevertheless, the reasons for this may also have to do with environment (nurture). They may have been raised by different families, yet the environments may have been quite similar.

3. Malcolm Gladwell wrote another book, *Outliers: The Story of Success*. It was published in 2008 and was number one on the *New York Times* bestseller list for eleven straight weeks. It followed *Tipping Point*, which was published in 2000. *Tipping Point* addresses the individual's ability to change society. This non-fiction bestseller was followed by *Blink* in 2005. *Blink* is about thinking. Why are some people able to make brilliant decisions in the blink of an eye while others seem to always make the wrong decision? *Blink* also was a non-fiction bestseller.

4 Now write the first draft of your summary paragraph. Use the information from Prepare to Write and complete the organizer below to plan your paragraph (use a separate piece of paper). Make sure you have a clear topic sentence and content that supports it. The topic sentence should introduce the genius that you are going to write about and include a controlling idea. Be sure to use grammar and vocabulary from the unit.

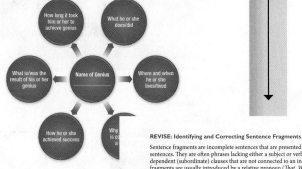

How long it took him or her to achieve genius

What he or she does/did

What is/was the result of his or her genius

Name of Genius

Where and when he or she lives/lived

How he or she achieved success

Why is c...
a...

EDIT: Writing the Final Draft

Go to MyEnglishLab and write the final draft of your paragraph. Carefully edit it for grammatical and mechanical errors, such as spelling, capitalization, and punctuation. Make sure you use some of the grammar and vocabulary from the unit. Use the checklist to help you write your final draft. Then submit your paragraph to your teacher.

FINAL DRAFT CHECKLIST

❑ Does the paragraph fully describe why the person is considered a genius and how he or she achieved expertise?

❑ Is there a topic sentence with a controlling idea that introduces the genius?

❑ Is the paragraph free of sentence fragments?

❑ Did you use modals and semi-modals correctly?

❑ Have you used the vocabulary from the unit?

UNIT PROJECT

Work with a partner to research an autistic savant. Take notes and write a report based on your findings. Follow these steps:

STEP 1: Choose one of these autistic savants:

Leslie Lemke, music	**Gregory Blackstock**, music, language
Henriett Seth-F, music, painting, literature	**Jedediah Buxton**, mathematical calculations
Stephen Wiltshire, accurate detailed drawings	**Ellen Bourdeaux**, music, "human clock"
Kim Peek, the real "Rain Man," calendar calculations, memory	Any other autistic savant based on your own research
Alonzo Clemons, sculptor	

STEP 2: Do research on the Internet about the person you chose. Answer the questions:

• When and where did/does the person live?

al abilities?

acquire these abilities?

isabilities? If so, what are they?

REVISE: Identifying and Correcting Sentence Fragments

Sentence fragments are incomplete sentences that are presented as if they were complete sentences. They are often phrases lacking either a subject or verb. Other fragments may be dependent (subordinate) clauses that are not connected to an independent clause. These fragments are usually introduced by a relative pronoun (*That, Who, Which, Whom,* etc. . . .) or a subordinating conjunction (*After, Although, Because, Since, When,* etc. . . .).

1 Work with a partner. Identify whether each item is **F** (a fragment) or **C** (a complete sentence).

_____ 1. Although autistic savants have many extraordinary skills and abilities.

_____ 2. Gladwell has written an interesting book. Which emphasizes the importance of hard work in achieving success.

_____ 3. Before Daniel received his counting book when he was four years old.

_____ 4. Before he had an epileptic seizure, there was no evidence that Daniel had extraordinary math abilities.

_____ 5. Because Dr. Levitin says that at least 10,000 hours of practice are needed to achieve success.

_____ 6. The book that Kim Peek was reading the day before he met Daniel Tammet at the library in Salt Lake City.

_____ 7. Practicing as much as ten hours a day before the math competition.

_____ 8. Einstein was voted the "Person of the 20th Century" by *Time* magazine after he received the Nobel Prize for Physics.

There are a variety of strategies for correcting sentence fragments.

• Connect the fragment to the sentence before or after it.

• Change the punctuation.

• Add a verb.

• Add more information and rewrite it as a complete sentence.

• Remove the subordinating conjunction or relative pronoun.

2 Work with a partner. Go back to Exercise 1. Using one of the strategies listed above, correct each item you identified as a sentence fragment. Use a separate piece of paper.

3 Look at the first draft of your summary paragraph. Make sure it does not include any sentence fragments.

GO TO MyEnglishLab FOR MORE SKILL PRACTICE.

With instant access to a wide range of online content and diagnostic tools, teachers can customize learning environments to meet the needs of every student.

USING MyEnglishLab,
NORTHSTAR TEACHERS CAN:

Deliver rich online content to engage and motivate students, including:

- student audio to support listening and speaking skills.
- engaging, authentic video clips, including reports adapted from ABC, NBC, and CBS newscasts, tied to the unit themes.
- opportunities for written and recorded reactions to be submitted by students.

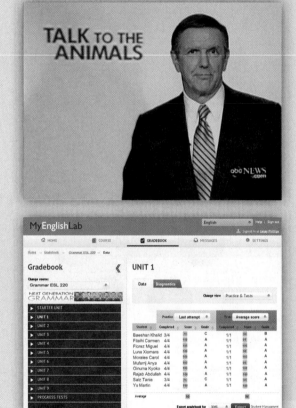

Use a powerful selection of diagnostic reports to:

- view student scores by unit, skill, and activity.
- monitor student progress on any activity or test as often as needed.
- analyze class data to determine steps for remediation and support.

Use Teacher Resource eText* to access:

- a digital copy of the student book for whole-class instruction.
- downloadable achievement and placement tests.
- printable resources including lesson planners, videoscripts, and video activities.
- classroom audio.
- unit teaching notes and answer keys.

---

* Teacher Resource eText is accessible through MyEnglishLab: *NorthStar*.

COMPONENTS PRINT or eTEXT

STUDENT BOOK and
MyEnglishLab

★ Student Book with MyEnglishLab

The two strands, Reading & Writing and Listening & Speaking, for each of the five levels, provide a fully blended approach with the seamless integration of print and online content. Students use MyEnglishLab to access additional practice online, view videos, listen to audio selections, and receive instant feedback on their work.

eTEXT and
MyEnglishLab

★ eText with MyEnglishLab

Offering maximum flexibility for different learning styles and needs, a digital version of the student book can be used on iPad® and Android® devices.

★ Instructor Access: Teacher Resource eText and MyEnglishLab (Reading & Writing 1–5)

Teacher Resource eText

Each level and strand of *NorthStar* has an accompanying Teacher Resource eText that includes: a digital student book, unit teaching notes, answer keys, downloadable achievement tests, classroom audio, lesson planners, video activities, videoscripts, and a downloadable placement test.

MyEnglishLab

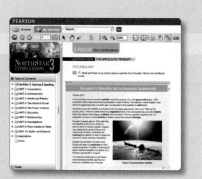

Teachers assign MyEnglishLab activities to reinforce the skills students learn in class and monitor progress through an online gradebook. The automatically-graded exercises in MyEnglishLab *NorthStar* support and build on academic skills and vocabulary presented and practiced in the Student Book/eText. The teacher-graded activities include pronunciation, speaking, and writing, and are assigned by the instructor.

★ Classroom Audio CD

The Listening & Speaking audio contains the recordings and activities as well as audio for the achievement tests. The Reading & Writing strand contains the readings on audio

SCOPE AND SEQUENCE

UNIT OUTCOMES	1 PRODIGIES **GENIUS: NATURE OR NURTURE?** pages 2–33 *Reading 1: A Genius Explains* *Reading 2: 10,000 Hours to mastery*	2 OVERCOMING OBSTACLES **FACING LIFE'S OBSTACLES** pages 34–61 *Reading 1: The Education of Frank McCourt* *Reading 2: Marla Runyan*
READING	• Make and confirm predictions • Identify the main idea of each paragraph in a reading • Identify and categorize details and examples • Scan a text to locate specific information • Distinguish voice in quotations **MyEnglishLab** Vocabulary and Reading Skill Practice	• Make and confirm predictions • Identify the main ideas in a reading • Construct chronology from a reading • Identify different types of supporting details • Scan a text to locate specific information • Recognize the use of synonyms and antonyms to reinforce word meaning **MyEnglishLab** Vocabulary and Reading Skill Practice
WRITING	• Identify and write the topic sentence and controlling idea of a summary paragraph • Distinguish between sentence fragments and complete sentences • Use strategies to correct sentence fragments • Edit and revise writing for content, language, and conventions **Task:** Write a summary paragraph **MyEnglishLab** Writing Skill Practice and Writing Task	• Write a comparison paragraph • Identify and write topic sentences, supporting sentences, and a concluding sentence in a paragraph • Recognize inappropriate supporting ideas within a text • Edit and revise writing for content, language, and conventions **Task:** Write a biographical paragraph **MyEnglishLab** Writing Skill Practice and Writing Task
INFERENCE	• Infer the writer's assumptions	• Infer the meaning of idioms and expressions from context
VOCABULARY	• Infer word meaning from context • Recognize and use word forms (nouns, verbs, adjectives, and adverbs) **MyEnglishLab** Vocabulary Practice	• Infer word meaning from context • Identify synonyms • Classify words • Analyze relationships between words **MyEnglishLab** Vocabulary Practice
GRAMMAR	• Identify and categorize a range of modal and semi-modal verbs **MyEnglishLab** Grammar Practice	• Recognize and use gerunds and infinitives **MyEnglishLab** Grammar Practice
VIDEO	**MyEnglishLab** *Small Wonders*, ABC News, Video Activity	**MyEnglishLab** *A Child's Voice*, ABC News, Video Activity
ASSESSMENTS	**MyEnglishLab** Check What You Know, Checkpoints 1 and 2, Unit 1 Achievement Test	**MyEnglishLab** Check What You Know, Checkpoints 1 and 2, Unit 2 Achievement Test

3 MEDICINE
MAKING MEDICAL DECISIONS
pages 62–89

Reading 1: Genetic Testing and Disease: Would you want to know?
Reading 2: Norman Cousins's Laughter Therapy

4 ANIMAL INTELLIGENCE
INSTINCT OR INTELLECT?
pages 90–121

Reading 1: Extreme Perception and Animal Intelligence
Reading 2: How smart are animals?

• Make and confirm predictions • Demonstrate understanding of and use a timeline to sequence events • Identify and categorize the main ideas in a reading • Identify different types of supporting details • Scan a text to locate specific information MyEnglishLab Vocabulary and Reading Skill Practice	• Make and confirm predictions • Identify the main ideas in a reading • Identify different types of supporting details • Scan a text to locate specific information • Recognize the role of quoted speech MyEnglishLab Vocabulary and Reading Skill Practice
• Organize ideas using a tree map and other organizers • Identify the introduction, body, and conclusion of an opinion essay • Identify the parts of an effective introduction • Write a comparison-and-contrast paragraph • Edit and revise writing for content, language, and conventions **Task:** Write an opinion essay MyEnglishLab Writing Skill Practice and Writing Task	• Organize ideas using *Wh-* questions • Summarize sources and data • Paraphrase details from text • Edit and revise writing for content, language, and conventions **Task:** Write a summary in journalistic style MyEnglishLab Writing Skill Practice and Writing Task
• Infer the degree of support	• Infer writer's meaning and identify hedging language
• Infer word meaning from context • Analyze relationships between words (similar and different meanings) MyEnglishLab Vocabulary Practice	• Infer word meaning from context • Identify synonyms • Analyze relationships between words (similar and different meanings) • Recognize Latin and Greek word roots MyEnglishLab Vocabulary Practice
• Recognize and use past unreal conditionals MyEnglishLab Grammar Practice	• Recognize and use identifying adjective clauses MyEnglishLab Grammar Practice
MyEnglishLab *A Sleep Clinic,* Video Activity	MyEnglishLab *Talk to the Animals,* ABC News, Video Activity
MyEnglishLab Check What You Know, Checkpoints 1 and 2, Unit 3 Achievement Test	MyEnglishLab Check What You Know, Checkpoints 1 and 2, Unit 4 Achievement Test

SCOPE AND SEQUENCE

UNIT OUTCOMES	5 LONGEVITY **TOO MUCH OF A GOOD THING?** pages 122–153 *Reading 1: Death Do Us Part* *Reading 2: Toward Immortality: The Social Burden of Longer Lives*	6 GENEROSITY **MAKING A DIFFERENCE** pages 154–187 *Reading 1: Justin Lebo* *Reading 2: Some Take the Time Gladly and Problems with Mandatory Volunteering*
READING	• Make and confirm predictions • Identify the main ideas in a reading • Identify different types of supporting details • Scan a text to locate specific information • Analyze titles and headings to improve comprehension MyEnglishLab Vocabulary and Reading Skill Practice	• Make and confirm predictions • Identify the main ideas in a reading • Identify different types of supporting details, examples and reasons • Scan a text to locate specific information • Recognize persuasive language MyEnglishLab Vocabulary and Reading Skill Practice
WRITING	• Organize ideas using a cause-and-effect diagram • Use an idea web to relate different topics to a central theme • Recognize and use figurative language to add depth to writing • Write an opinion paragraph • Edit and revise writing for content, language, and conventions **Task:** Write a descriptive essay MyEnglishLab Writing Skill Practice and Writing Task	• Organize ideas for an argument using a chart • Identify and organize positions, arguments, and counterarguments • Identify and write effective introductions, thesis statements, and conclusions • Write an opinion letter supported with examples from a text • Edit and revise writing for content, language, and conventions **Task:** Write a persuasive essay MyEnglishLab Writing Skill Practice and Writing Task
INFERENCE	• Infer characters' attitudes and feelings	• Infer the meaning of people's reactions
VOCABULARY	• Infer word meaning from context • Recognize connotations and implied meanings • Recognize and use common adjective suffixes MyEnglishLab Vocabulary Practice	• Infer word meaning from context • Analyze relationships between words (similar and different meanings) • Recognize and use word forms (nouns, verbs, adjectives, and adverbs) • Infer meaning of phrasal verbs MyEnglishLab Vocabulary Practice
GRAMMAR	• Distinguish between and use the simple past, present perfect, and present perfect continuous verb tenses MyEnglishLab Grammar Practice	• Recognize and use concessions to support an opinion while recognizing counterarguments MyEnglishLab Grammar Practice
VIDEO	MyEnglishLab *Living Longer*, ABC News, Video Activity	MyEnglishLab *Local Teen Awarded for Making Difference*, NBC News, Video Activity
ASSESSMENTS	MyEnglishLab Check What You Know, Checkpoints 1 and 2, Unit 5 Achievement Test	MyEnglishLab Check What You Know, Checkpoints 1 and 2, Unit 6 Achievement Test

7 EDUCATION
THE EMPTY CLASSROOM
pages 188–223

Reading 1: Teaching to the World from Central New Jersey
Reading 2: The Fun They Had

8 TECHNOLOGY
MANAGING YOUR SMARTPHONE
pages 224–259

Reading 1: Addicted to Your Smartphone? Here's What to Do
Reading 2: Unplugging Wired Kids: A Vacation from Technology and Social Media

7 EDUCATION	8 TECHNOLOGY
• Make and confirm predictions • Identify the main ideas in a reading • Identify different types of supporting details • Scan a text to locate specific information • Follow chronological sequence of a timeline • Recognize the speaker in direct speech MyEnglishLab Vocabulary and Reading Skill Practice	• Make and confirm predictions • Identify the main ideas in a reading • Identify different types of supporting details • Scan a text to locate specific information • Identify referents for the pronoun *it* • Identify and categorize problems and solutions from a text MyEnglishLab Vocabulary and Reading Skill Practice
• Organize ideas using a chart • Recognize various types of organization in a comparison-and-contrast essay • Identify and use subordinators and transitions to introduce points of comparison or contrast • Edit and revise writing for content, language, and conventions **Task:** Write a comparison-and-contrast essay MyEnglishLab Writing Skill Practice and Writing Task	• Write summary statements • Organize ideas using a flowchart • Use subordinators, prepositional phrases, and transitions to clearly signal cause-and-effect relationships • Edit and revise writing for content, language, and conventions **Task:** Write a cause-and-effect essay MyEnglishLab Writing Skill Practice and Writing Task
• Infer the writer's degree of concern about the topic	• Infer meaning of writer's appeal to authority with experts' quotes
• Infer word meaning from context • Recognize and use word forms (nouns, verbs, adjectives, and adverbs) MyEnglishLab Vocabulary Practice	• Infer word meaning from context • Understand implied meaning and degrees of intensity MyEnglishLab Vocabulary Practice
• Distinguish between and use direct and indirect speech MyEnglishLab Grammar Practice	• Recognize and use common phrasal verbs MyEnglishLab Grammar Practice
MyEnglishLab *Homework Holiday,* ABC News, Video Activity	MyEnglishLab *Kids and Video Games,* NBC News, Video Activity
MyEnglishLab Check What You Know, Checkpoints 1 and 2, Unit 7 Achievement Test	MyEnglishLab Check What You Know, Checkpoints 1 and 2, Unit 8 Achievement Test

ACKNOWLEDGMENTS

We would like to express our gratitude to the entire *NorthStar* team of authors, editors, and assistants. Special thanks go to Carol Numrich for her vision and especially her ideas and guidance. We are, as always, honored to work with her. Thanks also to Kathleen Smith for her unending support, ideas, and attention to detail. In addition, thanks to Massimo Rubini for his timely help researching articles. Lastly, kudos to Debbie Sistino for all her hard work and support bringing this fourth edition to fruition.

—Andrew K. English and
Laura Monahon English

REVIEWERS

Chris Antonellis, Boston University – CELOP; Gail August, Hostos; Aegina Barnes, York College; Kim Bayer, Hunter College; Mine Bellikli, Atilim University; Allison Blechman, Embassy CES; Paul Blomquist, Kaplan; Helena Botros, FLS; James Branchick, FLS; Chris Bruffee, Embassy CES; Nese Cakli, Duzce University; María Cordani Tourinho Dantas, Colégio Rainha De Paz; Jason Davis, ASC English; Lindsay Donigan, Fullerton College; Bina Dugan, BCCC; Sibel Ece Izmir, Atilim University; Érica Ferrer, Universidad del Norte; María Irma Gallegos Peláez, Universidad del Valle de México; Jeff Gano, ASA College; Juan Garcia, FLS; María Genovev a Chávez Bazán, Universidad del Valle de México; Heidi Gramlich, The New England School of English; Phillip Grayson, Kaplan; Rebecca Gross, The New England School of English; Rick Guadiana, FLS; Sebnem Guzel, Tobb University; Esra Hatipoglu, Ufuk University; Brian Henry, FLS; Josephine Horna, BCCC; Arthur Hui, Fullerton College; Zoe Isaacson, Hunter College; Kathy Johnson, Fullerton College; Marcelo Juica, Urban College of Boston; Tom Justice, North Shore Community College; Lisa Karakas, Berkeley College; Eva Kopernacki, Embassy CES; Drew Larimore, Kaplan; Heidi Lieb, BCCC; Patricia Martins, Ibeu; Cecilia Mora Espejo, Universidad del Valle de México; Kate Nyhan, The New England School of English; Julie Oni, FLS; Willard Osman, The New England School of English; Olga Pagieva, ASA College; Manish Patel, FLS; Paige Poole, Universidad del Norte; Claudia Rebello, Ibeu; Lourdes Rey, Universidad del Norte; Michelle Reynolds, FLS International Boston Commons; Mary Ritter, NYU; Minerva Santos, Hostos; Sezer Sarioz, Saint Benoit PLS; Ebru Sinar, Tobb University; Beth Soll, NYU (Columbia); Christopher Stobart, Universidad del Norte; Guliz Uludag, Ufuk University; Debra Un, NYU; Hilal Unlusu, Saint Benoit PLS; María del Carmen Viruega Trejo, Universidad del Valle de México; Reda Vural, Atilim University; Douglas Waters, Universidad del Norte; Leyla Yucklik, Duzce University; Jorge Zepeda Porras, Universidad del Valle de México

GENIUS: NATURE OR Nurture?

1. Why are some people geniuses and others are not? Does the environment a person is raised in (nurture) create a genius, or is it because the person was simply born that way (nature)? Which part do you think each of these plays in being a genius?

2. What is one special talent or ability that you have? When did you first become aware of it? Did it come naturally, or did you have to practice a long time to perfect it? Explain. (You may instead answer these questions about someone you know who has a talent or ability.)

GO TO MyEnglishLab *TO CHECK WHAT YOU KNOW.*

VOCABULARY

1 Read the short piece about Daniel Tammet, who is considered by many to be a genius. Being a genius does not mean that all aspects of your life are easy or even that you are good at everything. Daniel is very good at some things but challenged by others. Pay attention to the boldfaced words. Try to understand them from the context.

Autism and autistic spectrum disorder (ASD) are names given to groups of complex developmental disorders involving the brain. Some of the symptoms of these disorders are problems with verbal and non-verbal social **interaction**, the display of repetitive behavior, and an inability to be **flexible**. Many people with ASD **compensate** for these problems and are able to be high functioning and lead "normal" lives; others are more **disabled** by the disorder.

ASD is an umbrella term that includes many subcategories. One of these subcategories is autistic **savants**. Psychologists **estimate** that 10 percent of people with ASD have some savant abilities. An autistic savant is a person with an unusual ability, skill, or knowledge that is much more developed than that of an average person. Many savants are able to **retain** large amounts of information in their memory. For example, some autistic savants can recite entire dictionaries or telephone books word for word. Others are able to draw detailed maps of an area after flying over it once in a helicopter. Although the autistic savant has these specific abilities or skills, he or she may have difficulty with other types of mental or physical tasks.

Daniel Tammet is an autistic savant. Like many people with ASD, he **benefits** from leading a **predictable** life. In other words, he has fewer problems if his life has structure and routine. If it does not, he may become **anxious**. One of Daniel's special abilities is in mathematics; he is able to almost immediately solve complex multiplication problems. When he does this, he sees each number he is multiplying as an **image**. These images transform into a third image, which is the **sum**.

Why autistic savants have these special abilities is a question that still has no definitive answer.

2 Complete the sentences with the words in the boxes.

compensate	estimate	retain

1. No one is sure of the exact number of autistic savants there are in the world, but experts _____ that there are fewer than 100.

2. Studies indicate that one hemisphere of a savant's brain may _____ for damage to the other hemisphere.

3. It is amazing how much information a small USB drive can _____.

anxious	disabled	flexible	predictable

4. Children may feel _____ about their first day in a new school because they don't know what to expect.

5. For me, it is very hard to change my plans because I am not very _____.

6. Although savants have amazing abilities and knowledge, in other areas of their lives they may appear to be _____.

7. Because I know him so well, Sam's reaction to my suggestion was very _____.

benefit	image	interaction	savant	sum

8. It is sometimes hard for people who are shy to engage in social _____, especially with people they don't know well.

9. Finding the _____ of 20 × 3 in your head is not difficult.

10. A(n) _____ can exhibit amazing mental powers and is able to memorize huge amounts of information.

11. One _____ of my new job is health insurance, and another is two weeks of paid vacation.

12. Even though Daniel had not been to Paris in many years, he still had a clear _____ in his mind of what his hotel looked like.

GO TO MyEnglishLab FOR MORE VOCABULARY PRACTICE.

PREVIEW

You are going to read an article about Daniel Tammet, an autistic savant. Before you read, look at the statements below. Check (✓) three things about Daniel that you think you will read in the story.

_____ **1.** He can't drive a car.

_____ **2.** He has trouble remembering things.

_____ **3.** He loves going to the beach.

_____ **4.** He has lots of friends.

_____ **5.** He has invented his own language.

_____ **6.** He lives with his parents.

Now read the Daniel Tammet article.

A GENIUS EXPLAINS
By Richard Johnson
The Guardian

1   Daniel Tammet is talking. As he talks, he studies my shirt and counts the stitches. Ever since the age of three, when he suffered an epileptic fit, Tammet has been obsessed with counting. Now he is 26, and a mathematical genius who can figure out cube roots quicker than a calculator and recall pi to 22,514 decimal places. He also happens to be autistic, which is why he can't drive a car, wire a plug, or tell right from left. He lives with extraordinary ability and disability.

2   Tammet is calculating 377 multiplied by 795. Actually, he isn't "calculating": there is nothing conscious about what he is doing. He arrives at the answer instantly. Since his epileptic fit, he has been able to see numbers as shapes, colors, and textures. The number two, for instance, is a motion, and five is a clap of thunder. "When I multiply numbers together, I see two shapes. The **image** starts to change and evolve, and a third shape emerges. That's the answer. It's mental imagery. It's like maths without having to think."

3   Tammet is a "**savant**," an individual with an astonishing, extraordinary mental ability. An **estimated** 10% of the autistic population—and an estimated 1% of the non-autistic population—have savant abilities, but no one knows exactly why.

4   Scans of the brains of autistic savants suggest that the right hemisphere might be **compensating** for damage in the left hemisphere. While many savants struggle with language and comprehension (skills associated primarily with the left hemisphere), they often have amazing skills in mathematics and memory (primarily right hemisphere skills). Typically, savants have a limited vocabulary, but there is nothing limited about Tammet's vocabulary.

5   Tammet is creating his own language, strongly influenced by the vowel and image-rich languages of northern Europe. (He already speaks French, German, Spanish, Lithuanian, Icelandic, and Esperanto.) The vocabulary of his language—"Mänti," meaning a type of tree —reflects the relationships between different things. The word "ema," for instance, translates as "mother," and "ela" is what a mother creates: "life." "Päike" is "sun," and "päive" is what the

sun creates: "day." Tammet hopes to launch Mänti in academic circles later this year, his own personal exploration of the power of words and their inter-relationship.

6   Last year, Tammet broke the European record for recalling pi, the mathematical constant,[1] to the furthest decimal point. He found it easy, he says, because he didn't even have to "think." To him, pi isn't an abstract set of digits; it's a visual story, a film projected in front of his eyes. He learnt the number forwards and backwards and, last year, spent five hours recalling it in front of an adjudicator.[2] He wanted to prove a point. "I memorised pi to 22,514 decimal places, and I am technically **disabled**. I just wanted to show people that disability needn't get in the way."

7   Tammet is softly spoken, and shy about making eye contact, which makes him seem younger than he is. He lives on the Kent coast, but never goes near the beach—there are too many pebbles to count. The thought of a mathematical problem with no solution makes him feel uncomfortable. Trips to the supermarket are always a chore. "There's too much mental stimulus. I have to look at every shape and texture. Every price, and every arrangement of fruit and vegetables. So instead of thinking,'What cheese do I want this week?', I'm just really uncomfortable."

8   Tammet has never been able to work 9 to 5. It would be too difficult to fit around his daily routine. For instance, he has to drink his cups of tea at exactly the same time every day. Things have to happen in the same order: he always brushes his teeth before he has his shower. "I have tried to be more **flexible**, but I always end up feeling more uncomfortable. **Retaining** a sense of control is really important. I like to do things in my own time and in my own style, so an office with targets and bureaucracy just wouldn't work."

9   Instead, he has set up a business on his own, at home, writing e-mail courses in language learning, numeracy, and literacy for private clients. It has had the fringe **benefit** of keeping human interaction to a minimum. It also gives him time to work on the verb structures of Mänti.

10   Few people on the streets have recognised Tammet since his pi record attempt. But, when a documentary about his life is broadcast on Channel 5 later this year, all that will change. "The highlight of filming was to meet Kim Peek, the real-life character who inspired the film *Rain Man*. Before I watched *Rain Man*, I was frightened. As a nine-year-old schoolboy, you don't want people to point at the screen and say, 'That's you.' But I watched it and felt a real connection. Getting to meet the real-life Rain Man was inspirational."

11   Peek was shy and introspective, but he sat and held Tammet's hand for hours. "We shared so much—our love of key dates from history, for instance. And our love of books. As a child, I regularly took over a room in the house and started my own lending library. I would separate out fiction and non-fiction, and then alphabetise them all. I even introduced a ticketing system. I love books so much. I've read more books than anyone else I know. So I was delighted when Kim wanted to meet in a library." Peek can read two pages simultaneously, one with each eye. He can also recall, in exact detail, the 7,600 books he has read. When he is at home in Utah, he spends afternoons at the Salt Lake City public library, memorising phone books and address directories. "He is such a lovely man," says Tammet. "Kim says, 'You don't have to be handicapped to be different—everybody's different.' And he's right."

12   As a baby, he (Tammet) banged his head against the wall and cried constantly. Nobody knew what was wrong. His mother was

[1]**mathematical constant:** a special number that is usually a real number and is considered "significantly interesting is some way"

[2]**adjudicator:** a judge or arbitrator, especially in a dispute or competition

(continued on next page)

anxious, and would swing him to sleep in a blanket. She breastfed him for two years. The only thing the doctors could say was that perhaps he was understimulated. Then, one afternoon when he was playing with his brother in the living room, he had an epileptic fit.[3]

13   "I was given medication—round blue tablets—to control my seizures and told not to go out in direct sunlight. I had to visit the hospital every month for regular blood tests. I hated those tests, but I knew they were necessary. To make up for it, my father would always buy me a cup of squash to drink while we sat in the waiting room. It was a worrying time because my Dad's father had epilepsy and actually died of it, in the end. They were thinking, 'This is the end of Daniel's life.'"

14   He remembers being given a Ladybird book called *Counting* when he was four. "When I looked at the numbers, I 'saw' images. It felt like a place I could go where I really belonged. That was great. I went to this other country whenever I could. I would sit on the floor in my bedroom and just count. I didn't notice that time was passing. It was only when my Mum shouted up for dinner, or someone knocked at my door, that I would snap out of it."

15   One day his brother asked him a **sum**. "He asked me to multiply something in my head—like 'What is $82 \times 82 \times 82 \times 82$?' I just looked at the floor and closed my eyes. My back went very straight, and I made my hands into fists. But after five or 10 seconds, the answer just flowed out of my mouth. He asked me several others, and I got every one right. My parents didn't seem surprised. And they never put pressure on me to perform for the neighbours. They knew I was different but wanted me to have a normal life as far as possible."

16   Tammet could see the car park of his infant school from his bedroom window, which made him feel safe. "I loved assembly because we got to sing hymns. The notes formed a pattern in my head, just like the numbers did." The other children didn't know what to make of him and would tease him. The minute the bell went for playtime, he would rush off. "I went to the playground, but not to play. The place was surrounded by trees. While the other children were playing football, I would just stand and count the leaves."

17   Tammet may have been teased at school, but his teachers were always protective. "I think my parents must have had a word with them, so I was pretty much left alone." He found it hard to socialise with anyone outside the family, and, with the advent of adolesence, his shyness got worse.

18   After leaving school with three A-levels (History, French and German, all grade Bs), he decided he wanted to teach—only not the **predictable**, learn-by-rote type of teaching. For a start, he went to teach in Lithuania, and he worked as a volunteer. "It was also the first time I was introduced as 'Daniel' rather than 'the guy who can do weird stuff in his head.' It was such a pleasant relief." Later, he returned home to live with his parents and found work as a maths tutor.

19   When he isn't working, Tammet likes to hang out with his friends on the church quiz team. His knowledge of popular culture lets him down, but he's a shoo-in when it comes to the maths questions. "I do love numbers," he says. "It isn't only an intellectual or aloof thing that I do. I really feel that there is an emotional attachment, a caring for numbers. I think this is a human thing—in the same way that a poet humanises a river or a tree through metaphor, my world gives me a sense of numbers as personal. It sounds silly, but numbers are my friends."

---

[3]**epileptic fit:** (also referred to as an epileptic seizure) a brief symptom of epilepsy which may include loss of consciousness, convulsions, or losing muscle tone and slumping to the ground

MAIN IDEAS

1 Look again at your predictions from the Preview on page 6. How did they help you understand the article?

2 Many articles and textbooks contain paragraph headers. A paragraph header is like a title for the paragraph. It tells readers what they can expect to read about. Choose the best paragraph headers for each of the following sections in the article.

1. *For paragraphs 1 and 2:*

   a. Daniel Tammet—mathematical genius

   b. Daniel Tammet's abilities and disabilities

   c. Math—how he does it

2. *For paragraphs 4 and 5:*

   a. The autistic brain

   b. Mänti—Daniel's language

   c. Not the typical savant

3. *For paragraphs 7 and 8:*

   a. Everyday life can be difficult

   b. Overstimulation can be a problem

   c. Daniel's daily routine

4. *For paragraphs 10 and 11:*

   a. Kim Peek and Daniel's similarities

   b. Kim Peek and Daniel's love of books

   c. Daniel and Kim Peek connect

5. *For paragraphs 14 and 15:*

   a. Daniel starts counting

   b. Daniel's math skills emerge

   c. Numbers as images

6. *For paragraphs 16 and 17:*

   a. Daniel's love of singing

   b. Daniel's shyness

   c. Problems in school

DETAILS

Reading One gives information about Daniel's abilities and disabilities. Read the categories on the left in the chart below. Then write the details and examples from the box next to the appropriate categories. Finally, identify each detail or example as either an ability or a disability. Share your completed chart with a partner.

Daniel feels uncomfortable in the supermarket.	~~Daniel has invented his own language.~~	~~Daniel can calculate cube roots faster than a calculator.~~
Daniel can recall pi to 22,514 decimal points.	Daniel must drink his tea at exactly the same time every day.	It is hard for Daniel to socialize with anyone outside his family.
Daniel is able to read a lot of books.	Daniel has trouble making eye contact.	Daniel can multiply 377 × 795 in his head.
Daniel doesn't go to the beach because there are too many pebbles to count.	Daniel always has to brush his teeth before he showers.	The thought of a mathematical problem with no solution makes Daniel uncomfortable.
Daniel can easily remember key dates in history.	Daniel speaks seven languages.	

CATEGORY	DETAILS OR EXAMPLES	ABILITY	DISABILITY
MATH	1. Daniel can calculate cube roots faster than a calculator.	X	
	2.		
	3.		
	4.		
LANGUAGE	1. Daniel has invented his own language.	X	
	2.		
	3.		
MEMORY	1.		
	2.		
SOCIAL INTERACTION	1.		
	2.		
	3.		
NEED FOR ORDER	1.		
	2.		

MAKE INFERENCES

UNDERSTANDING ASSUMPTIONS

An inference is an educated guess about something that is not directly stated. In "A Genius Explains," there are quotes from Daniel Tammet and Kim Peek that show what others might assume about the two men's disabilities. What assumptions can you infer from these quotations?

Look at the example and read the explanation.

Daniel (*paragraph 6*): "I just wanted to show people that disability needn't get in the way."

People think that <u>someone with a disability cannot do as much as someone without a disability</u>.

When other people realized that Daniel had a disability, they assumed that he would have problems in other areas of his life. By showing people that he could achieve remarkable things, even though he was "technically disabled," he wanted to show that their assumptions were wrong. His disability wasn't going to hold him back.

Work with a partner. Read the following quotes from Daniel and Kim. What assumptions do the quotes show that people have made about them? Complete the sentences.

1. Daniel (*paragraph 18*): "It was also the first time I was introduced as 'Daniel' rather than 'the guy who can do weird stuff in his head.'"

   Others didn't think that Daniel was _____

   _____

2. Kim (*paragraph 11*): "You don't have to be handicapped to be different—everybody's different."

   Others think that _____

   _____

3. Daniel (*paragraph 19*): "It sounds silly, but numbers are my friends."

   Other people probably think that numbers _____

   _____

4. Daniel (*paragraph 19*): "It isn't only an intellectual or aloof thing that I do. I really feel that there is an emotional attachment, a caring for numbers."

   Other people probably assume that Daniel's relationship to numbers _____

   _____

5. Daniel (*paragraph 8*): " I like to do things in my own time and in my own style, so an office with targets and bureaucracy just wouldn't work."

   Other people might expect Daniel to _____

   _____

EXPRESS OPINIONS

Work in groups of three. Choose one of the questions and discuss your ideas. Then choose one person in your group to report the ideas to the class.

1. Which of Daniel's abilities would be most useful to you? How would having this ability change your life?

2. William James, the American psychologist and philosopher (1842–1910) said, "Genius means nothing more than the faculty of perceiving in an unhabitual way." How does this quotation apply to Daniel Tammet?

■■■■■■■■■■■■■■■■■■■■■■■■■■■■■■■■■ *GO TO* MyEnglishLab *TO GIVE YOUR OPINION ABOUT ANOTHER QUESTION.*

READING TWO | 10,000 HOURS TO MASTERY

READ

1 Look at the boldfaced words in the reading and think about the questions.

1. Which words do you know the meanings of?

2. Can you use any of the words or phrases in a sentence?

2 Read the article about Malcolm Gladwell's book, *Outliers: The Story of Success.* As you read, notice the boldfaced vocabulary. Try to guess the meaning of the words from the context.

10,000 HOURS TO MASTERY
by **Harvey Mackay**

1 For years, I have preached the importance of hard work, determination, **persistence**, and practice—make that perfect practice—as key ingredients of success. A nifty new book seems to support my theory.

2 Malcolm Gladwell has written a fascinating study, *Outliers: The Story of Success* (Little, Brown & Co.), which should make a lot of people feel much better about not achieving instant success. In fact, he says it takes about 10 years, or 10,000 hours, of practice to attain true **expertise**.

3 "The people at the very top don't just work harder or even much harder than everyone else," Gladwell writes. "They work much, much harder." Achievement, he says, is talent plus preparation. Preparation seems to play a bigger role.

4 For example, he describes the Beatles: They had been together seven years before their famous arrival in America. They spent a lot of time playing in strip clubs in Hamburg, Germany, sometimes for as long as eight hours a night. Overnight sensation? Not exactly. Estimates are the band performed 1,200 times before their big success in 1964. By comparison, most bands don't perform 1,200 times in their careers.

The Beatles

5 Neurologist Daniel Levitin has studied the formula for success extensively and shares this finding: "The **emerging** picture from such studies is that 10,000 hours of practice is required to achieve the level of mastery associated with being a world-class expert in anything. In study after study of composers, basketball players, fiction writers, ice skaters, concert pianists, chess players, master criminals, and what have you, the number comes up again and again. Of course, this doesn't address why some people get more out of their practice sessions than others do. But no one has yet found a case in which true world-class expertise was accomplished in less time. It seems it takes the brain this long to **assimilate** all that it needs to know to achieve true mastery."

6 Two computer giants, Bill Joy, who co-founded Sun Microsystems, and Bill Gates, co-founder of Microsoft, also were proof of the 10,000-hour theory.

7 As Gladwell puts it, "Practice isn't the thing you do once you're good. It's the thing you do that makes you good."

8 Consider these thoughts from successful folks in all walks of life:

9 • "No one can arrive from being talented alone. God gives talent; work **transforms** talent into genius."—Anna Pavlova, ballerina.

10 • "I know the price of success: dedication, hard work and an unremitting devotion to the things you want to see happen."—Frank Lloyd Wright, architect.

(continued on next page)

11 • "The way to learn to do things is to do things. The way to learn a trade is to work at it. Success teaches how to succeed. Begin with the determination to succeed, and the work is half done already."—Mark Twain, writer and humorist.

12 Do you detect a theme here?

13 The abilities these people possessed were far-ranging, yet the formula for success was the same: hard work and lots of it. I don't know anyone who has succeeded any other way. Some people just make it look easy. Of course, you probably didn't see the first 9,999 hours of hard work. And you don't just have to work hard; you have to work smart, too.

14 **Mackay's Moral:** Some people dream about success, and others wake up and do something about it.

COMPREHENSION

Work with a partner. Complete each statement according to information in the article.

1. According to Gladwell, achievement is _____
   _____.

2. The Beatles were different from most other bands because _____
   _____.

3. Daniel Levitin says about success that _____
   _____.

4. Levitin believes success takes so long to achieve because _____
   _____.

■■■ *GO TO* MyEnglishLab *FOR MORE VOCABULARY PRACTICE.*

READING SKILL

1 Go back to Reading Two. Underline the quotations. Why do you think Mackay includes these quotations?

DISTINGUISHING VOICE IN QUOTATIONS

Distinguishing voice is an important reading skill as it can sometimes be confusing whether we are reading the author's words or someone else's words. One indication of a change in voice is quotation marks. Another indication is a change in pronouns, for example, from third person (*he, she,* or *they*) to first person (*I* or *we*). In order to fully comprehend the text, you need to notice when a shift in voice takes place to know who is speaking.

Authors often shift the voice in their writing by using quoted speech. Quotations can:

- add first-hand validity to a point the author has made.
- provide details or examples of what the author has been talking about.
- continue the story in another voice for added interest.

In paragraph 3 of Reading Two, Mackay includes two quotations from Gladwell's book. This adds validity to what Mackay says, as the words are Gladwell's. In paragraph 5, the author includes an extended quotation from Daniel Levitin. This quotation gives several details and examples of how much time it takes for true mastery to occur.

2 Read the following excerpts from Reading One. All double quotation marks have been removed. Underline the sections where the voice changes from the author's to someone else's. Add quotation marks where necessary. Then discuss the following questions with a partner:

- How do you know where the change in voice occurs?
- Who is speaking where you added quotation marks?
- Why might the author have chosen to use quotations in the examples?

1. To [Tammet], pi isn't an abstract set of digits; it's a visual story, a film projected in front of his eyes. He learnt the number forwards and backwards and, last year, spent five hours recalling it in front of an adjudicator. He wanted to prove a point. I memorised pi to 22,514 decimal places, and I am technically disabled. I just wanted to show people that disability needn't get in the way. *(paragraph 6)*

2. [Tammet] lives on the Kent coast, but never goes near the beach—there are too many pebbles to count. The thought of a mathematical problem with no solution makes him feel uncomfortable. Trips to the supermarket are always a chore. There's too much mental stimulus. I have to look at every shape and texture. Every price, and every arrangement of fruit and vegetables. So instead of thinking, 'What cheese do I want this week?', I'm just really uncomfortable. *(paragraph 7)*

3. Peek was shy and introspective, but he sat and held Tammet's hand for hours. We shared so much—our love of key dates from history, for instance. And our love of books. . . . I've read more books than anyone else I know. So I was delighted when Kim wanted to meet in a library. Peek can read two pages simultaneously, one with each eye. He can also recall, in exact detail, the 7,600 books he has read. . . . 'He is such a lovely man,' says Tammet. Kim says, 'You don't have to be handicapped to be different—everybody's different.' And he's right. *(paragraph 11)*

(continued on next page)

4. He remembers being given a Ladybird book called *Counting* when he was four. When I looked at the numbers, I 'saw' images. It felt like a place I could go where I really belonged. *(paragraph 14)*

GO TO MyEnglishLab *FOR MORE SKILL PRACTICE.*

CONNECT THE READINGS

STEP 1: Organize

Reading One (R1) and Reading Two (R2) both talk about genius. A Venn diagram can show where the ideas about genius are found. Read the statements in the box. Write the number of the statement in the correct part of the diagram. Include the paragraph number where the information is found.

---

1. "Genius" may be the result of brain chemistry.

2. A person can be a genius and also be disabled.

3. People at the top (experts) work harder than other people.

4. Genius = talent + hard work.

5. "Genius" is being studied by scientists.

6. Expertise requires a lot of practice.

7. Special talents can also cause problems.

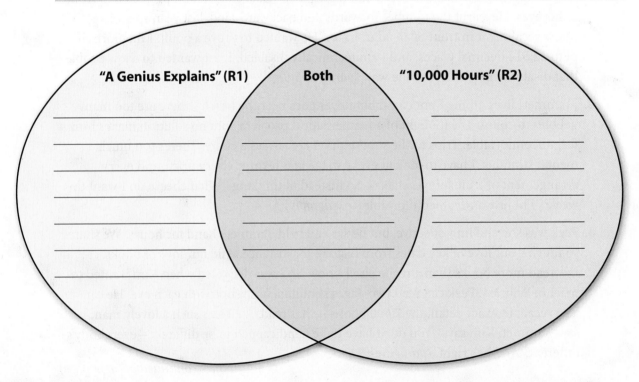

"A Genius Explains" (R1)   Both   "10,000 Hours" (R2)

STEP 2: Synthesize

Work with a partner. Imagine that one of you is Daniel Tammet and the other is Malcolm Gladwell. On a separate piece of paper, write three questions that you would like to ask each other. Use information from Step 1. Exchange your questions with your partner and write answers.

▪▪▪▪▪▪▪▪▪▪▪▪▪▪▪▪▪▪▪▪▪▪▪▪▪▪▪▪▪▪▪▪▪▪▪▪ *GO TO* MyEnglishLab *TO CHECK WHAT YOU LEARNED.*

3 FOCUS ON WRITING

VOCABULARY

REVIEW

Complete the word scramble puzzle. By rearranging the letters, you will be able to form vocabulary words used in the unit. Use the circled letter from each word to find the bonus word.

1. e a i t ⓒ t r n o n i	<u>i n t e r a c t i o n</u>	Communication or collaboration
2. l i a a m ⓢ t s i e	_ _ _ _ _ _ _ _ _ _	This is what takes the brain so long to do, according to Dr. Levitin.
3. v a n ⓣ a s	_ _ _ _ _ _ _	A person with extraordinary mental skills might be this.
4. f r o a m t r ⓝ s	_ _ _ _ _ _ _ _ _	To change
5. e ⓟ i r d b t e a l c	_ _ _ _ _ _ _ _ _ _ _	Because of his need for structure, Daniel Tammet's life is this.
6. p e i e e x ⓢ t r	_ _ _ _ _ _ _ _ _	What you may acquire after thousands of hours of practice
7. f n i t b e ⓔ	_ _ _ _ _ _ _	An advantage
8. n m ⓡ i e g g e	_ _ _ _ _ _ _ _	Starting to appear
9. u n x a o ⓘ s	_ _ _ _ _ _ _	Nervous or eager
10. m p n o ⓔ s a t e c	_ _ _ _ _ _ _ _ _ _	To make up for a weakness
11. b l d s i ⓔ a	_ _ _ _ _ _ _ _	Unable to perform certain activities

Bonus Word (This is the quality you might need to have to complete this puzzle!)

_ _ _ _ _ _ _ _ _ _ _ _ _

EXPAND

1 Complete the chart with the correct word forms. Use a dictionary if necessary. An **X** indicates there is no form in that category.

NOUN	VERB	ADJECTIVE	ADVERB
		predictable	
		estimated	X
sum		X	X
	X	anxious	
savant	X	X	X
		flexible	
interaction			
	transform	1. 2. 3.	X
	retain		X
benefit			X
		disabled	X
1. expertise 2.	X		
	assimilate		X
		emerging	X
		persistent	
	compensate	X	X

2 Complete the sentences with the words in the boxes. You may need to change the word form and/or the verb tense.

| expertise   flexible   persistence   predictable   transform |

1. According to Anna Pavlova, work has the _____ effect of turning talent into genius.

2. A lack of _____ is one of the symptoms of ASD.

3. Daniel Tammet's life is very _____; he always drinks his tea at the same time.

4. Gladwell believes that to achieve mastery you must _____ in your practice and never give up.

5. Gladwell says it takes about ten years to attain true world-class _____.

anxious	compensate	emerging	estimated	interaction

6. Mathematical problems with no solution cause a feeling of _____ for Daniel Tammet.

7. Scientists _____ that there are fewer than 100 autistic savants alive today.

8. Daniel Tammet's choosing to work at home instead of in an office is a type of _____ for the fact that he needs structure and has trouble with social _____.

9. The symptoms of ASD usually begin to _____ when a child is two or three years old.

CREATE

Rewrite the sentences by replacing the underlined word with the form in parentheses. Make any necessary grammatical changes.

1. Because I know Daniel Tammet well, I can <u>predict</u> how he will react in certain situations. (predictable)

   Because I know Daniel Tammet well, how he will react in certain situations is very predictable.

2. Many people who suffer from ASD have problems with <u>flexibility</u>. (flexible)

   _____

   _____

3. According to Gladwell, the <u>transformation</u> of talent into expertise requires at least 10,000 hours. (transform)

   _____

   _____

4. A lack of structure can cause <u>anxiety</u> for Daniel Tammet. (anxious)

   _____

   _____

(continued on next page)

5. For many people with ASD, being able to <u>interact</u> socially is difficult. (interaction)

_____

_____

6. Scans of the brains of autistic savants suggest that there might be some <u>compensation</u> being done by the right hemisphere for damage to the left. (compensate)

_____

_____

7. The <u>retention</u> of large amounts of information is usually not a problem for autistic savants. (retain)

_____

_____

8. Daniel Tammet memorized pi to 22,514 decimal places to show people that, although he is technically <u>disabled</u>, it doesn't stop him from being successful. (disability)

_____

_____

GO TO MyEnglishLab FOR MORE VOCABULARY PRACTICE.

GRAMMAR

1 Read the sentences based on the two readings. Look at the boldfaced verbs. Notice how they change the meaning of the underlined verbs that follow them. What added information do they provide?

a. Malcolm Gladwell has written a fascinating study, *Outliers: The Story of Success*, which **should** <u>make</u> a lot of people feel much better about not achieving instant success.

b. Scans of the brains of autistic savants suggest that the right hemisphere **might** <u>compensate</u> for damage in the left hemisphere.

c. For instance, Tammet **has to** <u>drink</u> his cups of tea at exactly the same time every day.

1. In sentence *a*, does **should** indicate advice or does it express likelihood?

2. In sentence *b*, does **might** indicate speculation or a conclusion?

3. In sentence *c*, does **has to** indicate a conclusion or necessity?

Modals and semi-modals are auxiliary ("helping") verbs. They are always followed by the base form of the verb.

MODALS AND SEMI-MODALS: ADVICE, LIKELIHOOD, NECESSITY, SPECULATION, AND CONCLUSIONS			
Advice: *should, ought to,* and *had better*			
SUBJECT	MODAL	VERB (BASE FORM)	THE REST OF THE SENTENCE
You	should (not)	practice	10 hours a day.
	ought (not) to*		
	had better (not)		
Likelihood: *should* and *ought to*			
SUBJECT	MODAL	VERB (BASE FORM)	THE REST OF THE SENTENCE
Gladwell	should (not)	explain	his theory.
	ought (not) to		

Ought to, like *have (got) to*, is considered a semi-modal because the word *to* is placed between it and the verb that it is modifying. *Had better* is also considered a semi-modal because it is two words. The meanings of these semi-modals are similar to their modal counterparts except that *had better* often implies a threat. "You had better listen to me (or else you are going to have a problem)." When asking a question, speakers generally use *should* instead of *ought to* or *had better*.

(continued on next page)

Necessity: *must, have to,* and *have got to*

SUBJECT	MODAL	VERB (BASE FORM)	THE REST OF THE SENTENCE
Daniel's brother	must (not)	eat	at exactly the same time.
	has to		
	has got to		

Be careful. The meaning of **must not** is very different from **doesn't have to** or **hasn't got to**.

- "You **must not** drive over 50 mph" means you are not allowed to drive faster than 50 mph.

- However, "You **don't have to** drive over 50 mph," means you are not obligated to drive faster than 50 mph, but you can if you want to. It is your choice.

Modals have only one form; however, *have* in *have (got) to* changes depending on the subject.

- He **has** got to go.

- They **have** got to go.

Speculation: *may, might,* and *could*

SUBJECT	MODAL	VERB (BASE FORM)	THE REST OF THE SENTENCE
Daniel	may (not)	know	Kim Peek's sister.
	might (not)		
	could		

Conclusions: *must, have to, have got to, can not,* and *could not*

SUBJECT	MODAL	VERB (BASE FORM)	THE REST OF THE SENTENCE
Daniel's brother	must (not)	live	in a very neat house.
	has to		
	has got to		
	can not		
	could not		

Be careful.

- Both **must** and **must not** can indicate a conclusion.

- However, **have to** and **have got to** only indicate a conclusion in the affirmative; in the negative, they indicate a choice. "You don't **have to** believe Dr. Levitin."

- **Can not** and **could not** can indicate a negative conclusion based on something being impossible. "Daniel **couldn't** (or **can not**) have crashed the car because he doesn't drive."

- However, **could** in the affirmative indicates speculation or possibility. "Daniel Tammet **could** know Kim Peek's sister."

- *Can* in the affirmative indicates ability or possibility. "Daniel **can** speak seven languages."

- *May* and *might* can also be used to indicate possibility.

2 Read each sentence and decide what meaning the boldfaced modal verb expresses. Write the letter indicating its meaning.

a. Advice	b. Likelihood	c. Necessity	d. Speculation	e. Conclusion

MEANING OF MODAL OR SEMI-MODAL	
b	1. No matter how hard the mathematical problem, Daniel **ought to** be able to solve it nearly as fast as a calculator.
	2. Daniel **could not** have met Kim's sister because she wasn't at the library when Daniel met Kim.
	3. Daniel **shouldn't** take the job at that office. It will interfere with his routine and make him very anxious.
	4. According to Gladwell, in order to be a world-class expert, you **have to** put in at least 10,000 hours of practice.
	5. Daniel has started to study Swedish. Because I know he is good with languages, I think he **might** be fluent by the time I see him next if he puts his mind to it.
	6. If you do not already have world-class expertise in some area, you **ought to** feel better after reading Gladwell's book. It takes up to ten years to reach expertise!
	7. Daniel **must** always brush his teeth before he takes his shower.
	8. Even though Kim Peek can read two books at the same time, one with each eye, I think he **may** really prefer to read only one at a time. I know I would.
	9. Kim Peek **has got to** have an incredible memory. He can remember all 7,600 books that he has ever read.
	10. You **had better not** expect to become the next Michael Jordan or Usain Bolt without putting in a lot of practice time.

3 Circle the best modal or semi-modal to complete the paragraphs.

1. Although Daniel Tammet has many abilities, he also has many disabilities. For

example, he can't drive a car; he has never learned how. For him not to be anxious,

his life _____ be very structured. In other words, things
          1. (could / has got to)

_____ happen randomly. Instead, they _____
2. (don't have to / must not)   3. (must / might)

happen in the same order every day. In addition, he never goes to the beach because

there are so many pebbles there, and he _____ feel he has to count
                    4. (might / should)

them. Making choices is also difficult for Daniel. That is perhaps why his parents

think that maybe he _____ also stay out of the supermarket.
          5. (should / must)

There are too many products for him to choose from! In terms of his abilities, Daniel

_____ solve complex mathematical problems so fast that for most
      6. (is able to / had better)

problems, he _____ be able to arrive at an answer faster than a
      7. (has got to / ought to)

calculator. He can also retain amazing amounts of information in his memory. In fact,

if you allow him to study a 100-digit number, he _____ have any
               8. (should not / could not)

trouble remembering it.

2. Malcolm Gladwell's book, *Outliers*, _____ make people who
          1. (had better / ought to)

have not attained instant success feel better. In it, he states that if you want to reach

true expertise, you _____ spend about 10,000 hours practicing.
      2. (might / have to)

The ballerina, Anna Pavlova, speaking from personal experience, commented that

no matter how talented you are, you _____ reach genius without
           3. (can't / shouldn't)

hard work. Therefore, don't expect to become an expert at anything overnight. You

_____ be prepared to work hard.
    4. (must / may)

■■■■■■■■■■■■■■■■■■ **GO TO** MyEnglishLab **FOR MORE GRAMMAR PRACTICE AND TO CHECK WHAT YOU LEARNED.**

FINAL WRITING TASK

In this unit, you read about different geniuses and how they achieved their expertise.

You are going to *write a summary paragraph about a current or past genius. Be sure to include why this person is considered a genius and how he or she achieved expertise.* Use the vocabulary and grammar from the unit.*

PREPARE TO WRITE: Group Brainstorming

Group brainstorming is a good way to get ideas for writing. In brainstorming, you think of as many ideas as you can. Don't think about whether the ideas are good or bad; just write down all ideas.

1 Work with a small group. Brainstorm a list of geniuses, past or present, that you know about. The person can be from any time period or culture. Don't stop to discuss the genius. Just concentrate on thinking of as many examples as possible.

Geniuses

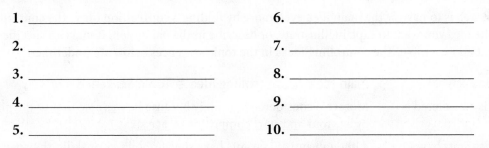

1. _____   6. _____

2. _____   7. _____

3. _____   8. _____

4. _____   9. _____

5. _____   10. _____

2 Individually, choose one genius that you find interesting and want to write about. Research this person to find information about his or her life and achievements. Be sure to include why this person is considered a genius and how he or she achieved expertise. Take notes about what you find out. Make sure the notes are in your own words and not copied word-for-word.

---

* For Alternative Writing Topics, see page 33. These topics can be used in place of the writing topic for this unit or as homework. The alternative topics relate to the theme of the unit but may not target the same grammar or rhetorical structures taught in the unit.

WRITE: A Summary Paragraph

A **paragraph** is a group of sentences that are related and support a controlling idea. A **summary paragraph** identifies and extracts the main idea from a text, leaving out less important details. All summary paragraphs have a **topic sentence** with a **controlling idea**.

TOPIC SENTENCE

The **topic sentence** is an essential part of all well-written paragraphs. The topic sentence controls the content of the rest of the paragraph. This control helps the writer focus on supporting ideas in the paragraph that are directly related to the topic sentence. The first step in writing a topic sentence is to choose a topic and find a point of view or **main idea** about it.

Topics	Main Idea
Mozart	Mozart is considered a prodigy.
Autistic savants	Autistic savants have specific abilities or skills.
Malcolm Gladwell	Malcolm Gladwell has written a fascinating book.

CONTROLLING IDEA

The next step is to narrow the main idea even more by finding a **controlling idea**. The controlling idea is the idea you want to explain, illustrate, or describe in the paragraph. It makes a specific statement about a topic. The controlling ideas in the topic sentences below are underlined.

Main Idea	Main Idea + Controlling Idea = Topic Sentence
Mozart is considered a prodigy.	Mozart is considered a prodigy <u>because he was able to play the piano by age four and start composing by age six</u>.
Autistic savants have specific abilities or skills.	Although autistic savants have specific abilities or skills, <u>they may have other limitations, especially problems with social interactions</u>.
Malcolm Gladwell has written a fascinating book.	Malcolm Gladwell has written a fascinating book, <u>which emphasizes the importance of hard work</u>.

Autistic savants have specific abilities or skills, but they are not without certain limitations in other areas of life. An autistic savant is a person with an unusual ability, skill, or knowledge that is much more developed than that of an average person. In fact, many savants have highly developed mathematical skills. Others are able to retain large amounts of information in their memory. For example, some autistic savants can recite entire dictionaries or telephone books word for word. Still others are able to draw detailed maps of an area after flying over it once in a helicopter. Despite the fact that the autistic savant has these specific abilities or skills, he or she may have difficulties with other types of mental or physical tasks and social interactions. For instance, some savants may have trouble doing simple tasks, such as tying their shoes or driving a car. Additionally, an autistic savant may have problems talking to people or even making eye contact. So, despite their advanced skills and abilities in certain areas, savants may encounter difficulty with seemingly simple tasks.

1. What is the topic of this paragraph?

_____

2. The first sentence is the topic sentence. What two ideas are presented in this sentence?

_____

_____

3. How does the content of the rest of the paragraph relate to the topic sentence?

_____

_____

Each paragraph is missing a topic sentence. Circle the topic sentence that best fits the paragraph. Discuss your answers with a partner.

1. Daniel suffered an epileptic seizure when he was very young, which may be the cause of his savant abilities. Soon after, when he was four, his mother gave him a counting book, and his love of mathematics was born. From an early age, he has been able to solve complicated mathematical problems in his head. Recently, he has been able to memorize pi to 22,514 digits.

   a. Daniel Tammet is very good at math and has a great memory.

   b. Daniel Tammet is an autistic savant with exceptional memory and mathematical abilities.

   c. Daniel Tammet is an autistic savant who loves solving mathematical problems.

2. What Levitin has found is that it appears that 10,000 hours of practice are required to reach world-class expertise in any field. In fact, he has found no world-class expert who has not put in at least that many hours of preparation. He believes that this is because it takes that much time for the brain to assimilate everything necessary to reach this level of expertise.

   a. Daniel Levitin, a neurologist, has extensively studied what is needed to reach success.

   b. To reach world-class expertise requires a lot of time and practice.

   c. Daniel Levitin believes that it takes the brain a long time to assimilate the information necessary to be an expert.

3. Parents create these hothouse kids because they are attempting to create a "genius." They may begin by playing classical music for the hothouse child when he or she is still in the crib. The parents start working with their children on math and language skills at an early age, using flashcards. They also enroll their children in music and dance lessons, often as early as age three or four. In addition, they try to get their kids into the most academically challenging preschools.

   a. Hothouse kids learn math and music at an early age.

   b. Parents take a variety of approaches to ensure that their kids become geniuses and can get into the best preschools.

   c. "Hothouse kids" is a term used to define children whose parents push them to learn more quickly and earlier than a "normal" child by providing a rich educational environment.

3 Read the paragraphs. The underlined topic sentences are incomplete because they do not have a controlling idea. On a separate piece of paper, rewrite each topic sentence to include both a topic and a controlling idea.

1. <u>Wolfgang Amadeus Mozart was a genius</u>. For one thing, Mozart was a child prodigy who was playing the violin and piano by age 4 and composing by age 6. Another reason that he is considered a genius is that he was able to create over 600 compositions, including symphonies, chamber music, sonatas, and choral music in his 34-year lifetime. Additionally, he is said to have been able to compose entire symphonies in his head. He could imagine the sounds of all the different instruments without using a piano to help him compose. He was not only the best pianist of his day in Europe but also one of the top three or four violinists.

2. <u>Scientists debate the importance of nature vs. nurture</u>. In other words, the debate of nature vs. nurture asks the question: "What part does nature—the genetic information that you have inherited from your parents—play in your development? And, conversely, what part does environment— what you eat, where you went to school, how your parents raised you—play?" In an effort to understand the importance of each of these factors, studies have been done using twins who were separated at birth. While these studies are not conclusive, there were instances where the

(continued on next page)

separated twins had developed in a remarkably similar manner. Nevertheless, the reasons for this may also have to do with environment (nurture). They may have been raised by different families, yet the environments may have been quite similar.

3. <u>Malcolm Gladwell wrote another book, *Outliers: The Story of Success*</u>. It was published in 2008 and was number one on the *New York Times* bestseller list for eleven straight weeks. It followed *Tipping Point,* which was published in 2000. *Tipping Point* addresses the individual's ability to change society. This non-fiction bestseller was followed by *Blink* in 2005. *Blink* is about thinking. Why are some people able to make brilliant decisions in the blink of an eye while others seem to always make the wrong decision? *Blink* also was a non-fiction bestseller.

4 Now write the first draft of your summary paragraph. Use the information from Prepare to Write and complete the organizer below to plan your paragraph (use a separate piece of paper). Make sure you have a clear topic sentence and content that supports it. The topic sentence should introduce the genius that you are going to write about and include a controlling idea. Be sure to use grammar and vocabulary from the unit.

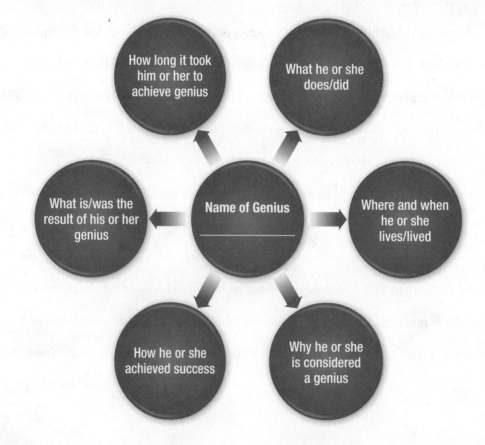

How long it took him or her to achieve genius

What he or she does/did

What is/was the result of his or her genius

Name of Genius
_____

Where and when he or she lives/lived

How he or she achieved success

Why he or she is considered a genius

REVISE: Identifying and Correcting Sentence Fragments

Sentence fragments are incomplete sentences that are presented as if they were complete sentences. They are often phrases lacking either a subject or verb. Other fragments may be dependent (subordinate) clauses that are not connected to an independent clause. These fragments are usually introduced by a relative pronoun (*That, Who, Which, Whom,* etc. . . .) or a subordinating conjunction (*After, Although, Because, Since, When,* etc. . . .).

1 Work with a partner. Identify whether each item is **F** (a fragment) or **C** (a complete sentence).

_____ **1.** Although autistic savants have many extraordinary skills and abilities.

_____ **2.** Gladwell has written an interesting book. Which emphasizes the importance of hard work in achieving success.

_____ **3.** Before Daniel received his counting book when he was four years old.

_____ **4.** Before he had an epileptic seizure, there was no evidence that Daniel had extraordinary math abilities.

_____ **5.** Because Dr. Levitin says that at least 10,000 hours of practice are needed to achieve success.

_____ **6.** The book that Kim Peek was reading the day before he met Daniel Tammet at the library in Salt Lake City.

_____ **7.** Practicing as much as ten hours a day before the math competition.

_____ **8.** Einstein was voted the "Person of the 20th Century" by *Time* magazine after he received the Nobel Prize for Physics.

There are a variety of strategies for correcting sentence fragments.

- Connect the fragment to the sentence before or after it.
- Add more information and rewrite it as a complete sentence.
- Change the punctuation.
- Remove the subordinating conjunction or relative pronoun.
- Add a verb.

2 Work with a partner. Go back to Exercise 1. Using one of the strategies listed above, correct each item you identified as a sentence fragment. Use a separate piece of paper.

3 Look at the first draft of your summary paragraph. Make sure it does not include any sentence fragments.

GO TO MyEnglishLab *FOR MORE SKILL PRACTICE.*

EDIT: Writing the Final Draft

Go to MyEnglishLab and write the final draft of your paragraph. Carefully edit it for grammatical and mechanical errors, such as spelling, capitalization, and punctuation. Make sure you use some of the grammar and vocabulary from the unit. Use the checklist to help you write your final draft. Then submit your paragraph to your teacher.

FINAL DRAFT CHECKLIST

❏ Does the paragraph fully describe why the person is considered a genius and how he or she achieved expertise?

❏ Is there a topic sentence with a controlling idea that introduces the genius?

❏ Is the paragraph free of sentence fragments?

❏ Did you use modals and semi-modals correctly?

❏ Have you used the vocabulary from the unit?

UNIT PROJECT

Work with a partner to research an autistic savant. Take notes and write a report based on your findings. Follow these steps:

STEP 1: Choose one of these autistic savants:

Leslie Lemke, music	**Gregory Blackstock**, music, language
Henriett Seth-F, music, painting, literature	**Jedediah Buxton**, mathematical calculations
Stephen Wiltshire, accurate detailed drawings	**Ellen Bourdeaux**, music, "human clock"
Kim Peek, the real "Rain Man," calendar calculations, memory	Any other autistic savant based on your own research
Alonzo Clemons, sculptor	

STEP 2: Do research on the Internet about the person you chose. Answer the questions:

- When and where did/does the person live?
- What are the person's special abilities?
- When or how did he or she acquire these abilities?
- Does the person also have disabilities? If so, what are they?

STEP 3: To proceed with your research:

1. Go to a search engine and type in the name of the savant you have chosen or key words such as "famous autistic savants" or "prodigious savant abilities."

2. Read the entries that relate to your topic.

3. Takes notes in your own words for a written report.

Be sure to check information on two or more websites.

STEP 4: Prepare a written report for the class.

ALTERNATIVE WRITING TOPICS

Write an essay about one of the topics. Use the vocabulary and grammar from the unit.

1. Kim Peek says, "You don't have to be handicapped to be different—everybody's different." What do you think he means by this? Do you agree? Explain.

2. Daniel Levitin states that it takes 10,000 hours of practice to achieve true world-class expertise. Nevertheless, many people have put in that amount of practice in their fields and still have not achieved world-class expertise. Why do you think they were not successful? What makes the experts different from the others who have also put in 10,000 hours of practice? Explain.

■■■■■■■■■■■■■■■■■■■■■■■■ *GO TO* MyEnglishLab *TO WRITE ABOUT ONE OF THE ALTERNATIVE TOPICS, WATCH A VIDEO ABOUT CHILD PRODIGIES, AND TAKE THE UNIT 1 ACHIEVEMENT TEST.* ■■■■■■■■■■■■■■

FACING LIFE'S Obstacles

1 FOCUS ON THE TOPIC

1. There are many different kinds of obstacles: Physical and economic are two examples. What are some other examples of the kinds of obstacles that people face?

2. What are some ways that people overcome their obstacles?

3. What obstacles have you faced in your life? How have you tried to overcome them?

GO TO MyEnglishLab *TO CHECK WHAT YOU KNOW.*

VOCABULARY

1 Read the passage about author Frank McCourt. Try to understand the boldfaced words from the context.

Frank McCourt was born in Brooklyn, New York, in 1930. His parents, Angela and Malachy, had moved to New York from Ireland in search of a better life. Unfortunately, life was not easy in New York. His father could not earn enough money to support his family. The McCourts returned to Ireland hoping their life would improve. Again, it didn't. Life in Ireland was equally hard if not harder than in New York. Three of Frank's siblings died as babies. Eventually, his father's **abandonment** of the family forced his four sons and Angela to live a very **meager** existence.

Frank's childhood was filled with **misery**. There was never enough food. Their house was small, dirty, and very cold in the winter. When it rained, the floor would flood with water. Frank and his brothers **yearned for** a better life.

Frank did, however, have ways to escape from his **tormented** childhood. He loved to read, and because his **dilapidated** house had no electricity, he would read under the street lamp outside his home. He also had an excellent sense of humor. Humor was the McCourts' defense against their life of relentless **poverty** and **hopelessness**. Even in the worst of times, the McCourts could find something to laugh about.

In 1949, Frank returned to the United States. He was 19 years old and only had an eighth-grade education. He was full of **shame** about his past and often invented stories about his **sordid** childhood instead of telling the truth. However, Frank was never **defeated** by his obstacles; in fact, Frank eventually used his humor and his storytelling talents to overcome the challenges life had set before him.

2 Answer the questions with a partner.

1. Frank had a hard life growing up. What were some of the obstacles or challenges he had to overcome?

2. What did Frank enjoy doing as a child?

3. Why did Frank reinvent his past when he came to America?

3 Find the boldfaced words in the reading passage. Write each word next to its synonym.

1. _____misery_____ sadness

2. _____ poor, sparse

3. _____ embarrassment

4. _____ beaten, overcome by

5. _____ strongly desired, wanted

6. _____ painful

7. _____ immoral, dishonest

8. _____ having little money or few material things

9. _____ leaving someone behind

10. _____ being without hope

11. _____ falling apart, in terrible condition

GO TO MyEnglishLab *FOR MORE VOCABULARY PRACTICE.*

PREVIEW

Read the first two paragraphs of *The Education of Frank McCourt*. Work with a partner to answer the questions. Then read the rest of the article.

1. Where is Frank McCourt now?

2. What do you think he means by "They gave me so much more than I gave them?"

3. What do you think happened to Frank between 1949 and 1997?

THE EDUCATION OF FRANK McCOURT

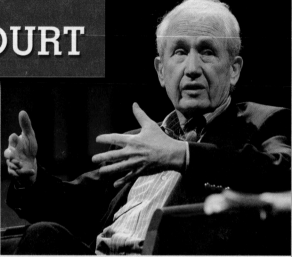

By Barbara Sande Dimmitt
(*from Reader's Digest*)

1   Frank McCourt sat on a stage in New York City's Lincoln Center, his white hair glistening under the lights overhead. He was still boyish of expression at 66, and smile lines radiated from hazel eyes bright with inquisitiveness. Soon he would be addressing the 1997 graduating class of Stuyvesant High School, where he had taught English for 18 years.

2   He let his mind wander as he gazed out at the great hall. *I've learned so much from kids like these*, he thought. *They gave me much more than I gave them.*

3   "Yo, Teach!" a voice boomed. Frank McCourt scanned the adolescents in his classroom. It was the fall of 1970 and his first week of teaching at Seward Park High School, which sat in the midst of **dilapidated** tenement buildings on Manhattan's Lower East Side. McCourt located the speaker and nodded. "You talk funny," the student said, "Where ya from?"

4   "Ireland," McCourt replied. With more than ten years of teaching experience under his belt, this kind of interrogation[1] no longer surprised him. But one question in particular still made him squirm[2] "Where'd you go to high school?" someone else asked.

5   *If I tell them the truth, they'll feel superior to me*, McCourt thought. *They'll throw it in my face.* Most of all, he feared an accusation he'd heard before—from himself: You come from nothing, so you are nothing.

6   But McCourt's heart whispered another possibility: Maybe these kids are **yearning for** a way of figuring out this new teacher. Am I willing to risk being humiliated in the classroom to find out?

---

[1] **interrogation:** intense questioning
[2] **squirm:** feel embarrassed or ashamed

7   "Come on, tell us! Where'd you go to high school?"

8   "I never did," McCourt replied.

9   "Did you get thrown out?"

10   *I was right*, the teacher thought. *They're curious.* McCourt explained he'd left school after the eighth grade to take a job.

11   "How'd you get to be a teacher, then?" they asked. "When I came to America," he began, "I dreamed bigger dreams. I loved reading and writing, and teaching was the most exalted profession I could imagine. I was unloading sides of beef[3] down on the docks when I decided enough was enough. By then I'd done a lot of reading on my own, so I persuaded New York University to enroll me."

12   McCourt wasn't surprised that this story fascinated his students. Theirs wasn't the kind of **poverty** McCourt had known; they had electricity and food. But he recognized the telltale signs of need in some of his students' threadbare[4] clothes and sensed the bitter **shame** and **hopelessness** he knew all too well. If recounting his own experiences would jolt these kids out of their defeatism so he could teach them something, that's what he would do.

13   A born storyteller, McCourt drew from a repertoire of accounts about his youth. His students would listen, spellbound[5] by the gritty details, drawn by something more powerful than curiosity. He'd look from face to face, recognizing a bit of himself in each sober gaze.

14   Since humor had been the McCourts' weapon against life's **miseries** in Limerick, he used it to describe those days. "Dinner usually was bread and tea," he told the students. "Mam[6] used to say, 'We've got our balanced diet: a solid and a liquid. What more could we want?'"

15   The students roared with laughter.

16   He realized that his honesty was helping forge a link with kids who normally regarded teachers as adversaries. At the same time, the more he talked about his past, the better he understood how it affected him.

17   While at college, a creative-writing professor had asked him to describe an object from his childhood. McCourt chose the decrepit bed he and his brothers had shared. He wrote of their being scratched by the stiff stuffing protruding from the mattress and of ending up jumbled together in the sagging center with fleas[7] leaping all over their bodies. The professor gave McCourt an A, and asked him to read the essay to the class.

18   "No!" McCourt said, recoiling at the thought. But for the first time, he began to see his **sordid** childhood, with all the miseries, betrayals, and longings that **tormented** him still, as a worthy topic. *Maybe that's what I was born to put on the page,[8]* he thought.

19   While teaching, McCourt wrote occasional articles for newspapers and magazines. But his major effort, a memoir of 150 pages that he churned out in 1966, remained unfinished. Now he leafed through his students' transcribed essays. They lacked polish, but somehow they worked in a way his writing didn't. *I'm trying to teach these kids to write*, he thought, *yet I haven't found the secret myself.*

20   The bell rang in the faculty lounge at Stuyvesant High School in Manhattan. When McCourt began teaching at the prestigious[9] public high school in 1972, he joked that he'd finally made it to paradise. Some 13,000 students sought admission each year, competing for approximately 700 vacancies. Part of the fun of working with these bright students was keeping them a few degrees off-balance. McCourt asked at the beginning

(continued on next page)

---

[3] **sides of beef:** very large pieces of meat

[4] **threadbare:** very thin from being used a lot

[5] **spellbound:** very interested in something you are listening to

[6] **Mam:** a word for *mother*

[7] **fleas:** tiny insects that bite

[8] **put on the page:** to write

[9] **prestigious:** admired or respected as one of the best or most important

of a creative writing class, "What did you have for dinner last night?" The students stared at him as if he'd lost his wits.

21   "Why am I asking this? Because you need to become good observers of detail if you're going to write well." As answers trickled in, McCourt countered with more questions. "Where did you eat?" "Who else was there?" "Who cleaned up afterward?"

22   Student after student revealed families fragmented by divorce and loneliness. "We always argue at the table." "We don't eat together." As he listened, McCourt mentally catalogued the differences and similarities between his early life and theirs. He began to appreciate more the companionship that enriched the **meager** meals his mother had struggled to put on the table.

23   That night McCourt lay awake in bed, harvesting the bounty of his chronic insomnia.[10] He visualized himself standing on a street in Limerick and took an imaginary walk about. He looked at shops and pubs, noting their names, and peered through their windows. He read street signs and recognized people walking past. Oblivious to time, he wandered the Limerick of his mind, collecting the details of scenery and a cast for the book that festered inside him.

24   Yet when he later picked up a notebook and tried to set down the previous night's travels, he stopped. McCourt knew that he was still holding back. Before, he had done it out of respect for his mother, who would have been mortified to see the darkest and most searing episodes of his childhood in print.[11] But she had died in 1981, and with her had died his excuse.

25   At least the bits and pieces that bubbled into his consciousness enlivened the stories he told in class. "Everyone has a story to tell," he said. "Write about what you know with conviction, from the heart. Dig deep," he urged. "Find your own voice and dance your own dance!"

26   On Fridays the students read their compositions aloud. To draw them out, McCourt would read excerpts from his duffel bag full of notebooks. "You had such an interesting childhood, Mr. McCourt," they said. "Why don't you write a book?" They threw his own words back at him: "It sounds like there's more to that story; dig deeper . . ."

27   McCourt was past 50 and painfully aware of the passage of time. But despite his growing frustration at his unfinished book, he never tired of his students' work.

28   *These young people have been giving you lessons in courage*, he thought. *When will you dare as mightily as they?*

29   It was October 1994. Frank McCourt, now retired, sat down and read his book's new opening, which he had written a few days before and still found satisfying. But many blank pages lay before him. *What if I never get it right?* he wondered grimly.

30   He stared at the logs glowing in the fireplace and could almost hear students' voices from years past, some angry, some **defeated**, others confused and seeking guidance. "It's no good, Mr. McCourt. I don't have what it takes."

31   Then Frank McCourt, author, heard the steadying tones of Frank McCourt, teacher: Of course you do. Dig deeper. Find your own voice and dance your own dance.

32   He scribbled a few lines. "I'm in a playground on Classon Avenue in Brooklyn with my brother Malachy. He's two, I'm three. We're on the seesaw." In the innocent voice of an unprotected child who could neither comprehend nor control the world around him, Frank McCourt told his tale of poverty and **abandonment**.

33   In September 1996 *Angela's Ashes* hit bookstores. Within weeks McCourt received an excited call from his agent: His book was getting warm reviews and selling at an unbelievable rate. The most surprising call came on April 7, 1997, when McCourt learned

---

[10] **insomnia:** sleeplessness

[11] **in print:** in a book, newspaper, or magazine

that *Angela's Ashes* had received America's most coveted literary award: the Pulitzer Prize.

34   McCourt laid his hands on the lectern, finishing his commencement address[12] at Lincoln Center. "Early in my teaching days, the kids asked me the meaning of a poem," he said. "I replied, 'I don't know any more than you do. I have ideas. What are your ideas?' I realized then that we're all in the same boat. What does anybody know?

35   "So when you go forth tonight, fellow students—for I'm still one of you—remember that you know nothing! Be excited that your whole life is before you for learning."

36   As he gave them a crooked smile, the students leapt to their feet, waving and whistling. *This is too much*, he thought, startled by the intensity of their response. During months of speeches and book signings, he had received many accolades.[13] But this—this left him fighting back tears. It's the culmination of everything, coming from them.

37   Their standing ovation continued long after Frank McCourt, the teacher who had learned his own lessons slowly but well, returned to his seat.

---

[12] **commencement address:** speech given at a graduation
[13] **accolades:** praise and approval for someone's work

MAIN IDEAS

1 Look again at the Preview on page 38. How did your answers to the questions help you understand the story?

2 Complete the timeline with information from Vocabulary on pages 36–37 and Reading One.

1934	Frank McCourt's family returned to Ireland.
1949	Frank McCourt returned to the United States.
1970	Frank McCourt first week teaching at Seward Park High School.
1981	Frank McCourt's mother died and her excuse too.
1994	Frank McCourt's retired, sat down and read his book's new opening
1996	He received an exicited call from his Agent. His book was getting warm reviews and selling at an unavibble rate.
1997	He recived America's most coveted literary award: the Pulitzer Prize.

DETAILS

Complete the left side of the chart using information from Main Ideas on page 41. Then complete the right side of the chart with details about why the event took place and what happened as a result. Look at Vocabulary on pages 36–37 and Reading One for the information.

1934 Event: Frank McCourt's family returned to Ireland.	*The McCourts wanted a better life, so they returned to Ireland. Their life was still very hard. Three children died. The family remained very poor and very hungry.*
1949 Event:	
1970 Event:	
1981 Event:	
1994 Event:	
1996 Event:	
1997 Event:	

MAKE INFERENCES

INFERRING THE MEANING OF IDIOMS AND EXPRESSIONS FROM CONTEXT

An inference is an educated guess about meaning. Readers can often infer the meaning of idioms and expressions from the context of a story. By closely reading the information in the sentence where the idiom or expression is used, as well as reading the sentences before and after that sentence, readers can often determine the meaning of an idiom or expression.

Look at the example and read the explanation.

What does the idiom in bold mean? *(paragraph 4)*

"With more than ten years of teaching experience **under his belt**, this kind of interrogation no longer surprised him."

In the sentence we read that McCourt has more than ten years of teaching experience; we also read that the students' questions do not surprise him. We can infer that McCourt's teaching experience makes him feel strong enough to face his students. We can guess that the meaning of the idiom is "already achieved or experienced."

Read the following idioms and expressions in context. Refer to the paragraphs in parentheses. Use context clues to determine meaning. Write a synonym or definition of the idiom or expression. Compare your answers with another student's and discuss context clues that helped you figure out the meaning.

1. throw it in my face *(paragraph 5)* You come from nothing, so you are nothing

   use that information againt him

2. forge a link *(paragraph 16)*

   to from strong connection

3. churned out *(paragraph 19)*

   to churned

4. leafed through *(paragraph 19)*

   I haven't found the secreat myself

5. lost his wits *(paragraph 20)*

   feel superior me

6. harvesting the bounty *(paragraph 23)*

   humiliated in the classroom

(continued on next page)

7. bubbled into his consciousness *(paragraph 25)*

_____bits and pieces_____

8. dig deep *(paragraph 25)*

_____Write about what you know! with conviction_____

9. dance your own dance *(paragraph 25)*

_____Find your voice :- be himself, be your self_____

10. in the same boat *(paragraph 34)*

_____We are all in same boat._____

EXPRESS OPINIONS

Discuss the questions with a partner. Then share your answers with the class.

1. Frank McCourt had many obstacles in his life. What do you think was Frank McCourt's greatest obstacle? How did he overcome it?

2. How did Frank McCourt's students give him the courage he had been lacking to overcome his obstacles?

■■■■■■■■■■■■■■■■■■■■■■■■■■■■■■■ **GO TO** MyEnglishLab **TO GIVE YOUR OPINION ABOUT ANOTHER QUESTION.**

READING TWO | MARLA RUNYAN

READ

1 Look at the boldfaced words in the reading and think about the questions.

1. Which words do you know the meanings of?

2. Can you use any of the words or phrases in a sentence?

Marla Runyan is an accomplished athlete who is legally blind. Despite her blindness, she has excelled in many fields in addition to athletics. How has she been able to do so much? She explains it by saying, "A poor attitude can be far more disabling than blindness."

2 Read the article about Marla Runyan. As you read, notice the boldfaced vocabulary. Try to guess its meaning from the context.

MARLA RUNYAN
By Peter Rugg

1   Marla Runyan is a woman used to questions. There are the interviews about how she made history chasing an Olympic dream, runners who want to know how she trains, people looking for advice on how to overcome the obstacles in their lives. They come to her looking for answers sometimes mundane and sometimes profound. But since she was a child, there has been one question that has followed her above all others. What do you see?

2   At the age of nine, Runyan was diagnosed with Stargardt's Disease. It's a genetic condition that causes progressive vision loss, and most who suffer from it have their sight degenerate[1] to the point of legal blindness.

3   Now 44, Runyan's vision is reduced to shadows and indistinct shapes, though she retains some peripheral sight.

4   "Here's what I do see: a permanent blot in front of my eyes that almost has physical properties," she described in her autobiography, *No Finish Line: My Life As I See It*. "Imagine that someone took a flash picture, and the flash got in your eyes. For a few moments, you'd see a purplish or grey splotch. In a few minutes it would fade away, and the world around you would appear normal again. For me, it stays."

5   However, she has refused to be defined by her condition. Today she holds the Paralympic World Records in the B3 division for the 100m, 200m, 400m, 800m, 1500m, High Jump, Long Jump, and Pentathlon.

6   Her success has extended far beyond athletics. She has been a teacher, a public speaker, a coach, the race director for the Camarillo Half Marathon, a philanthropist[2] for Camp Ability, and, with the publication of her autobiography *No Finish Line: My Life as I See It*, a bestselling author.

7   This was not the life most thought Runyan would have. As a child, the specialists told her to lower her expectations. They told her she shouldn't expect to get the same grades as her fellow students because she wouldn't be able to learn the way they did. They told her that meant she likely wouldn't get into a good college.

8   While Runyan may not have been graced with perfect eyes, she was given a loving mother who instilled in her a sense of hard work, **self-reliance**, and pride.

9   "A poor attitude can be far more disabling than blindness," Runyan would later say.

10   All of the specialists were wrong. Runyan refused to give up because of her disability. In 1987, she graduated from Adolfo Camarillo High School, then went on to attend the University of San Diego to complete her Master's Degree in 1994. She studied education for deaf and blind students.

11   Still, none of it came easily.

(continued on next page)

---

[1]**degenerate:** to become worse

[2]**philanthropist:** a person who donates his or her time or money to help others

12   As an adult, Runyan admitted to struggling in the classroom because schoolwork was so **laborious** for her. However, one place she felt free was on the field. She'd always been an athletic girl, and in college she found herself drawn to the track.

13   When she was running, the divisions between herself and the students with perfect vision fell away. She felt as if she could do as well as everyone else.

14   It was a feeling she would chase the rest of her life, and following it would lead her into history.

15   In 2000, when she journeyed to Sydney, she became the first legally blind person ever to compete in the Olympic Games.

16   Then, in 2002, she finished the New York Marathon in fourth place with a time of 2 hours, 27 minutes, and ten seconds, becoming the fastest American in that year's competition and the second fastest American woman ever to cross the finish line.

17   In preparation for those games, Runyan told reporters that her biggest challenge was to keep track of the people just ahead of her as she navigated the field.

18   To compensate for her handicap, Runyan prepared for a style of racing she described as "fast and tactical—a combination of both."

19   The one thing she didn't plan for, or want, was sympathy.

20   "I don't expect any mercy, no mercy whatsoever," she said. "They're not going to say, 'Go ahead Marla.' That's not going to happen."

21   Runyan's unique story put her in the international spotlight and brought her fans across the globe.

22   Runyan explained to reporters that, though she loves knowing that she inspires people, seeing how strongly some people react to her story can be shocking.

23   In that interview, Runyan went on to recount how she received an email from a woman whose son wanted to be a skateboarder but had also been diagnosed with Stargardt's. At first the mother refused to allow him, but once she read Runyan's story, she told him "Go get the ramp."

24   As much as these stories inspire Runyan to continue her example, she admits that even reading them can be a **struggle**. Reading is extremely difficult, and she can only do so with a voice output system on her computer. The words have to be enlarged so much that sometimes only three letters at a time can fit on the screen.

25   There are moments when she simply **gives up** for the day. Even the simple act of reading an email is too much.

26   Those moments never last long.

27   "I've never known anyone to be successful if all they do is blame, if they choose to be a victim," she told reporters. "If you choose to be a victim of this or that, or of what others have done to you, or what you believe to be someone else's fault, [you're] just constantly making excuses. I think the secret to achieving something is holding yourself **accountable** for your choices, good and bad, and learning from your mistakes, and then re-grouping and moving on. It's an ongoing process."

COMPREHENSION

Two of the three choices for each question are correct. Cross out the answer that is incorrect.

1. What does Marla "see"?

    a. a permanent blot

    b. shadows and indistinct shapes

    c. blindness

2. How has her life defied the experts' predictions?

    a. She graduated from college.

    b. She struggled in the classroom.

    c. She became a bestselling author.

3. How did she feel on the field?

    a. She felt equal to everyone else.

    b. She felt free.

    c. She felt she needed sympathy.

4. What strategies have helped her to be successful?

    a. lowering her expectations

    b. having a good attitude

    c. working hard

5. How does she feel about her effect on other people?

    a. She is shocked.

    b. She is inspired.

    c. She is self-reliant.

GO TO MyEnglishLab FOR MORE VOCABULARY PRACTICE.

READING SKILL

1 Go back to Reading Two and see how many synonyms and antonyms you can find.

RECOGNIZING POSITIVE REDUNDANCY

Authors often use synonyms and antonyms in their writing for positive redundancy. This use of synonyms and antonyms in a text allows readers to read ideas more than once but with different vocabulary. In this way, meaning is reinforced, but language is new. The writer's ideas stay with the reader as related vocabulary is threaded through a text.

Look at the example and read the explanation.

Reread paragraph 4 of Reading Two, "Marla Runyan."

"Here's what I do see: a permanent **blot** in front of my eyes that almost has physical properties," she described in her autobiography, *No Finish Line: My Life As I See It*. "Imagine that someone took a flash picture, and the flash got in your eyes. For a few moments, you'd see a purplish or grey splotch. In a few minutes it would fade away, and the world around you would appear normal again. For me, it stays."

In the first sentence, Marla uses the word *blot*. What synonym for the word *blot* does she use later in the paragraph?

Answer: splotch

This synonym adds interest to her description. Instead of repeating the word *blot*, the author uses a synonym to repeat an idea, but with new language.

Noticing synonyms and antonyms will help you see where the author emphasizes important information and ideas.

2 Work with a partner to identify synonyms and antonyms for the words given. Then discuss the effect of using different language rather than repeating the same words or expressions.

1. In paragraph 3, the author mentions *shadows*. What similar expression is also used in this paragraph? indistinct shape

2. In paragraph 8, the author uses the word *graced*. What synonym is also used in this paragraph? given

3. In paragraph 10, the author uses the phrase *give up*. What antonym is also used in this paragraph? go on, went on

4. In paragraph 12, the author talks about *struggling*. What two-word expression with an opposite meaning is also used in this paragraph? felt free

5. In paragraph 19, the author uses the word *sympathy*. What synonym is used in paragraph 20? _____ mercy _____

6. In paragraph 24, the author says reading can be a *struggle*. What similar phrase is also used in this paragraph? _____ extremely difficult and _____

7. In paragraph 27, the author talks about *blame*. What similar expression is also used in this paragraph? _____ victim _____

■■■■■■■■■■■■■■■■■■■■■■■■■■■■■■■■■■■■ *GO TO* MyEnglishLab *FOR MORE SKILL PRACTICE.*

CONNECT THE READINGS

STEP 1: Organize

Both Frank McCourt in Reading One (R1) and Marla Runyan in Reading Two (R2) faced many obstacles and challenges in their lives. These same challenges also helped them to discover and develop their talent and become successful. Complete the chart comparing Frank McCourt and Marla Runyan.

	FRANK MCCOURT (R1)	MARLA RUNYAN (R2)
1. Obstacles they faced	He was poor. He learned a lot, He passed exams.	She wasn't see clearly. Low expectation.
2. Person or people who influenced and inspired them	He was learned so much in childhood. He had a experiences.	Her Mother : Pride, Hard working
3. Personal values, traits, or characteristics that helped them face their obstacles	Dreams, Self-talk, self reliene	Hard work, Pride and Possative attitude.
4. Talent or gift that resulted from the challenges they faced	His books sold a lot. He recelcoved America's most coveted literary Award the Pulitzer Prize.	She has a woorb record in Paralympic in B3 Division. and She became the first legally blind person ever to complet in olempic Games.

STEP 2: Synthesize

On a separate piece of paper, write a short paragraph comparing the lives of Frank McCourt and Marla Runyan. Use the information from Step 1. Describe their obstacles and triumphs.

■■■■■■■■■■■■■■■■■■■■■■■■■■■■■■■■■■■■ *GO TO* MyEnglishLab *TO CHECK WHAT YOU LEARNED.*

VOCABULARY

REVIEW

The chain diagram below shows the three stages of overcoming obstacles: facing an obstacle, dealing with an obstacle, and overcoming an obstacle. Write the words from the box in the correct circles. Some of the words may be put in more than one circle. Discuss your answers with a partner.

responsibible.

accountable	exalted	inquisitiveness	pride
confused	expectations	laborious	self-reliance
darkest	free	misery	struggle
defeated	give up	mortified	suffer
disability	hopelessness	paradise	yearning for

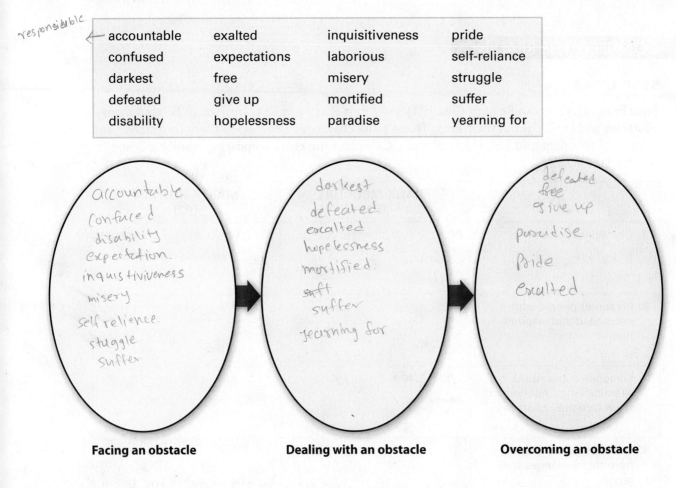

Facing an obstacle

accountable
confuced
disability
expectation.
inquistiviveness
misery
self relience.
stuggle
suffer.

Dealing with an obstacle

darkest
defeated
excalted
hopelessness
mortisied:
suft
suffer
yearning for

Overcoming an obstacle

defeated
free
give up
paradise.
Pride
excalted.

EXPAND

An **analogy** is a comparison between two words that seem similar or are related in some way. In this exercise, the word pairs are either synonyms or antonyms. For example, in item 1, *struggle* is a synonym of *fight*; in the same way, *embarrassment* is a synonym of *shame*.

Work with a partner. Discuss the relationship between the words. Circle the word that best completes each analogy. Then circle *synonym* or *antonym* for each set of words. Use a dictionary if you need help.

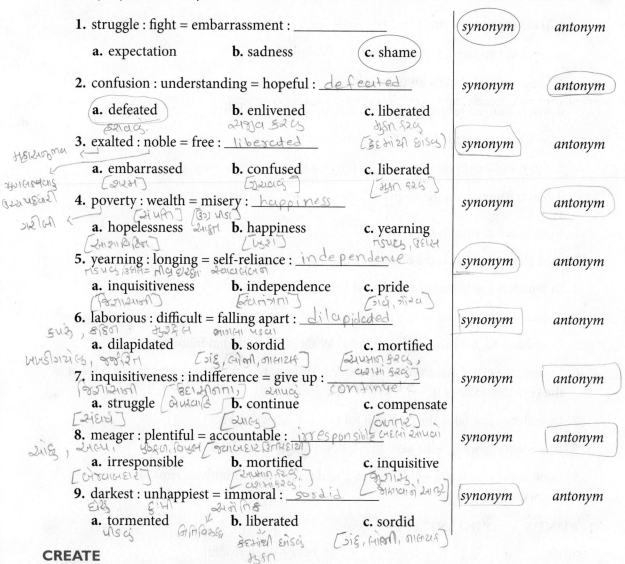

1. struggle : fight = embarrassment : _____   (*synonym*)   *antonym*

   a. expectation   **b.** sadness   (**c.** shame)

2. confusion : understanding = hopeful : _defeated_   *synonym*   (*antonym*)

   (**a.** defeated)   **b.** enlivened   **c.** liberated

3. exalted : noble = free : _liberated_   (*synonym*)   *antonym*

   a. embarrassed   **b.** confused   **c.** liberated

4. poverty : wealth = misery : _happiness_   *synonym*   (*antonym*)

   a. hopelessness   **b.** happiness   **c.** yearning

5. yearning : longing = self-reliance : _independence_   (*synonym*)   *antonym*

   a. inquisitiveness   **b.** independence   **c.** pride

6. laborious : difficult = falling apart : _dilapidated_   *synonym*   *antonym*

   a. dilapidated   **b.** sordid   **c.** mortified

7. inquisitiveness : indifference = give up : _continue_   *synonym*   (*antonym*)

   a. struggle   **b.** continue   **c.** compensate

8. meager : plentiful = accountable : _irresponsible_   *synonym*   (*antonym*)

   a. irresponsible   **b.** mortified   **c.** inquisitive

9. darkest : unhappiest = immoral : _sordid_   (*synonym*)   *antonym*

   a. tormented   **b.** liberated   **c.** sordid

CREATE

Choose one of the situations. On a separate piece of paper, write a letter using words and phrases from Review and Expand.

1. Imagine you are the skateboarder's mother. Write a letter to Marla Runyan. Explain how she helped and inspired you and your son.

2. Imagine you are one of Frank McCourt's former students. You have just graduated from college. Write a letter to Frank McCourt. Explain how he helped and inspired you to overcome an obstacle.

GO TO MyEnglishLab *FOR MORE VOCABULARY PRACTICE.*

GRAMMAR

1 Examine the sentences and answer the questions with a partner.

    a. Teaching was the most exalted profession I could imagine.

    b. McCourt enjoyed **writing** about his childhood.

    c. McCourt had done a lot of **reading**.

    d. Marla Runyan refused **to give up** because of her disability.

    e. McCourt persuaded New York University **to enroll** him.

    f. After McCourt's mother died, he felt free **to write** his memoirs.

    g. Marla Runyan has the ability **to inspire** others with her actions.

1. In sentence *a*, what is the subject?

2. In sentence *b*, what is the object of the verb *enjoyed*?

3. In sentence *c*, what word follows the preposition *of*?

4. Look at the boldfaced words in *a*, *b*, and *c*. They are gerunds. How are gerunds formed?

5. In sentence *d*, the main verb is *refused*. What is the verb that follows it?

6. In sentence *e*, the main verb is *persuaded*. What is the object of the main verb? What is the verb that follows it?

7. In sentence *f*, what is the verb that follows the adjective *free*?

8. In sentence *g*, what is the verb that follows the noun *ability*?

9. Look at the boldfaced words in *d*, *e*, *f*, and *g*. They are infinitives. How are infinitives formed?

GERUNDS AND INFINITIVES

Gerunds	read + ing = reading
To form a gerund, **use the base form of the verb + -ing**.	write + ing = writing* *Note that for verbs ending in a consonant and final "e," drop the "e" before adding "ing".*
1. Use the gerund as the **subject** of a sentence.	**Writing** is very important to Frank McCourt.
2. Use the gerund as the **object** of a sentence after certain verbs (such as *enjoy, acknowledge, recall*).	Frank McCourt enjoys **writing**. McCourt recalled **not wanting** to offend his mother, and that held him back.
3. Use the gerund **after a preposition** (such as *of, in, for, about*).	Frank McCourt is interested in **writing**.

Infinitives

To form an infinitive, use *to* + **the base form of the verb**.	to read to write
4. Use the infinitive **after certain verbs.**	
a. some verbs are followed directly by an infinitive (such as *learn, decide, agree, refuse*)	McCourt's students **learned to write** about their personal experiences.
b. some verbs are followed by an object + an infinitive (such as *urge, persuade*)	McCourt **urged his students to write** about their personal experiences.
c. some verbs are followed by an infinitive or an object + an infinitive (such as *want, ask, need*)	McCourt **wanted to write** about his personal experiences. McCourt **wanted them to write** their personal experiences.
5. Use the infinitive **after certain adjectives** (such as *free, able, hard*).	McCourt's students were **free to write** about whatever they wanted.
6. Use the infinitive **after certain nouns** (such as *ability, freedom*).	McCourt's students had the **freedom to write** about whatever they wanted.

2 Work with a partner. Underline the gerund or infinitive in each sentence. Write the number of the grammar rule that applies to each.

__1__ **a.** <u>Doing</u> schoolwork was very laborious for Marla Runyan.

_____ **b.** Marla Runyan has the ability to run as fast as sighted competitors.

_____ **c.** McCourt acknowledged not going to high school.

_____ **d.** Marla Runyan was able to compete in the 2000 Olympics.

_____ **e.** A professor asked McCourt to describe an object from his childhood.

_____ **f.** Marla Runyan has refused to be defined by her condition.

_____ **g.** Many people don't feel free to write about their lives.

_____ **h.** Recounting his experiences inspired McCourt's students.

_____ **i.** McCourt couldn't think about writing his memoirs while his mother was alive.

_____ **j.** McCourt's students urged him to write a book.

3 Read the information about Frank McCourt and Marla Runyan. Rewrite each situation using a form of the first verb given and the gerund or infinitive form of the second verb.

1. McCourt was worried that his memoirs would embarrass his mother. After she died, he didn't have to worry about this. (feel free / write)

   After his mother died, McCourt felt free to write his memoirs.

2. Before Marla runs a marathon, she spends months preparing. It takes a long time to get ready for a 26-mile race. (need / train)

   _____

3. McCourt had no high school education, but he had read a lot. He told New York University it should admit him. (persuade / allow)

   _____

4. Marla's unique story has brought her fans from around the globe. She is happy that her story is helping others. (enjoy / inspire)

   _____

5. Frank McCourt hadn't gone to high school. He was afraid of what his students would think about him. (worry about / tell)

   _____

6. At first the boy's mother did not want him to skateboard, but after she read about Marla's story, she changed her mind. (decide / let)

   _____

7. McCourt's students didn't think they were able to write. He gave them lots of encouragement and told them "everyone has a story to tell." (urge / write)

   _____

8. Because Marla is legally blind, it is a struggle for her to read the words on a computer screen. (be hard / see)

   _____

9. McCourt remembered the town of Limerick. He could see and imagine what it was like when he was a child. (recall / live)

   _____

10. Specialists told Marla she couldn't expect to get good grades. Despite their predictions, Marla attended the University of San Diego and completed her Master's degree. (be able / graduate)

    _____

GO TO MyEnglishLab *FOR MORE GRAMMAR PRACTICE AND TO CHECK WHAT YOU LEARNED.*

FINAL WRITING TASK

In this unit, you read personal accounts of how people overcame obstacles.

You are going to *write a biographical paragraph about how you or someone you know overcame an obstacle*. Use the vocabulary and grammar from the unit.*

PREPARE TO WRITE: Listing

Listing is a prewriting activity in which you list information about a topic or category before you begin to write a paragraph or essay.

Look back at Connect the Readings on page 49 to complete the first column of the chart. In the second column, write three or more obstacles that you or someone you know has faced.

OBSTACLES FACED BY FRANK MCCOURT AND MARLA RUNYAN	OBSTACLES FACED BY ME OR SOMEONE I KNOW

WRITE: A Biographical Paragraph

A **paragraph** is a group of sentences that are related and that support a controlling idea. A **biographical paragraph** describes a person's life and sometimes focuses on one particular aspect. All paragraphs have three parts: the **topic sentence**, the **supporting sentences**, and the **concluding sentence**.

TOPIC SENTENCE

The **topic sentence** introduces the main idea and the controlling idea, which is your idea or opinion about the main idea. The topic sentence controls what you write in the rest of the paragraph. All the sentences in the paragraph must relate to, describe, or illustrate the controlling idea in the topic sentence.

(continued on next page)

---

* For Alternative Writing Topics, see page 61. These topics can be used in place of the writing topic for this unit or as homework. The alternative topics relate to the theme of the unit but may not target the same grammar or rhetorical structures taught in the unit.

SUPPORTING SENTENCES

The second part of the paragraph includes **supporting sentences** that give details or examples that develop your ideas about the topic. This is usually the longest part of the paragraph, since it discusses and explains the controlling idea.

CONCLUDING SENTENCE

The **concluding sentence** is the last part of the paragraph. It can do one or more of the following: summarize the paragraph, offer a solution to the problem, restate the topic sentence, or offer an opinion.

1 Read the paragraph. Then answer the questions with a partner.

Michael Jordan said, "Obstacles don't have to stop you. If you run into a wall, don't turn around and give up. Figure out how to climb it, go through it, or work around it." This attitude can be seen all around us. Many people have faced great obstacles in their lives but have found ways to overcome and actually benefit from these obstacles. For example, Greg Barton, the 1984, 1988, and 1992 U.S. Olympic medalist in kayaking, was born with a serious disability. He had club feet, his toes pointed inward, and as a result, he could not walk easily. Even after a series of operations, he still had limited mobility. Even so, Greg was never defeated. First, he taught himself to walk, and even to run. Then he competed on his high school running team. He knew, though, he would never become an Olympic runner, so he looked for other sports that he could play. Happily, he discovered kayaking, a perfect sport for him because it required minimal leg and foot muscles. Using his upper body strength, he was able to master the sport. Finally, after many years of training and perseverance, Greg made the 1984 Olympic team. He says of his accomplishments, "Each step of the road has been made easier by looking just as far as necessary—yet not beyond that." In short, even though that road was paved with obstacles, he was able to overcome them and achieve the impossible.

1. What is the topic of the paragraph? How do you know?

_____

_____

2. What is the controlling idea?

_____

_____

3. Underline the sentences that support the topic and controlling ideas. How do they relate to the controlling idea?

_____

_____

4. What is the concluding sentence? What does it do?

_____

_____

Note: For more information on topic sentences and controlling ideas, see Unit 1.

2 Now write the first draft of your biographical paragraph. Use the information from Prepare to Write and complete the chart below to plan your paragraph. Make sure you have a topic sentence, supporting sentences, and a concluding sentence. Be sure to use grammar and vocabulary from the unit.

Topic Sentence:

1.

Supporting Sentences:

2.

3.

4.

5.

6.

Concluding Sentence:

7.

REVISE: Choosing Appropriate Support

The **supporting sentences** in a paragraph help the reader to better understand the controlling idea. Supporting sentences provide examples, details, and facts, and must relate directly to the topic sentence.

 Read each topic sentence. Two ideas support the topic sentence and one does not. Cross out the idea that does not support the topic sentence.

1. Ever since Greg Barton was in high school, he longed to be an Olympic champion.

   a. Greg's sports records

   b. How Greg trained for the Olympics

   c. ~~Greg's academic achievements~~

2. The achievements of people like Greg Barton and Marla Runyan have inspired many others.

   a. Explanation of how they have inspired others

   b. How many people have read about Greg Barton and Marla Runyan

   c. Greg Barton's and Marla Runyan's obstacles

3. The poverty-stricken lives of Frank McCourt's students deeply affected him.

   a. How Frank saw himself in his students

   b. How Frank taught his students to write

   c. How the students inspired Frank to write

4. Training to run a marathon is a very difficult and time-consuming process.

   a. The patience needed to run a marathon

   b. Reasons why people should run a marathon

   c. The amount of practice and time needed to run a marathon

2 Each paragraph has one supporting sentence that does not directly relate to the topic sentence. Cross out the sentence and explain why it is unrelated.

1. Helen Keller lost her sight at a very early age and, so, was very frustrated as a child. First of all, because she could neither hear nor speak, she couldn't understand what was happening around her. She felt her mother's lips moving as she spoke, but this made no sense to her. She couldn't understand what her mother was doing. ~~Her mother could hear and speak.~~ Secondly, once she learned what words were, she felt she could never communicate with them as quickly as sighted people could. As a result of all her frustration, she would often cry and scream until she was exhausted.

   Explanation: _The sentence focuses on her mother's abilities, not Helen's frustrations._

2. Succeeding in sports liberated Marla Runyan and Greg Barton. They both faced overwhelming obstacles, but sports freed them from their hardest struggles. For example, when Marla was on the field, she finally felt she could do as well as everyone else. Similarly, when Greg found the best sport for his physical limitations, he excelled. In addition, Marla has become a bestselling author. They are both great athletes who were freed from their struggles by sports.

Explanation: _____

_____

3. Some of the world's most talented and famous people have overcome some of the hardest obstacles. For example, Ludwig van Beethoven became deaf at age 46. Franklin D. Roosevelt was paralyzed by polio and was often in a wheelchair, but he was elected president of the United States four times. Finally, Steven Hawking is a world-famous scientist who is completely paralyzed and cannot speak. Furthermore, he lives in England. These people show us that we should never give up or let obstacles defeat us.

Explanation: _____

_____

3 Look at your first draft. Make sure your supporting sentences give clear examples and details that connect with and support the controlling idea.

■■■■■■■■■■■■■■■■■■■■■■■■■■■■■■■■■■ *GO TO* MyEnglishLab *FOR MORE SKILL PRACTICE.*

EDIT: Writing the Final Draft

Go to MyEnglishLab and write the final draft of your paragraph. Carefully edit it for grammatical and mechanical errors, such as spelling, capitalization, and punctuation. Make sure you use some of the grammar and vocabulary from the unit. Use the checklist to help you write your final draft. Then submit your paragraph to your teacher.

FINAL DRAFT CHECKLIST

❑ Does the paragraph describe a person who was faced with challenges and overcame them?

❑ Is there a topic sentence stating the obstacle that the person overcame?

❑ Do all the supporting sentences relate directly to the topic sentence?

❑ Is there a concluding sentence that restates the main idea of the paragraph, offers an opinion, or suggests a solution?

❑ Did you use gerunds and infinitives correctly?

❑ Have you used vocabulary from the unit?

UNIT PROJECT

RESEARCH: A Famous Person Who Has Overcome an Obstacle

In this unit, you have read about two people who have overcome obstacles. Many famous people have overcome great obstacles, including emotional, physical, and political obstacles. You are going to write a biographical essay about a famous person who has overcome an obstacle. Follow these steps:

STEP 1: Choose a famous person you admire or a person from the list below who has overcome an obstacle.

Artists / Performers	**Writers / Scientists**
Christopher Reeve	Steven Hawking
Mary Cassat	Sigmund Freud
50 Cent	Charles Darwin
Vincent van Gogh	Thomas Edison
Michelangelo	Hans Christian Andersen
Oprah Winfrey	Jorge Luis Borges
Stevie Wonder	

Sports Figures	**Politicians / Leaders**
Jackie Robinson	The Dalai Lama
Magic Johnson	Mahatma Ghandi
Natalie du Toit	John F. Kennedy
Jeremy Lin	Golda Meir
Bethany Hamilton	Franklin D. Roosevelt
Tahmina Kohistani	Nelson Mandela

STEP 2: Do research on the Internet about the person you chose. Check information on two or more websites.

1. If you need help getting started with Internet research, go back to Unit 1, pages 32–33.

2. Read the entries that relate to your topic.

3. Takes notes in your own words for a written report.

STEP 3: Use your notes to write a biographical essay. Be sure it includes the answers to these questions:

- When and where did/does the person live?

- What is/was the person famous for?

- What did this person achieve?

- What obstacles did this person have to overcome? How did he or she overcome them?

- What personal characteristics helped this person overcome his or her obstacles?

- What has researching this person taught you about life and overcoming obstacles?

STEP 4: Present your biography to the class by giving an oral presentation that summarizes your research.

ALTERNATIVE WRITING TOPICS

Write a paragraph about one of the topics. Use the vocabulary and grammar from the unit.

1. Read the quotation.

"I've missed more than 9,000 shots in my career. I've lost almost 300 games. 26 times, I've been trusted to take the game winning shot and missed. I've failed over and over and over again in my life. And that is why I succeed."

—Michael Jordan

How does this quotation apply to a person you have read about in the unit, to another famous person, or to yourself?

2. What are two of the most important values and personal characteristics people need in order to overcome obstacles? How do people apply these values and characteristics to their lives?

■■■■■■■■■■■■■■■■■■■■■■■■■■■■■ *GO TO* MyEnglishLab *TO WRITE ABOUT ONE OF THE ALTERNATIVE TOPICS, WATCH A VIDEO ABOUT A GIRL WITH AUTISM, AND TAKE THE UNIT 2 ACHIEVEMENT TEST.* ■■■■■■■■■■■■■

MAKING MEDICAL
Decisions

1 FOCUS ON THE TOPIC

1. What role can genes play in medicine?

2. Do you think medical treatment could be more effective if doctors had genetic information about their patients?

3. Genetic testing is now available very cheaply. Would you want to be tested to find out if you have the gene for a certain disease, even if there were no cure for the disease?

GO TO MyEnglishLab *TO CHECK WHAT YOU KNOW.*

VOCABULARY

1 Read the timeline about the history of medicine and medical decision-making. Try to understand the boldfaced words from the context.

PRIMITIVE TRIBAL SOCIETIES	A shaman (holy person) held all the existing medical knowledge. By **interpreting** the patient's symptoms, he would decide on a treatment.
ANCIENT GREECE (5TH CENTURY B.C.E.)	Socrates began the practice of questioning and testing beliefs to discover knowledge. This "Socratic method" had a tremendous **impact** on medical decision-making because it allowed physicians to evaluate treatment methods. As a result, treatments became more **reliable**.
4TH CENTURY B.C.E.	Medical practice was **revolutionized** by Hippocrates, the "father of western medicine." He changed medicine in many ways. For example, he was an **advocate** for publishing medical knowledge, focusing on patient care rather than diagnosis, and demanding physicians act professionally. He also recognized that disease could be caused by the **environment**. That is, diet and living habits are **linked** to disease, and their modification can be beneficial in reducing disease.
2ND CENTURY C.E.	The Skeptics saw the life-saving **potential** of *trial and error* as the basis of medical decision-making.
17TH CENTURY C.E.	Rene Descartes wrote about the mind-body **interaction**, which is the basis of psychology and psychiatry today.
2003	The Human Genome Project identified all the genes in the human body. Now patients are able to make medical decisions based on their own genetic **risk factor**. However, even with the knowledge provided by human gene mapping, there is not always **consensus** about what the best treatment is for a specific patient. Different doctors may recommend different treatments. That is why in the end, patients must weigh the emotional and medical **aspects** of each option and then make their own decision.

2 Find the boldfaced words in the timeline in Exercise 1. Write each word next to its definition.

1. _____ (n.) something that is likely to hurt you or be dangerous

2. _____impact_____ (n.) the effect that an event or situation has on someone or something

3. _____potential_____ (n.) the possibility that something will develop or happen in a particular way

4. _____environment_____ (n.) the circumstances, objects, or conditions that surround you

5. _____interaction_____ (n.) the action or influence of people, groups, or things on one another

6. _____aspect_____ (n.) parts or features of a situation, idea, problem, etc.

7. _____consensus_____ (n.) an agreement that everyone in a group reaches

8. _____advocate_____ (n.) strong supporter of a particular way of doing things

9. _____interpreting_____ (n.) explaining or deciding on the meaning of an event

10. _____reliable_____ (adj.) able to be trusted; dependable

11. _____link_____ (v.) made a connection between two or more events, people, or ideas

12. _____revolutionized_____ (v.) to have completely changed the way people think or do things

GO TO MyEnglishLab *FOR MORE VOCABULARY PRACTICE.*

PREVIEW

Read the first two paragraphs of *Genetic testing and disease: Would you want to know?* Work with a partner to answer the questions. Then read the rest of the article.

1. Why do you think Kristen wants to know?

2. How can knowing if she has the gene for Huntington's disease help her live her life better?

3. What do you think Kristen's father thinks about her being tested?

Genetic testing and disease: Would you want to know?

By Janice Lloyd, USA TODAY

1   Kristen Powers finishes packing her lunch and opens the kitchen door to leave for high school with her brother, Nate, in tow.[1] "I drive but always let him pick the music," she says, smiling. He gives her a gentle nudge[2] and they set off to the car.

2   Nothing like having a kid brother behind you, especially when you are embarking[3] on a courageous journey. Kristen, 18, is having blood work done May 18 to find out whether she inherited the defective gene for Huntington's disease, a fatal, neurodegenerative disorder that can debilitate victims as early as their mid-30s. The siblings have a 50-50 chance of developing the rare disease, which claimed their mother's life last year at age 45.

3   Nate, 16, doesn't know whether he'll follow his sister's lead. Only people 18 or older can be tested, unless they're exhibiting symptoms, because a positive result can be shattering news. There's also no cure. Huntington's is devastating on so many levels: People lose coordination, developing wild jerky movements; they suffer behavioral changes, often becoming depressed and psychotic; and in the end, they develop dementia and require total care. One of their last images of their mother was in a wheelchair in a nursing home.

4   Nate "has been amazingly supportive of my wanting to get tested," Kristen says. "He is interested in the whole process, but he's been hesitant over the years to commit to testing, while I've known since I was 15 that I wanted to do this."

5   "Know thyself" has taken on a scientific meaning for a growing number of people who, like Kristen, want a crystal ball to look into their DNA. Ever since the Human Genome Project identified the 20,000 to 25,000 genes in 2003, researchers have continued to identify the ones that play roles in diseases, from Alzheimer's to type 2 diabetes to certain types of cancer. Though lifestyle and environment are big pieces of the puzzle, consider this: Genetic tests could become part of standard care for everyone and **revolutionize** the way medicine is practiced, proponents say.

6   Gone would be the days of waiting to develop a disease. People would know about diseases they are at risk for and could change their living habits or consider treatments.

---

[1] **in tow:** following closely behind someone or something

[2] **nudge:** push

[3] **embarking:** starting something new, difficult, or exciting

Opponents warn about the **potential** for invasion of privacy—threatening employment and insurance—and the possibility that people equipped with the knowledge of their genetic makeup might make risky and unhealthy decisions.

7 Kristen has had counseling at the University of North Carolina to prepare her for dealing with her testing news, and she copes with stress by walking with her rescue dog, Jake. "Walking is critical for me," she says. She will return to the campus at the end of May with her father, Ed Powers, to get the results.

8 "She's always wanted to take matters into her own hands," her father says. "She's constantly asking what we can do to make things better. I am her biggest backer and want to be there for her every step of the way during this."

Leaning on social media

9 Kristen leans on her kitchen table and explains in a quiet, clear voice that she is ready to handle the news and has no plans to keep it secret. "I started out trying to find answers on the Internet about Huntington's disease," she says, "but I quickly became very disappointed. There's not a good video or an **advocate** for it, like Michael J. Fox is for Parkinson's disease."

10 She has raised $17,580 on the website Indiegogo.com and hired a video crew to make a documentary about the emotional and medical **aspects** of testing on her and her family. "Social media can be a real unifier. There's not much out there yet for young people on Huntington's. I want to change that."

11 Her mother, Nicola Powers, was diagnosed in 2003 after struggling with symptoms for several years. "I remember watching her stumble and walk like a drunk person at times," Kristen says. "That was before we knew what was wrong with her. She was really struggling. It was very scary."

12 Nicola Powers didn't know the disease ran in her family. She grew apart from her biological father after her parents divorced. Once she looked into his medical history because of her symptoms, she discovered he had Huntington's.

13 Kristen doesn't want the gene to be passed on again. She says she won't have children if she tests positive: "I can be candid with potential partners and be responsible," she says.

14 Genetic counselors warn about the emotional **impact** of testing on the person and family. "Some people like to plan everything out," says Brenda Finucane, president of the National Society of Genetic Counselors. "They think the information is empowering, while some people want to see how life plays out."

15 Robert Green has found that most people will not seek out risk information about late-onset Alzheimer's disease if they're not psychologically prepared to handle it. But "it turns out many people handle this kind of information quite well," says Green, associate director for research in genetics at Brigham and Women's Hospital in Boston. "Some changed their wills,[4] and some made lifestyle changes. Taking these tests is all about actionability.[5]"

16 Timing can be tricky, though. Kristen's father and stepmother, Betsy Banks Saul, suggested she hold off until she has a support system at college. "She's a very intelligent,

---

[4] **wills:** legal documents that show whom you want to have your money and property after you die

[5] **actionability:** being able to act upon

(continued on next page)

strong young woman, and we trust her, but we wish we could be nearby to support her," Betsy says.

17 After high school graduation in June, she will attend Stanford, in California — far from her farm, family, and friends. Kristen listened to her parents' concerns and considered putting off testing, "but I am a type A person who has always craved getting information. I want to know."

Not all tests are equal

18 Her test will look for the single gene that causes Huntington's, but most diseases have a more complicated genetic profile. A growing number of tests look at multiple genes that might increase or decrease a person's risk for developing thousands of diseases. Companies market the tests for as little as $100 on the Internet and don't require a physician's signature. But those kinds of results are not always **reliable**, says Ardis Dee Hoven, former chair of the American Medical Association.

19 "In the absence of a medical professional, a patient might have difficulty **interpreting** the test and make decisions that are not healthy decisions," Hoven says. For instance, someone who tests negative for BRCA1 and BRCA2—genes that put people at a higher risk for developing certain breast and ovarian cancers—might not know there are other **risk factors**. Unless the patient has a physician guiding her, Hoven says, she might think she's home-free[6] and skip routine screening tests.

20 David Agus, author of the new book *The End of Illness*, says that's why the company he co-founded, Navigenics, requires customers to get a signature from their doctors before being tested. Navigenics also offers genetic counseling as part of the $300–$400 fee. "Genetics are a small piece of the puzzle, but they're a very important piece," says Agus, head of the Center for Applied Molecular Medicine at the University of Southern California.

21 A cancer specialist, Agus discovered he has an above-average risk for cardiovascular disease and a slightly lower-than-average risk for colon cancer. His doctor put him on a statin to help prevent heart disease, and, he says, "my kids took it upon themselves to keep me away from french fries." He also had a colonoscopy at age 43, earlier than medical standards call for, and had a polyp removed. "Could my polyp have turned into cancer? Who knows? But why should I wait for that to happen? Unless our country can focus on prevention, which testing is all about, our health care costs will be completely out of control."

22 A study of 1,200 patients that was presented in March at an American College of Cardiology meeting found that those who were told they had a gene **linked** to heart disease improved their adherence to statin therapy by 13% compared with those who had not been tested for the gene.

23 "I could see how testing could become embedded[7] in how we treat our patients," Hoven says. "It's always better to prevent disease than to treat it, and quality of life is so much better for people."

How accessibility could change

24 Since the human genome was unraveled[8] a dozen years ago, genetic testing has been

---

[6] **home-free:** safe and without problems

[7] **embedded:** put something firmly and deeply into something else

[8] **was unraveled:** something very complicated was understood or explained

cost-prohibitive for the average person. The promise was that this breakthrough would lead to a better understanding of myriad[9] diseases and, ultimately, individualized treatments. Whole genome testing studies the **interaction** of our 20,000 to 25,000 genes with one another and with a person's **environment**. The $10,000 price tag, though, is expected to drop to $1,000 within the decade. When the tests become mainstream, doctors could face a dilemma.[10]

25   A study in March reports that 10 of 16 specialists (62%) favored telling a patient he carried the gene for Huntington's if the finding was incidental to why the test was ordered. The study noted that the specialists unanimously agreed on disclosing 21 of 99 commonly ordered genetic conditions for adults, and "multiple expert panels" might be needed to agree on what to tell patients.

26   "This is one of the toughest issues facing the rollout of clinical sequencing (whole genome sequencing)," Green says. He adds that after the study, he co-chaired a forum March 28 of the American College of Medical Genetics to discuss how to form a **consensus**.
     agreement

27   That's a non-issue for Kristen. She knows she will get an answer. One of her hardest decisions has been picking who will be in the room when she gets her results. She knows she wants the videographers taping. At first she didn't want her father to be there, but she relented when he asked her to reconsider.

28   "I know I can take the news," she says, "Knowledge is power. But I didn't think I could get a positive result and then watch my father cry. I've never seen him cry before."*

---

[9] **myriad:** a very large number of something

[10] **dilemma:** situation in which you have to make a choice between two or more difficult actions

*Kristin tested negative for Huntington's disease.

MAIN IDEAS

1 Look again at your answers to the questions from the Preview on page 65. How did your answers help you understand the article?

Reading One presents the pros and cons of genetic testing. Complete the chart with the information in the box. Then compare answers with a partner.

can choose appropriate treatment plan	There are other risk factors in addition to genes.	can change lifestyle	Positive result can lead to risky, unhealthy decisions.
can prevent diseases rather than just treat them	Positive result can be shattering for patient and family.	Patient may interpret test results incorrectly.	may threaten employment and insurance

POSITIVE	NEGATIVE

I. Can revolutionize medicine
  a.
  b. Quality of life is better.
	I. Emotional and physical impact
	  a.
	  b.

II. Information is empowering for patient.
  a.
  b.
	II. Invasion of privacy
	  a.

	III. Results are not always reliable.

	IV. Professional interpretation is not required.
	  a.
	  b.

DETAILS

Reading One mentions many people, places, and names of diseases connected with genetic testing. Match the people, places, and diseases on the left with the information on the right.

1. _____ Ardis Dee Hoven

   a. A progressive, degenerative disorder that attacks the brain's nerve cells, or neurons, resulting in loss of memory, thinking and language skills, and behavioral changes. It can be identified through genetic testing.

2. _____ Robert Green

   b. Head of the Center for Applied Molecular Medicine at the University of Southern California, author of *The End of Illness*, and co-founder of Navigenics, a genetic testing company

3. _____ Human Genome Project

   c. Location of Kristen Powers' counseling center

4. _____ Alzheimer's disease

5. _____ David Agus

6. _____ BRCA1 & BRCA2

7. _____ Huntington's disease

8. _____ University of North Carolina

9. _____ Indiegogo.com

10. _____ Brenda Finucane

11. _____ Michael J. Fox

d. An incurable fatal, neurodegenerative disorder that can debilitate victims as early as their mid-30s. It can be identified through genetic testing.

e. A 2003 study which identified the 20,000–25,000 genes in the human body

f. A well-known advocate for Parkinson's disease

g. Website where Kristen Powers raised money to hire a video crew

h. Former chair of the American Medical Association who warned that genetic test results are not always reliable

i. President of the National Society of Genetic Counselors who talks about the emotional impact of testing

j. Genes that indicate a high risk factor for developing certain breast and ovarian cancers

k. Associate director for research in genetics at Brigham and Women's Hospital. He talks about using the test results to take (positive) action.

MAKE INFERENCES

INFERRING DEGREE OF SUPPORT

When reading a text dealing with a controversial topic, it is important to be able to infer the degree of support that different people express about it. Some may be more supportive than others. Some may not be supportive at all. How do we "read between the lines" to get a sense of how supportive a person is? What language is used? How often does a statement of support occur? What reservations are expressed?

Look at the example and read the explanation.

Reading One deals with genetic testing. This is clearly a controversial topic as evidenced by the varying viewpoints of the people mentioned in the story.

How strong is Kristen's support of genetic testing?

Very Weak	Weak	Neutral	Strong	Very Strong

In paragraph 4, she notes, "I've known since I was 15 that I wanted to do this." She adds in paragraph 17, "I am a type A person who has always craved getting information. I want to know." Finally, in paragraph 28, she states, "I know I can take the news. Knowledge is power."

From these statements, we can infer that Kristen's support of genetic testing is *Very Strong*.

Understanding the position of people mentioned in a text concerning controversial topics enables the reader to understand the text more thoroughly.

Think about the people mentioned in Reading One. Rate their support of genetic testing, based on what they say and do, by putting an **X** in the correct column. Reread the indicated paragraph(s) to support your choice. Compare your answers with a partner's.

	Paragraph(s)	Very Weak	Weak	Neutral	Strong	Very Strong
NATE, KRISTEN'S BROTHER	3		✓			
KRISTEN'S FATHER	7, 8				✓	
BRENDA FINUCANE	14			✓		
ROBERT GREEN	15, 26				✓	
BETSY BANK SAUL	16				✓	
ARDIS DEE HOVEN	18, 19				✓	
DAVID AGUS	20, 21					✓

EXPRESS OPINIONS

Discuss the questions in a small group. Then share your answers with the class.

1. If you were in Kristen's position, would you have chosen to be tested?

2. Do you think genetic testing has more potential benefits than possible problems? Explain.

3. If you had a genetic test and it indicated you were at risk for a certain disease, who would you share the information with? Would you tell your children, brothers and sisters, cousins? How would you make this decision? Explain.

■■■■■■■■■■■■■■■■■■■■■■■■■■■■■■■■ *GO TO* MyEnglishLab *TO GIVE YOUR OPINION ABOUT ANOTHER QUESTION.*

READ

Norman Cousins was a well-known American writer and editor. When he was diagnosed with a serious illness, he was not content to let the doctor make all of his medical decisions. He decided to use his own type of alternative therapy. He focused on the importance of a positive attitude in healing. After writing about his successful recovery, he received mail from all over the world. Many letters came from doctors who supported his ideas.

1 Look at the boldfaced words in the reading and think about the questions.

1. Which words do you know the meanings of?

2. Can you use any of the words or phrases in a sentence?

2 Read the article about Norman Cousins. As you read, notice the boldfaced vocabulary. Try to guess its meaning from the context.

Charlie Chaplin

Norman Cousins's Laughter Therapy

1   In the summer of 1964, well-known [famous] writer and editor Norman Cousins became very ill. His body ached, and he felt constantly tired. It was difficult for him to even move around. He **consulted** his physician, who did many tests. Eventually, he was diagnosed as having ankylosing spondylitis, a very serious and destructive form of arthritis.[1] His doctor told him that he would become immobilized[2] and eventually die from the disease. He was told he had only a 1 in 500 chance of survival.

2   Despite the diagnosis,[3] Cousins was determined to overcome the disease and survive. He had always been interested in medicine and had read the work of organic chemist Hans Selye, *The Stress of Life* (1956). This book discussed the idea of how body chemistry and health can be damaged by emotional stress and negative attitudes. Selye's book made Cousins think about the possible benefits of positive attitudes and emotions. He thought, "If negative emotions produce (negative) changes in the body, wouldn't positive emotions produce positive chemical changes? Is it possible that love, hope, faith, laughter, confidence, and the will to live have positive therapeutic value?"

---

[1] **arthritis:** a disease that causes pain and swelling in the joints of the body
[2] **immobilized:** not able to move
[3] **diagnosis:** identification of what illness a person has

(continued on next page)

3   He decided to concentrate on positive emotions as a remedy to heal some of the symptoms of his ailment. In addition to his **conventional** medical treatment, he tried to put himself in situations that would **elicit** positive emotions. "Laughter Therapy" became part of his treatment. He scheduled time each day for watching comedy films, reading humorous books, and doing other activities that would bring about laughter and positive emotions. Within eight days of starting his "Laughter Therapy" program, his pain began to decrease, and he was able to sleep more easily. His body chemistry even improved. Doctors were able to see an improvement in his condition! Within a few months' time, he was able to walk wearing a metal brace. Soon after that, he was able to return to work. He actually reached complete recovery in a few years. He lived for 26 years after he became ill. He died in 1990 at the age of 75.

4   **Skeptical** readers may question the doctor's preliminary diagnosis, but Cousins believed his recovery was the result of a mysterious mind-body interaction. His "Laughter Therapy" is a good example of one of the many **alternative**, or nonconventional, medical treatments people look to today.

COMPREHENSION

Write answers to the questions. Use a separate piece of paper.

1. What was Norman Cousins' original diagnosis and how did he respond?

2. What is the connection between mind and body in Laughter Therapy?

3. What are some examples of Laughter Therapy?

4. How did Cousins benefit from his Laughter Therapy?

■■ GO TO MyEnglishLab FOR MORE VOCABULARY PRACTICE.

READING SKILL

1 In Reading Two, the author describes a number of events that take place around the year 1964: Cousins's diagnosis with arthritis, his reading books by Hans Selye, his invention of Laughter Therapy, etc. What is the order in which these different events take place? How do you know?

USING A TIMELINE TO ORGANIZE THE SEQUENCE OF EVENTS

Making a timeline of events in a narrative is a useful way to organize and remember information. This organization can help readers understand the text. In the article about Norman Cousins, a number of events happen before, during, and after the summer of 1964.

Look at paragraph 3. The author states, "Within eight days of starting his 'Laughter Therapy' program [later in the summer of 1964], his pain began to decrease, and he was able to sleep more easily. His body chemistry even improved."

How would you complete the timeline?

Later in the summer of 1964	
8 days later	

What happened later in the summer of 1964?
Cousins was diagnosed with a severe form of arthritis and started his Laughter Therapy program.

What happened eight days later?
Cousins's pain decreased, he was able to sleep better, and his body chemistry improved.

Understanding how events are related chronologically can increase the comprehension and retention of the information you read. Using a timeline is one way to do this.

---

2 Go back to Reading Two. Complete the timeline using information from the article.

Sometime before the summer of 1964	He had a dress
Summer 1964	He was tired, difficut to move around.
Later in the summer of 1964	Cousins was diagnosed with a severe form of arthritis and started his Laughter Therapy program.
8 days later	Cousins's pain decreased, he was able to sleep better, and his body chemistry improved.
A few months later	able to walk, wearing a metal brace.
Soon after that	able to return to work.
A few years later	complet recovery
1990	He died at the age 75

·······■·····■■·····■·····■·····■···■·····■···■·····■·■··■·■■·■■ GO TO MyEnglishLab FOR MORE SKILL PRACTICE.

STEP 1: Organize

You have read about genetic testing in Reading 1 (R1) and Norman Cousins's Laughter Therapy in Reading 2 (R2). What are the similarities and differences between them? Complete the Venn diagram with information from both readings. In the left circle, write notes that are true only about the genetic testing. In the right circle, write notes that are true only about Norman Cousins. In the middle, write notes that are true for both.

Genetic Testing (R1)

Expensive

ugly result
rist factor
take medicine
you gi+ts test

Both

take some action
therapy s

Laughter Therapy (R2)

Little cost

hope result.
treuding, watching
possotive attitude
more flexible

STEP 2: Synthesize

On a separate piece of paper, write a short paragraph explaining the similarities and differences between the genetic testing story and Norman Cousins's story. Use the information from Step 1.

GO TO MyEnglishLab TO CHECK WHAT YOU LEARNED.

VOCABULARY

REVIEW

Complete the paragraph using the words in the boxes.

advocates	impact	potential	revolutionize	risk factors
2	5	3	1	4

Many people believe that genetic testing will __revolutionize__ the
1.

practice of medicine. These __advocates__, who support genetic testing,
2.

believe it has the __potential__ to save many lives. They point out that
3.

the __risk factors__ indicated by genetic test results can help patients
4.

choose an appropriate treatment plan. These supporters acknowledge that the

admit

__impact__ of a positive test could be devastating, but point out that with
5.

proper counseling this negative aspect of genetic testing will not be a problem.

> Dependable

consult	environment	linked	reliable	skeptical	→ daughted people
3	5	4	2	1	

ask for advise

connected

However, others are __skeptical__ of the value of genetic testing. For
6.

one thing, some people don't believe it is __reliable__. In addition,
7.

they note that without professional help to interpret the results, patients may

experience more harm than good from the tests. Of course, if patients were required to

__consult__ with their doctors about the results, this problem would be
8.

eliminated. Another problem they see is that some diseases are not caused by genetics.

They are __linked__ to the __environment__.
9.   10.

(continued on next page)

alternative	consensus	conventional	interaction

→ Agreement

3   *2*   *4*   *1*

→ comunnication

A further area of concern is that doctors still do not fully understand the

_____interaction_____ between specific genes and how this affects the possibility
11.

for disease. Although there may never be _____consensus_____ on the value
12.

of genetic testing, the way the public and the medical establishment view specific

treatments and therapies may change over time. Don't forget that when Norman

Cousins first used Laughter Therapy in the summer of 1964, it was definitely viewed as

a(n) _____alternative_____ therapy. Nowadays, it is used in many hospitals around
13.

the world, and has entered the realm of _____conventional_____ medicine.
14.

EXPAND

1 Work with a partner. Write **S** if the word pairs have a similar meaning and **D** if they have a different meaning.

1. reliable / dependable __S__
2. impact / interaction __D__
3. conventional / alternative __D__
4. interpret / elicit __D__
5. revolutionize / change __S__
6. environment / surroundings __S__
7. treatment / diagnosis __D__
8. linked / connected __S__

9. elicit / produce __S__
10. consensus / disagreement __D__
11. consulted / asked advice of __S__
12. potential / ability __S__
13. aspect / factor __S__
14. skeptical / doubtful __S__
15. advocate / supporter __S__

2 Write the word that best completes each sentence.

1. The _____impact_____ *(impact / interaction)* of a positive test result can be devastating for a patient.

2. A medical professional can help a patient _____interpret_____ *(elicit / interpret)* genetic test results.

3. After the doctor told Norman Cousins he was suffering from ankylosing spondylitis, Cousins had to decide on his _treatment_ (treatment / diagnosis).

4. The idea of genetic testing is still a controversial topic. There is ongoing _disagreement_ (disagreement / consensus) on when it should be used.

5. When Norman Cousins first used Laughter Therapy, it was considered a(n) _alternative_ (alternative / conventional) treatment.

6. Norman Cousins watched comedy films as a way to _elicit_ (revolutionize / elicit) positive emotions.

7. Some people are skeptical of Cousins's original _diagnosis_ (diagnosis / treatment). They don't think he was really suffering from a severe form of arthritis.

CREATE

Imagine that you are going to interview Kristen Powers or Norman Cousins. On a separate piece of paper, write four interview questions that you would like to ask. Use at least one word from the box in each question. Then work with a partner. Answer each other's questions as if you were Kristen Powers or Norman Cousins.

advocate	consensus	elicit	impact	link	revolutionize
alternative	consult	environment	interaction	potential	skeptical
aspect	conventional	factor	interpret	reliable	

GO TO MyEnglishLab FOR MORE VOCABULARY PRACTICE.

GRAMMAR

1 Examine the sentences with a partner. Write **T** (true) or **F** (false) for the statements that follow the sentences.

a. If Kristen Power's mother **hadn't died** of Huntington's disease, Kristen **might not have wanted** to be tested.

b. If Kristen's mother **had been** closer to her biological father, Kristen **could have known** that Huntington's disease ran in her family.

c. If Norman Cousins **hadn't read** Hans Selye's book, Cousins **wouldn't have invented** Laughter Therapy.

(continued on next page)

1. In sentence *a*: Kristen's mother died. _____

   Kristen didn't want to be tested. _____

2. In sentence *b*: Kristen's mother wasn't close to her father. _____

   Kristen didn't know Huntington's disease ran in her family. _____

3. In sentence *c*: Norman Cousins didn't read Hans Selye's book. _____

   Norman Cousins invented Laughter Therapy. _____

PAST UNREAL CONDITIONALS

1. A **past unreal conditional** sentence has two clauses: the **if clause**, which gives the condition, and the **result clause**, which gives the result. The sentence can begin with the *if* clause or the result clause, and the meaning is the same.

2. There are two important things to notice in past unreal conditional sentences:
   - the use of the comma when the *if* clause comes at the beginning of the sentence
   - the verb forms used in each clause

If Clause	Result Clause
If + subject + past perfect,	subject + *would (not) have* + past participle *could (not) have* *might (not) have*
If Kristen's father **hadn't supported** her,	she **might not have wanted** a genetic test.

Result Clause	*If* Clause
Subject + *would (not) have* + past participle *could (not) have* *might (not) have*	if + subject + past perfect
Norman Cousins **might not have survived**	if he **hadn't used** Laughter Therapy.

3. The past unreal conditional talks about past unreal, untrue, or imagined conditions and their results. Both parts of the sentence describe events that are the opposite of what happened.

   Conditional statement: Kristen **could not have been tested if** the Human Genome Project **hadn't identified** all the genes in the human body.

   What really happened: Kristen was tested. The Human Genome Project did identify all the genes in the human body.

4. The past unreal conditional is often used to express regret about what really happened. In sentences like this, use *would have* in the result clause. To express possibility or uncertainty about the result, use *might have* or *could have* in the result clause.

2 Read the conditional sentences. Write **T** (true) or **F** (false) for each statement that follows the sentences.

1. If David Agus hadn't taken a genetic test, he wouldn't have discovered his risk for cardiovascular disease.

   __T__ He took a genetic test.

   __F__ He didn't discover his risk for cardiovascular disease.

2. If Norman Cousins had been healthy, he wouldn't have had to try Laughter Therapy.

   _____ Norman Cousins was healthy.

   _____ He didn't have to try Laughter Therapy.

3. Kristen's parents might not have been so worried if she had decided to go to a nearby college.

   _____ Kristen decided to go to a nearby college.

   _____ Her parents were worried.

4. The family wouldn't have understood Kristen's mother's symptoms if she hadn't been diagnosed with Huntington's disease.

   _____ The family understood her symptoms.

   _____ Kristen's mother was not diagnosed with Huntington's disease.

5. If there had been a famous advocate for Huntington's disease, Kristen might not have decided to make a documentary about her genetic testing.

   _____ There is not a famous advocate for Huntington's disease.

   _____ Kristen decided to make a documentary.

6. If Kristen hadn't had counseling, she might not have been prepared to deal with the test results.

   _____ Kristen didn't have counseling.

   _____ Kristen was prepared to deal with the test results.

7. If Norman Cousins hadn't survived for 26 more years, Laughter Therapy might not have received so much publicity.

   _____ Norman Cousins survived for 26 more years.

   _____ Laughter Therapy received a lot of publicity.

   (continued on next page)

8. If Norman Cousins hadn't believed in a mind-body interaction, Laughter Therapy would not have been effective for him.

_____ Norman Cousins didn't believe in a mind-body interaction.

_____ Laughter Therapy didn't work for him.

 3 Write a sentence about each situation. Use the past unreal conditional.

1. A female patient chose a treatment plan based on her genetic test results. She soon felt better. _If she hadn't chosen the correct treatment plan, she might not have felt better._

2. Kristen Powers always wanted all the information available. She chose to be genetically tested. _____

_____

3. Norman Cousins read *The Stress of Life* by Hans Seyle. When Cousins was diagnosed with ankylosing spondylitis, he already had some ideas about the mind-body connection. _____

_____

4. Norman Cousins was sick. He tried to cure himself by using Laughter Therapy. He made a complete recovery. _____

_____

5. David Agus had a genetic test, and he found out that he was at risk for cardiovascular disease. His children made him change his diet. _____

_____

6. Kristen's mom contacted her biological father. She learned that Huntington's disease ran in their family. _____

_____

7. Norman Cousins wasn't satisfied with his doctor's treatment plan. He developed his own Laughter Therapy treatment. _____

_____

■■■■■■■■■■■■■■■■■■ **GO TO** MyEnglishLab *FOR MORE GRAMMAR PRACTICE AND TO CHECK WHAT YOU LEARNED.*

FINAL WRITING TASK

In this unit, you have read about genetic testing. Genetic testing can be ordered and interpreted by medical professionals. It can also be done at home by sending saliva samples to private companies. In these cases, there is often no consultation or interpretation offered.

You are going to *write a four-paragraph opinion essay expressing your opinion on making medical decisions based on genetic testing*. Use the vocabulary and grammar from the unit.*

PREPARE TO WRITE: Tree Mapping

Tree mapping helps you to organize ideas about a topic. The topic is written on the top line. Your ideas are written in branches leading from the topic. You can include reasons and evidence on smaller branches.

Complete the tree map. Then discuss your tree map with a partner. Notice how the ideas become more detailed as the branches extend.

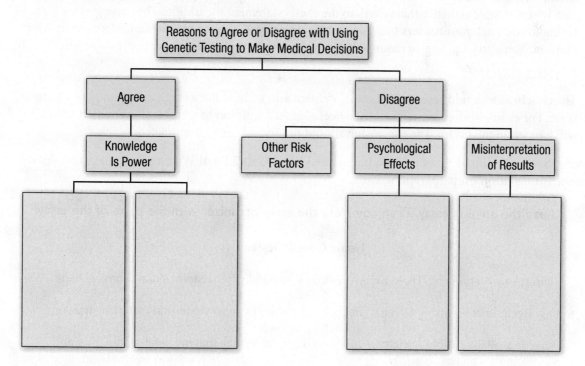

---

* For Alternative Writing Topics, see page 89. These topics can be used in place of the writing topic for this unit or as homework. The alternative topics relate to the theme of the unit but may not target the same grammar or rhetorical structures taught in the unit.

WRITE: An Opinion Essay

An **essay** is a group of paragraphs about one topic. An **opinion essay** is written to persuade or convince the reader that your opinion is "the right way of thinking." An opinion essay has three parts: the **introduction**, the **body**, and the **conclusion**.

INTRODUCTION

The **introduction** is the first paragraph of your essay. It includes a thesis statement that introduces the topic and states the main idea. The introduction should capture the readers' attention and make them want to read on. Many introductions begin with general background information on the topic and often end with the thesis statement as the last sentence of the paragraph. In an opinion essay, the thesis statement should state your opinion about the topic. *Tip*: Some writers find it helpful to write their introductory paragraph after they have completed their essay.

BODY

The **body** is one to three paragraphs. The body supports the thesis statement by giving examples, details, reasons, and facts to support the thesis statement. Each paragraph should start with a clearly stated topic sentence that relates to the thesis statement. In addition, because you are trying to convince your readers to accept your opinion, you need to give evidence to support your opinion. You also need to give reasons that explain why the evidence supports your opinion.

CONCLUSION

The **conclusion** should restate the thesis statement and include the writer's final thoughts on the topic. For example, the writer can give advice, suggest a solution to a problem, or predict what will happen in the future. The conclusion should not include new or unrelated topics.

Note: See Unit 1 Final Writing Task, pages 25–32 and Unit 2 Final Writing Task, pages 55–59 for more information on paragraph writing.

1 Read the opinion essay. Then complete the essay organizer with the parts of the essay.

Home Genetic Testing

Disastrous. Depressing. These two words come to mind when reading about home genetic testing. Because of the many adverse effects it can cause, I cannot understand why this type of 'service' is available without stricter regulations. First, let me say that my great-grandfather and my grandmother both suffered from Huntington's disease. I am a well-educated college graduate with a Master's degree in biology. I am thirty years old and so far show no signs of developing Huntington's. I don't think knowing whether I have the potential to develop an incurable disease will, in any way, enhance the quality of my life, nor would I be able to interpret the test results without the help of a medical professional. From this personal perspective, I believe that home genetic testing should be much more strictly regulated, if not prohibited all together.

I have witnessed the devastating effects that home genetic testing can have. A 55 year-old co-worker of mine whose family had a history of cancer submitted a DNA sample to an Internet genetic testing company. He was told that he had an 83% chance of developing colon cancer. He was convinced that because of this test result, he was going to die. After the test, this was all he could think about. This fear of impending tragedy made it impossible for him to concentrate on his work. As a result, his work suffered, and eventually he was let go. Finally, he went to a doctor and was retested. The doctor was able to interpret the results and explain to him that by taking the correct medications and changing his lifestyle, he could expect to live for many more years and very possibly never develop colon cancer. This is exactly why genetic testing must have stricter regulations.

The results of genetic testing are seen as infallible and definitive. Neither of these assumptions is true. Genetic testing is currently in its infancy, and even doctors and researchers do not fully understand the interaction between different genes. Very few diseases can be indicated by a single gene, so, until the link between diseases and multiple genes has been further studied, there is the potential for false positives and false negatives. In addition, environmental factors play a large part in who develops a disease and who doesn't. DNA is not the only factor affecting disease. For example, some cancers and other diseases are caused by exposure to chemicals or even to the sun. They have nothing to do with genetics. Knowledge is power, but it is important that that knowledge be accurate.

If we, as a society, truly believe that genetic testing has more benefits than negative effects, it is our responsibility to regulate it so all testing includes counseling and interpretation by professionals. In this way, patients can choose the treatment that is appropriate and effective for their genetic profile and lifestyle. Do we, as a society, truly believe that home genetic testing can be an effective method of choosing treatment without this professional counseling and interpretation?

Remember, the key is that to truly be able to make the best medical choices, medical professionals need to be involved in any decision.

2 Create an essay organizer like the one below with information for your opinion essay about making medical decisions based on genetic testing.

THREE PARTS OF AN ESSAY	NOTES
I. Introduction Thesis Statement:	**Background Information:**
II. Body Paragraph 1 Topic:	**Body Paragraph 1** Support/Evidence:
Body Paragraph 2 Topic:	**Body Paragraph 2** Support/Evidence:
III. Conclusion Restate the Thesis: Final Thought/Wrap Up:	

3 Now write the first draft of your opinion essay. Use the information from Prepare to Write and your essay organizer to plan your essay. Make sure you have four paragraphs: an introductory paragraph, two body paragraphs, and one concluding paragraph. Be sure to use grammar and vocabulary from the unit.

REVISE: Writing Introductions and Hooks

The **introductory paragraph** is very important in all essays. The reader will decide whether or not your essay is worth the time and effort to read, depending on how interesting your introductory paragraph is. The introduction for an opinion essay should:

- state who you are and why your opinion matters;
- provide background information about the topic;
- provoke the reader's interest with a hook;
- include a thesis statement.

A **hook** is a sentence or two meant to grab the reader's attention. The hook could be:

- a shocking or surprising sentence;

- an anecdote (story);

- an interesting point;

- a quote.

1 Is there a hook in the essay "Home Genetic Testing" on page 84? What is it? Is it effective? Why or why not? Share your answer with a partner.

2 Read the hooks from introductions of opinion essays. Check (✓) the hooks you think are effective. Discuss your answers with a partner.

1. _____ "Genetic testing definitely saved my life! If I hadn't been tested, I would never have known that I had an elevated risk of type-2 diabetes. Because of my test results, I was able to change my lifestyle before developing the disease," says Dr. Neville Clynes of Columbia Presbyterian Hospital.

2. _____ People are becoming more interested in genetic testing. Genetic testing can be very useful in making medical decisions.

3. _____ Stop! Don't go to the doctor! You can cure all problems with genetic testing. Or at least that's what people who believe in genetic testing would have you believe.

4. _____ People should stick with conventional medicine because it has been proven. There is no proof that genetic testing is an effective tool in making medical decisions.

5. _____ There are some studies that prove genetic testing can help with medical decision-making. This is why genetic testing should be a regular part of medical treatment.

6. _____ Dr. Robert Grasberger finally, after almost 3 months of consultation, understood what was wrong with his patient. What had he done? He had ordered a genetic test; the results explained everything.

7. _____ Imagine a world in which people are given jobs entirely based on their genes. Marriages are permitted only between couples whose genetic matchup ensures a "perfect" child. This is the future genetic testing will bring! Is this the future you want?

3 Look at the introductory paragraph in your first draft. Make sure you have all the parts of an effective introduction. If you don't have a hook, add one.

GO TO MyEnglishLab *FOR MORE SKILL PRACTICE.*

EDIT: Writing the Final Draft

Go to MyEnglishLab and write the final draft of your essay. Carefully edit it for grammatical and mechanical errors, such as spelling, capitalization, and punctuation. Make sure you use some of the grammar and vocabulary from the unit. Use the checklist to help you write your final draft. Then submit your essay to your teacher.

FINAL DRAFT CHECKLIST

❑ Does the essay have an introduction, two body paragraphs, and a conclusion?

❑ Does the introduction include a thesis statement, background information about the topic, and a hook?

❑ Does each paragraph have a topic sentence?

❑ Do all the topic sentences support the thesis statement?

❑ Does the essay have a conclusion that restates the thesis and includes a final thought?

❑ Did you use the past unreal conditional correctly?

❑ Have you used vocabulary from the unit?

UNIT PROJECT

In this unit, you have read about using genetic testing to make medical decisions. Genetic testing is also used for a variety of other reasons. You are going to research two genetic testing companies and find out what services they offer. Do they provide information about ancestry, ethnicity, paternity, or different health-related issues? Follow these steps:

STEP 1: In small groups, report on two genetic testing companies. Do research on the Internet to complete the following information.

DOES THE COMPANY TEST FOR:	COMPANY #1: _____	COMPANY #2: _____
ANCESTRY?		
ETHNICITY?		
HEALTH? (EXPLAIN)		
PATERNITY?		
OTHER? _____		
MORE QUESTIONS		
WHAT IS THE COST?		
IS THE COST DIRECT TO CONSUMERS?		
HOW IS DNA COLLECTED AND SUBMITTED?		
IS COUNSELING AND INTERPRETATION PROVIDED?		
WHEN WAS THE COMPANY ESTABLISHED?		

STEP 2: Compile your information and prepare a poster or PowerPoint™ presentation with your findings. Present the information to the class.

ALTERNATIVE WRITING TOPICS

Write an essay about one of the topics. Use the vocabulary and grammar from the unit.

1. Ethicists worry that genetic testing will be used not just to help make medical decisions, but to discriminate against people. They foresee a world in which test results could prevent people from getting high-paying jobs, insurance and welfare benefits, and even being able to marry. Do you believe such uses of test results will happen and be a problem? If so, does this issue outweigh the potential medical benefits of genetic testing?

2. What do you think of Norman Cousins's Laughter Therapy? Do you think there is any truth to the idea of a mind-body interaction? Have you, or someone you know, had a medical experience where the mind was stronger than the body?

■■■■■■■■■■■■■■■■■■■■■■■■■■■ *GO TO* MyEnglishLab *TO WRITE ABOUT ONE OF THE ALTERNATIVE TOPICS,*
WATCH A VIDEO ABOUT A SLEEP CLINIC, AND TAKE THE UNIT 3 ACHIEVEMENT TEST. ■■■■■■■■■■■■■■■■

INSTINCT OR
Intellect?

1 FOCUS ON THE TOPIC

1. Do you think an animal's ability to imitate human behavior is a sign of high intelligence? Explain.

2. Do you think domesticated animals (dogs, horses, monkeys, parrots) that can be trained are more intelligent than animals living in the wild?

3. Work in a small group. Think of three animals you believe are intelligent. What do they do that makes them seem intelligent?

GO TO MyEnglishLab *TO CHECK WHAT YOU KNOW.*

2 FOCUS ON READING

VOCABULARY

Reading One is an excerpt from the book *Animals in Translation* by Temple Grandin. In this excerpt, the author discusses animal intelligence. Many other scientists and researchers are also studying animal intelligence.

Read the imaginary interview with Dr. Clara Bell, a noted researcher in animal intelligence. Complete the interview with synonyms for the words in parentheses. Use the words in the box.

achieve	approach	cognition	perception
acquired	behavior	controversy	unconscious
apparently	category	obvious	unique

→ plues

Reporter: Dr. Bell, can you tell us a little bit about your work studying animal intelligence?

Dr. Bell: Sure, but let me start by saying that there has always been ___controversy___ about
                                                                          1. (serious disagreement)
exactly what animal intelligence is. For many years, those animals that could act most human were

put into the ___category___ of 'intelligent.'
              2. (group)

R: But that is not really the case, is it? Maybe you could give us some historical background.

Dr. B.: Well, during the 19th and early 20th centuries, people believed animals possessed

human emotions and mental abilities. Those animals that could be trained to imitate human

___behavior___ were judged to be intelligent. In fact, shows involving these trained
   3. (conduct)
animals were very popular. One such animal was the famous horse, Clever Hans, who seemed to

be able to solve mathematical problems. The ___obvious___ conclusion was that he was
                                             4. (clear)
intelligent. Actually, Clever Hans was reacting to ___unconscious___ movements made by
                                                    5. (done without realizing it)
people watching him. His answers had nothing to do with a knowledge of mathematics.

R: But doesn't the fact that an animal can be trained show that it is intelligent?

Dr. B.: Not really. When trying to assess animal intelligence, it is easy to confuse trainability with

_____cognition_____. However, just because you can train an animal to perform certain
    6. (thinking)

behaviors doesn't mean it really knows what it is doing. Dogs at John F. Kennedy Airport in New

York sniff suitcases and signal their handlers when they perceive illegal drugs. These dogs are

_____apparently_____ behaving in an intelligent manner, but they have no concept of drugs
    7. (seeming to be true)

being illegal.

R: So, what is actually happening?

Dr. B.: These dogs possess extreme _____preception_____ with their sense of smell, but this
        8. (use of senses)

doesn't necessarily make them intelligent. In fact, smell is not the only sense in which animals

outdo humans. For example, eagles can clearly see a rabbit when flying almost a mile above it.

They also see more colors than humans. In fact, eagles are not _____unique_____ in regard
        9. (special)

to extreme vision. Hammerhead sharks have a visual field of 360 degrees. In other words, they can

see fish both in front of and behind them, but again, this alone does not make them intelligent.

R: So, how can we really know if an animal is intelligent?

Dr. B.: As Albert Einstein said, "Everybody is a genius. But, if you judge a fish by its ability to

climb a tree, it'll spend its whole life believing it is stupid." Therefore, in order to assess animal

intelligence, it is important to test the animal in ways that are meaningful for their lives. This is the

_____approach_____ most researchers are using in the 21st century.
    10. (method)

R: Using this method, how do researchers today define intelligence?

Dr. B.: First of all, it is necessary to separate what animals are born with, instinct, from what they

have _____acquried_____ by learning. Learning how to respond to new situations in ways
    11. (developed/obtained)

that allow them to _____achive_____ the goals that are important in their lives is the most
    12. (accomplish)

effective measure of their intelligence.

GO TO MyEnglishLab *FOR MORE VOCABULARY PRACTICE.*

PREVIEW

In Reading One, Temple Grandin talks about animals that are considered intelligent. She mentions two types of dogs that help people with medical problems, seizure[1] alert dogs and seizure response dogs. She also gives her own definition of what animal intelligence is.

Answer the questions with a partner.

1. What do you think the difference is between a seizure response dog and a seizure alert dog?

   _____

   _____

   _____

2. Which of these dogs might the author think is showing more intelligence?

   _____

   _____

   _____

3. How do you think Temple Grandin defines intelligence in animals?

   _____

   _____

   _____

Now read the article about animal intelligence.

---

[1] **seizure:** a short time when someone is unconscious and cannot control the movements of his or her body

EXTREME PERCEPTION AND ANIMAL INTELLIGENCE
By Temple Grandin and Catherine Johnson
(from *Animals in Translation*)

1   Many animals have extreme **perception**. Forensic[1] dogs are three times as good as any X-ray machine at sniffing out contraband,[2] drugs, or explosives, and their overall success rate is 90 percent.

Seizure alert dog with owner Donna Jacobs

2   The fact that dogs can smell things a person can't doesn't make him a genius; it just makes him a dog. Humans can see things dogs can't, but that doesn't make us smarter. But when you look at the jobs some dogs have invented for themselves using their advanced perceptual abilities, you're moving into the realm of true **cognition**, which is solving a problem under novel conditions. The seizure alert dogs are an example of an animal using advanced perceptual abilities to solve a problem no dog was born knowing how to solve. Seizure alert dogs are dogs who, their owners say, can *predict* a seizure before it starts. There's still **controversy** over whether you can train a dog to predict seizures, and so far people haven't had a lot of luck trying. But there are a number of dogs who have figured it out on their own. These dogs were trained as seizure response dogs, meaning they can help a person once a seizure has begun. The dog might be trained to lie on top of the person so he doesn't hurt himself, or bring the person his medicine or the telephone. Those are all standard helpful **behaviors** any dog can be trained to perform.

3   But some of these dogs have gone from responding to seizures to perceiving signs of a seizure ahead of time. No one knows how they do this because the signs are invisible to people. No human being can look at someone who is about to have a seizure and see (or hear, smell, or feel) what's coming. Yet one study found that 10 percent of owners said their seizure response dogs had turned into seizure alert dogs.

4   The *New York Times* published a terrific article about a woman named Connie Standley, in Florida, who has two huge Bouvier de Flandres dogs who predict her seizures about thirty minutes ahead of time. When they sense Ms. Standley is heading into a seizure, they'll do things like pull on her clothes, bark at her, or drag on her hand to get her to someplace safe so she won't get hurt when the seizure begins. Ms. Standley says they predict about 80 percent of her seizures. Ms. Standley's dogs **apparently** were trained as seizure alert dogs before they came to her, but there aren't many dogs in that **category**. Most seizure alert dogs were trained to respond to seizures, not predict seizures.

(continued on next page)

---

[1] **forensic:** relating to methods for finding out about a crime
[2] **contraband:** goods that are brought into or taken out of a country illegally

5   The seizure alert dogs remind me of Clever Hans. Hans was the world-famous German horse in the early 1900s whose owner, Wilhelm von Osten, thought he could count. Herr von Osten could ask the horse questions like, "What's seven and five?" and Hans would tap out the number twelve with his hoof. Hans could even tap out answers to questions like, "If the eighth day of the month comes on Tuesday, what is the date for the following Friday?" He could answer mathematical questions posed to him by complete strangers, too.

6   Eventually, a psychologist named Oskar Pfungst managed to show that Hans wasn't really counting. Instead, Hans was observing subtle, **unconscious** cues the humans had no idea they were giving off. He'd start tapping his foot when he could see it was time to start tapping; then he'd stop tapping his foot when he could see it was time to stop tapping. His questioners were making tiny, unconscious movements only Hans could see. The movements were so tiny the humans making them couldn't even *feel* them.

7   Dr. Pfungst couldn't see the movements, either, and he was looking for them. He finally solved the case by putting Hans's questioners out of view and having them ask Hans questions they didn't know the answers to themselves. It turned out Hans could answer questions only when the person asking the question was in plain view and already knew the answer. If either condition was missing, his performance fell apart.

8   Psychologists often use the Clever Hans story to show that humans who believe animals are intelligent are deluding themselves. But that's not the **obvious** conclusion as far as I'm concerned. No one has ever been able to *train* a horse to do what Hans did. Hans trained himself. Is the ability to read a member of a different species as well as Hans was reading human beings really a sign that he was just a "dumb animal" who'd been classically conditioned to stamp his hoof? I think there is more to it than that.

9   What makes Hans similar to seizure alert dogs is that both Hans and the dogs **acquired** their skills without human help. As I mentioned, to my knowledge, so far no one has figured out how to take a "raw" dog and teach it how to predict seizures. About the best a trainer can do is reward the dogs for helping when a person is having a seizure and then leave it up to the dog to start identifying signs that predict the onset of a seizure on his own. That **approach** hasn't been hugely successful, but some dogs do it. I think those dogs are showing superior intelligence the same way a human who can do something few other people can do shows superior intelligence.

10   What makes the actions of the seizure alert dogs, and probably of Hans, too, a sign of high intelligence—or high talent—is the fact that they didn't have to do what they did. It's one thing for a dog to start recognizing the signs that a seizure is coming; you might chalk that up to **unique** aspects of canine hearing, smell, or vision, like the fact that a dog can hear a dog whistle while a human can't. But it's another thing for a dog to start to recognize the signs of an impending seizure and *then decide to do something about it*. That's what intelligence is in humans; intelligence is people using their built-in perceptual and cognitive skills to **achieve** useful and sometimes remarkable goals.

MAIN IDEAS

1 Look again at your answers to the Preview questions on page 94. Were they correct? How did they help you understand the story?

2 Work with a partner. Read the statements and decide which three represent the main ideas of Reading One. Then discuss the reasons for your choice.

1. Many animals have extreme perception.

2. The author believes that true cognition, or intelligence, is defined as solving problems under novel conditions.

3. Ms. Standley's seizure alert dogs are able to predict about 80 percent of her seizures before they happen.

4. Some psychologists believe animals like Clever Hans are not really intelligent.

5. Some animals are able to read human behavior by observing subtle signs that even humans don't recognize.

6. The psychologist Oskar Pfungst was able to show that Hans wasn't really counting.

7. For Clever Hans to correctly answer a question, two conditions had to be met. He had to be able to see the person asking the question, and the person had to know the answer to the question.

8. The author believes seizure alert dogs and Clever Hans are showing high intelligence because they are able to recognize a sign and then choose to do something about it.

DETAILS

Reading One mentions many people and animals connected with animal intelligence. Match these people and animals with their descriptions.

1. __f__ Forensic dogs

2. __c__ Seizure response dogs

3. __d__ Seizure alert dogs

4. __b__ Ms. Connie Standley

5. __a__ Wilhelm von Osten

6. __g__ Oskar Pfungst

7. __e__ Clever Hans

a. Clever Hans's owner who thought he could count

b. Owner of two seizure alert dogs

c. Dogs that have been trained to help people once their seizures have started

d. Dogs that are able to predict seizures before they happen and warn their owners

e. German horse who apparently could count and answer questions

f. Dogs that use their sense of smell to find contraband such as drugs or explosives =Tigle

g. Psychologist who proved that Clever Hans wasn't really counting

MAKE INFERENCES

HEDGING

Sometimes authors employ cautious language, called hedging, when they are not entirely sure that their information is supported by facts. This caution can be denoted by verb choice (*seem, look like, say, indicate, suggest, think, believe*), the use of modals (*might, may, could*), adverbs (*really, sometimes, possibly, perhaps, apparently*), adjectives (*most, some, obvious*), or certain phrases (*to my knowledge, as far as I'm concerned*).

Look at the example and read the explanation.

Look at the excerpt from paragraph 2. What cautious language does Temple Grandin use to show that the information may not be factual?

"The seizure alert dogs are an example of an animal using advanced perceptual abilities to solve a problem no dog was born knowing how to solve. Seizure alert dogs are dogs who, their owners say, can predict a seizure before it starts."

She doesn't say that seizure alert dogs *can* predict seizures, but rather that *their owners say* that they can.

Why does she include the phrase "their owners say"? She does not have scientific proof but only anecdotal evidence.

It is important to recognize hedging language as it indicates that the author is not 100 percent certain of the information he or she writes.

Look at the indicated paragraphs in Reading One and write the words or phrases used by the author that indicate hedging. Compare your answers with a partner's.

1. *Paragraph 4*

   What hedging language does the author use? _____ apperently.

   Why does the author use this hedging language? _____

2. *Paragraph 5*

   What hedging language does the author use? _____

   Why does the author use this hedging language? _____

3. *Paragraph 6*

   What hedging language does the author use? _____

   Why does the author use this hedging language?_____

4. *Paragraph 8*

   What hedging language does the author use? _____

   Why does the author use this hedging language? _____

5. *Paragraph 9*

   What hedging language does the author use? _____ my knowledge. _____

   Why does the author use this hedging language? _____

EXPRESS OPINIONS

Discuss the questions with a partner.

1. Oskar Pfungst proved that Clever Hans wasn't able to solve mathematical problems. Do you still believe that Hans showed intelligence by learning to "read" the movements of his questioners and audience members?

2. Temple Grandin feels that seizure alert dogs are showing signs of high intelligence. Others may say that what they do is really just an example of animals reacting based on instinct. What is your opinion? Explain.

3. Share examples of animal behavior you have witnessed that you think exhibit intelligence. Do these examples relate to Temple Grandin's idea of what animal intelligence is?

■■■■■■■■■■■■■■■■■■■■■■■■■■■■■■ *GO TO* MyEnglishLab *TO GIVE YOUR OPINION ABOUT ANOTHER QUESTION.*

READ

Reading Two talks about why it is difficult to judge animal intelligence. One problem is that we often use human standards to evaluate animal intelligence.

1 Look at the boldfaced words in the reading and think about the questions.

1. Which words or phrases do you know the meanings of?

2. Can you use any of the words or phrases in a sentence?

2 Read the article, *How smart are animals?* As you read, notice the boldfaced vocabulary. Try to guess its meaning from the context.

How smart are animals?
By Gita Simonsen

1   We think that crows are smart, but what do we really know? Intelligence takes on diverse meanings for different species, and researchers think we are too prone to use human standards.

2   We've all heard talk of animal intelligence. We speak of crafty crows, clever foxes, discerning dolphins, and brilliant squids, but can we really use the word intelligence with regard to animals?

3   Researchers are concerned with learning mechanisms and other cognitive abilities— thinking, acquiring knowledge, **sensory** perception, memory, and language. These are the thought processes which form the basis for what we experience and comprehend of the world around us.

4   The problem is that we often look for human traits when we study animal behaviour. But what may be clever for us needn't be a **viable** attribute in other members of the animal kingdom.

5   "Animals are often given tasks based on human behaviour, such as the use of tools," says Peter Bøckman, a zoologist at the Natural History Museum in Oslo.

6   "If you turn it around and visualise a flock[1] of screaming chimpanzees hauling you up into a treetop and **confronting** you with a complicated problem involving nuts, how intelligently do you think you would perform?" he asks.

---

[1] **flock:** group

7   Indeed, we can easily fail to notice animal intelligence if we only look for human qualities, says Bjarne Braastad, an animal behaviourist at the Norwegian University of Life Sciences.

8   "It can be limiting if your point of departure is human traits. Animals have other abilities and can have elements of intelligence that humans lack," he says.

IQ by the kilo

9   We often measure intelligence, particularly in mammals, in accordance with how much the brain weighs in relation to total body weight. Humans lead by a long shot on this list, and the animal right behind us is not one of the apes—it's the dolphin.

10   Dolphins can thus be said to have the potential for very high intelligence, but we can't measure this optimally. Dolphins come from a completely different world, in a way, and have a language we can't fathom.[2] Communication is definitely a great barrier in the understanding of animal behaviour.

11   "Human intelligence is strongly linked to the language we use to communicate with one another," says Bøckman. "As long as we can't communicate with animals, it's really hard to decide how smart they are."

12   "Language is such an integral part of being human, and that makes it hard to avoid using human traits as a framework for considering the intelligence of animals."

Bees smarter than babies?

13   A group of scientists from Queen Mary University in London examined studies of animal intelligence to find out what scientists currently think about comparable cognition in different species.

14   They found that concepts and terms used to calculate the intelligence of animals are often borrowed from studies of human psychology.

15   One recent study charting the learning speed of bees, human infants, birds, and fish ended with the bees on top and our offspring[3] at bottom. So the researchers behind the experiment concluded that learning speed couldn't be used to measure intelligence— because humans weren't first across the finish line.[4]

16   The British scientists point out that the bees beat the babies in a learning test because the lab tested characteristics that bees have been perfecting during aeons[5] of evolutionary development.

17   In comparisons of intelligence among species, it's hard to avoid dealing trump cards[6] to one species or another.

18   "It's difficult to **discern** between reasoning, learned reflexes, and pure instincts. This makes it challenging for humans to create tests that don't remind animals of their natural behaviour," says Bøckman.

(continued on next page)

---

[2] **fathom:** understand what something means after thinking about it carefully
[3] **offspring:** someone's child or children
[4] **first across the finish line:** the winner
[5] **aeons:** extremely long periods of time
[6] **dealing trump cards to:** giving an advantage to

Bottom-up

19   The British scientists suggest what they term a bottom-up method. This differs from what they regard as top-bottom studies in animal behaviour research. In these, researchers pick out a cognitive **trait** and investigate how the animal's nerve system guides this trait.

20   With more emphasis on a bottom-up method, they would study the species' neural networks in attempts to perceive what uses these networks can have.

21   "The advantage of the bottom-up methods is that we can find traits that we didn't know existed in animals," says Braastad.

22   Bøckman comments that one of the challenges of this method is the extreme difficulty of investigating tiny neural circuitry in minuscule brains, such as in small insects.

Better tools required

23   There are now numerous studies that compare the cognitive capabilities of various species through investigations of their brains' neural circuitry. This has contributed toward answering questions about whether some of our human qualities can also exist in other species and help lay the groundwork for better comparisons.

24   For instance, multiple studies have been conducted with regard to facial recognition, imitation, social behaviour and empathy, and these can be found among many of our animal cousins.

25   "If the neural paths that are active in animals are the same ones acting in humans, we could have kindred[7] abilities," says Bøckman.

26   Gro Amdam conducts research on bees and what happens to their brains as they age. She is a professor at Arizona State University, and a researcher at the Norwegian University of Life Sciences.

27   "Scientists need to develop better tools, methods, and theories for comparing the brain skills in different species, but we are well on our way," she says.

---

[7] **kindred:** of the same family

COMPREHENSION

Two of the three answers for each question are correct. Cross out the answer that is incorrect.

1. It is difficult to define animal intelligence because

   a. animals have extreme sensory perception.

   b. intelligence has different meanings depending on the species of animal.

   c. what is intelligent for one species may not be for another.

2. The presence of human traits in animal behavior may not be a good indicator of animal intelligence because

   a. an animal's ability to imitate human behavior may have no value in its own life.

   b. animals may have other types of intelligence that humans lack.

   c. animals are given tasks based on human behavior.

3. Despite the fact that dolphins apparently are very intelligent based on their brain size, we cannot optimally measure their intelligence because

   a. we cannot use language to communicate.

   b. the concepts and terms used to calculate animal intelligence are often borrowed from human psychology.

   c. they live in a very different environment.

4. If humans do not come out on top in intelligence tests compared to animals, then researchers assume that

   a. it is due to comparable cognition in different species.

   b. there is something wrong with the assessment.

   c. the test must have been similar to the animal's, and not the human's, natural environment.

5. A new way of assessing animal intelligence, the bottom-up method, involves finding a cognitive trait and investigating how the neural system guides this trait. An advantage of this method is that

   a. many animals have minuscule brains.

   b. researchers can find traits they didn't even know existed in animals.

   c. it allows researchers to understand the use of neural networks.

6. For scientists to eventually be able to effectively assess animal intelligence, they need to

   a. develop better tools and methods.

   b. develop new theories.

   c. develop facial recognition.

GO TO MyEnglishLab FOR MORE VOCABULARY PRACTICE.

READING SKILL

1 Look at paragraphs 6–8 of Reading Two. The author uses a quotation in paragraph 8 to support a point she has made previously in the article. Which of her points is she supporting?

RECOGNIZING THE ROLE OF QUOTED SPEECH IN A READING

One way that authors use quotations is to support a point they are trying to make. By doing this, they are giving the reader an example of why their assertion is correct. Seeing how the quotation is related to an author's point helps the reader to understand the author's point and its importance.

In paragraph 11, the author quotes Peter Bøckman, a zoologist, who says, "As long as we can't communicate with animals [dolphins], it's really hard to decide how smart they are."

Which of the author's points does this quotation support?

Look at paragraph 10:

"Dolphins can thus be said to have the potential for very high intelligence, but we can't measure this optimally. Dolphins come from a completely different world, in a way, and have a language we can't fathom. Communication is definitely a great barrier in the understanding of animal behaviour."

The author's assertion that the quotation supports is "Communication is definitely a great barrier in the understanding of animal behaviour."

In fact, this statement is a paraphrase of the quotation that the author included for support. Seeing the connection between an author's point and the quotations he or she uses as support can give you a deeper understanding of the ideas that the author is presenting.

2 In Reading Two, Gita Simonsen often makes a statement about animal intelligence and then supports it with an appropriate quotation. Look at the quotations in the paragraphs indicated. Then look at the preceding paragraph(s) and underline the author's words that the quotations support. Compare your answers with a partner's.

1. *(paragraph 6):* "If you turn it around and visualise a flock of screaming chimpanzees hauling you up into a treetop and confronting you with a complicated problem involving nuts, how intelligently do you think you would perform?"

2. *(paragraph 18):* "It's difficult to discern between reasoning, learned reflexes and pure instincts. This makes it challenging for humans to create tests that don't remind animals of their natural behaviour."

3. *(paragraph 21):* "The advantage of the bottom-up method is that we can find traits that we didn't know existed in animals."

4. *(paragraph 25):* "If the neural paths that are active in animals are the same ones acting in humans, we could have kindred abilities."

■■ *GO TO* MyEnglishLab *FOR MORE SKILL PRACTICE.*

STEP 1: Organize

Both Reading One (R1) and Reading Two (R2) talk about what intelligence is for animals, how it differs from instinct and learned reflexes, and the problems associated with assessing animal intelligence. Complete the chart with examples from each reading. Use the information in the box.

For humans, intelligence is linked to language, but we can't understand animal language. (dolphins)	Extreme perception	Using human standards (Clever Hans can count→ he is smart; He is not really counting→ he is a dumb animal.)
Looking for human traits and qualities (the use of tools)	Using extreme perception to invent jobs (Recognizing something and then deciding to act)	Learned reflexes
Diverse meanings for different species	Instinct	Brain weight of mammals

	R1	R2
WHAT IS INTELLIGENCE?	Problem solving Use language use math be creative	extreme perception diverse
PROBLEMS WITH ASSESSING ANIMAL INTELLIGENCE		1. 2. 3.
OTHER ABILITIES VS. INTELLIGENCE	Forensic dogs: Clever Hans:	Bees:

Read the imaginary interview with the authors of Reading One and Reading Two. Complete the interview using information from Step 1 and from the readings.

REPORTER: Today we are lucky to have with us two animal experts, Temple Grandin and Gita Simonsen. They are both especially interested in the question of animal intelligence. Ms. Grandin, how would you define animal intelligence?

TEMPLE GRANDIN: Let me start by saying that many people confuse extreme perception with intelligence. Many animals have extreme perception at least compared to humans, but that alone _any animals_ . I think seizure alert dogs are a good example of animal intelligence because

_____.

This is not something they need to do or have been taught to do, but something that _____. This is what shows intelligence.

GITA SIMONSEN: I definitely agree that seizure alert dogs are showing intelligence, but, in my opinion, what can be considered intelligence in animals ____is not same in human._____.

REPORTER: How can animal intelligence be assessed?

TEMPLE GRANDIN: One problem that we have in assessing animal intelligence is that ____human condition._____

_____.

GITA SIMONSEN: Yes, I agree. For example, ____A dog playing soccer.____

_____.

TEMPLE GRANDIN: In the case of the "counting" horse, Clever Hans, many people judged him to be intelligent when ____tab to show answer____

the question, _____. However, as soon as they realized that he was getting unconscious cues from the audience, then

_____. I don't agree with them. I think Clever Hans was showing intelligence because _he was read_

to able what was required them.

GITA SIMONSEN: That's a good point. However, let me say one more thing about the problems with assessing animal intelligence. Because for humans intelligence is so linked to language, the fact that we don't understand animal language _we don't understand them language._

REPORTER: Are all of these apparently amazing things that animals are capable of doing really a sign of intelligence, or are there other explanations for their actions?

TEMPLE GRANDIN: Sometimes there are other explanations. For example, forensic dogs that work at airports looking for explosives or illegal drugs

_____

_____.

GITA SIMONSEN: Yes, similarly, a recent test of intelligence across species (including humans) found bees to be smarter than all other species including humans. However, the explanation might not be intelligence, but rather

_____.

REPORTER: Thank you both very much. I am afraid we have run out of time. I know I have learned a lot, and I am sure our viewers have, too. Thanks again.

■■■■■■■■■■■■■■■■■■■■■■■■■■■■■■■■■■■ *GO TO* MyEnglishLab *TO CHECK WHAT YOU LEARNED.*

VOCABULARY

REVIEW

Two of the three words in each row have similar meanings to the boldfaced word from the reading. Cross out the word that does not belong. If you need help, use a dictionary.

READING ONE

1. **achieve**	assess	accomplish	attain
2. **acquire**	obtain	need	gain
3. **apparently**	seemingly	allegedly	visually
4. **approach**	method	attempt	procedure
5. **behavior**	ability	action	conduct
6. **category**	section	group	aspect
7. **cognition**	understanding	instinct	intelligence
8. **controversy**	consensus	disagreement	debate
9. **obvious**	clear	evident	possible
10. **perception**	thought	awareness	observation
11. **unconscious**	cautious	involuntary	unintentional
12. **unique**	singular	normal	solitary

READING TWO

13. **confront**	remind	challenge	present
14. **discern**	differentiate	figure out	dislike
15. **sensory**	auditory	visual	habitual
16. **trait**	characteristic	path	feature
17. **viable**	usable	applicable	achievable

EXPAND

Many academic words, especially those used in the sciences, have Latin or Greek roots. For example, the word *psychologist* comes from the Greek root, *psych*, meaning *mind*. A **psych**ologist is someone who is trained to study the mind and how it works.

Work with a partner to complete the chart.

1. For each root (column 1), find a word with that root in the reading(s) and paragraph(s) indicated.

2. Write the word in column 4.

3. Guess the meaning of the word using the meaning of the root and the context of the sentence in which you found the word. Write the meaning in column 5.

4. In the last column, write other words you can think of with the same root.

If you need help, use a dictionary. Share your answers with the class.

1 ROOT	2 MEANING	3 READING and PARAGRAPH(S)	4 WORD	5 MEANING	6 OTHER WORDS WITH THE SAME ROOT
1. PSYCH-	mind	R1-6	psychologist	Someone who is trained to study the mind	psychic
2. COGNI-	know / learn	R1-2, 10	Cognition.		
		R2-3, 13			
3. DICT-	say / tell	R1-2	Dictonary	Dectetion	Prodict.
4. ACT-	do	R1-10	Action	Active	
		R2-25			
5. CEPT-	taken	R1-2	Accept	Receptive	Perception.
		R2-14			
6. NUMER-	number	R2-23	Numerize		
7. NOV-	new	R1-2	Novel		
8. SENS-	feeling	R1-4	Sensetive		
		R2-3			
9. CENT-	one hundred	R1-3	Century	Percent	
10. SCI-	know	R1-6	Science	Scintific	
		R2-7			
11. NEUR-	nerve	R2-20	Neuronlogical.		

CREATE

On a separate piece of paper, write five questions about Clever Hans. Use at least one word from the Review or Expand sections in each question. Then exchange papers with a partner and answer the questions. You can write or discuss your answers.

■■■■■■■■■■■■■■■■■■■■■■■■■■■■■■■ *GO TO* MyEnglishLab *FOR MORE VOCABULARY PRACTICE.*

GRAMMAR

1 Examine the sentences and answer the questions with a partner.

    a. Animals have other abilities and can have elements of intelligence **that humans lack**.

    b. No human being can look at someone **who is about to have a seizure** and see (or hear, smell, or feel) what's coming.

    c. Oskar Pfungst thought back proudly on the afternoon **when he was finally able to figure out how Clever Hans was able to answer the questions**.

    1. In sentence *a*, what elements of intelligence is the writer describing?

    2. In sentence *b*, what type of person does the writer say no human being can look at and see what's coming?

    3. In sentence *c*, which afternoon is the writer describing?

    4. What words begin the boldfaced phrases? Are the words that come just before these phrases verbs, adjectives, nouns, or adverbs?

IDENTIFYING ADJECTIVE CLAUSES

1. Identifying adjective clauses, sometimes called restrictive relative clauses, are groups of words (phrases) that act as adjectives to describe or identify a noun. These phrases come directly after the nouns they describe and begin with relative pronouns that refer to the noun. Sentences with adjective clauses can be seen as a combination of two shorter sentences about the same noun.

He had **a horse**. + **The horse** could answer mathematical questions.
= He had **a horse that could answer mathematical questions**.

Clever Hans lived in **a small town**. + **The small town** was in Germany.
= **The small town where Clever Hans lived** was in Germany.

2. Identifying adjective clauses begin with a **relative pronoun**. The noun that the clause describes determines the choice of pronoun.

who = person or people (and sometimes animals)
which = thing or things
that = thing, things, person, or people (less formal than *which* or *who*)
when = a time or times
where or *in which* = a place or places
whose or *in whose* = possession

3. Remember that the relative pronoun replaces the noun it describes; the noun is not repeated.

I saw **the horse**. + The scientist was testing **the horse**.
= I saw **the horse** *that* the scientist was testing.

INCORRECT: I saw **the horse** *that* the scientist was testing **the horse**.

2 Read the sentences and circle *Correct* or *Incorrect* for the underlined relative pronouns. If the pronoun is correct, add an alternative, or other, pronoun that could also be used. If the pronoun is incorrect, write one or two pronouns that could be used.

1. The scientist <u>which</u> observed Clever Hans wrote a book.

   Correct   Alternative: _____

   (Incorrect)   Correction(s): ___ *who or that* ___

2. The museum <u>where</u> Peter Bøckman works is in Oslo, Norway.

   Correct   Alternative: _____

   Incorrect   Correction(s): _____

3. Seizure alert dogs are dogs <u>whose</u> can predict a seizure before it starts.

   Correct   Alternative: _____

   Incorrect   Correction(s): _____

4. Hans was the world-famous horse <u>which</u> owner, Wilhelm von Osten, was a retired school teacher.

   Correct   Alternative: _____

   Incorrect   Correction(s): _____

5. On the day <u>when</u> Oskar Pfungst discovered Clever Hans's secret, Wilhelm von Osten was visiting his sister.

   Correct   Alternative: _____

   Incorrect   Correction(s): _____

6. Zoolologists are now developing tests <u>that</u> assess animal intelligence more accurately.

   Correct   Alternative: _____

   Incorrect   Correction(s): _____

7. Many people <u>when</u> study animals are convinced that they are able to understand some human language.

   Correct   Alternative: _____

   Incorrect   Correction(s): _____

(continued on next page)

8. Oskar Pfungst put the questioners in a place <u>which</u> they could not be seen by Clever Hans.

Correct ____ Alternative: _____

Incorrect ____ Correction(s): _____

3 Combine each pair of sentences into one sentence using an identifying adjective clause.

1. **a.** Clever Hans was trained by a retired school teacher.

   b. The school teacher had taught science for many years.

   Clever Hans was trained by a retired school teacher who had taught science for many years.

2. **a.** The afternoon was cold and rainy.

   b. That afternoon Clever Hans was ready to perform in front of an audience.

   The afternoon when Clever Hans was ready to perform in front of an audience was cold and rainy.

3. **a.** Binti the gorilla is best known for an amazing incident.

   b. The incident occurred on August 16, 1996.

   _____

   _____

4. **a.** I spoke with a man.

   b. The man had trained dolphins and killer whales.

   _____

   _____

5. **a.** Psychologists study many animals.

   b. Animals live in zoos.

   _____

   _____

6. **a.** I saw my friend.

   b. Her dog could predict seizures before they started.

   _____

   _____

7. a. We saw the dolphin.

   b. The dolphin performed some spectacular feats.

_____

_____

8. a. The psychologist had studied at the University of Berlin.

   b. The psychologist developed a new test of animal intelligence.

_____

_____

9. a. The morning was sunny and hot.

   b. That morning the dogs saved Ms. Standley.

_____

_____

10. a. The contraband was in an old brown suitcase.

    b. It was discovered by the forensic dog.

_____

_____

■■■■■■■■■■■ *GO TO* MyEnglishLab *FOR MORE GRAMMAR PRACTICE AND TO CHECK WHAT YOU LEARNED.*

FINAL WRITING TASK

In this unit, you read two passages on animal intelligence. How would you summarize the important information from one of the readings?

You are going to *write a summary of Reading One as if you were a journalist writing for a newspaper or magazine*. Use the vocabulary and grammar from the unit.*

PREPARE TO WRITE: Asking and Answering *Wh-* Questions

To help you to plan your summary of Reading One, you will **ask and answer the *Wh-* questions *Who, What, Where, When, Why,* and *How***. Many writers, especially journalists, use the *Wh-* questions when they are writing a summary of an important story or news event.

_____

* For Alternative Writing Topics, see page 121. These topics can be used in place of the writing topic for this unit or as homework. The alternative topics relate to the theme of the unit but may not target the same grammar or rhetorical structures taught in the unit.

Write one or two questions for each *Wh-* question. Share your questions with a partner and answer them.

Q: What: What is the main idea (paragraph) or thesis (essay or longer article)? What does the person have to say? What issues are discussed?

A: _____

_____

Q: Who: Who wrote the article or passage?

A: _____

_____

Q: When: _____

A: _____

_____

STORY

Q: Where: _____

A: _____

_____

Q: Why: _____

A: _____

_____

Q: How: _____

A: _____

WRITE: A Summary

A **summary** is a shortened version of a text that focuses on the thesis or main idea. It does not include many details or examples. It does not include personal opinions. Here are some important points:

1. **Read and reread the text**. As you read, think about the *Wh-* questions. Make sure you understand the text.

2. **Highlight or underline the thesis**. To find the thesis, think about the purpose of the text. What is the author's main idea?

3. **Rewrite the thesis in one sentence**. Use your own words.

4. **Continue reading**. Highlight the main idea and key words and phrases for each paragraph. Write one-sentence summaries in your own words for each paragraph.

5. **Check your sentences against the text**. Again, use your own wording.

6. **Make sure you have not included irrelevant examples or your own opinion**.

7. **Write your summary**.

8. **Return later and check it again** with fresh eyes.

9. **Polish summary for flow**; it needs to read well.

1 Read the summary of Reading Two and answer the questions.

In *How smart are animals?*, author Gita Simonsen discusses the problems scientists face in assessing animal intelligence. The first problem is defining animal intelligence. Too often our tests of animal intelligence are based on how well animals can imitate human behavior. This method does not recognize other elements of intelligence that animals use in their own lives that humans may not possess.

Another method that scientists use with mammals is brain weight as a proportion of total weight. This measurement finds dolphins high in intelligence. However, since human intelligence is linked to language, and we can't communicate with dolphins, or other animals, it is not possible to fully assess their intelligence.

A further problem of animal intelligence testing, especially when comparing intelligence across species, is the assumption that humans must be smarter than any other animal. In a study where bees outperformed human babies, scientists reassessed the test itself. They concluded that the test must have been flawed, and the bees came out on top because of instinct, not intelligence.

A new method of assessment involves studying animals' neural networks and trying to figure out what traits they are designed to allow. This helps scientists to identify traits they had not even thought about. Nevertheless, the minuscule size of some animal brains makes this method very challenging.

Simonsen concludes by quoting Gro Amdam, a professor at Arizona State University, who states, "Scientists need to develop better tools, methods, and theories for comparing the brain skills in different species, but we are well on our way."

1. Who is the author? What is the title of the article? _____

_____

2. What is the thesis? _____

_____

(continued on next page)

3. What are some of the problems of testing an animal's intelligence? _____

_____

_____

4. What is the author's conclusion about testing animal intelligence? _____

_____

_____

2 Before you begin to write a summary of Reading One, practice by summarizing sections of the reading, individual paragraphs, or groups of paragraphs. For paragraphs 1–7, circle the sentence that best describes the main idea. For paragraphs 8–10, write the one-sentence summary yourself. Check your answers with a partner's.

1. Read paragraph 1 of Reading One. Which statement best describes the main idea of the paragraph?

    a. Animals that display a deep understanding of the world around them are plentiful.

    b. There are some dogs that can sniff out dangerous materials at a very successful rate.

    c. Some forensic dogs are so good at their jobs that they are much better than X-ray machines.

2. Read paragraph 2. Which statement best describes the main idea of the paragraph?

    a. Some seizure response dogs have trained themselves to be seizure alert dogs.

    b. Dogs who are truly intelligent will apply their thinking skills to new situations.

    c. Seizure response dogs are trained to save their owners' lives.

3. Read paragraphs 3 and 4. Which statement best describes the main idea of the paragraphs?

    a. Connie Standley's dogs predict her seizures before they happen.

    b. No one knows how seizure response dogs read signs given off by humans before a seizure.

    c. Some seizure response dogs have become seizure alert dogs without any training.

4. Read paragraphs 5, 6, and 7. Which statement best describes the main idea of the paragraphs?

   a. Clever Hans was not really counting but was able to detect and understand human signs that even humans could not see, just as seizure alert dogs can.

   b. Oskar Pfungst, a psychologist, eventually proved that Clever Hans was not really counting.

   c. Clever Hans looked like he was counting but was really just tapping his foot until he knew to stop.

5. Read paragraph 8. Write a one-sentence summary of the main idea.

   _____

   _____

6. Read paragraphs 9 and 10. Write a one-sentence summary of the main idea.

   _____

   _____

3 Now write your first draft of your summary of Reading One. Use the information from Prepare to Write and Write to plan your summary. Make sure you state the thesis and eliminate any unimportant details. Be sure to use grammar and vocabulary from the unit.

Summary writing often requires the writer to restate an author's ideas. It is very important to restate the author's ideas in your own words while keeping true to the author's ideas. This is called **paraphrasing**. (*Note:* When you choose to use an author's direct words, you must use quotation marks.)

AUTHOR'S OWN WORDS	PARAPHRASED TEXT
"A group of scientists from Queen Mary University in London examined studies of animal intelligence to find out what scientists currently think about comparable cognition in different species. One recent study, charting the learning speed of bees, human infants, birds and fish, ended with the bees on top and our offspring at bottom. So the researchers behind the experiment concluded that learning speed couldn't be used to measure intelligence—because humans weren't first across the finish line. The British scientists point out that the bees beat the babies in a learning test because the lab tested characteristics that bees have been perfecting during aeons of evolutionary development."	A further problem of animal intelligence testing is comparing intelligence across species. Scientists from Queen Mary University in London recently studied the learning speed of different species. When bees outperformed all the other species, including human babies, scientists reassessed the test itself. They concluded that the test must have been flawed and the bees came out on top because of instincts they had developed over millions of years, not intelligence.

When using a direct quote, use these punctuation rules:

1. Lift the quote directly as is from the text. Do not change the capitalization or punctuation.

2. Place a comma before the quote: Simonsen concludes by quoting Gro Amdam who states, "Scientists need to develop better tools, methods, and theories for comparing the brain skills in different species, but we are well on our way."

3. Place the final punctuation mark at the end of the sentence before the final quotation mark: Simonsen concludes by quoting Gro Amdam who states, "Scientists need to develop better tools, methods, and theories for comparing the brain skills in different species, but we are well on our way."

When paraphrasing or quoting, use a variety of reporting verbs to introduce an author's ideas:

says	*notes*
tells	*mentions*
acknowledges	*thinks*
concedes	*writes*
states	*believes*
explains	*concludes*

When paraphrasing, first think of the main idea or what the author is trying to tell you. Think of ways to say the same thing using your own words. Do not just replace words in a sentence with synonyms.

Original

Many animals have extreme perception.

Incorrect Paraphrase

Many animals have excellent awareness.

Rules for Paraphrasing

1. Read the original text. Make sure you understand it. Highlight the main idea and key words or phrases.

2. Read the text again. Put the text aside.

3. Write the idea in your own words without looking at the text. Try to use different words than the text.

4. Try to reorder the ideas in the sentence. Start with the middle or the end. Put the paraphrased text aside for a while.

5. With fresh eyes, check your paraphrased sentence against the original. Make sure it is not too close to the original.

Original

Many animals have extreme perception.

Correct Paraphrase

Animals that display a deep understanding of their world are common.

1 Paraphrase the sentences from Reading Two in your own words.

1. The problem is that we often look for human traits when we study animal behaviour. But what may be clever for us needn't be a viable attribute in other members of the animal kingdom.

   _____

   _____

2. "Human intelligence is strongly linked to the language we use to communicate with one another," says Bøckman. "As long as we can't communicate with animals, it's really hard to decide how smart they are."

   _____

   _____

(continued on next page)

3. There are now numerous studies that compare the cognitive capabilities of various species through investigations of their brains' neural circuitry. This has contributed toward answering questions about whether some of our human qualities can also exist in other species and help lay the groundwork for better comparisons.

_____

_____

 Look at your first draft. Make sure you have paraphrased the author of Reading One using your own words. Check against the original text and make any changes necessary. Add a quote if you think it will be effective. Watch your punctuation with your quote!

■■■ *GO TO* MyEnglishLab *FOR MORE SKILL PRACTICE.*

EDIT: Writing the Final Draft

Go to MyEnglishLab and write the final draft of your summary. Carefully edit it for grammatical and mechanical errors, such as spelling, capitalization, and punctuation. Make sure you use some of the grammar and vocabulary from the unit. Use the checklist to help you write your final draft. Then submit your essay to your teacher.

> **FINAL DRAFT CHECKLIST**
>
> ❏ Does the summary include the author's name and the title of the reading?
>
> ❏ Does the summary include a thesis statement?
>
> ❏ Does the summary answer some of the *Wh-* questions?
>
> ❏ Is the summary in your own words?
>
> ❏ Did you use a variety of reporting verbs?
>
> ❏ If you are using quotes, are they properly punctuated?
>
> ❏ Did you use identifying adjective clauses?
>
> ❏ Have you used the vocabulary from the unit?

UNIT PROJECT

In this unit, you have read about animal intelligence and a few specific "intelligent" animals: Clever Hans and Connie Standley's dogs. Other famous animals have equally remarkable abilities. From the list below, choose an "intelligent" animal to research. Take notes and write a report based on your findings. Follow these steps:

STEP 1: Use the Internet and other sources to research an animal from the list.

Koko the gorilla	Twiggy the squirrel
Bimbo the killer whale	Jonathan and Chantek the orangutans
Betty the crow	Lulu the pig
Ruby the elephant	Washoe the chimpanzee
Akeakemai the dolphin	Siri the elephant
Michael the gorilla	Orky and Corky the killer whales
Alex the parrot	Willow the dog
Rio the sea lion	

STEP 2: Write a summary of the information you find, including answers to some of the *Wh-* questions. Conclude by explaining whether you think the animal is exhibiting intelligence and why.

STEP 3: Combine your research with all of your classmates' research and create a class book.

ALTERNATIVE WRITING TOPICS

Write an essay about one of the topics. Use the vocabulary and grammar from the unit.

1. Noted animal intelligence expert Dorothy Hinshaw believes, "The things that are important to animals can be different than those that matter to humans. When studying animals, we must test them in situations that have meaning for their lives, not ours, and not just look to see how much they resemble us." Think of a specific animal or group of animals. What situations would have meaning for them? Why? How could you test them in these situations?

2. "If a rabbit defined intelligence the way man does, then the most intelligent animal would be a rabbit, followed by the animal most willing to obey the commands of a rabbit."
   —Robert Brault (writer, born 1938)

   How does the quotation apply to the problems of testing animal intelligence that is discussed in Reading One and Reading Two?

■■■■■■■■■■■■■■■■■■■■■■■■■■ *GO TO* MyEnglishLab *TO WRITE ABOUT ONE OF THE ALTERNATIVE TOPICS,*
WATCH A VIDEO ABOUT TALKING TO ANIMALS, AND TAKE THE UNIT 4 ACHIEVEMENT TEST. ■■■■■■■■■■■■■

TOO MUCH OF A GOOD Thing?

1. It has been projected that by the year 2050, the average lifespan will reach 125, and by 2087 it will be 150! Do you think living longer is a good thing? Why or why not? Think about how such issues as relationships, marriage, family structure, and career might be affected.

2. Immortality means living forever. Do you know stories or myths about the desire or search for immortality?

3. If scientists could create a pill that would allow you to live twice as long while staying healthy, would you take it?

GO TO MyEnglishLab *TO CHECK WHAT YOU KNOW.*

VOCABULARY

Reading One is a story about Marilisa and her husband, Leo. Read the letter Marilisa wrote to a friend about Leo. Then choose the definition that best defines each boldfaced word.

1. **a.** mean
   b. energetic
   c. lazy

2. **a.** on time
   b. well dressed
   c. considerately

3. **a.** understandably
   b. incredibly
   c. to some extent

4. **a.** difficult
   b. fascinating
   c. different

5. **a.** slightly
   b. always
   c. completely

6. **a.** complicated
   b. impressive
   c. terrible

7. **a.** doing things slowly after much thinking
   b. doing things because somebody said to
   c. doing things quickly without thinking

Dear Joan,

I know you're worried about my marrying Leo, but please realize that he has many good qualities. For example, he is quite **(1) vigorous**. Despite his age, he still exercises for hours and then works in the garden. In addition, he's very thoughtful. Unlike some of my friends, he always arrives **(2) punctually**. If he says he'll meet me at 10 o'clock, he'll be there exactly at 10.

He is also **(3) immeasurably** wise. He has so much knowledge and experience and is interested in so many **(4) disparate** subjects like Greek history, diamond mining, dinosaurs, and alternative medicine. Even though they're not related, he enjoys them all. I find this quality **(5) utterly** fascinating, and I'm totally amazed by his vast knowledge. Leo really has had an **(6) awesome** life when you think about everything he's done. It's so exciting living with someone who has had so many incredible experiences.

However, I'm not claiming that Leo is perfect. For one thing, he can be very **(7) impetuous**. Just last week, he bought a new car. He didn't even think about the fact that we needed that money to pay our credit card bills!

8. **a.** annoying
b. friendly
c. interesting

9. **a.** pleasant
b. very unfriendly
c. unhappy

10. **a.** rude or arrogant
b. modest or shy
c. admired or respected

11. **a.** accustomed to
b. feeling love or affection for
c. drawn toward

12. **a.** maybe
b. currently
c. in the end

Furthermore, at times, he can be **(8) insufferable**. I was trying to watch television last night, and he was constantly interrupting me to ask questions. Couldn't he understand that I was trying to concentrate on the show? His family is another problem. Take his ex-wife, Katrin, for example. I don't understand why he ever married her. Leo, of course, is very nice and friendly to everyone.

She, however, always seems very **(9) chilly**, especially toward me. Also, one of his sons from a previous marriage can be very **(10) presumptuous**. He expects me to do things for him just because I am now married to his father . . . even though I barely know him! His daughter, however, is lovely. I am really quite **(11) fond of** her. I think you would really like her, too.

Despite my complaints, I know that Leo is **(12) ultimately** the best first husband I could ever wish for, so don't worry. I'm sure we'll always be happy together. Joan, I hope all is well with you.

Love,

Marilisa

GO TO MyEnglishLab *FOR MORE VOCABULARY PRACTICE.*

You are going to read a science fiction story. Science fiction is a genre of writing that describes imaginary future developments in science and technology and their effects on people. It often includes elements that seem familiar to our lives today, making the story seem "real."

Read the first two paragraphs of *Death Do Us Part.* Then work with a partner to answer the questions.

1. What do you think was "her first, his seventh"?

2. What is happening with Marilisa and Leo?

3. Where and when do you think this story takes place?

4. What seems real?

5. What seems unreal?

6. What do you think "the Process" is?

Now read the rest of the story.

DEATH DO US PART

By Robert Silverberg

1 It was her first, his seventh. She was thirty-two, he was three hundred and sixty-three: the good old May/December[1] number. They honeymooned in Venice, Nairobi, the Malaysia Pleasure Dome, and one of the posh[2] L-5 resorts, a shimmering glassy sphere with round-the-clock sunlight and waterfalls that tumbled like cascades of diamonds, and then they came home to his lovely sky-house suspended on tremulous guy-wires[3] a thousand meters above the Pacific to begin the everyday part of their life together.

2 Her friends couldn't get over it. "He's ten times your age!" they would exclaim. "How could you possibly want anybody that old?" Marilisa admitted that marrying Leo was more of a lark[4] for her than anything else. An <u>impulsive</u> thing: a sudden **impetuous** leap. Marriages weren't forever, after all—just thirty or forty years and then you moved along. But Leo was sweet and kind and actually

[1] **May/December:** term used to describe a romantic relationship where there is a big difference in the ages of the two people
[2] **posh:** expensive and used by rich people
[3] **tremulous guy-wires:** shaking cables (metal ropes)
[4] **lark:** something you do to amuse yourself or as a joke

quite sexy. And he had wanted her so much. He genuinely did seem to love her. Why should his age be an issue? He didn't appear to be any older than thirty-five or so. These days you could look as young as you like. Leo did his Process faithfully and **punctually**, twice each decade, and it kept him as dashing and **vigorous** as a boy.

3   There were little drawbacks, of course. Once upon a time, long, long ago, he had been a friend of Marilisa's great-grandmother: They might have even been lovers. She wasn't going to ask. Such things sometimes happened, and you simply had to work your way around them. And then also he had an ex-wife on the scene, Number Three, Katrin, two hundred and forty-seven years old and not looking a day over thirty. She was constantly hovering[5] about. Leo still had warm feelings for her. "A wonderfully dear woman, a good and loyal friend," he would say. "When you get to know her, you'll be as **fond of** her as I am." That one was hard, all right. What was almost as bad, he had children three times Marilisa's age and more. One of them—the next-to-youngest, Fyodor—had an **insufferable** and **presumptuous** way of winking[6] and sniggering[7] at her. "I want you to meet our father's newest toy," Fyodor said of her once, when yet another of Leo's centenarian sons, previously unsuspected by Marilisa, turned up. "We get to play with her when he's tired of her." Someday Marilisa was going to pay him back[8] for that.

4   Still and all, she had no serious complaints. Leo was an ideal first husband: wise, warm, loving, attentive, and generous. She felt nothing but the greatest tenderness for him. And then too he was so **immeasurably** experienced in the ways of the world. If being married to him was a little like being married to Abraham Lincoln or Augustus Caesar, well, so be it: They had been great men, and so was Leo. He was endlessly fascinating. He was like seven husbands rolled into one. She had no regrets, none at all, not really.

5   In the spring of eighty-seven they go to Capri for their first anniversary. Their hotel is a reconstructed Roman villa on the southern slope of Monte Tiberio: alabaster wall frescoed in black and red, a brilliantly colored mosaic of sea-creatures in the marble bathtub, a broad travertine terrace that looks out over the sea. They stand together in the darkness, staring at the **awesome** sparkle of the stars. A crescent moon slashes across the night. His arm is around her; her head rests against his breast. Though she is a tall woman, Marilisa is barely heart-high to him.

Blue Grotto

6   "Tomorrow at sunrise," he says, "we'll see the Blue Grotto.[9] And then in the afternoon we'll hike down below here to the Cave of the Mater Magna. I always get a shiver when I'm there. Thinking about the ancient islanders who

(continued on next page)

---

[5] **hovering:** staying in the same place especially because you are waiting for something
[6] **winking:** closing and opening one eye quickly, usually to show that you are joking, being friendly, or telling a secret
[7] **sniggering:** laughing quietly in a way that is not nice
[8] **pay (someone) back:** to do something unpleasant to someone as a punishment because that person has done something unpleasant to you
[9] **Blue Grotto:** a famous sea cove on the coast of the Italian island of Capri

worshipped their goddess under that cliff, somewhere back in the Pleistocene. Their rites and rituals, the offerings they made to her."

7   "Is that when you first came here?" she asks, keeping it light and sly. "Somewhere in the Pleistocene?"

8   "A little later than that, really. The Renaissance, I think it was. Leonardo and I traveled down together from Florence-"

9   "You and Leonardo, you were like *that*?"

10   "Like that, yes. But not like *that*, if you take my meaning."

11   "And Cosimo di'Medici. Another one from the good old days. Cosimo gave such great parties, right?"

12   "That was Lorenzo," he says. "Lorenzo the Magnificent, Cosimo's grandson. Much more fun than the old man. You would have adored him."

13   "I almost think you're serious when you talk like that."

14   "I'm always serious. Even when I'm not." His arm tightens around her. He leans forward and down, and buries a kiss in her thick dark hair. "I love you," he whispers.

15   "I love you," she says. "You're the best first husband a girl could want."

16   "You're the finest last wife a man could ever desire."

17   The words skewer[10] her. *Last* wife? Is he expecting to die in the next ten or twenty or thirty years? He is old—ancient—but nobody has any idea yet where the limits of the Process lie. Five hundred years? A thousand? Who can say? No one able to afford the treatments has died a natural death yet, in the four hundred years since the Process was invented. Why then does he speak so knowingly of her as his last wife? He may live long enough to have seven, ten, fifty wives after her.

18   Marilisa is silent a long while.

19   Then she asks him, quietly, uncertainly. "I don't understand why you said that."

20   "Said what?"

21   "The thing about my being your last wife."

22   He hesitates[11] a moment. "But why would I ever want another, now that I have you?"

23   "Am I so **utterly** perfect?"

24   "I love you."

25   "You loved Tedesca and Thane and Iavilda too," she says. "And Miaule and Katrin." She is counting on her fingers in the darkness. One wife is missing from the list. "And . . . Syantha. See, I know all their names. You must have loved them but the marriage ended anyway. They have to end. No matter how much you love a person, you can't keep a marriage going forever."

26   "How do you know that?"

27   "I just do. Everybody knows it."

28   "I would like this marriage never to end," he tells her. "I'd like it to go on and on and on. To continue to the end of time. Is that all right? Is such a sentiment[12] permissible, do you think?"

29   "What a romantic you are, Leo!"

30   "What else can I be but romantic, tonight? This place, the spring night, the moon, the stars, the sea, the fragrance of the flowers in the air. Our anniversary. I love you. Nothing will ever end for us. Nothing."

[10] **skewer:** to hurt
[11] **hesitates:** pauses before doing or saying something because of uncertainty
[12] **sentiment:** an opinion or feeling that you have about something

31   "Can that really be so?" she asks.

32   "Of course. Forever and ever, as it is this moment."

33   She thinks from time to time of the men she will marry after she and Leo have gone their separate ways. For she knows that she will. Perhaps she'll stay with Leo for ten years, perhaps for fifty; but **ultimately**, despite all his assurances to the contrary,[13] one or the other of them will want to move on. No one stays married forever. Fifteen, twenty years, that's the usual. Sixty or seventy tops.

34   She'll marry a great athlete, next, she decides. And then a philosopher; and a political leader; and then stay single for a few decades, just to clear her palate, so to speak, an intermezzo[14] in her life, and when she wearies of that she'll find someone entirely different, a simple rugged man who likes to hunt, to work in the fields with his hands, and then a yachtsman with whom she'll sail the world, and then maybe when she's about three hundred she'll marry a boy, an innocent of eighteen or nineteen who hasn't even had his first Prep yet, and then—then a childish game. It always brings her to tears, eventually. The unknown husbands that wait for her in the misty future are vague **chilly** phantoms, fantasies, frightening, and inimical.[15] They are like swords that will inevitably fall between her and Leo, and she hates them for that.

35   The thought of having the same husband for all the vast expanse[16] of time that is the rest of her life, is a little disturbing—it gives her a sense of walls closing in, and closing and closing and closing—but the thought of leaving Leo is even worse. Or of his leaving her. Maybe she isn't truly in love with him, at any rate not as she imagines love at its deepest to be, but she is happy with him. She wants to stay with him. She can't really envision parting with him and moving on to someone else.

36   But of course she knows that she will. Everybody does in the fullness of time. *Everybody*.

37   Leo is a sand-painter. Sand-painting is his fifteenth or twentieth career. He has been an architect, an archeologist, a space-habitats developer, a professional gambler, an astronomer, and a number of other **disparate** and dazzling things. He reinvents himself every decade or two. That's as necessary to him as the Process itself. Making money is never an issue, since he lives on the compounding interest of investments set aside centuries ago. But the fresh challenge—ah, yes, always the fresh challenge.

38   Marilisa hasn't entered on any career path yet. It's much too soon. She is, after all, still in her first life, too young for the Process, merely in the Prep stage yet. Just a child, really. She has dabbled[17] in ceramics, written some poetry, composed a little music. Lately she has begun to think about studying economics or perhaps Spanish literature. No doubt her actual choice of a path to follow will be very far from any of these. But there's time to decide. Oh, is there ever time.

---

[13] **to the contrary:** showing that the opposite is true
[14] **intermezzo:** a short period of time between two longer periods
[15] **inimical:** harmful
[16] **vast expanse:** large, wide area
[17] **dabbled:** did something in a way that wasn't very serious

MAIN IDEAS

 1 Look again at your predictions from the Preview on page 126. How did your answers to the questions help you understand the story?

2 Reading One discusses Marilisa's and Leo's views on marriage, family structure and relationships, careers, and longevity. Write sentences about how their views are different from the present-day society views described.

Marriage

Present-day society: *Marriage is seen as a lifelong commitment, although in some societies divorce is common. Some people may have more than one or two marriages.*

"Death Do Us Part": _____

_____

_____

Family structure / Relationships

Present-day society: *Three generations of a family living at the same time is common.*

"Death Do Us Part": _____

_____

_____

Careers

Present-day society: *Although many people have many different jobs throughout their lives, they don't frequently change careers.*

"Death Do Us Part": _____

_____

_____

Longevity

Present-day society: *The average lifespan varies around the world, but in developed countries the average lifespan is mid-seventies.*

"Death Do Us Part": _____

_____

_____

DETAILS

Marilisa and Leo have different perspectives on the topics in the chart. Complete the chart with examples of their differing views.

TOPIC	MARILISA	LEO
MARRIAGE	*First marriage* *Assumes she'll be married again to a variety of men*	
FAMILY STRUCTURE / RELATIONSHIPS		
CAREERS		
LONGEVITY		

MAKE INFERENCES

UNDERSTANDING CHARACTERS' ATTITUDES AND FEELINGS

Writers sometimes suggest relationships between characters in a story without stating them directly. We use inference to understand characters' attitudes and feelings on a deeper level.

Look at the example and read the explanation.

How does Marilisa feel about Leo? *(paragraph 2)*

a. That he is too old for her.

b. That he is a joke.

c. That he is youthful.

The best answer is *c*.

Evidence: In paragraph 2, we learn that Marilisa's friends are concerned about Leo's age. Marilisa doesn't seem as bothered because marriages aren't forever. We also learn that her marriage was a lark, but she doesn't say that Leo himself is a joke. He is actually sweet, kind, and sexy. This makes him appear youthful to Marilisa.

After reading the text closely, we can infer that Marilisa's strongest feeling about Leo is that he is youthful.

Circle the best answer. Refer to the paragraph in parentheses. Cite the evidence from the story that supports your answer.

1. How does Marilisa feel about Katrin? *(paragraph 3)*

   a. warm

   b. loyal

   c. jealous

   Evidence: _____

   _____

   _____

2. How does Fyodor feel toward Marilisa? *(paragraph 3)*

   a. playful

   b. disrespectful

   c. bored

   Evidence: _____

   _____

   _____

3. How does Leo feel about his marriage with Marilisa? *(paragraphs 23–32)*

   a. tired

   b. unclear

   c. secure

   Evidence: _____

   _____

   _____

4. How does Marilisa feel about her marriage to Leo? *(paragraphs 29–34)*

    a. It's romantic.

    b. She wants it to be permanent.

    c. She is resigned that it will end.

Evidence: _____

_____

_____

5. Which best describes Marilisa's feeling about her marriage to Leo? *(paragraph 35)*

    a. conflicted

    b. committed

    c. insecure

Evidence: _____

_____

_____

EXPRESS OPINIONS

Discuss the questions with a partner.

1. Leo was "ten times her age." Would you marry someone older than you? By how much? What possible advantages or disadvantages are there to marrying someone much older than you?

2. The story mentions that with the Process, "these days you could look as young as you like." What age would you choose to look if you were having the Process? Why?

3. Leo has had many different careers. "He reinvents himself every decade or two. That's as necessary to him as the Process itself." Why do you think he changes careers so often? Would you want to reinvent yourself every decade or two? Why or why not?

■■■■■■■■■■■■■■■■■■■■■■■■■ *GO TO* MyEnglishLab *TO GIVE YOUR OPINION ABOUT ANOTHER QUESTION.*

Scientific understanding of aging at the cellular and molecular level may be the key to a longer lifespan. More and more scientists now believe that the human lifespan could be increased to 140 or more in the future. This may be achieved through genetic manipulation or caloric restriction (eating less). These strategies have proved effective with worms, flies, and mice. Maybe someday they will work on humans.

READ

1 Look at the boldfaced words in the reading and think about the questions.

1. Which words do you know the meanings of?

2. Can you use any of the words in a sentence?

2 Read *Toward Immortality: The Social Burden of Longer Lives*. As you read, notice the boldfaced vocabulary. Try to guess the meaning of the words from the context.

TOWARD IMMORTALITY: THE SOCIAL BURDEN OF LONGER LIVES

By Ker Than   LiveScience Staff Writer

A doubled lifespan

1   If scientists could create a pill that let you live twice as long while remaining free of infirmities,[1] would you take it?

2   If one considers only the personal benefits that longer life would bring, the answer might seem like a no-brainer[2]: People could spend more quality time with loved ones; watch future generations grow up; learn new languages; master new musical instruments; try different careers or travel the world.

3   But what about society as a whole? Would it be better off if lifespans were doubled? The question is one of growing relevance, and serious debate about it goes back at least a few years to the Kronos Conference on Longevity Health Sciences in Arizona. Gregory Stock, director of the Program on Medicine, Technology, and Society at UCLA's School of Public Health, answered the question with an **emphatic** "Yes." A doubled lifespan, Stock said, would "give us a chance to recover from our mistakes, lead us towards longer-term thinking and reduce healthcare costs by delaying the onset of expensive diseases of aging. It would also raise productivity by adding to our prime years."

---

[1] **infirmities:** sicknesses, diseases

[2] **no-brainer:** something that you do not have to think about because it is easy to understand

4   Bioethicist Daniel Callahan, a cofounder of the Hastings Center in New York, didn't share Stock's enthusiasm. Callahan's objections were practical ones. For one thing, he said, doubling lifespans won't solve any of our current social problems. "We have war, poverty, all sorts of issues around, and I don't think any of them would be at all helped by having people live longer," Callahan said in a recent telephone interview. "The question is, 'What will we get as a society?' I suspect it won't be a better society."

5   Others point out that a doubling of the human lifespan will affect society at every level. Notions[3] about marriage, family, and work will change in fundamental ways, they say, as will attitudes toward the young and the old.

Marriage and family

6   Richard Kalish, a psychologist who considered the social effects of life extension technologies, thinks a longer lifespan will **radically** change how we view marriage.

7   In today's world, for example, a couple in their 60s who are stuck in a **loveless** but **tolerable** marriage might decide to stay together for the remaining 15 to 20 years of their lives out of inertia[4] or familiarity. But if that same couple knew they might have to suffer each other's company for another 60 or 80 years, their choice might be different. Kalish predicted that as lifespans increase, there will be a shift in emphasis from marriage as a lifelong union to marriage as a long-term commitment. Multiple, brief marriages could become common.

8   A doubled lifespan will reshape notions of family life in other ways, too, says Chris Hackler, head of the Division of Medical Humanities at the University of Arkansas. If multiple marriages become the norm as Kalish predicts, and each marriage produces children, then half-siblings will become more common, Hackler points out. And if couples continue the current trend of having children beginning in their 20s and 30s, then eight or even ten generations might be alive simultaneously, Hackler said. Furthermore, if life extension also increases a woman's period of fertility, siblings could be born 40 or 50 years apart. Such a large age difference would radically change the way siblings or parents and their children interact with one another.

9   "If we were 100 years younger than our parents or 60 years apart from our siblings, that would certainly create a different set of social relationships," Hackler told *LiveScience*.

The workplace

10   For most people, living longer will **inevitably** mean more time spent working. Careers will necessarily become longer, and the retirement age will have to be pushed back, not only so individuals can support themselves, but to avoid overtaxing a nation's social security system.

11   Advocates of anti-aging research say that working longer might not be such a bad thing. With skilled workers remaining in the workforce longer, economic productivity would go up. And if people got bored with their jobs, they could switch careers.

12   But such changes would carry their own set of dangers, critics say. Competition for jobs would become fiercer as "mid-life re-trainees" beginning new careers vie with young workers for a limited number of entry-level positions. Especially **worrisome** is the

---

[3] **notions:** ideas, beliefs, or opinions
[4] **inertia:** the feeling that you do not want to do anything at all

(continued on next page)

problem of workplace mobility, Callahan said. "If you have people staying in their jobs for 100 years, that is going to make it really tough for young people to move in and get ahead," Callahan explained.

13   Callahan also worries that corporations and universities could become dominated by a few individuals if executives, managers, and tenured professors refuse to give up their posts.[5] Without a constant infusion of youthful talent and ideas, these institutions could stagnate.[6]

movement

Time to act

14   While opinions differ wildly about what the ramifications for society will be if the human lifespan is extended, most ethicists agree that the issue should be discussed now, since it might be impossible to stop or control the technology once it's developed. "If this could ever happen, then we'd better ask what kind of society we want to get," Callahan said. "We had better not go anywhere near it until we have figured those problems out."

---

[5] **give up their posts:** leave their jobs
[6] **stagnate:** to stop developing or improving

COMPREHENSION

Discuss the questions with the class.

1. Some people in Reading Two think a longer lifespan is a good idea. Discuss the reasons.

2. Some people in Reading Two don't think a longer lifespan is a good idea. Discuss the reasons.

▪▪▪▪▪▪▪▪▪▪▪▪▪▪▪▪▪▪▪▪▪▪▪▪▪▪▪▪▪▪▪▪▪▪▪▪▪▪▪ **GO TO** MyEnglishLab **FOR MORE VOCABULARY PRACTICE.**

READING SKILL

1 Go back to Reading Two. Did you look at the title and the headings before you read the article? If so, did they help you understand the article? Why or why not?

USING TITLES AND HEADINGS TO IMPROVE COMPREHENSION

The title of a reading and the headings give the reader information. Good readers use the clues provided by titles and headings to help them predict the content of the whole reading and the individual sections in the reading. Based on the title and headings, readers can ask themselves questions they think the reading or section will answer.

Think about the title, *Toward Immortality: The Social Burden of Longer Lives*. From this title, what questions would you expect this article to answer? Two of the choices are correct.

a. How long will people live in the future?

b. Why will there be fewer diseases in the future?

c. What problems may longer lives cause for society?

The best answers are *a* and *c*. Answer *a* is correct because the words "immortality" and "longer lives" are in the title. Therefore, we know that the author will probably mention how long people will live. Answer *c* is also correct because the words "social burden" suggest there will be problems or issues with longer lives. Answer *b* is not a good choice because there is no indication in the title that the article will discuss medical issues associated with longer lives.

Just as with titles, headings and subheadings also provide clues as to what you can expect to find in those sections of the text. Predicting content from headings can improve your reading comprehension.

2 Imagine that you are looking at the headings from Reading Two for the first time. For each heading, write two questions you might ask.

1. A doubled lifespan

_____

_____

2. Marriage and family

_____

_____

3. The workplace

_____

_____

3 Share your questions with a partner. Try to use these comprehension skills whenever you read a new article.

GO TO MyEnglishLab *FOR MORE SKILL PRACTICE.*

STEP 1: Organize

Reading One (R1) and Reading Two (R2) discuss both positive and negative effects of longer lifespans. Complete the cause and effect diagram with information from the readings.

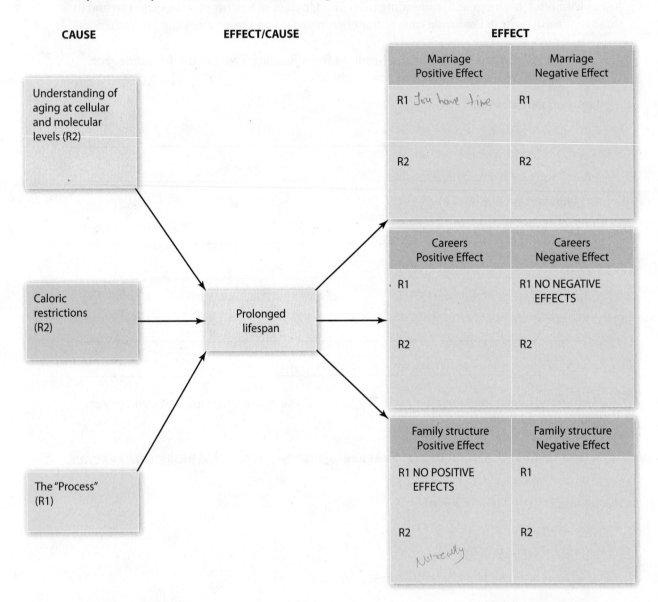

CAUSE	EFFECT/CAUSE	EFFECT

Marriage

Marriage Positive Effect	Marriage Negative Effect
R1 You have time	R1
R2	R2

Careers

Careers Positive Effect	Careers Negative Effect
R1	R1 NO NEGATIVE EFFECTS
R2	R2

Family structure

Family structure Positive Effect	Family structure Negative Effect
R1 NO POSITIVE EFFECTS	R1
R2	R2

Not really

Causes:
- Understanding of aging at cellular and molecular levels (R2)
- Caloric restrictions (R2)
- The "Process" (R1)

Effect/Cause: Prolonged lifespan

STEP 2: Synthesize

Bioethicist Daniel Callahan asked, when talking about the potential for doubled lifespans, "'What will we get as a society?' I suspect it won't be a better society." On a separate piece of paper, write a paragraph about whether you agree or disagree with his statement. Support your answer with at least three pieces of information from Step 1.

▪▪ *GO TO* MyEnglishLab *TO CHECK WHAT YOU LEARNED.*

VOCABULARY

REVIEW

Work with a partner. Discuss the meanings of the adjectives and adverbs in the box. Decide if the words give you positive, negative, or neutral feelings. Then write the words in the chart. Note that some words can be interpreted in more than one way. Discuss why.

P awesome	emphatic	impetuous	N loveless	radically	completely utterly
NG chilly	Pos fond → to like	inevitably	presumptuous	NG tolerable	vigorous → energy
NE disparate NT	immeasurably	insufferable	E punctually	ultimately nt	worrisome → to worry NG

POSITIVE	NEGATIVE	NEUTRAL
fond	tolerable	radically
Positive	worrisome	to.

EXPAND

ADJECTIVE SUFFIXES

Many adjectives are formed by combining a base word with a suffix. (*vigor* + *ous* = *vigorous*). Look at the boldfaced adjectives in the excerpts from the readings.

- They stand together in the darkness, staring at the **awesome** sparkle of the stars.
- A couple in their 60s who are stuck in a loveless but **tolerable** marriage might decide to stay together.
- Fyodor had a **presumptuous** way of winking and sniggering at her.

Suffixes can sometimes change the meaning of the base word.

- love → loveless (without love)
- care → careful (with care)
- tolerate → tolerable (able to be tolerated)

In addition, suffixes always change the form of the word.

- vigor (noun) → vigorous (adjective)

(continued on next page)

COMMON ADJECTIVE SUFFIXES

-al	-ous	-ful	-able	-less	-ive
-ed	-ing	-ant	-ic	-ent	-ial
-ible	-ar	-en	-ical	-y	-ary
-ese	-ish	-some			

Adjective suffixes can be added to nouns or verbs.

adventure (n.) → adventurous   fascinate (v.) → fascinating

care (n.) → careful

Suffixes can also be added to base/root words. Sometimes there are spelling changes when a suffix is added.

- Leave out the final *e*.
    - measure → measurable
- Double the final consonant.
    - sun → sunny
- Leave out the final *s* before *-al*.
    - politics → political

Complete the chart with synonyms from Reading One (R1) and Reading Two (R2) that have the suffixes listed. Then think of your own example of an adjective with the same suffix.

DEATH DO US PART (R1)			
SUFFIXES	EXAMPLE FROM TEXT	DEFINITION OR SYNONYM	EXAMPLE OF A NEW ADJECTIVE WITH THE SAME SUFFIX
Paragraphs 1–2			
-ing		sparkling	
-ive	*impulsive*	impetuous	*active*
Paragraphs 3–5			
-able		intolerable	
-al		perfect	
Paragraphs 6–15			
-ent		very old	
-ous		sincere	

Paragraphs 26–33			
-ible		allowable	
-ic		passionate	
Paragraphs 34–38			
-y		foggy	

TOWARD IMMORTALITY (R2)			
SUFFIXES	**EXAMPLE FROM TEXT**	**DEFINITION OR SYNONYM**	**EXAMPLE OF A NEW ADJECTIVE WITH THE SAME SUFFIX**
Paragraphs 1–2			
-al		individual	
Paragraphs 3–4			
-ic		forceful	
-ical		sensible	
Paragraphs 5–7			
-less		without love	
-ing		still left	
Paragraphs 10–13			
-ly		without doubt	
-ed		restricted	
-some		troublesome	
-ant		steady	
-ful		young	

CREATE

Imagine that you are either the bioethicist Daniel Callahan or Gregory Stock of UCLA's School of Public Health. On a separate piece of paper, write five questions for Leo (R1), about his extended lifespan. Use at least one word from the Review or Expand section in each question. Then exchange papers with a partner and answer the questions as if you were Leo.

GO TO MyEnglishLab *FOR MORE VOCABULARY PRACTICE.*

GRAMMAR

1 Examine the sentences and answer the questions with a partner.

   a. Marilisa and Leo **went** to Nairobi and Venice on their honeymoon three years ago.

   b. Leo **has been** an architect, an archeologist, a space-habitats developer, a professional gambler, an astronomer, and a number of other disparate and dazzling things.

   c. People **have been searching** for the "fountain of youth" since the beginning of recorded history.

   1. In sentence *a*, is Leo and Marilisa's honeymoon over? How do you know?

   2. In sentence *b*, is Leo still an architect, an archeologist . . . ? How do you know?

   3. In sentence *c*, are people still searching for the fountain of youth? How do you know? When did people start searching?

   4. What verb tenses are used in sentences *a, b,* and *c*?

CONTRASTING THE SIMPLE PAST, PRESENT PERFECT, AND PRESENT PERFECT CONTINUOUS

The Simple Past

1. Use the simple past for things that happened in the past and were completed.	Leo **watched** the movie. *(Leo is no longer watching the movie. He finished watching the movie.)*
2. Use past time expressions such as: *last, ago, in, on, at, yesterday, when . . .* to indicate that an action or event was completed at a definite time in the past.	Leo **watched** the movie **yesterday**. *(Leo is no longer watching the movie. He finished watching the movie yesterday.)*

The Present Perfect

3. Use the present perfect for completed actions that happened at an indefinite time in the past.	Marilisa **has eaten** breakfast. *(She has finished her breakfast, but we don't know exactly when she ate it, or it is not important.)*
4. You can also use the present perfect for repeated actions that were completed in the past, but that may happen again in the future.	Leo **has visited** Paris six times. *(Those six visits are finished. However, he may visit Paris again in the future.)*

5. Use the present perfect with *for* or *since* for actions that began in the past. These actions were not completed, have continued up to the present, and may continue into the future. Use *for* or *since* for this meaning especially with non-action verbs, such as *be, feel,* and *know*. *For* is followed by a length of time, for example, *six years*. *Since* is followed by a specific point in time, for example, *2099*.

Leo **has been** a sand painter **for** six years. (*Leo began to be a sand painter six years ago. He is still a sand painter today, and may continue to be a sand painter in the future.*)

Leo **has been** a sand painter **since** 2099. (*Leo began to be a sand painter in 2099. He is still a sand painter today, and may continue to be a sand painter in the future.*)

6. Compare the present perfect without *for* or *since.*

Leo **has been** a sand painter. (*Leo was a sand painter at some time in the past, but he is not anymore. We don't know exactly when he was, or it is not important.*)

The Present Perfect Continuous

7. Use the present perfect continuous for actions that began in the past. These actions were not completed, have continued up to the present, and may continue into the future. The use of *for* or *since* with the present perfect continuous is optional. Using *for* or *since* gives additional information about when the action began or how long it has been in progress, but it does not change the meaning of the verb.

Daniel Callahan **has been studying** about the ramifications of increasing human lifespans.

(*Daniel Callahan began studying sometime in the past. He is still studying and will probably continue to study in the future.*)

8. Non-action verbs are not usually used in the continuous. Use the present perfect with *for* or *since* for this meaning with a non-action verb.

Callahan **has been** at the Hastings Center **for** many years.

Callahan **has been** at the Hastings Center **since** 1969.

2 Complete the conversations by circling the correct forms of the verbs.

Conversation 1

REPORTER: Our readers may already know about the "fountain of youth," but can you give us some historical perspective? Also, do you think scientific advancements will turn out to be a "fountain of youth," allowing people to live forever?

DANIEL CALLAHAN: People **(1) have been searching / searched** for the "fountain of youth" since the beginning of recorded history. People believed that drinking from this fountain would allow them to be healthy and vigorous forever. They would never get sick and would be full of energy. So far, the "fountain" **(2) has been / was** impossible to find. People **(3) have not been / were not** able to truly achieve eternal life. Human lifespans have been increasing, but we are still far from reaching immortality. Even considering the scientific advancements that **(4) have taken / took** place in the twentieth century, I, as a scientist, believe that ultimately the limit of human life will be no more than 150 years.

Conversation 2

DR. KALISH: I know you have been very busy attending conferences this month. I believe you have recently attended a conference on longevity. Did you learn a lot?

Dr. Gregory Stock: What a month! The conference on longevity I **(5) attended / have been attending** last week did not begin very punctually. It was supposed to begin at 9:00 A.M. but **(6) didn't actually start / hasn't actually started** until 9:45! On top of that, the first speaker was insufferable; he finished every sentence with, "you know." Luckily, I **(7) have gone / have been going** to three other conferences this month that had awesome speakers who provided us with lots of interesting facts and ideas about longevity. At the first conference, the speaker **(8) discussed / has been discussing** how restricting the amount of food eaten may increase lifespans. At the next conference, I learned about some ongoing research that Dr. Clynes **(9) did / has been doing** with mice that has ramifications for human longevity.

Conversation 3

Marilisa's Friend, Joan: Leo has such a large family. Now that you are married, how are you getting along with them?

Marilisa: Not as well as I would like, but I suppose the problems I am having are quite normal for a newlywed. I **(10) have had / had** problems with Leo's son, Fyodor, since the first time I met him, but I am willing to tolerate him for Leo's sake. Other than Fyodor, and one or two of Leo's ex-wives, I **(11) have enjoyed / enjoyed** getting to know Leo's family. I really like Leo's brother, Max. Max is a writer and scientist who **(12) has completed / completed** a book on "the Process" two years ago. Ever since that was published, he **(13) worked / has been working** on his autobiography.

3 Complete the sentences with the verb in the correct tense: simple past, present perfect, or present perfect continuous.

1. Leo (**meet**) _____ many important historical figures during his life, and he looks forward to meeting many more.

2. Marilisa and Leo (**visit**) _____ Capri in '87 on their first anniversary.

3. Leo (**have**) _____ at least 10 different careers so far.

4. Marilisa (**talk**) _____ to Fyodor for at least 30 minutes. Do you think they will be done soon?

5. Leo (**meet**) _____ Leonardo da Vinci over 500 years ago.

6. Doctors at the Hastings Center (**study**) _____ longevity for many years and plan to continue for many more years.

7. Daniel Callahan doesn't believe that scientists should continue working on extending lifespans until they (**figure**) _____ out the ramifications longer life will have for society.

8. The conference that Dr. Kalish (**attend**) _____ last August dealt with the future of marriage in a society with prolonged lifespans.

9. Dr. Chris Hackler (**do**) _____ research concerning family relationships of siblings born 40–50 years apart. He expects to finish his research next year.

10. Although it is only March, Gregory Stock (**write**) _____ four papers on how increased lifespans can decrease healthcare costs. He is expecting to write at least two more papers before the end of the year.

■■■■■■■■■■■■■■■■■ *GO TO* MyEnglishLab *FOR MORE GRAMMAR PRACTICE AND TO CHECK WHAT YOU LEARNED.*

FINAL WRITING TASK

In this unit, you read about immortal life in the future. Imagine that scientists have discovered a way to make you immortal, and it is now the year 2175. What is your life like? What jobs have you had? What relationships have you had? Who have you married? What is your family like? What have been the advantages of living so long? What have been the disadvantages?

You are going to *write a descriptive essay about the positive and negative aspects of your life in 2175*. Use the vocabulary and grammar from the unit.*

PREPARE TO WRITE: Using an Idea Web

An **idea web** helps you see how different topics are related to one central theme.

Imagine your life in the year 2175. Look at the topics in the idea web. Close your eyes and try to create a mental picture of yourself and your life. Think about the topics in the circles as they relate to your life. Write your ideas about each topic in the circles. Be sure to include details and adjectives.

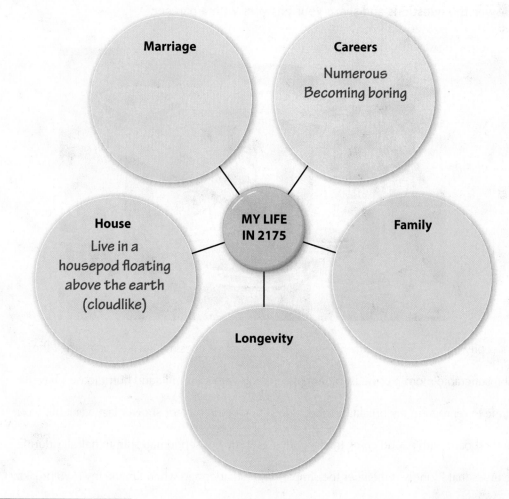

Marriage

Careers
Numerous
Becoming boring

House
Live in a
housepod floating
above the earth
(cloudlike)

MY LIFE
IN 2175

Family

Longevity

---

* For Alternative Writing Topics, see page 153. These topics can be used in place of the writing topic for this unit or as homework. The alternative topics relate to the theme of the unit but may not target the same grammar or rhetorical structures taught in the unit.

WRITE: A Descriptive Essay

A **descriptive essay** describes a place, person, or situation. The writer uses such vivid or descriptive language that the reader can create a clear mental picture of the description. Here are some important points:

1. **Have an introduction.** Capture the reader's attention by telling an interesting anecdote or story.

2. **Use strong imagery.** Try to create mental pictures for your reader by using descriptive adjectives and details.

3. **Rely on sensory details.** Create strong sensory images by describing smells, sights, sounds, tastes, and senses of touch.

4. **Have a conclusion.** Bring the ideas of the essay to a close by providing final thoughts or predictions.

1 Read the introductory paragraph from a descriptive essay about life in the future. Then answer the questions and share your answers with a partner.

I sleepily open my eyes as my alarm robot vigorously shakes me awake. I can smell the usual insufferable morning smells: bitter coffee made with sour milk and burnt toast. I haven't had time to reprogram my breakfast robot since the electric meteor shower last week blew out its motherboard with a loud *crack* that sounded as if my housepod had split in half. It's during these times that I fondly remember the simple days decades ago when I made my own breakfast and lived on Earth, not floating above it like a lonely cloud. No matter. I'll glide through a convenient coffee shop's hovercraft window on the way to work. Work. I used to be so punctual. "As utterly dependable as a Swiss watch," my bosses always said, even with a half a world commute every day. After more than 150 years of work, it's hard to get excited. But I am getting ahead of myself. In the past 200 years, I have had numerous wives, careers, countless numbers of children, and awesome experiences. My life has been an endless roller coaster ride filled with immeasurable happiness and sadness.

1. Circle the thesis statement.

2. What do you expect the next paragraphs of the essay will be about?

3. Descriptive essays often include sensory details and create mental imagery. What are some examples of sensory details in the paragraph above?

TOUCH	SMELL	SIGHT	TASTE	SOUND
Vigorously	burned toust	homePod gliding	coffee	

4. What mental picture does this writing create? Underline the words or sentences in the paragraph that create these images for you.

2 Now write the first draft of your descriptive essay. Use your notes from Prepare to Write. Make sure you have multiple paragraphs and use descriptive language that includes adjectives and sensory details. Be sure to use grammar and vocabulary from the unit.

REVISE: Using Figurative Language

Many descriptive essays and stories include **figurative language**, such as **similes**, **metaphors**, and **personification**, to add depth and imagery.

A **simile** is a way of describing something through a comparison using *like* or *as*.

The comparison is with something not normally connected with the subject.

Simile: *The snow was like a blanket.*

Explanation: The subject, snow, is being compared to a blanket because it covers the ground in the same way a blanket covers a bed.

1 Look at the introductory paragraph in Write on pages 148–149. With a partner, find the two similes and complete the information.

_____ is being compared to _____ because _____

_____

_____ is being compared to _____ because _____

_____

2 Look at Reading One. With a partner find the similes and complete the information.

Paragraph 1: _____ are being compared to _____

because _____

Paragraph 2: _____ is being compared to _____

because _____

Paragraph 34: _____ are being compared to _____

because _____

A **metaphor** is another way of describing something through a comparison but without using *like* or *as*. Instead, the metaphor explicitly states what a thing "is." The subject and its complement are the same.

Metaphor: *The setting sun is a red ball of fire falling into the sea.*

Explanation: The sun is not *like* a red ball of fire, it **is** a red ball of fire.

3 Work with a partner. Look at Reading One, paragraph 34. What metaphor does Marilisa use to describe her unknown future husbands? Why does she use this metaphor?

Personification gives human qualities to animals or objects. This helps the reader better connect with the image.

Without Personification	With Personification
The leaves blew around in the wind.	The leaves danced in the wind.
The sun was shining in the sky.	The sun sang its happy summer song.

4 Look at Reading One, paragraph 17. Find an example of personification. With a partner, discuss how personification helps the description come alive.

5 Look at your first draft. Are your descriptions clear? Do they create vivid mental imagery? Add at least one simile, one metaphor, or one example of personification.

■■ *GO TO* MyEnglishLab *FOR MORE SKILL PRACTICE.*

EDIT: Writing the Final Draft

Go to MyEnglishLab and write the final draft of your essay. Carefully edit it for grammatical and mechanical errors, such as spelling, capitalization, and punctuation. Make sure you use some of the grammar and vocabulary from the unit. Use the checklist to help you write your final draft. Then submit your essay to your teacher.

FINAL DRAFT CHECKLIST

❏ Does the essay have an interesting introduction?

❏ Does the essay have multiple paragraphs?

❏ Does the essay include clear descriptive language including lots of adjectives?

❏ Does the essay contain vivid mental imagery, including sensory details and a simile, a metaphor, or an example of personification?

❏ Does the essay have a conclusion?

❏ Did you use tenses correctly?

❏ Have you used the vocabulary from the unit?

UNIT PROJECT

In this unit, you have read a science fiction story about people living longer lives. Even today, there are areas of the world as well as specific groups of people who are already living lives that are significantly longer than average. Areas where these people live are called "blue zones." There are a number of reasons why people in these longevity hotspots seem to live longer than most people.

In a small group, research one of these areas. Compare your findings and write a report. Follow these steps:

STEP 1: Choose one of these blue zones:

Okinawa, Japan	Campodimele, Italy
Loma Linda, California, USA	Sardinia, Italy
Nicoya Peninsula, Costa Rica	Ikaria, Greece
Symi, Greece	Your own idea based on your research.
Hunza, Pakistan	

STEP 2: Do research on the Internet about the blue zone you chose. Read two or more articles describing the area or group you are studying. Answer the questions:

- How long do the people live?
- Where do they live, and what is their environment like?
- What is their diet?
- What is their lifestyle?
- What do they do that is different from what most people do?
- How do experts explain their longevity?
- What can we learn from these people?

STEP 3: Work in your small group to compare your findings and prepare a report for the class.

ALTERNATIVE WRITING TOPICS

Write an essay about one of the topics. Use the vocabulary and grammar from the unit.

1. If scientists created a pill that would allow you to live twice as long while remaining free of infirmities, would you take it? Why or why not?

2. As with all new medical technology, life extension technology will probably be very expensive, at least at first. Because of this, the people able to afford the treatments will be wealthy. How will this affect all areas of society? Think about politics, business, entertainment, the economy, and so on.

GO TO MyEnglishLab TO WRITE ABOUT ONE OF THE ALTERNATIVE TOPICS, WATCH A VIDEO ABOUT LONGEVITY, AND TAKE THE UNIT 5 ACHIEVEMENT TEST.

MAKING A
Difference

1. What do you think the people in the photo are doing?

2. Philanthropy is a way of showing concern for other people by giving money or volunteering (working without pay) to help people in need or organizations that help people in need. What do you think people can learn from volunteering?

3.   Have you ever done any volunteering? If so, what motivated you to volunteer? What did you learn from this experience?

GO TO MyEnglishLab *TO CHECK WHAT YOU KNOW.*

VOCABULARY

1 Two of the three words in each row have meanings similar to the boldfaced word. Cross out the word that doesn't belong. If you need help, use a dictionary.

1. **passion**	enthusiasm	~~decision~~	interest
2. **proudly**	modestly	self-satisfyingly	contentedly
3. **challenge**	pride	test	demand
4. **satisfaction**	happiness	pleasure	amusement
5. **determined**	insistent	stubborn	uncertain
6. **proposal**	suggestion	order	recommendation
7. **donate**	contribute	give	sell
8. **admiring**	complimentary	approving	boring
9. **devote**	dedicate	appreciate	commit
10. **inspired**	saddened	encouraged	motivated
11. **manage**	handle	cope with	respond
12. **thrilled**	happy	scared	excited

Across the United States, more and more organizations—including corporate, educational, religious, and government groups—are supporting volunteer programs. In addition, more people are volunteering in a wide range of ways. People volunteer for many different reasons: some for political or religious reasons; some for personal or social reasons. Others volunteer because it's mandatory, or required, in certain situations, for example, as part of a school's curriculum or as a requirement for graduation.

2 Read what people say about volunteering. Complete each statement with the words in the boxes. Then write the reasons you think they volunteer. (Note: Not all words are used, and some people may have more than one reason.)

Reasons for Volunteering

environmental	medical research	political	aged care
mandatory	tutoring	personal	religious

1. Matt Olsen, age 60: Raised $2,000 for AIDS research in the annual Boston-to-New York AIDS bicycle ride

| admiring | challenge | ~~donate~~ | manage |

"I'm trying to raise money for AIDS research in memory of my brother. I'm hoping to _____*donate*_____ more than $2,000 this year. Maybe this way what happened to him won't happen to others. The ride is certainly a physical _____, especially since I hurt my leg last weekend. However, I still think I can _____ to finish the ride. In any case, I enjoy biking, and this way I can combine my favorite sport with a good cause."

Reasons: _*personal; medical research*_____

2. Steve Hooley, age 36: Donates his time as a Boy Scout leader

| inspired | manage | passion | thrilled |

"I've always loved the outdoors and camping. In fact, preserving the environment is a _____ for me. Therefore, I'm _____ to be a Scout leader. By being a Scout leader, I can do something I like and share my love of nature with the next generation. If they are _____, maybe they'll take better care of the environment than our generation has.

Reasons: _____

3. Hannah Bullard, age 27: Volunteers in a shelter for homeless women

| inspired | passion | proudly | satisfaction |

"I've always been taught that we should help those who are less fortunate than we are. Reverend Woodson spoke at church last Sunday about all the good work being done here. He spoke with such _____ that I knew I wanted to participate. It gives me a lot of _____ to work with these women. Some of them have been through so much: alcoholism, drug addiction, and in many cases, abuse. I am very _____ by how far some of them have come. Despite their many problems, many of these women have now taken back control of their lives."

Reasons: _____

(continued on next page)

4. Louisa Deering, age 17: Spends three hours a week playing guitar for senior citizens in a nursing home

determined	devoting	proposal	satisfaction

"I started coming here last year because it was a school requirement. After I completed my requirement, I didn't want to stop. In order to continue volunteering, I made a _____ to the director of the program—I asked him if I could come back again this year after school and on weekends because I really have a good time with the people. I want to continue _____ time to them because I truly enjoy being with them and I think they like to listen to my music, too."

Reasons: _____

5. Ted Sirota, age 23: Spends five hours a week volunteering at a politician's office

admiring	determined	donate	inspire

"I feel that this person is the best candidate. I find her truly amazing; she's someone I can really look up to and want to be like. However, I'm not just one of her _____ supporters. I also volunteer for her. By volunteering, I can do more than just vote. I am _____ to help her get elected. That way I can be more involved in the whole political process."

Reasons: _____

■■■■■■■■■■■■■■■■■■■■■■■■■■■■■■■■■■■■ **GO TO** MyEnglishLab **FOR MORE VOCABULARY PRACTICE.**

PREVIEW

Justin Lebo is a boy who volunteers his time and energy to help others in a unique way.

Read the first two paragraphs of *Justin Lebo*. **Work with a partner to answer the questions.**

1. What condition is the bicycle in?

2. Why do you think Justin would be interested in a bike in that condition?

3. What do you think Justin will do with the bicycle?

Now read the rest of the article.

JUSTIN LEBO

BY PHILLIP HOOSE (from *It's Our World, Too*)

1   Something about the battered old bicycle at the garage sale[1] caught ten-year-old Justin Lebo's eye. What a wreck! It was like looking at a few big bones in the dust and trying to figure out what kind of dinosaur they had once belonged to.

2   It was a BMX bike with a twenty-inch frame. Its original color was buried beneath five or six coats of gunky paint. Everything—the grips, the pedals, the brakes, the seat, the spokes—was bent or broken, twisted and rusted. Justin stood back as if he were inspecting a painting for sale at an auction. Then he made his final judgment: perfect.

3   Justin talked the owner down to $6.50 and asked his mother, Diane, to help load the bike into the back of their car.

4   When he got it home, he wheeled the junker into the garage and showed it **proudly** to his father. "Will you help me fix it up?" he asked. Justin's hobby was bike racing, a **passion** the two of them shared. Their garage barely had room for the car anymore. It was more like a bike shop. Tires and frames hung from hooks on the ceiling, and bike wrenches dangled from the walls.

5   Now Justin and his father cleared out a work space in the garage and put the old junker up on a rack. They poured alcohol on the frame and rubbed until the old paint began to yield, layer by layer. They replaced the broken pedal, tightened down a new seat, and restored the grips. In about a week, it looked brand new.

6   Soon he forgot about the bike. But the very next week, he bought another junker at a yard sale[2] and fixed it up, too. After a while, it bothered him that he wasn't really using either bike. Then he realized that what he loved about the old bikes wasn't riding them: It was the **challenge** of making something new and useful out of something old and broken.

7   Justin wondered what he should do with them. They were just taking up space in the garage. He remembered that when he was younger, he used to live near a large brick building called the Kilbarchan Home for Boys. It was a place for boys whose parents couldn't care for them for one reason or another.

8   He found "Kilbarchan" in the phone book and called the director, who said the boys would be **thrilled** to get two bicycles. The next day when Justin and his mother unloaded the bikes at the home, two boys raced out to greet them. They leapt aboard the bikes and started tooling around the semicircular driveway, doing wheelies and pirouettes, laughing and shouting.

---

[1] **garage sale:** a sale of used furniture, clothes, toys, etc. that you no longer want, usually held in your garage
[2] **yard sale:** another phrase for garage sale

(continued on next page)

9   The Lebos watched them for a while, then started to climb into their car to go home. The boys cried after them, "Wait a minute! You forgot your bikes!" Justin explained that the bikes were for them to keep. "They were so happy," Justin remembers. "It was like they couldn't believe it. It made me feel good just to see them happy."

10   On the way home, Justin was silent. His mother assumed he was lost in a feeling of **satisfaction**. But he was thinking about what would happen once those bikes got wheeled inside and everybody saw them. How could all those kids decide who got the bikes? Two bikes could cause more trouble than they would solve. Actually they hadn't been that hard to build. It was fun. Maybe he could do more . . .

11   "Mom," Justin said as they turned onto their street, "I've got an idea. I'm going to make a bike for every boy at Kilbarchan for Christmas." Diane Lebo looked at Justin out of the corner of her eye. She had rarely seen him so **determined.** → made a decision.

12   When they got home, Justin called Kilbarchan to find out how many boys lived there. There were twenty-one. It was already June. He had six months to make nineteen bikes. That was almost a bike a week. Justin called the home back to tell them of his plan. "I could tell they didn't think I could do it," Justin remembers. "I knew I could."

13   Justin knew his best chance to build bikes was almost the way General Motors or Ford builds cars: in an assembly line. He figured it would take three or four junkers to produce enough parts to make one good bike. That meant sixty to eighty bikes. Where would he get them?

14   Garage sales seemed to be the only hope. It was June, and there would be garage sales all summer long. But even if he could find that many bikes, how could he ever pay for them? That was hundreds of dollars.

15   He went to his parents with a **proposal**. "When Justin was younger, say five or six," says his mother, "he used to give away some of his allowance[3] to help others in need. His father and I would **donate** a dollar for every dollar Justin donated. So he asked us if it could be like the old days, if we'd match every dollar he put into buying old bikes. We said yes."

16   Justin and his mother spent most of June and July hunting for cheap bikes at garage sales and thrift shops.[4] They would haul the bikes home, and Justin would start stripping them down in the yard.

17   But by the beginning of August, he had **managed** to make only ten bikes. Summer vacation was almost over, and school and homework would soon cut into his time. Garage sales would dry up when it got colder, and Justin was out of money. Still he was determined to find a way.

18   At the end of August, Justin got a break. A neighbor wrote a letter to the local newspaper describing Justin's project, and an editor thought it would make a good story. In her **admiring** article about a boy who was **devoting** his summer to help kids he didn't even know, she said Justin needed bikes and money, and she printed his home phone number.

19   Overnight, everything changed. "There must have been a hundred calls," Justin says. "People would call me up and ask me to come over and

---

[3] **allowance:** money you are given regularly or for a special reason
[4] **thrift shops:** stores that sell used goods, especially furniture, clothes, and toys, often in order to raise money for a charity

pick up their old bike. Or I'd be working in the garage, and a station wagon would pull up. The driver would leave a couple of bikes by the curb. It just snowballed.[5]"

20   The week before Christmas Justin delivered the last of the twenty-one bikes to Kilbarchan. Once again, the boys poured out of the home and leapt aboard the bikes, tearing around in the snow.

21   And once again, their joy **inspired** Justin. They reminded him how important bikes were to him. Wheels meant freedom. He thought about how much more the freedom to ride must mean to boys like these who had so little freedom in their lives. He decided to keep on building.

22   "First I made eleven bikes for the children in a foster home[6] my mother told me about. Then I made bikes for all the women in a battered women's shelter. Then I made ten little bikes and tricycles for children with AIDS. Then I made twenty-three bikes for the Paterson Housing Coalition."

23   In the four years since he started, Justin Lebo has made between 150 and 200 bikes and given them all away. He has been careful to leave time for his homework, his friends, his coin collection, his new interest in marine biology, and of course, his own bikes.

24   Reporters and interviewers have asked Justin Lebo the same question over and over: "Why do you do it?" The question seems to make him uncomfortable. It's as if they want him to say what a great person he is. Their stories always make him seem like a saint, which he knows he isn't. "Sure it's nice of me to make the bikes," he says, "because I don't have to. But I want to. In part, I do it for myself. I don't think you can ever really do anything to help anybody else if it doesn't make you happy."

25   "Once I overheard a kid who got one of my bikes say, 'A bike is like a book; it opens up a whole new world.' That's how I feel, too. It made me happy to know that kid felt that way. That's why I do it."

---

[5] **snowballed:** got bigger quickly or got harder to control
[6] **foster home:** a home where a child is taken care of for a period of time by someone who is not a parent or legal guardian

MAIN IDEAS

1 Look again at your answers to the questions from the Preview on page 158. How did your answers help you understand the story?

2 Work with a partner. Read the statements and decide which three represent the main ideas of Reading One. Then discuss the reasons for your choices.

1. Justin paid $6.50 for the first bike he fixed up.

2. Justin needed to find a way to get a lot of used bikes.

3. Justin was able to fix up and donate hundreds of bikes because of the support of his parents and community.

4. Justin's hobby was bike racing.

5. Justin is a special boy because he likes to help others.

6. After the newspaper article, people called Justin and offered him their old bikes.

DETAILS

The chart lists some benefits of doing community service. Complete the chart with examples of how Justin Lebo benefited from his experience.

THE BENEFITS OF COMMUNITY SERVICE	EXAMPLES OF JUSTIN LEBO
Encourages people to use their free time constructively	*Justin spent his free time in the summer making bicycles for the children at the Kilbarchan Home for Boys.*
Gives a sense of satisfaction; builds self-esteem	
Opens volunteers' eyes to the great variety of people in need by providing opportunities to meet new and different types of people	
One successful community service experience leads to performing other services	
Volunteers learn they can help solve real social problems and needs	
Helps people to find out who they are, what their interests are, and what they are good at	

MAKE INFERENCES

INFERRING PEOPLE'S REACTIONS

By reading carefully, it is often possible to increase your understanding by inferring how different people in a story react to an event or to a person's decisions.

Look at the example and read the explanation.

In Reading One, paragraph 15, the author writes, "He [Justin] went to his parents with a proposal. 'When Justin was younger, say five or six,' says his mother, 'he used to give away some of his allowance to help others in need. His father and I would donate a dollar for every dollar Justin donated. So he asked us if it could be like the old days, if we'd match every dollar he put into buying old bikes. We said yes.'"

How would you describe the reaction of Justin's parents to his proposal?

a. excited   **b.** skeptical   **c.** supportive

The correct answer is *c*. His parents agreed to help Justin buy more old bikes. They supported him by agreeing to give him money.

Work with a partner. Think about the people mentioned in Reading One. How do they react to Justin and his ideas? Read the questions and look at the paragraphs indicated. Then choose the best answer.

1. What was the Kilbarchan boys' first reaction when Justin started to leave without taking his bikes? *(paragraph 9)*

   a. confused   **b.** admiring   **c.** appreciative

2. How do you think Justin's mother felt about his idea to build one bike for every boy at Kilbarchan? *(paragraph 11)*

   a. excited   **b.** unsure   **c.** appreciative

3. How would you characterize the Kilbarchan director's reaction to Justin's proposal to build a bike for every boy at Kilbarchan? *(paragraph 12)*

   a. confused   **b.** helpful   **c.** skeptical

4. How did the people who called and left bikes react to the letter in the newspaper? *(paragraph 19)*

   a. stubbornly   **b.** enthusiastically   **c.** resentfully

5. How do you think the kid who Justin overheard felt about getting a bike? *(paragraph 25)*

   a. proud   **b.** surprised   **c.** appreciative

EXPRESS OPINIONS

Work with a partner. Discuss your ideas. Then report your ideas to the class.

1. Justin was able to combine something he loved to do with philanthropic work. Is it very important to love what you are volunteering to do? Why?

2. Who do you think received more from Justin's philanthropic work, Justin or the people that he gave the bikes to? Explain.

3. No one forced Justin to do what he did. Do you believe this makes Justin an exceptional young man? Explain.

■■■■■■■■■■■■■■■■■■■■■■■■■■■■■■■■■■■ *GO TO* MyEnglishLab *TO GIVE YOUR OPINION ABOUT ANOTHER QUESTION.*

READING TWO | SOME TAKE THE TIME GLADLY PROBLEMS WITH MANDATORY VOLUNTEERING

READ

Many educational organizations in the United States require high school students to devote a certain number of hours outside of the classroom to community service in order to graduate. Supporters of mandatory volunteering believe that the school's role should include both preparing children to be academically successful and helping them to be responsible citizens who are active participants in their communities.

However, not everybody believes that mandatory volunteering is a good idea. Those opposed to the requirement believe that the term "mandatory volunteering" is an oxymoron, a contradiction; they believe that volunteering should be something you do of your own free will. It is not something that is forced on you.

1 Look at the boldfaced words in the two opinions and think about the questions.

1. Which words do you know the meanings of?

2. Can you use any of the words in a sentence?

2 Read the two opinions about mandatory volunteering. As you read, notice the boldfaced vocabulary. Try to guess its meaning from the context.

SOME TAKE THE TIME GLADLY

By Mensah Dean (from the *Washington Times*)

1   Mandatory volunteering made many members of Maryland's high school class of '97 grumble with **indignation**. angry, upset

2   Future seniors,[1] however, probably won't be as resistant now that the program has been broken in. Some, like John Maloney, already have completed their required hours of approved community service. The Bowie High School sophomore[2] earned his hours in eighth grade[3] by volunteering two nights a week at the Larkin-Chase Nursing and Restorative Center in Bowie.

3   He played shuffleboard, cards, and other games with the senior citizens.[4] He also helped plan parties for them and visited their rooms to keep them company.

4   John, fifteen, is not finished volunteering. Once a week he videotapes animals at the Prince George County animal shelter in Forestville. His footage is shown on the Bowie public access television channel in hopes of finding homes for the animals.

5   "Volunteering is better than just sitting around," says John, "and I like animals; I don't want to see them put to sleep."[5]

6   He's not the only volunteer in his family. His sister, Melissa, an eighth grader, has completed her hours also volunteering at Larkin-Chase.

7   "It is a good idea to have kids go out into the community, but it's frustrating to have to

write essays about the work," she said. "It makes you feel like you're doing it for the requirement and not for yourself."

8   The high school's service learning office, run by Beth Ansley, provides information on organizations seeking volunteers so that students will have an easier time **fulfilling** their hours.

9   "It's ridiculous that people are opposing the requirements," said Amy Rouse, who this summer has worked at the Ronald McDonald House[6] and has helped to rebuild a church in Clinton.

10   "So many people won't do the service unless it's mandatory," Rouse said, "but once they start doing it, they'll really like it and hopefully it will become a part of their lives—like it has become a part of mine."

---

[1] **seniors:** students in the last year of high school, approximately 17–18 years old

[2] **sophomore:** a student in the second year of high school, approximately 15–16 years old

[3] **eighth grade:** The U.S. public school system begins with kindergarten and continues with grades 1–12. A student in eighth grade is approximately 13–14 years old.

[4] **senior citizens:** people over the age of 65

[5] **put to sleep:** give an animal drugs so that it dies without pain

[6] **Ronald McDonald House:** a residence, usually near a hospital, which provides a home and other support services for the families of children who require a lot of time in the hospital because of serious illness

Source: "Some Take the Time Gladly" by Mensah Dean from *The Washington Times*, May 14, 1997. Copyright © 1997 The Washington Times LLC. Reprinted by permission. This reprint does not constitute or imply any endorsement or sponsorship of any product, service, company, or organization.

Problems with Mandatory Volunteering

1   I think the school board's plan to implement a mandatory volunteering program is a terrible idea.

2   First of all, let me say that I am already a volunteer and proud of it. In fact, I do volunteer work at my local library as well as tutor elementary school kids at my church's after-school program. I believe that, at least in part, the reason that I enjoy volunteering and am effective at it is that I am not being forced to do it. In addition, I can choose to volunteer with people and organizations that interest me; that is not always the case with mandatory volunteering.

3   I am a new transfer student in this district and am very happy that we currently do not have a mandatory volunteering program here; however, my last school did, and for many students it was not a good experience. Imagine how new students must feel when they are told that to graduate they will have to volunteer hundreds of hours! They are already overwhelmed by schoolwork and so often end up just completing their hours, but not putting in any effort. As a result, the quality of their volunteer work is much worse than the work done by volunteers who actually choose to volunteer. In addition, students who are told they must volunteer may become **resentful** and not want to volunteer in the future. Volunteering becomes a negative experience. On the other hand, many students do already volunteer, and those who choose to do so make a real difference.

4   Another problem is that many students have busy after-school schedules: they have family, work, and athletic responsibilities. For example, many students need to be able to work after school in order to help out their families or to save money for college. Some have to take care of younger siblings or grandparents, and still others use this time to participate in athletics. School starts and ends at set times, and any school-related activity after those times is extracurricular, such as the football team or science club. To participate in these activities is a personal choice, just as volunteering should be. Nothing should be required of a student after school except homework.

5   Finally, the term 'mandatory volunteering' is an **oxymoron**. Volunteering is something you do of your own free will. If it is mandatory, it is not volunteering. For all these reasons, I am totally **opposed** to our school implementing a mandatory volunteering program and suggest that volunteering be left as a personal choice. It should not be made mandatory.

COMPREHENSION

Both writers give reasons to support their opinions in the editorials. Complete the chart with reasons found in the editorials. Share your list with the class.

FOR MANDATORY VOLUNTEERING	AGAINST MANDATORY VOLUNTEERING
1.	1. Volunteering is a personal choice.
2. Community and like	2. after School No time
3. Investing in future	3. Part time Job, life responsibility
	4. They don't like it
	5. oxymoron
	6.

GO TO MyEnglishLab FOR MORE VOCABULARY PRACTICE.

READING SKILL

1 Go back to the two opinions in Reading Two. What words do the authors use to show that the opposing point of view makes no sense? Why do they choose to use these words?

RECOGNIZING PERSUASIVE LANGUAGE

When trying to persuade a reader to agree with their ideas, writers use persuasive language. These words or phrases add structure and depth to writers' ideas. Writers use persuasive language to support their own points of view and also to oppose ideas they are trying to refute. In many cases, persuasive language evokes strong emotions.

Look at this quote from paragraph 9 of "Some Take the Time Gladly": "'It's ridiculous that people are opposing the requirements,' said Amy Rouse, who this summer has worked at the Ronald McDonald House and has helped to rebuild a church in Clinton."

What words does the author use to persuade the reader that his point of view is the only sensible way to think?

He uses a quotation that connects the words *ridiculous* and *opposing* to support his point of view and dismiss those who don't agree with him. The writer could have stated the same idea without evoking such strong emotions. For example, instead of using that quotation, he could have written, "It *doesn't make sense* that people *don't like* the requirements," but that would not be as persuasive. The word *ridiculous* suggests that it is impossible to take people's reactions seriously; they make no sense. With *opposing*, the writer shows that it is not just that people don't like the idea of mandatory volunteering but that they are actively trying to stop it. This choice of words is strong and creates a clear difference in attitudes toward mandatory volunteering.

Reread Reading Two and find the persuasive words that describe the opposing point of view. Look in the indicated paragraphs.

SOME TAKE THE TIME GLADLY

Paragraph and number of words or phrases	Persuasive words that evoke negative emotions
1 (2)	
2 (1)	
7 (1)	
9 (2)	*ridiculous* *opposing*

PROBLEMS WITH MANDATORY VOLUNTEERING

Paragraph and number of words or phrases	Persuasive words that evoke negative emotions
1 (1)	
3 (5)	
5 (2)	

3 With a partner, look at the words and phrases you have selected and discuss the questions.

1. How do these words influence your thinking about the topic of mandatory volunteering?

2. Do these words make you agree more or less with the writers' opinions?

3. Which two words from each of the articles were most effective in making you agree with the authors?

GO TO MyEnglishLab FOR MORE SKILL PRACTICE.

STEP 1: Organize

The readings in this unit address four issues relating to volunteering.

- Personal enrichment
- Time commitment
- Personal choice
- Dedication to work

Go back to the indicated paragraphs in the readings and find quotes or statements that relate—either positively or negatively— to one or more of the issues. Underline the passages in the text. Then write the issue(s) next to the correct paragraph number in the chart. Some issues may be used more than once.

JUSTIN LEBO (R1)	
PARAGRAPH	**ISSUE**
22	*Dedication to work*
23	
24	
SOME TAKE THE TIME GLADLY (R2)	
PARAGRAPH	**ISSUE**
2	
5	
PROBLEMS WITH MANDATORY VOLUNTEERING (R2)	
PARAGRAPH	**ISSUE**
2	
3	
4	

STEP 2: Synthesize

Imagine you are Justin Lebo. Use a separate piece of paper or go to MyEnglishLab and write a letter to one of the two authors of the editorials in Reading Two. Be sure to clearly state your opinion about mandatory volunteering. Use Justin's experience as a volunteer to either disagree with or support the position stated in the editorial and explain why. Use the quotes or statements that you underlined in Step 1.

GO TO MyEnglishLab TO CHECK WHAT YOU LEARNED.

VOCABULARY

REVIEW

 Look at the word forms chart. The vocabulary from the unit is boldfaced.

NOUN	VERB	ADJECTIVE	ADVERB
admiration	admire	**admiring**	admiringly
challenge	challenge	challenging	X
determination	determine	**determined**	X
devotion	**devote**	devoted	devotedly
donation	**donate**	donated	X
fulfillment	fulfill	fulfilled **fulfilling**	X
indignation	X	indignant	indignantly
inspiration	**inspire**	inspired inspirational	inspirationally
management	**manage**	manageable	manageably
opposition	**oppose**	opposite opposing	X
oxymoron	X	oxymoronic	X
passion	X	passionate	passionately
pride	X	proud	**proudly**
proposal	propose	proposed	X
resentment	resent	**resentful**	resentfully
ridicule	ridicule	**ridiculous**	ridiculously
satisfaction	satisfy	satisfied satisfying satisfactory	satisfactorily
thrill	thrill	**thrilled** thrilling	thrillingly

2 Complete the sentences using words from the word form chart in Exercise 1. Pay attention to verb tense and subject-verb agreement.

1. Justin Lebo had to rely on _____donations_____ from people in order to complete the
   (donate)
   bicycles for the children at Kilbarchan.

2. Justin felt _____inspired_____ when he saw how the boys enjoyed the first two
   (inspire)
   bicycles he had made.

3. Many people hope that after experiencing mandatory volunteering, students will

   become _____passion_____ about volunteering in general.
   (passion)

4. Justin Lebo met the _____challenge_____ of making a bike for each boy at Kilbarchan.
   (challenge)

5. When Justin _____proposed_____ that his parents give a dollar for every dollar he
   (proposal)
   donated, they agreed.

6. Critics worry that students who are forced to volunteer and have a bad experience may

   become _____resentful_____ and never volunteer again.
   (resent) angry

7. Although many people support mandatory volunteering, there is still a lot of

   _____opposition_____ to it.
   (oppose) against

8. Justin feels a lot of _____pride_____ in the fact that he was able to donate so many
   (proudly)
   bikes.

9. Justin's neighbor _____admired_____ his accomplishments.
   (admiring)

10. In many schools, students are not able to graduate without _____fulfilling_____ a
    (fulfill)
    volunteering requirement.

11. Mandatory volunteering is an emotionally charged issue. Many critics are

    _____indignant_____ that volunteering is not left up to the individual.
    (indignation)

EXPAND

A **phrasal verb** consists of a verb and a particle. The combination often has a meaning that is different from the meaning of the separate parts.

Work in a small group. Read the sentences. Circle the best explanation for each underlined phrasal verb.

1. Supporters of mandatory volunteering say volunteering for community service is time better spent than <u>sitting around</u> all day watching television or playing computer games.

   a. doing nothing special or useful

   b. sitting with friends in a circle

   c. not taking part in something

2. Justin Lebo has <u>fixed up</u> between 150 and 200 bikes and has given them all away.

   a. arranged a date for someone

   b. repaired or restored something to working order

   c. bought at a low price

3. Supporters of mandatory volunteering hope that students will <u>keep on</u> volunteering after they have fulfilled their requirement.

   a. hold

   b. consider

   c. continue

4. At first, Justin could not <u>figure out</u> what to do with his two bikes.

   a. satisfy

   b. make a plan for

   c. take part in

5. Justin had so many bikes that he had to <u>clear out</u> his basement and start building them there.

   a. make room on a table

   b. clean an area or place

   c. empty an area or place

6. When the students <u>found out</u> the new graduation requirements, they were indignant and completely opposed to them.

   a. created something

   b. discovered something lost

   c. learned new information about something

7. After the newspaper article was published, many people <u>called</u> Justin <u>up</u> and offered him their old bikes.

   a. discussed a situation

   b. spoke disrespectfully to someone

   c. got in touch with by phone

8. People fear that if students do not do community service, they will <u>end up</u> being uncaring and unsympathetic individuals.

   a. complete a project

   b. be in a situation without planning it

   c. stop something

9. When people donate old clothes to a community center, the center staff will often come to the house and <u>pick up</u> the donations.

   a. start to increase

   b. clean something

   c. collect something

10. Justin was afraid that the garage sales would <u>dry up</u> by the end of the summer.

   a. be dull and uninteresting

   b. slowly come to an end

   c. become useless

CREATE

Imagine you are a reporter interviewing the people below. How would they respond to the questions? Write answers using the words given. Change the word form or tense if necessary. Use a separate piece of paper or go to MyEnglishLab.

1.

| ~~devote~~ | ~~determined~~ | ~~keep on~~ | ~~proudly~~ |

REPORTER: Your son Justin is quite remarkable, isn't he?

DIANE LEBO: *Yes, he is. After Justin saw the boys having so much fun on their bicycles, he became devoted to the project. He was determined to get every boy on a bicycle, so he kept on working hard. I'm very proud of him.*

2.

| challenge | inspired | passion | sit around |

REPORTER: After fixing the first bike, did you ever think you would end up repairing and donating over 150 more?

JUSTIN LEBO: _____

_____

_____

_____

3.

| donate | end up | manage | proposal |

REPORTER: What did you think when Justin first told you he was planning on building a bicycle for every boy at Kilbarchan?

DIRECTOR OF THE
KILBARCHAN SCHOOL: _____

_____

_____

_____

4. | donate   figure out   fulfilling   proudly

REPORTER: Why do you support mandatory volunteering?

STUDENT SUPPORTING
MANDATORY VOLUNTEERING: _____

_____

_____

_____

5. | find out   indignant   manage   oxymoron

REPORTER: Why are you opposed to mandatory volunteering?

STUDENT OPPOSING
MANDATORY VOLUNTEERING: _____

_____

_____

_____

GO TO MyEnglishLab *FOR MORE VOCABULARY PRACTICE.*

GRAMMAR

1 Examine the sentences and answer the questions with a partner.

a. **Even though** <u>Justin was not required by his school to volunteer</u>, he chose to work on bikes and donate them.

b. **Despite the fact that** <u>many students initially don't want to volunteer</u>, they learn to love it and continue after the school requirements are fulfilled.

c. It is a good idea to get students to go out into the community **although** <u>it can be frustrating to have to write about it.</u>

1. Each sentence is composed of two clauses.[1] What are the clauses in each sentence?

2. Do the clauses that begin with the concessions *although, even though,* and *despite the fact that* introduce a positive or negative opinion of mandatory volunteering?

3. Do the three sentences have the same punctuation? If not, why not?

4. Which clauses express the writer's main idea: the clauses with the concessions *although, even though,* and *despite the fact that . . .* or the other clauses?

CONCESSIONS

1. Use **concessions** when expressing an opinion, where you need to support your opinion but, at the same time, recognize and describe the opposing opinion. Presenting similarities and differences in contrasting points of view makes your argument stronger.

2. Use these words to concede or acknowledge similarities or differences between two contrasting ideas.

although	even though	despite the fact that
though	in spite of the fact that	

   Note that these words do not introduce a complete thought—they introduce **dependent clauses.** A dependent clause cannot stand alone as a sentence. It must be joined to an independent (main) clause.

3. The **main clause** usually describes the point that is more important.

   a. **Even though Justin was not required by his school to volunteer,** he chose to work on bikes and donate them.

   <u>Writer's opinion</u>: Justin's school had no requirement for volunteering, but he still wanted to use his time to help others.
   <u>Acknowledging the opposite view</u>: You would expect Justin not to volunteer unless he was forced to.

   b. It is a good idea to get students to go out into the community **although it can be frustrating to have to write about it.**

---

[1] **clause**: a group of words containing a subject and verb that forms part of a sentence. Clauses can be dependent or independent.

Writer's opinion: There may be problems with assignments relating to mandatory volunteering, but students should still be required to go out into the community.
Acknowledging the opposite view: Being forced to write about your volunteering takes away from any benefit you may receive from it.

4. When a sentence begins with a dependent clause, use a comma to separate it from the main clause.

   Even though garage sales had dried up by the end of August, Justin got enough old bikes as the result of a letter to the newspaper.

5. When the sentence begins with an independent clause, do not use a comma.

   Justin got enough old bikes as the result of a letter to the newspaper **even though garage sales had dried up by the end of August**.

2 Combine each pair of sentences using the words in parentheses. Does your new sentence support mandatory volunteering or oppose mandatory volunteering?

1. Supporters of mandatory volunteering say that it is a good way for students to get valuable work experience. Critics say students should be paid if they are doing work. (even though)

   Supporters of mandatory volunteering say it is a good way for students to get

   valuable experience even though they are not paid.

   (supports mandatory volunteering) / opposes mandatory volunteering

2. Critics of mandatory volunteering maintain that a school should not require a student to do anything after school except homework. Supporters of mandatory volunteering say that volunteering is better than just sitting around watching TV or playing video games. (though)

   _____

   _____

   supports mandatory volunteering / opposes mandatory volunteering

3. Opponents argue that volunteering is a personal choice, and so it shouldn't be mandatory. Supporters note that schools have many required classes that may not be a student's personal choice. (although)

   _____

   _____

   supports mandatory volunteering / opposes mandatory volunteering

(continued on next page)

Making a Difference 177

4. Critics worry that a bad volunteering experience will stop people from volunteering again in the future. Supporters maintain that most student volunteers have successful experiences, and many continue to volunteer later in life. (in spite of the fact that)

_____

_____

supports mandatory volunteering / opposes mandatory volunteering

5. Supporters believe that mandatory volunteering can benefit the community. Critics feel that mandatory volunteers may do a bad job and, therefore, cause more harm than good. (despite the fact that)

_____

_____

supports mandatory volunteering / opposes mandatory volunteering

3 Write sentences expressing your opinion about each educational issue. Use the concession words in the box. Does your sentence support mandatory volunteering (**S**) or oppose mandatory volunteering (**O**)? Write **S** or **O** on the line.

although	even though	though
despite the fact that	in spite of the fact that	

1. busy after-school schedules ___S___

Although many students do have busy after-school schedules, with planning,

most should be able to find some time to volunteer either after school or

during free class periods.

2. personal choice _____

_____

_____

_____

3. good to get students out into the community _____

_____

_____

_____

4. volunteer may do a bad job _____

_____

_____

_____

5. builds self-esteem _____

_____

_____

_____

■■■■■■■■■■■■■ *GO TO* MyEnglishLab *FOR MORE GRAMMAR PRACTICE AND TO CHECK WHAT YOU LEARNED.*

FINAL WRITING TASK

In this unit, you read about the pros and cons of mandatory volunteering. Imagine that your school has proposed a mandatory community service program. Students can choose an organization to volunteer for and are required to give at least five hours of time a month. Students must volunteer after school but will receive academic credit.

You are going to **write a persuasive essay explaining your opinion about the volunteering program**. Use the vocabulary and grammar from the unit.*

PREPARE TO WRITE: Using a T-Chart

A **T-chart** is a prewriting tool that helps you examine two aspects of a topic, such as the pros and cons associated with it. When you want to persuade someone to agree with your point of view, you need to have strong reasons to support your opinion (pros). You also need to acknowledge and address possible arguments against your opinion (cons).

1 Work in a small group. On a separate piece of paper, complete a T-chart like the one below with reasons to support a mandatory community service program (pros) and reasons against it (cons). Share your ideas with the class.

PROS	CONS

---

* For Alternative Writing Topics, see page 187. These topics can be used in place of the writing topic for this unit or as homework. The alternative topics relate to the theme of the unit but may not target the same grammar or rhetorical structures taught in the unit.

2 Use your T-chart to decide if this program should be implemented or not. Write a thesis statement stating your opinion.

WRITE: A Persuasive Essay

In a **persuasive essay**, your goal is to convince the reader to agree with your position. Here are some important points:

1. **State your position in the thesis statement**. The reader must know how you feel at the start of the essay.

2. **Present strong arguments to support your position**.

3. **Present strong support for your arguments**. Provide detailed examples, anecdotes, quotes, and statistics.

4. **Acknowledge the counterarguments presented by the opposing side**. Then refute the counterarguments by showing why they are weak. This will make your argument stronger.

1 Read the persuasive essay and answer the questions with a partner.

Cutting Our Sports Teams Is Not a Healthy Decision

Obesity rates are escalating! Students are more stressed than ever before! These are just a couple of recent news headlines. At the same time, ironically, our school administration has recently proposed eliminating all sports teams, citing a decrease in team participation, low attendance, and overall high cost of maintaining these teams. While cutting team sports from the budget would save money, the immediate and long-term negative results would not be worth the money saved.

First, though it is true that many teams have not had high numbers of participants, this is not a reason to cut *all* teams. A few teams still do have high participation rates and very dedicated players. One solution is to keep one or two high participation sports per season, for example, fall football, winter basketball and swimming, and spring track and baseball.

Second, the school is concerned about poor audience attendance at the games and uses this argument to support the idea that there is a decreasing interest in our teams. Although there may be lower audience numbers than in the past, the students who do go are loyal fans. Moreover, this devoted fan base has helped build a community that promotes school spirit across the campus.

This school spirit affects all students whether or not they attend each game. For example, after last year's baseball finals, more baseball hats were sold in the campus store than ever before even though most of the students wearing the hats had not attended one game! Adam Deering, a student, stated, "Even though I don't go to all of the games, I am still supportive of my school and proud of it. School can be really stressful, and the teams help reduce that stress and give students something else to focus on and bring them together besides academics."

Finally, the administration states that the cost of keeping team sports is just too costly. Though the cost of sports teams may be high, the price paid for cutting the teams in the long term is even higher. Sports teams are a daily reminder of the importance of maintaining a balanced, healthy life style. School sports help promote life-long healthy habits. With this in mind, shouldn't the school be putting more money into sports rather than taking it away?

1. What is the student's main position in regards to cutting school sports?

   _____

2. What are the three main arguments the school uses to support cutting school sports? Complete the left side of the chart.

3. What are the counterarguments the student presents? Complete the right side of the chart.

ARGUMENTS TO CUT SCHOOL SPORTS	COUNTERARGUMENTS

4. Do you think the counterarguments are convincing? Why or why not?

   _____

   _____

5. What examples are used to strengthen the student's argument? Underline them.

Start planning your essay by looking at your list of pros and cons in Prepare to Write. Choose three of the strongest arguments you will use to support your position and write them in sections 2–4 in the brace map below. Add details on the lettered lines to support your arguments.

1. Introduction and Thesis Statement:

2.

    a. _____

    b. _____

    c. _____

3.

    a. _____

    b. _____

    c. _____

4.

    a. _____

    b. _____

    c. _____

5. Conclusion

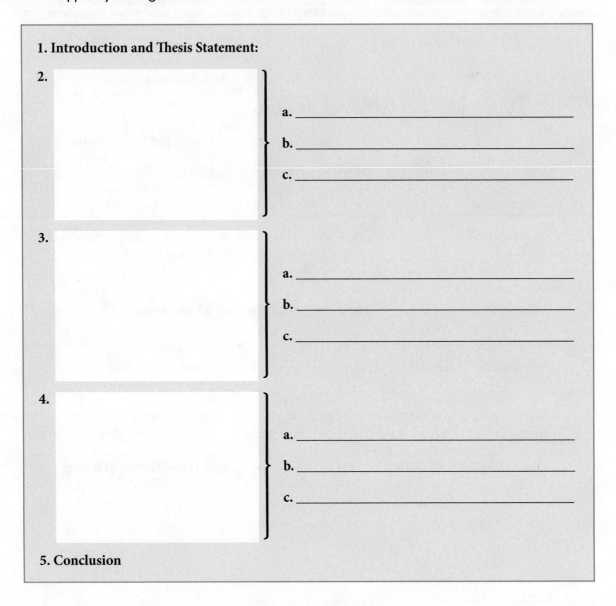

3 Look at the arguments in support of your position in your brace map. Write them in the left column. What are the possible counterarguments? Write them in the middle column. Why are those counterarguments weak? Write the reasons in the right column. You will acknowledge the counterarguments in your essay using a concession clause and then refute them.

ARGUMENTS FOR / AGAINST COMMUNITY SERVICE PROGRAMS	COUNTERARGUMENTS	REFUTATION (REASONS WHY THE COUNTERARGUMENT IS WEAK)

4 Now write the first draft of your persuasive essay. Use the information in Prepare to Write and your brace map to plan your essay. Include an introductory and a concluding paragraph. When writing the body, be sure to acknowledge the counterarguments by using a concession clause. Be sure to use vocabulary and grammar from the unit.

REVISE: Writing Introductions and Conclusions

The Introduction

The **introduction** to an essay can have several functions. It states the thesis, or controlling idea, and gives the reader an idea of what will be discussed. It can also provide background information on the topic. However, one of the most important functions is to engage the reader's interest and make the reader want to continue reading. Here are three common techniques used in introductions:

1. State why the topic is important.

2. Ask a provocative question.

3. Tell a relevant story or anecdote.

1 Work with a partner. Read the three introductions. Underline the thesis statements. Then label each introduction with the letter of the technique used.

Introduction 1   Technique: _____

Society today is obsessed with commercialism. People think only about making money and buying more and more possessions. Many college students choose their majors by deciding which careers will pay the most money. Young people today are not learning enough about the nonfinancial rewards in life. They are not learning about the joy and fulfillment of helping others. This is a very serious problem with education today. It is important to support the proposal for a mandatory community service program so that young people will learn the value of giving to others.

Introduction 2   Technique: _____

When I was in high school, I was required to take part in a community service project. At first, I really didn't want to do it. I thought it would be boring and a waste of time. The school let us choose our project, and I decided to work at an animal shelter. I like animals, and I thought the work wouldn't be too difficult. I worked all semester helping the veterinarian take care of sick and abandoned animals. I was surprised to find that by the end of the semester, I really liked my community service job. In fact, it was my favorite part of the week, and I signed up to work another semester. So I am a perfect illustration of the benefits of mandatory community service programs in school. This is why I support a program of mandatory community service in our university.

Introduction 3   Technique: _____

We all want to live in a better world, don't we? Poor children do not get enough to eat. The school system is not educating our kids. The environment is getting more and more polluted. What would happen if we all did something to solve the problems around us? Well, we can do something, and we should. A mandatory community service program in our school will give students a valuable experience and also help solve important problems in our community.

2 Look at the introduction of your essay. Make sure you have a thesis statement and use one of the three techniques for writing an effective introduction.

The Conclusion

The **conclusion** of an essay should bring the ideas of the essay to a close. Most commonly, the conclusion restates the thesis of the essay and offers the writer's final thoughts on the topic. Here are three common techniques used in conclusions:

1. Tell a relevant story or anecdote.

2. Ask a final question that the reader can think about.

3. Make a prediction about the future.

3 Work with a partner. Read the three conclusions. Underline the sentences that restate the thesis of the essay. Label the conclusion with the letter of the technique used.

Conclusion 1   Technique: _____

I urge everyone to support the mandatory community service program in our university. It has many benefits for both students and the community, including teaching students new skills, building bridges between students and community members, and exposing students to new experiences. I believe that if students try volunteering, many of them will discover that community service can be an enjoyable and rewarding experience.

Conclusion 2   Technique: _____

As you can see, community service benefits everyone. I know my life will never be the same after my experience in the veterinary clinic. Before I did my service, I wasn't sure what I wanted to do for a career. This experience has broadened my future and helped shape my goals. Now I know for certain that I want to do something in the animal sciences. Without this experience, I'm not sure I would have known what I wanted to do. Isn't this called a win-win situation?

Conclusion 3   Technique: _____

On a final note, I'd like to share a personal experience. Last year I started tutoring an elementary school student whose parents don't speak English. At first, he was resentful that he had to stay after school and do more schoolwork. Truthfully, it was also hard for me knowing he did

(continued on next page)

not want to be there. But as the year progressed, I got to know him and the kind of books he liked to read. He began to look forward to our weekly sessions and was eager to see what books I had brought for him. Now we are not just reading friends, but we are real friends. I know I have made a difference in his life, and he has certainly made a difference in mine. If I hadn't been required to do community service, I know I would not have had this experience. And I would not have discovered what a difference I can make.

4 Look at the conclusion of your essay. Make sure you have restated the thesis and have included your final thoughts by using one of the three conclusion techniques.

■■ GO TO MyEnglishLab *FOR MORE SKILL PRACTICE.*

EDIT: Writing the Final Draft

Go to MyEnglishLab and write the final draft of your essay. Carefully edit it for grammatical and mechanical errors, such as spelling, capitalization, and punctuation. Make sure you use some of the grammar and vocabulary from the unit. Use the checklist to help you write your final draft. Then submit your essay to your teacher.

FINAL DRAFT CHECKLIST

❏ Does the essay have an introduction, three body paragraphs, and a conclusion?

❏ Does the introduction include a thesis statement? Does it engage the interest of the reader?

❏ Does each body paragraph have a topic sentence? Do all the topic sentences support the thesis statement?

❏ Do the body paragraphs present your arguments for or against mandatory volunteering? Do you acknowledge and then refute possible counterarguments?

❏ Did you use concessions to introduce the counterargument?

❏ Does the conclusion restate the thesis and offer final thoughts?

❏ Have you used the vocabulary from the unit?

UNIT PROJECT

What are ways that people are incorporating philanthropy into their lives in your area? Research a community center or project. Follow these steps:

STEP 1: As a class, brainstorm a list of community centers or community work in your area, or list community centers you have heard about. Discuss the services these centers offer, such as serving food, offering shelter, meeting medical or educational needs, helping repair homes, and cleaning up the neighborhood.

STEP 2: Work in a small group. Research a community center or project. Then, individually or in groups, go to a center or project headquarters and gather information to organize your ideas on a separate piece of paper. You may also take photos and collect brochures. If there is no center or project near you, go to the library or use the Internet to find information about activities in another area.

- Name of center or project
- History: When was it started? Who started it? Why?
- Type of people helped

- Types of services offered
- Type of people who work there. Are there volunteers? How many?
- Funding: How are activities paid for? Where does the funding come from?

STEP 3: Prepare a PowerPoint™ presentation or a poster with photos and present your findings to the class.

ALTERNATIVE WRITING TOPICS

Write an essay about one of the topics. Use the vocabulary and grammar from the unit.

1. Imagine you are responsible for setting up a community service program in your city. What kind of program would you start? Who would it serve? Would there be volunteers? Who would they be? What would you hope to accomplish? Be specific.

2. Read John Bunyan's quotation about philanthropy.

   "He who bestows[1] his goods upon the poor,
   Shall have as much again, and ten times more."
   —John Bunyan, *Pilgrim's Progress,* Part Two, Section VII

   What is Bunyan trying to say? There are many different ways to "[bestow your] goods upon the poor." What are some ways, and why do people perform these acts?

   ---
   [1] **bestows:** gives someone something important

■■■■■■■■■■■■■■■■■■■■■■■■■ *GO TO* MyEnglishLab *TO WRITE ABOUT ONE OF THE ALTERNATIVE TOPICS, WATCH A VIDEO ABOUT A LOCAL TEEN MAKING A DIFFERENCE, AND TAKE THE UNIT 6 ACHIEVEMENT TEST.* ■■■

THE EMPTY Classroom

1 FOCUS ON THE TOPIC

1. Look at the unit title and the photograph. Fewer students are studying in the classroom. Where are they studying?

2. A new model of online distance learning, called a Massive Online Open Course or MOOC,[1] is becoming increasingly popular. What do you think the benefits and the challenges of this type of model are?

3. What would happen if online distance learning were the future of education?

---

[1] **MOOC:** online courses designed to have open access that are offered by many universities as well as private organizations. They are typically tuition-free because they do not offer academic credit.

GO TO MyEnglishLab TO CHECK WHAT YOU KNOW.

VOCABULARY

1 Read the timeline of the history of distance education. Try to understand the boldfaced words from the context.

Distance Education Timeline	
1728	Caleb Phillips, of Boston, challenges the **assumption** that education must take place in a classroom. He offers a correspondence course in shorthand.[2] He communicates with students using the mail.
1840	Because of a newly established affordable postage rate, the **issue** of cost is eliminated from distance education. Sir Isaac Pittman from London is able to successfully market his shorthand correspondence course, which **enhances** the existing method of shorthand.
1858	Distance education takes a **crucial** step forward as University of London becomes the first university in the world to offer distance-learning degrees.
1873	Anna Ticknor **analyzes** the existing educational opportunities for women and decides to create the *Society to Encourage Study at Home*, which offers correspondence courses to more than 10,000 women over the next two decades.
1885	William Rainey Harper, future president of the University of Chicago, predicts, in **anticipation** of the direction distance education is moving, "the day is coming when the work done by correspondence will be greater in amount than that done in the classrooms of our academies and colleges."
1906	University of Wisconsin, in a **subsequent** advance, records lectures and sends them to students on phonograph records.
1920s	Schools experiment with course delivery **via** radio broadcasts.
1930s	Television is first used as a method of course delivery.
1950s	College credit courses are offered via television. Television instruction in **collaboration** with correspondence study is used.
1989	Options for course delivery **significantly** change as a result of the World Wide Web, which allows online document sharing.
1995	First course delivered over the Internet is taught at Penn State University.

---

[2] **shorthand:** a fast method of writing using special signs or shorter forms to represent letters, words, and phrases

2000s	Distance education courses are delivered using **virtual** classrooms—multimedia resources, video conferencing, webcams etc. . . .
2008	The term MOOC is first used.
2012	The **diversity** of the student body grows as students from around the world enroll in MOOC courses. More than 150,000 students sign up for one MOOC course, "Introduction to Artificial Intelligence."

2 Write the words from the box next to their definitions.

analyze	collaboration	enhance	subsequent
anticipation	crucial	issue	via
assumption	diversity	significantly	virtual

1. _____anticipation_____ the act of expecting something to happen

2. _____ a range of different people or things; variety

3. _____ extremely important

4. _____issue_____ a subject or problem that people discuss

5. _____virtual_____ made, done, seen etc. on the Internet or on a computer, rather than in the real world

6. _____subsequed_____ something that you think is true although you have no proof

7. _____collaboractio_____ the act of working together to make or produce something

8. _____analyze_____ to examine or think about something carefully in order to understand it

9. _____singnifica_____ noticeably or importantly

10. _____via_____ by way of or through

11. _____subsec____ coming after or following something else

12. _____enhane____ to make something better

GO TO MyEnglishLab FOR MORE VOCABULARY PRACTICE.

You are going to read an article about a Princeton University professor's experience teaching 40,000 students from 113 countries.

Read the first paragraph of "Teaching to the World from Central New Jersey." Then work with a partner to answer the questions.

1. What challenges do you think Professor Duneier will face teaching so many students?

2. What do you predict will be the positive impact of having students from 113 countries in the course?

3. What do you predict will be some of the problems resulting from having students from so many different countries in the course?

Keep your discussion in mind as you read the rest of the article.

TEACHING TO THE WORLD FROM CENTRAL NEW JERSEY
By Mitchell Duneier

1   A few months ago, just as the campus of Princeton University had grown nearly silent after commencement, 40,000 students from 113 countries arrived here via the Internet to take a free course in introductory sociology. The noncredit Princeton offering came about through a collaboration between Coursera, a new venture in online learning, and 16 universities, including my own.

2   When my class was announced last spring, I was both excited and nervous. Unlike computer science and other subjects in which the answers are pretty much the same around the globe, sociology can be very different depending on the country that you come from. As letters and e-mail messages began arriving in **anticipation** of my course, I wondered how I, an American professor, could relate my subject to people I didn't know from so many different societies.

3   Would my lectures become yet another example of American ethnocentrism[3] and imperialism as I presented my sociological concepts like so many measuring sticks for the experiences of others around the world? Was it really possible, I asked myself, to provide quality education to tens of thousands of students in more than 100 countries at the same time? And in a way that would respond to the **diversity** of viewpoints represented from six continents?

4   My concerns grew deeper as I sat before the cold eye of the camera to record my first lecture. With nobody to ask me a question, or give me bored looks, or laugh at my jokes, I had no clues as to how the students might be responding. Staring into this void, it was hard for me to imagine that anyone was listening. Can we even call these "lectures" when there is no audience within the speaker's view? Aren't those interpersonal cues—those knowing nods and furrowed brows—that go

---

[3] **ethnocentrism:** based on the idea that your own race, nation, group, etc. is better than any other; used in order to show disapproval

from the audience to the professor as **crucial** to the definition of a lecture as the cues that go from the lecturer to the audience?

5   My opening discussion of C. Wright Mills's classic 1959 book, *The Sociological Imagination*, was a close reading of the text, in which I reviewed a key chapter line by line. I asked students to follow along in their own copies, as I do in the lecture hall. When I give this lecture on the Princeton campus, I usually receive a few penetrating questions. In this case, however, within a few hours of posting the online version, the course forums came alive with hundreds of comments and questions. Several days later there were thousands.

6   Although it was impossible for me to read even a fraction of the pages of students' comments as they engaged with one another, the software allowed me to take note of those that generated the most discussion. I was quickly able to see the **issues** that were most meaningful to my students.

7   In addition to the course lectures, I arranged live exchanges **via** a video chat room, in which six to eight students from around the world—some selected from the online class, others volunteers here at Princeton—participated with me in a seminar-style discussion of the readings while thousands of their online classmates listened in to the live stream or to recordings later. During these weekly sessions, I found that I was able to direct the discussion to issues that had been raised in the online postings.

8   Along with two Princeton students, our online seminar included university students from Nepal, Siberia, Iran, and Nigeria, a travel agent from Georgia, a civil servant from Singapore, and a fireman from Philadelphia. Their comments often revealed precisely how American sociology's **assumptions** about social life need to be **analyzed** and reconstructed in light of experiences elsewhere.

9   With so much volume, my audience became as visible to me as the students in a traditional lecture hall. This happened as I got to know them by sampling their comments on the forums and in the live, seminar-style discussions. As I developed a sense for them as people, I could imagine their nods and, increasingly, their critical questions. Within three weeks I had received more feedback on my sociological ideas than I had in a career of teaching, which **significantly** influenced each of my **subsequent** lectures and seminars.

10   Before the class began, I had played down this kind of teaching as inevitably a pale reflection of on-campus learning, both in terms of student-faculty interaction and the residential-college experience. Yet as I got to know some of my students, I came to feel that the difference was not of the sort I had imagined. For most of them, the choice was not between an online course and a traditional university. It was, as one student put it, "a choice between online class versus no class."

11   Nor had I imagined the **virtual** and real-time continuous interaction among the students. There were spontaneous and continuing in-person study groups in coffee shops in Katmandu and in pubs in London. Many people developed dialogues after following one another's posts on various subjects, while others got to know those with a common particular interest, such as racial differences in IQ, the prisoner abuses that took place at Abu Ghraib, or ethnocentrism— all topics covered in the lectures.

12   As one of hundreds who posted in the past few days wrote, "It has been an incredible experience for me, one that has not only taught me sociology, but the ways in which other cultures think, feel, and respond. I have many new 'friends' via this class. . . ." Another wrote, "It started as intellectual activity but

(continued on next page)

it's ending in an indescribable emotional relationship with all my classmates."

13 This is my cue. As I prepare to re-enter the lecture hall at Princeton this September and go back online in February, I am asking myself how I can translate the benefits of online technology to **enhance** the dialogue with and among my on-campus students, and between them and my online students around the globe. I had begun worrying about how I could bring the New Jersey campus experience to them; I ended by thinking about how to bring the world back to the classroom in Princeton.

Mitchell Duneier is a professor of sociology at Princeton University.

MAIN IDEAS

1 Look again at the Preview on page 192. How did your discussion help you understand the article?

2 Reading One discusses professor Duneier's feelings and concerns before, during, and after his MOOC. Circle the sentence that best answers the question. Share your answers with a partner.

1. **Before:** What was Professor Duneier's biggest concern about teaching the online course?

   a. No one would laugh at his jokes or be able to make eye contact with him.

   b. It might not be possible to provide quality education to students from more than 100 countries.

   c. Students wouldn't do the reading or participate in the forums because the course was free.

2. **During:** How did student participation affect Professor Duneier's feelings about his new course?

   a. Professor Duneier was overwhelmed by the number of student comments and so wasn't sure what issues were important to the students.

   b. Professor Duneier didn't know when students had a problem understanding him because of the lack of interpersonal cues.

   c. Student feedback influenced the direction Professor Duneier took in subsequent video chats.

3. **After:** What was the most important conclusion that Professor Duneier drew about online teaching after teaching this course?

   (a.) There were many benefits to online teaching that he would like to incorporate into his on-campus classes.

   b. It was a pale reflection of on-campus learning.

   c. For some students, the choice was an online class or no class at all.

DETAILS

Read each statement. Decide if it is **T** (true) or **F** (false) according to the reading. Write the number of the paragraph that supports your answer. If the statement is false, change it to make it true. Discuss your answers with a partner.

___T___ 1. Professor Duneier realized that teaching sociology to students from many different societies would not be as easy as teaching them computer science.
paragraph: ___2___

___T___ 2. Before the first class even had ended, it was obvious from the number of comments and questions that students were interested.
paragraph: _____

___F___ 3. The fact that Professor Duneier recorded his lectures in an empty classroom made it easy because no one would interrupt or distract him.
paragraph: _____

___F___ 4. Although it was impossible to answer all the student comments and questions, he did answer the majority of them.
paragraph: _____

___F___ 5. All the participants in the online seminar were Princeton students.
paragraph: _____

___F___ 6. Because the course was delivered over the Internet, Professor Duneier felt disconnected from his students.
paragraph: _____

___T___ 7. Students in the class did not remain anonymous to each other.
paragraph: _____

___F___ 8. Professor Duneier's next online course will be in September.
paragraph: _____

MAKE INFERENCES

INFERRING DEGREE OF CONCERN

Writers sometimes suggest their level of concern about something without stating it directly.

Look at the example and read the explanation.

In the text, Professor Duneier expresses several worries and concerns about the new course he will be teaching online.

How concerned is Professor Duneier that he is able to relate his sociology course to people he doesn't know from so many different societies?

(*paragraph 2*)

Where would you place his concern on the continuum?

Not very concerned	Somewhat concerned	Concerned	Very concerned

Answer: Somewhat concerned

- In the last sentence of paragraph 2, Professor Duneier uses the word "wonder" as he considers his new student population. This word does not express very much worry; he is asking himself questions.

- In the first sentence of paragraph 2, he says he is both "excited" and "nervous." These words express both positive and negative feelings.

After reading the text closely, we can infer that Professor Duneier is "somewhat concerned" about how he will be able to relate his course to this new student population. The language he uses suggests a concern but also an interest or excitement about his new endeavor.

For each concern or worry expressed by Professor Duneier in the reading, decide how concerned he is. Write an **X** in the column that best corresponds to his degree of concern. Refer to the paragraphs in parentheses.

HOW CONCERNED IS PROFESSOR DUNEIER THAT . . .	NOT VERY CONCERNED	SOMEWHAT CONCERNED	CONCERNED	VERY CONCERNED
1. his course will be perceived as ethnocentric and imperialistic? (paragraph 3)				
2. he will be able to deliver quality education? (paragraph 3)				
3. he will be able to respond to the diversity of his recorded lectures? (paragraph 4)				
4. he will not be able to see his audience during comments and questions? (paragraph 4)				

HOW CONCERNED IS PROFESSOR DUNEIER THAT . . .	NOT VERY CONCERNED	SOMEWHAT CONCERNED	CONCERNED	VERY CONCERNED
5. he would be able to respond to his students' questions, comments, and discussions? *(paragraphs 5, 6, 7)*				
6. he would be able to direct the discussion? *(paragraph 7)*				
7. he would develop a sense of his students as people? *(paragraph 9)*				
8. there would be student-faculty interaction? *(paragraph 10)*				
9. he would be able to take his online experience back to the classroom in Princeton? *(paragraph 13)*				

EXPRESS OPINIONS

Discuss the questions in a small group. Then share your ideas with the class.

1. Do you think it is possible to teach all subjects as MOOCs, or are there some subjects that must be taught face-to-face in a classroom or with a smaller enrollment? Explain.

2. Would you enjoy and be successful in a MOOC? Why or why not? Be specific.

3. Do you think distance learning is the future of education? Do you think we will still have classrooms as we know them in 50 or 100 years?

■■■■■■■■■■■■■■■■■■■■■■■■ *GO TO* MyEnglishLab *TO GIVE YOUR OPINION ABOUT ANOTHER QUESTION.*

READ

1 Look at the boldfaced words in the reading and think about the questions.

1. Which words do you know the meanings of?

2. Can you use any of the words in a sentence?

This story was written by Isaac Asimov in 1951. It addresses the question of distance learning using a computer. At that time, the idea of this type of learning was science fiction, and having a home computer was unimaginable. Most people did not even own a television set at the time!

2 Read the story, *The Fun They Had*. As you read, notice the boldfaced vocabulary. Try to guess its meaning from the context.

THE FUN THEY HAD
By Isaac Asimov
(from *Earth Is Room Enough*)

1   Margie even wrote about it that night in her diary. On the page headed May 17, 2157, she wrote, "Today Tommy found a real book!"

2   It was a very old book. Margie's grandfather once said that when he was a little boy, his grandfather told him that there was a time when all stories were printed on paper.

3   They turned the pages, which were yellow and crinkly,[1] and it was awfully funny to read words that stood still instead of moving the way that they were supposed to—on a screen, you know. And then, when they had turned back to the page before, it had the same words on it that it had had when they read it the first time.

4   "Gee," said Tommy, "what a waste. When you're through with the book, you just throw it away, I guess. Our television screen must have had a million books on it, and it's good for plenty more. I wouldn't throw it away."

5   "Same with mine," said Margie. She was eleven and hadn't seen as many books as Tommy had. He was thirteen.

6   She said, "Where did you find it?"

7   "In my house." He pointed without looking, because he was busy reading. "In the attic." *→ under the roof.*

8   "What's it about?"

9   "School."

10   Margie was scornful.[2] "School? What's there to write about school? I hate school."

---

[1] **crinkly:** having many folds or wrinkles; dried out
[2] **scornful:** critical of someone or something that you think is not good

11   Margie had always hated school, but now she hated it more than ever. The mechanical teacher[3] had been giving her test after test in geography, and she had been doing worse and worse until her mother had shaken her head sorrowfully and sent for the County Inspector.

12   He was a round little man with a red face and a whole box of tools with dials and wires. He smiled at Margie and gave her an apple, then took the teacher apart. Margie hoped he wouldn't know how to put it together again, but he knew how all right, and after an hour or so, there it was again, large and square and ugly, with a big screen on which all the lessons were shown and the questions were asked. That wasn't so bad. The part Margie hated most was the slot[4] where she had to put homework and test papers. She always had to write them out in a punch code[5] they made her learn when she was six years old, and the mechanical teacher calculated the mark[6] in no time.

13   The Inspector had smiled after he was finished and patted Margie's head. He said to her mother, "It's not the little girl's fault, Mrs. Jones. I think the geography **sector**[7] was geared a little too quick. Those things happen sometimes. I've slowed it up to a ten-year level. Actually, the **overall** pattern of her progress is quite satisfactory." And he patted Margie's head again.

14   Margie was **disappointed**. She had been hoping they would take the teacher away altogether. They had once taken Tommy's teacher away for nearly a month because the history sector had blanked out[8] completely.

15   So she said to Tommy, "Why would anyone write about school?"

16   Tommy looked at her with very superior eyes. "Because it's not our kind of school, stupid. This is the old kind of school that they had hundreds and hundreds of years ago." He added loftily, pronouncing the word very carefully, "Centuries ago."

17   Margie was hurt. "Well, I don't know what kind of school they had all that time ago." She read the book over his shoulder for a while, then said, "Anyway, they had a teacher."

18   "Sure they had a teacher, but it wasn't a regular teacher. It was a man."

19   "A man? How could a man be a teacher?"

20   "Well, he just told the boys and girls things and gave them homework and asked them questions."

21   "A man isn't smart enough."

22   "Sure he is. My father knows as much as my teacher."

23   "He can't. A man can't know as much as a teacher."

---

[3] **mechanical teacher:** a computer (in this story)

[4] **slot:** an opening for a paper

[5] **punch code:** a pattern of holes put on a card that was used in past times for putting information in a computer

[6] **mark:** a number score or letter grade

[7] **sector:** an area

[8] **blanked out:** been erased

(continued on next page)

24   "He knows almost as much, I betcha."[9]

25   Margie wasn't prepared to **dispute** that. She said, "I wouldn't want a strange man in my house to teach me."

26   Tommy screamed with laughter. "You don't know much, Margie. The teachers didn't live in the house. They had a special building and all the kids went there."

27   "And all the kids learned the same thing?"

28   "Sure, if they were the same age."

29   "But my mother says a teacher has to be **adjusted** to fit the mind of each boy and girl it teaches and that each kid has to be taught differently."

30   "Just the same, they didn't do it that way then. If you don't like it, you don't have to read the book."

31   "I didn't say I didn't like it," Margie said quickly. She wanted to read about those funny schools.

32   They weren't even half-finished when Margie's mother called, "Margie! School!"

33   Margie looked up. "Not yet, Mama."

34   "Now!" said Mrs. Jones. "And it's probably time for Tommy, too."

35   Margie said to Tommy, "Can I read the book some more with you after school?"

36   "Maybe," he said nonchalantly.[10] He walked away whistling, the dusty old book tucked beneath his arm.

37   Margie went into the schoolroom. It was right next to her bedroom, and the mechanical teacher was on and waiting for her. It was always on at the same time every day except Saturday and Sunday, because her mother said little girls learned better if they learned at regular hours.

38   The screen was lit up, and it said: "Today's arithmetic lesson is on the addition of proper fractions. Please insert yesterday's homework in the proper slot."

39   Margie did so with a sigh. She was thinking about the old schools they had when her grandfather's grandfather was a little boy. All the kids from the whole neighborhood came, laughing and shouting in the schoolyard, sitting together in the schoolroom, going home together at the end of the day. They learned the same things, so they could help one another on the homework and talk about it.

40   And the teachers were people . . .

41   The mechanical teacher was flashing on the screen: "When we add the fractions $1/2$ and $1/4$—"

42   Margie was thinking about how the kids must have loved it in the old days. She was thinking of the fun they had.

---

[9] *I betcha:* "I'll bet you"; "I'm sure"
[10] **nonchalantly:** calmly, in an informal way

COMPREHENSION

Discuss the questions in a small group. Then share your ideas with the class.

1. What does Tommy discover in his attic, and why is it such an important discovery?

2. What does Margie think about the discovery?

3. How does Margie feel about the "old days"?

4. How do you think the writer feels about the future of books?

■■■■■■■■■■■■■■■■■■■■■■■■■■■■■■■■■■■■■■■ GO TO MyEnglishLab *FOR MORE VOCABULARY PRACTICE.*

READING SKILL

1 In Reading Two, paragraph 13, the author writes, "The Inspector had smiled after he was finished and patted Margie's head. He said to her mother, 'It's not the little girl's fault, Mrs. Jones. I think the geography sector was geared a little too quick.'"

Who is speaking in the quoted section of the excerpt (underlined)? How do you know?

RECOGNIZING THE SPEAKER IN DIRECT SPEECH

Authors often include direct speech (quoted dialogue) in their writing. This can be confusing for readers, especially if more than two people are conversing. As a reader, you can use clues such as pronoun referents or the back and forth order of conversations to understand exactly who is speaking. You can also use background knowledge of a character's opinions or ideas. If you misinterpret who is speaking, it can be hard to understand the story.

Look at the example and read the explanations.

Read the paragraphs from *The Fun They Had* and complete the exercise.

4 "Gee," said Tommy, "what a waste. When you're through with the book, you just throw it away, I guess. Our television screen must have had a million books on it, and it's good for plenty more. I wouldn't throw it away."

5 "Same with mine," said Margie. She was eleven and hadn't seen as many books as Tommy had. He was thirteen.

6 She said, "Where did you find it?"

7 "In my house." He pointed without looking, because he was busy reading. "In the attic."

8 "What's it about?"

9 "School."

Identify the person who is speaking in each paragraph and explain how you know.

Paragraphs 4–5: Tommy, Margie; the authors state the names of the speakers.

Paragraphs 6–7: Margie, Tommy; the authors use pronoun referents—*she* for Margie, *he* for Tommy.

Paragraphs 8–9: Margie, Tommy; the reader must rely on the back and forth order of most conversations to identify the speakers.

Go back to Reading Two, *The Fun They Had.* Reread paragraphs 15–42. Work with a partner to underline or highlight what each speaker says (Margie, Tommy, Margie's mother, the mechanical teacher). Write the speaker's name in the margin or use a different color highlight for each speaker. Be prepared to explain how you know.

GO TO MyEnglishLab FOR MORE SKILL PRACTICE.

CONNECT THE READINGS

STEP 1: Organize

Reading One (R1) and Reading Two (R2) describe different models of education. Complete the chart comparing the readings.

	TEACHING TO THE WORLD (R1)	THE FUN THEY HAD (R2)
1. Is there a teacher? If yes, describe the teacher.	Human teacher siru logy	like Machine, It's bem ugly, slod
2. Where does the "school" take place?	It's Online	In home.
3. When does "class" take place?	Any time.	Parents deside time
4. Are students exposed to a variety of academic opinions?	Yes	No
5. What options are there for students who don't understand or who need more support?	They can ask question with email.	Ask inspector
6. When and where do students socialize with friends or classmates?	all time	They do not
7. What do the students and/ or teacher think about the learning experience?	excited, like it, love	hateing, bored.

STEP 2: Synthesize

Choose one of the scenarios. For number 1, write a response from Margie. For number 2, write a response from Professor Duneier. Use the information from Step 1. Write on a separate piece of paper.

1. **From a MOOC student to Margie:** "You are really lucky that you learn via technology. Before I took this MOOC course, I had always wanted to have the flexibility that an online course allows. I also enjoy the international perspective offered by my cyber-classmates; now I am so happy. You must be, too."

2. **From Tommy to Professor Duneier:** "Margie and I hate learning at home without other students. We don't understand why your students would choose to take online courses. Wouldn't they have more fun and friends in a school? Also, wouldn't they learn more?"

GO TO MyEnglishLab TO CHECK WHAT YOU LEARNED.

3 FOCUS ON WRITING

VOCABULARY

REVIEW

Read the prompt and the forum response posted by one of Professor Duneier's MOOC students. Complete her response using the words above each paragraph.

Now that the course has finished, please write about your experience taking a MOOC. Include information about your past online learning experience, your expectations, the problems and benefits of taking a MOOC, and the overall experience.

guess   assumption   via   anticipation   crucial → very important.
                true   →to wait

When I heard about Professor Duneier's Sociology MOOC, I was excited but also a bit anxious because I had never taken a completely online course before. In ___anticipation___ **1.** of the class, I e-mailed Professor Duneier with many of my questions. He graciously → politely. replied, but for him, too, this was going to be a new experience. Knowing this actually helped me to relax a little. One ___assumption___ I had about distance learning was that **2.** self-motivation and self-discipline would play a ___crucial___ role in my success. I **3.** knew it would be easy to fall behind because the classes were not going to be at a set time. This turned out to be true. I also knew that learning ___via___ the Internet **4.** might also pose other problems.

(continued on next page)

virtual   adjust   collaboration   diversity

[handwritten annotations: change, adapt → adjust; co-operate → collaboration; differences → diversity; not real → virtual; communicate]

I would have to ___adjust___ to a completely different method of interacting with
5.
my teacher and classmates. For example, it seemed to me that ___collaboration___ between
6.
students would be more difficult and, therefore, less common than in a traditional

classroom. This actually didn't turn out to be the case. I was able to have ___virtual___
7.
interactions with as many students as I wanted or had time for. In addition, because the

class included students from more than 100 countries, I was exposed to a

___diversity___ of viewpoints.
8.

issue   significantly   sector   enhanced

[handwritten annotations: subject/topic, problem → issue; a lot, big → significantly; part, area → sector; to make better, improve → enhanced]

Being exposed to so many different opinions actually ___enhanced___ learning.
9.
In fact, I think I learned ___significantly___ more from my online classmates than I would
10.
have from classmates in a small traditional classroom setting. I chose to take this class

instead of a traditional class at my university, but this was not the case for a

___sector___ of the student population. For these students, the ___issue___ was
11.   **12.**
not whether to take an online course or a traditional course; their only option was an

online course.

dispute   overall   analyze   disappointed

[handwritten annotations: disagreement → dispute; comprehension → overall; something happen against your expectation → disappointed]

Now that the course is over, I have been able to ___analyze___ my MOOC experience.
13.
I cannot ___dispute___ that there are many drawbacks to taking a completely online
14.
course. However, I can truthfully say that I was not ___disappointed___ with the class, the
15. *[disadvantage]*
method of course delivery, or the amount that I learned. Despite some minor problems,

the ___overall___ experience by far surpassed my expectations. I look forward to
16.
taking another MOOC in the future. *[be more than expectation]*

—Jacqui

EXPAND

Complete the chart with the forms of the words from the readings. If you need help, use a dictionary. (Note: An **X** indicates there is no form in that category.)

NOUN	VERB	ADJECTIVE	ADVERB
adjustment adjustability	adjust	(well) adjusted adjustable	X
enylysis	analyze	*analytic*	X
anticipation	*anicipate → to predict to wait*	*anticipated*	X
assumption	*to assume*	*assumed*	X
collaboration	*collaborte*	*collaborated*	*collaborative → team work*
X	X	crucial	*crucially*
disappointment	disappoint	*disappointed*	*disappointly*
dispute	dispute	*disputed*	X
diversity	*to diversify (v)*	*diverse (adj)*	*diversely*
enhancement	enhance	*enhanced*	X
issue	*to issue*	X	X
sector	X	X	X
significetion	*significetion*	*signify*	significantly
X	X	subsequent	*subsequently*
X	X	virtual	*virtually*

CREATE

Imagine you are a reporter interviewing the students and the professor from Reading One and Reading Two. How would they respond to the questions? Write answers using the words in the boxes. Change the word form or tense if necessary.

~~adjustment~~	~~crucial~~	~~subsequent~~	~~via~~

1. **REPORTER:** How difficult was it for you to adjust to this new format of course delivery?

   MOOC STUDENT: _The adjustment was not too difficult once I realized that self-discipline and self-motivation were crucial to my success. Because a "normal" class is at set times, it makes it easier to stay on track. However, learning via the Internet allows you the option of "going to class" whenever you want, in the early morning or late at night. A MOOC student needs to learn to control this freedom. In any subsequent MOOC that I take, this knowledge will help me avoid some of the problems I faced in this course._

(continued on next page)

anticipation	assume	disappointment	issue

2. **REPORTER:** This is the first MOOC that you were involved in. What were your expectations before you took the course, and how did it turn out to be different from what you expected?

MOOC STUDENT: _____

_____

_____

collaboration	diversity	significantly	virtual

3. **REPORTER:** Were you able to feel a connection to your classmates and teacher, or did you feel isolated?

MOOC STUDENT: _____

_____

_____

analyze	overall	sector	subsequent

4. **REPORTER:** This was the first MOOC that you have taught. How do you think it went, and what will you do differently in the next MOOC you teach?

PROFESSOR DUNEIER: _____

_____

_____

collaborate	dispute	enhance	significantly

5. **REPORTER:** What do you think about the schools of the twenty-first century compared to your school?

TOMMY: _____

_____

_____

GO TO MyEnglishLab FOR MORE VOCABULARY PRACTICE.

GRAMMAR

1 Examine the pairs of sentences and answer the questions with a partner.

Direct Speech	Indirect Speech
• One student said, "It was a choice between online class versus no class."	• A student said it had been a choice between online class versus no class.
• Professor Duneier told his students, "Sociological concepts may change from country to country."	• Professor Duneier told his students that sociolgical concepts might change from country to country.
• Professor Duneier commented, "I am excited about teaching this course. I think it will be really interesting."	• Professor Duneier commented that he was excited about teaching that course. He thought it would be really interesting.

1. What are the differences in punctuation between direct and indirect speech?

2. What other differences are there between direct and indirect speech? Which words are different? How do they change?

DIRECT AND INDIRECT SPEECH

Speech (and writing) can be reported in two ways:

Direct speech (also called *quoted speech*) reports the speaker's exact words.
Indirect speech (also called *reported speech*) reports what the speaker said without using the exact words.

Punctuation

For direct speech, put quotation marks before and after the words being quoted. Use a comma to separate the words in quotation marks from the reporting verbs such as *say, tell,* and *report.*

For indirect speech, there is no special punctuation.

Verb Tense Changes

For indirect speech, when the reporting verb is in the past tense (**said, told, reported**), the verbs inside the quotation marks change.

DIRECT SPEECH		INDIRECT SPEECH
Margie said, "I **do** my homework at night."		Margie said she **did** her homework at night.
do / does	→	**did**
(simple present)		(simple past)
am / is / are doing	→	**was / were doing**
(present progressive)		(past progressive)
did	→	**had done**
(simple past)		(past perfect)

(continued on next page)

DIRECT SPEECH		INDIRECT SPEECH
was / were doing	→	**had been doing**
(past progressive)		(past perfect progressive)
has / have done	→	**had done**
(present perfect)		(past perfect)
will	→	**would**
(modal)		(past modal)
can	→	**could**
(modal)		(past modal)
may	→	**might**
(modal)		(past modal)

Time and Location Word Changes

For indirect speech, time and location words may change to keep the speaker's original meaning.

DIRECT SPEECH		INDIRECT SPEECH
Tommy said, "I don't have to study **now**."		Tommy said he didn't have to study **at that time.**
now	→	**then / at that time**
tomorrow	→	**the next (following) day**
ago	→	**before / earlier**
here	→	**there**
this	→	**that**

Pronoun and Possessive Changes

For indirect speech, pronouns and possessives change to keep the speaker's original meaning.

DIRECT SPEECH	INDIRECT SPEECH
Professor Duneier said, "**I** . . ."	Professor Duneier said **he** . . .
Professor Duneier said, "**My** students . . ."	Professor Duneier said **his** students . . .

2 Read the first sentence in each item. It is indirect speech. Then circle the speaker's exact words.

1. The MOOC student said that he learned more in Professor Duneier's MOOC than he did in a traditional class.

    a. "I have learned more in Professor Duneier's MOOC than I have in a traditional class."

    b. "I had learned more in Professor Duneier's MOOC than I did in a traditional class."

    c. "I learn more in Professor Duneier's MOOC than I do in a traditional class."

2. A Nigerian student reported that he had never participated in a MOOC.

    a. "I have never participated in a MOOC."

    b. "I never participate in a MOOC."

    c. "I may never participate in a MOOC."

3. A Princeton student noted that in order to get the most out of the MOOC experience, she had to organize in-person study groups.

    a. "In order to get the most out of the MOOC experience, I will have to organize in-person study groups."

    b. "In order to get the most out of the MOOC experience, I have to organize in-person study groups."

    c. "In order to get the most out of the MOOC experience, I have had to organize in-person study groups."

4. The sociology department chairperson told us that Professor Duneier would teach two MOOCs the next year.

    a. "Professor Duneier teaches two MOOCs next year."

    b. "Professor Duneier taught two MOOCs last year."

    c. "Professor Duneier will teach two MOOCs next year."

5. Tommy argued that he didn't think that a man could know as much as a teacher.

    a. "I didn't think that a man could know as much as a teacher."

    b. "I don't think that a man can know as much as a teacher."

    c. "I don't think that a man could have known as much as a teacher."

(continued on next page)

6. Margie admitted that they hadn't had time to think about the book.

   a. "We didn't have time to think about the book."

   b. "We don't have time to think about the book."

   c. "We may not have time to think about the book."

7. Professor Duneier explained that many of his colleagues were teaching MOOCs, too.

   a. "Many of my colleagues were teaching MOOCs, too."

   b. "Many of his colleagues are teaching MOOCs, too."

   c. "Many of my colleagues are teaching MOOCs, too."

3 Write the direct speech statements in indirect speech. Remember to keep the speaker's original meaning.

1. Tommy said, "My father knows as much as my teacher."

   Tommy said that his father knew as much as his teacher.

2. The inspector told Margie's mother, "I think the geography sector was a little too quick."

   _____

3. He added, "I've slowed it up to a ten-year level."

   _____

4. Tommy said, "This is the old kind of school that they had hundreds and hundreds of years ago."

   _____

5. Margie told Tommy, "My mother says a teacher has to be adjusted to fit the mind of each boy and girl it teaches."

   _____

6. Tommy told Margie, "You can read the book with me again tomorrow."

   _____

GO TO MyEnglishLab **FOR MORE GRAMMAR PRACTICE AND TO CHECK WHAT YOU LEARNED.**

FINAL WRITING TASK

In this unit, you read about how Professor Duneier and his students feel about their educational experience as a result of the MOOC. You also read about how Tommy and Margie feel about their educational experience in the year 2157.

Now you are going to *write a comparison-and-contrast essay describing two different educational experiences you have participated in.* You can write about two different classes that you have taken, two different teachers that you have had, two different schools you have attended, etc. . . . Use the vocabulary and grammar from the unit.*

PREPARE TO WRITE: Charting

Charting is a prewriting activity that helps you organize information before you write. It is especially useful when you are comparing and contrasting, because you can easily make sure that you included similar information for both things that you are going to write about.

1 Think of different schools that you have attended, different classes you have taken, or different teachers that you have had. Write some notes about how they were the same and how they were different. Then discuss with a partner.

_____

_____

_____

_____

_____

_____

_____

_____

_____

_____

---

* For Alternative Writing Topics, see page 223. These topics can be used in place of the writing topic for this unit or as homework. The alternative topics relate to the theme of the unit but may not target the same grammar or rhetorical structures taught in the unit.

2 Look at the chart. The writer has described her experience taking a course in a traditional school and taking a MOOC course.

POINTS TO COMPARE / CONTRAST	MOOC	TRADITIONAL SCHOOL CLASS
Where the class takes place	Wherever there is an Internet connection	In a classroom in a school
When the class takes place	Sometimes at specific times, but generally whenever the student wants	At set times
Mode of student-teacher communication	Via Internet videos, e-mail, online forums, live-stream seminar-style discussions etc.	Listening and taking notes, face-to-face talking, writing papers, e-mail
Mode of student-student communication	Forums, in-person study groups (rare)	Face-to-face talking, texting, e-mail, in-person study groups
Ability to communicate nonverbally (nods, eye contact, intonation . . .)	Only for professor and videoed students in seminars, but not for the majority of students	For students and professors ·
Class size and makeup	100,000 + students from 100 + countries	Generally 25–30, although some large lecture classes could be for a hundred or more students; Students are predominantly from one country.
Socializing with classmates	Yes, through virtual and real-time communication via forums In-person study groups (rare)	Yes, before, between, and after classes; in clubs, sports teams, in-person study groups etc.

3 Brainstorm a list of areas to compare for your essay. Make a chart like the one above. Complete it with details about the two different educational experiences that you are comparing.

WRITE: A Comparison-and-Contrast Essay

A **comparison-and-contrast essay** explains the similarities and differences between two topics (ideas, people, or things).

Here are some important points:

1. **Have an introduction**. Include relevant background information about the two topics being compared and contrasted.

2. **Include a thesis statement**. Make sure it indicates the purpose for comparing and contrasting.

3. **Support your thesis throughout the essay**. Make sure your examples and details relate directly to the thesis.

4. **Include all points of comparison and contrast**. All points need to be discussed for each topic.

5. **Add specific details and examples**. Make sure they illustrate the similarities and differences.

6. **Have a conclusion**. Summarize the main ideas of the essay and include any final thoughts.

There are two common ways to organize a comparison-and-contrast essay. With **point-by-point organization**, you write about the similarities and differences of different aspects of each of the two topics you are comparing. With **block organization**, you first write a paragraph only about all aspects of the first topic and then another paragraph only about all aspects of the second topic. Note that in the block method, you usually compare the same aspects of each topic, but in separate paragraphs. It is also possible to put all similarities in one paragraph and all differences in another. This is another type of block organization.

1 Look at the outlines of an essay comparing and contrasting MOOCs and a traditional classroom experience. One outline is using point-by-point organization and the other block organization. Are the differences between them clear? Discuss with a partner.

POINT-BY-POINT ORGANIZATION

I. **Where and when the class takes place**

   A. Wherever there is an Internet connection; sometimes at set times, but generally when the student wants

   B. In a classroom in a school; at set times

II. **Student-teacher communication**

   A. Via Internet videos, e-mail, online forums, live-stream seminar-style discussions, etc.

   B. Face-to-face talking and listening, writing papers, e-mail

III. **Class size and makeup**

   A. Up to 100,000 or more students from 100 or more countries

   B. Generally 25–30, but possibly more than a hundred; students are usually predominantly from one country.

(continued on next page)

BLOCK ORGANIZATION

I. MOOC

    A. Location—Wherever there is an Internet connection

    B. Time—Sometimes at set times, but generally when the student wants

    C. Student-teacher communication—Via Internet videos, e-mail, online forums, live-stream seminar-style discussions, etc.

    D. Class size—Up to 100,000 or more students

    E. Class makeup—Students from 100 or more countries

II. Traditional School Class

    A. Location—In a classroom in a school

    B. Time—At set times

    C. Student-teacher communication—Face-to-face talking and listening, writing papers, e-mail

    D. Class size—Generally 25–30, but possibly more than a hundred

    E. Class makeup—Students are usually predominantly from one country.

2 Read the essay excerpts. How are they organized? How do you know? Circle *Point-by-Point* or *Block*. Discuss your answers with a partner.

1. I am taking five courses this semester. I am happy with all my teachers, but my English and history teachers are definitely my favorites. They are both extremely enthusiastic and knowledgeable about their subjects. In fact, my English teacher, Mr. Dadio, has recently received an award for his teaching. My history teacher, Ms. Mantell, has written history textbooks that are being used by many school systems. They both have a good sense of humor. Mr. Dadio likes to joke with the students, which helps us relax. Ms. Mantell is witty, and her comments also help reduce the stress many students feel because of our school's demanding curriculum. Both teachers insist that we work hard, and we do. The type of work that they give is different. Mr. Dadio expects us to read complete novels in only a couple of days, and he grades us on our essays comparing the characters or plots. Ms. Mantell expects us to read a chapter every two classes, and, instead of grading us on papers, she gives us tests that are usually short answer or multiple-choice questions. Despite their differences, they are both excellent teachers.

(Point-by-Point / Block)

2. My old school in Lima was very small. There were only about 75 students, and we all knew each other well. The teachers knew every student by name. My school was only for boys; girls went to another school. In Lima, we spoke only Spanish at school. Students had to wear uniforms. We had very little technology in Lima. There were only a couple of computers in the whole school, and students rarely got to use them.

In New York, my school is gigantic. There are over 1,400 students. The immense halls are filled with unfamiliar faces, male and female. Here we mostly speak English but sometimes Spanish. Uniforms are not required in New York, and students wear all different kinds of clothes. In New York, every student is given a laptop at the beginning of ninth grade, and assignments are posted on class websites. I often e-mail my homework and questions to teachers. I like school in New York, but sometimes I miss the intimacy of my old school.

(Point-by-Point / Block)

3. Two English courses that many students take in college are Creative Writing and English Literature. Both of these courses involve a lot of reading and writing. The types of reading assignments given are different in each course. In a literature course, students read entire books by famous authors. The books often deal with a central topic or a certain time in history. The reading assignments for a Creative Writing class are usually much shorter. They are often excerpts or news articles chosen to elicit an opinion from the student.

The types of writing assignments are also different. The writing assignments in a literature class are directly related to the books being read. They may involve analyzing structure and symbolism and comparing and contrasting different books or authors. In a creative writing class, the assignments are more general. Students may be given a broad topic but are expected to find their own personal way of approaching the writing. Journals and other types of reflection pieces may also be required.

(Point-by-Point / Block)

3 Look at your chart from Prepare to Write, Exercise 3. Make outlines for your essay using both types of organization. Then share your outlines with a partner. In what ways are the two types of organization different? Which outline was easier to read and which was easier to write? Discuss which of your outlines you think works better and why.

4 Now write the first draft of your comparison-and-contrast essay. Use the outline you have chosen and the information from Prepare to Write to plan your essay. Include relevant information about the two educational experiences you are comparing. Include a thesis statement that indicates how these experiences are similar and different. Be sure to add specific details and examples to illustrate the similarities and differences. In your conclusion, summarize the main ideas in the essay and include any final thoughts about your experience. Be sure to use vocabulary and grammar from the unit.

REVISE: Using Subordinators and Transitions

Certain words act as signals to introduce points of comparison or contrast.

1 Examine the paragraph and answer the questions with a partner.

I am quite happy with all my courses this semester, but I have two favorites, Intermediate Algebra and Biology I, and they are very different. First is the amount of time we spend in class. Algebra has two one-hour classes a week **while** biology has three one-hour classes plus a lab section that sometimes takes more than two hours. The teachers are very different, too. The biology teacher is young and somewhat inexperienced, but she has a lot of enthusiasm and current knowledge. **In contrast**, my algebra teacher has over 30 years of teaching experience and knows how to relate to all types of learners. In addition, he is available every day after class for extra help **whereas** my biology teacher can never help us right after class because she has another class then. However, she does have office hours before class two days a week and will answer e-mail questions very quickly. My algebra teacher expects students to do all homework and reading before class **in the same way** the biology teacher does; if you don't, you won't be successful in the class. Since I love both of these classes, this is not a problem for me.

1. Look at the boldfaced words. Which words introduce ideas that are similar? Which words introduce ideas that are different?

2. Four topics are compared and contrasted in this paragraph. What are they?

COMPARISONS AND CONTRASTS

Comparisons point out ideas that are similar. **Contrasts** point out ideas that are different.

Subordinators

Subordinators are used to compare or contrast the ideas in two clauses. They join the independent clause to the dependent clause being compared or contrasted. Examples of subordinators include *while, whereas, just as, as.* These words introduce dependent clauses, not complete thoughts. The independent clause usually describes the point that is being emphasized or is more important.

COMPARISON SUBORDINATORS INCLUDE:	CONTRAST SUBORDINATORS INCLUDE:
just as	whereas
as	while

Transitions

Transitions show the connection between two independent clauses (two sentences).

COMPARISON TRANSITIONS INCLUDE:	CONTRAST TRANSITIONS INCLUDE:
similarly	in contrast
in the same way	on the other hand
likewise	however

- Two independent clauses can be combined in one sentence by using a semicolon (;) and a comma (,):

   I love my biology class; **however**, I don't like all the memorization it requires.

- The two independent clauses can also be written as separate sentences:

   Our grade in algebra is based entirely on three tests and a final exam. **However**, our biology grade is based on tests, a final exam, lab reports, and a research paper.

- Two independent clauses can also be combined as a simple sentence using the phrase *in the same way*.

   The biology teacher expects a lot of hard work from her students *in the same way* the algebra teacher does.

2 Combine the pairs of sentences to make comparisons and contrasts.

1. likewise

- A MOOC student receives his or her assignments via the Internet.
- Tommy and Margie's computer is their teacher, and it tells them what to do and study.

   MOOC students are taught and submit papers via the Internet; likewise, Tommy and Margie also are taught via the computer.

(continued on next page)

2. in the same way

- Professor Duneier enjoyed the new course delivery method of a MOOC.

- The MOOC students were excited about the use of educational technology in their sociology course.

_____

_____

3. similarly

- Margie thought a man couldn't know enough to be a teacher.

- Professor Duneier was worried he wouldn't be able to effectively teach students from so many different countries.

_____

_____

4. on the other hand

- Margie wanted to go to a traditional school like in the old days.

- Many students today are tired of traditional school and want to incorporate distance learning in their education.

_____

_____

5. in contrast

- Many of Professor Duneier's MOOC students chose his course instead of a traditional sociology course.

- For others, the choice was his MOOC or no sociology course at all.

_____

_____

6. while

- _The Fun They Had_ describes the future as it was imagined in 1951.

- "Teaching the World from Central New Jersey" describes a present that may seem futuristic to some people.

_____

_____

3 Work with a partner. Read the paragraphs. Decide where the writer is comparing and where he or she is contrasting. Add transitions or subordinators of comparison or contrast to each paragraph to make the writer's meaning clear. Discuss which type of organization requires more transitions and subordinators.

1.   I am taking five courses this semester. I am happy with all my teachers.

_____, my English and history teachers are definitely my favorites. They are both extremely enthusiastic and knowledgeable about their subjects. For example, my English teacher, Mr. Dadio, has recently received an award for his teaching. _____, my history teacher, Ms. Mantell, also clearly knows her subject. In fact, she has written history textbooks that are being used by many school systems. They both have a good sense of humor. Mr. Dadio likes to joke with the students, which helps us relax. _____, Ms. Mantell's witty comments also help reduce the stress many students feel because of our school's demanding curriculum. Both teachers insist that we work hard, and we do.

_____, the type of work that they give is different. Mr. Dadio expects us to read complete novels in only a couple of days, and he grades us on our essays comparing the characters or plots. _____, Ms. Mantell expects us to read a chapter every two classes, and, instead of grading us on papers, she gives us tests that are usually short answer or multiple-choice questions. Despite their differences, they are both excellent teachers.

2.   Each new level of education brings new challenges and demands to students. Moving from high school into college can be especially difficult because of the freedom students experience in college along with a new set of expectations.

    In high school, students usually live at home, and their parents take care of all their physical needs such as food and housing. Students do not usually have to shop for their food, take time to pay bills, or even do their own laundry. Parents are also there to help with and make sure that the student's homework is done. During the school day, students rarely have free time. They go directly from one class to the other. Teachers are always around to tell the students what to

(continued on next page)

do. Finally, the work itself is not so challenging. Students can often complete their homework and reading in a short time.

_____, in college, students often live away from home in dorms or apartments. They may be responsible for shopping, paying bills, and laundry. They also may have to cook their own meals. Their parents are not around to help with homework or even to check that it has been done. _____ to students in high school, students in college may have a lot of free time between classes, but must discipline themselves to use this time productively for homework and other assignments. Most important, college requires a higher level of thinking and a lot more work than high school.

3. My old school in Lima was very small. _____, my school In New York is gigantic. There were only about 75 students in my Lima school, and we all knew each other well. The teachers knew every student by name. _____, in New York there are over 1,400 students, and the immense halls are filled with unfamiliar faces, male and female. _____, my school in Lima was only for boys; girls went to another school. In Lima, we spoke only Spanish at school _____ here we mostly speak English but sometimes Spanish. The teachers in Lima were very good and always were able to answer any question that we had. _____, in New York the teachers are also excellent. Use of technology is another difference between the two schools. We had very little technology in Lima. There were only a couple of computers in the whole school, and students rarely got to use them. _____, in New York, every student is given a laptop at the beginning of ninth grade, and assignments are posted on class websites. In fact, I often e-mail my homework and questions to teachers. I like school in New York, but sometimes I miss the intimacy of my old school.

4 Look at your first draft. Add comparison-and-contrast transitions and/or subordinators as needed.

GO TO MyEnglishLab *FOR MORE SKILL PRACTICE.*

EDIT: Writing the Final Draft

Go to MyEnglishLab and write the final draft of your essay. Carefully edit it for grammatical and mechanical errors, such as spelling, capitalization, and punctuation. Make sure you use some of the vocabulary and grammar from the unit. Use the checklist to help you write your final draft. Then submit your essay to your teacher.

FINAL DRAFT CHECKLIST

❑ Does the essay have an introduction which includes relevant background information about the two educational experiences?

❑ Does the essay have a thesis statement that indicates how these experiences are similar and different?

❑ Does your essay clearly follow a point-by-point or block organization?

❑ Does the essay use effective subordinators and transitions to show comparison and contrast?

❑ Does the essay include specific details and examples to illustrate the similarities and differences?

❑ Does the essay have a conclusion summarizing the main ideas of the essay?

❑ Does the essay use reported speech?

❑ Have you used vocabulary from the unit?

UNIT PROJECT

Distance education has changed substantially since it was first used in 1728. Many different models have been used over the last three centuries. You are going to work in a small group and choose a model of distance learning. The model you choose can be from the past and does not have to be used currently. You will write a report about the model based on your research. Follow these steps:

STEP 1: Research a current or past model of distance learning. Go to the library or use the Internet to do your research.

STEP 2: Prepare a list of questions you would like to find answers to as you research distance learning. Divide your questions among the members of your group and conduct your research. Some possible questions could include:

- How long has this model of distance learning been in existence?
- Where and how did it originate?
- How is the course delivered? What technology is necessary?
- Do/Did students have to be in "class" at a specific time?
- Where does/did student learning take place?
- How do/did students and teachers interact?
- Can/Could students interact with other students? If so, how?
- Where are/were the students from?
- Who is/was allowed to take the course? Do/Did you have to be a high school graduate or enrolled in college?
- What is/was the cost of the course?
- Do/Did students receive credit for the course?

STEP 3: Share your research with your group. Combine your information and write a report using this outline.

Part I: Introduction

- A brief introduction to your topic (distance learning)
- An explanation of what information you were looking for (your original questions)
- An explanation of where and how you found your information

Part II: Results

- The information you collected and the answers to your questions

Part III: Conclusions

- Final conclusions and opinions about distance learning

STEP 4: Present your report to the class.

ALTERNATIVE WRITING TOPICS

Write about one of the topics. Use the vocabulary and grammar from the unit.

1. Different subjects require different teaching methods. Do you think any subject could be effectively taught as a MOOC, or are certain subjects more easily adapted to the MOOC format? Explain.

2. How do you envision education in the future? Do you think the traditional classroom with one teacher, 20–25 students, and a chalkboard is a thing of the past? What role do you think technology will play in education in the future? What effects will these changes have on the student?

■■■■■■■■■■■■■■■■■■■■■■■ *GO TO* MyEnglishLab *TO WRITE ABOUT ONE OF THE ALTERNATIVE TOPICS, WATCH A VIDEO ABOUT A HOLIDAY FROM HOMEWORK, AND TAKE THE UNIT 7 ACHIEVEMENT TEST.* ■■■■■■■■■■■■■■■■■■■■■■■■■■■■■■■■■■■■■■

MANAGING YOUR Smartphone

1 FOCUS ON THE TOPIC

1. In addition to making calls, what are cell phones used for?

2. *Nomophobia* is the fear of being without your mobile phone. *Phantom vibration syndrome* is an associated problem in which people think they feel or hear their phone vibrate and check it expecting to find a message or a call—but the phone did not vibrate. Do you think you suffer from nomophobia and/or have you experienced phantom vibration syndrome? If so, explain.

3. Do you think you would be able to happily "survive" a week without your phone? What would be hardest about not having a phone for a week?

GO TO MyEnglishLab *TO CHECK WHAT YOU KNOW.*

VOCABULARY

Reading One is an article about smartphone dependency. Read the letter a woman wrote to a newspaper advice columnist about her husband's smartphone usage. Circle the letter of the definition that best defines each boldfaced word or phrase.

1. **a.** aversion
   b. strong need
   c. understanding

2. **a.** normal
   b. boring
   c. uncontrollable

3. **a.** fix
   b. make something happen
   c. stop

4. **a.** strong desire
   b. message
   c. distraction

5. **a.** awake
   b. aware
   c. unclear

6. **a.** taking money from a bank
   b. bad feelings when you stop doing something
   c. learning

7. **a.** decision
   b. reliance
   c. technology

8. **a.** inability to work normally
   b. disease
   c. mood

9. **a.** worry
   b. relaxation
   c. experience

10. **a.** benefit from
    b. learn to use better
    c. gradually stop doing

ASK HELPFUL HANNAH

Dear Helpful Hannah,

I've got a problem with my husband, Sam. He bought a smartphone a couple of months ago, and he took it on our recent ski vacation to Colorado. It was a great trip except for one problem. He has a constant **(1) urge** to check for text messages; he checks his phone every five minutes! He's **(2) compulsive** about it. He can't stop checking even at inappropriate times like when we are eating in a restaurant and I am talking to him! It is almost as if any small amount of boredom can **(3) trigger** a need for him to check his phone even when he knows he shouldn't. The **(4) temptation** to see who is contacting him is just too great. When I ask him to please put down the phone and stop ignoring me, he says, "In a minute," but still checks to see if there is an important text or if someone has posted something new on Facebook. I don't think he is even **(5) conscious** that he is being rude! If we go somewhere and I ask him to leave the phone at home, he suffers from **(6) withdrawal** symptoms. I just keep thinking that maybe this **(7) dependency** on his smartphone has become more than an everyday problem.

I recently read an article about "nomophobia." It's a real illness people can suffer from: the fear of being without your phone! I am worried that Sam may be suffering from this **(8) dysfunction**. Why? Because he experiences a great deal of **(9) anxiety** if he doesn't have his phone with him, even for a short time. It is so bad that he sometimes brings it into the bathroom with him.

While we were in Colorado, we talked a little about his "problem," and he agreed to try to slowly **(10) wean** himself **away from** the phone. But, so far, I don't think the amount of time he spends using his phone each day is

11. **a.** increasing
    b. decreasing
    c. finishing

12. **a.** tools or machines
    b. plans
    c. methods

really **(11) diminishing**. He's got to do something, or I am going to throw his phone away while he is sleeping!

Who would have thought that little **(12) devices** like these could be such a blessing and yet such a curse!

Sick and Tired Sadie

GO TO MyEnglishLab *FOR MORE VOCABULARY PRACTICE.*

PREVIEW

You are going to read an article about smartphone addiction. Read the questions and discuss your answers with a partner.

1. What behaviors have you noticed about people and their smartphones?

2. Why do people enjoy their smartphones so much?

3. Are there any negative consequences of owning a smartphone? Explain.

Keep your ideas in mind as you read Davis's article.

Addicted to Your Smartphone?

Here's What to Do. Why smartphones hook us in, plus tips on reclaiming your time and concentration

By Susan Davis

1 I'll admit it: I check my smartphone compulsively. And the more I use it, the more often the **urge** to look at it hits me.

2 In the orthodontist's office. Walking my kids to school. In meetings. Even while making breakfast. Sometimes it is in my hand before I even know what I'm searching for. Sometimes I tap the screen absentmindedly—looking at my e-mail, a local blogger, my calendar, and Twitter.

3 I'm not the only one struggling with this very modern compulsion. According to a 2012 survey by the Pew Research Center, 46% of all American adults now own a smartphone—up a whopping 25% from 2011.

4 And smartphone use can get very heavy. In a study of 1,600 managers and professionals, Leslie Perlow, PhD, the Konosuke Matsushita professor of leadership at the Harvard Business School, found that:

- 70% said they check their smartphone within an hour of getting up.
- 56% check their phone within an hour of going to sleep.

(continued on next page)

Managing Your Smartphone 227

- 48% check over the weekend, including on Friday and Saturday nights.

- 51% check continuously during vacation.

- 44% said they would experience "a great deal of **anxiety**" if they lost their phone and couldn't replace it for a week.

5   "The amount of time that people are spending with the new technology, the apparent preoccupation, raises the question 'why?'" says Peter DeLisi, academic dean of the information technology leadership program at Santa Clara University in California. "When you start seeing that people have to text when they're driving, even though they clearly  know that they're endangering their lives and the lives of others, we really have to ask what is so compelling about this new medium?"

Hook or Habit?

6   Whether smartphones really "hook" users into **dependency** remains unclear.

7   But "we already know that the Internet and certain forms of computer use are addictive," says David Greenfield, PhD, a West Hartford, Conn., psychologist and author of *Virtual Addiction: Help for Netheads, Cyber Freaks, and Those Who Love Them.*

8   "And while we're not seeing actual smartphone addictions now," Greenfield says, "the potential is certainly there."

9   A true addiction entails a growing tolerance to a substance (think drugs or alcohol) so you need more to get "high," uncomfortable symptoms during **withdrawal**, and a harmful impact on your life, Greenfield says.

10   Computer technologies can be addictive, he says, because they're "psychoactive." That is, they alter mood and often **trigger** enjoyable feelings.

11   E-mail, in particular, gives us satisfaction due to what psychologists call "variable ratio reinforcement." That is, we never know when we'll get a satisfying e-mail, so we keep checking, over and over again. "It's like slot machines," Greenfield says. "We're seeking that pleasurable hit."

12   Smartphones, of course, allow us to seek rewards (including videos, Twitter feeds, and news updates, in addition to e-mail) anytime and anywhere. Is such behavior unhealthy?

13   "That really depends on whether it's disrupting your work or family life," Greenfield says.

14   Such a disruption could be small—like ignoring your friend over lunch to post a Facebook status about how much you're enjoying lunch with your friend.

15   Or it could be big—like tuning out a distressed spouse or colleagues in a meeting to check e-mail, or feeling increasingly stressed by the fact that everyone else seems to be on call 24/7, so perhaps we should be, too.

16   Other researchers are seeing clear signs of **dysfunction**, if not an "addiction."

17   According to a 2011 study published in the journal *Personal and Ubiquitous Computing*, people aren't addicted to smartphones themselves as much as they are addicted to "checking habits" that develop with phone use—including repeatedly (and very quickly) checking for news updates, e-mails, or social media connections.

18   That study found that certain environmental triggers—like being bored or listening to a lecture—trigger the habits. And while the average user checks his or her smartphone 35 times a day—for about 30 seconds each time, when the information rewards are greater (e.g., having contact info linked to the contact's whereabouts), users check even *more* often.

The Interrupted Life

19   Besides creating a compulsion, smartphones pose other dangers to our mental life, says Nicholas Carr, author of *The Shallows: What the Internet Is Doing to Our Brains*.

20   "The smartphone, through its small size, ease of use, proliferation of free or cheap apps, and constant connectivity, changes our relationship with computers in a way that goes well beyond what we experienced with laptops," he says. That's because people keep their smartphones near them "from the moment they wake up until the moment they go to bed," and throughout that time the **devices** provide an almost continuous stream of messages and alerts as well as easy access to a myriad[1] of compelling information sources.

21   "By design," he says, "it's an environment of almost constant interruptions and distractions. The smartphone, more than any other gadget,[2] steals from us the opportunity to maintain our attention, to engage in contemplation and reflection, or even to be alone with our thoughts."

22   Carr, who writes extensively in *The Shallows* about the way that computer technology in general may be **diminishing** our ability to concentrate and think deeply, does not have a smartphone.

23   "One thing my research made clear is that human beings have a deep, primitive desire to know everything that's going on around them," he says.

24   "That instinct probably helped us survive when we were cavemen and cavewomen. I'm sure one of the main reasons people tend to be so **compulsive** in their use of smartphones is that they can't stand the idea that there may be a new bit of information out there that they haven't seen. I know that I'm not strong enough to resist that **temptation**, so I've decided to shun[3] the device altogether."

(continued on next page)

---

[1] **myriad:** a very large number of something

[2] **gadget:** a small tool or machine that makes a particular job easier

[3] **shun:** to deliberately avoid someone or something

Managing Your Smartphone Use

25   Can't give up your phone altogether? Experts suggest these steps to control your usage:

- **Be conscious** of the situations and emotions that make you want to check your phone. Is it boredom? Loneliness? Anxiety? Maybe something else would soothe you.

- **Be strong** when your phone beeps or rings. You don't always have to answer it. In fact, you can avoid temptation by turning off the alert signals.

- **Be disciplined** about not using your device in certain situations (such as when you're with children, driving, or in a meeting) or at certain hours (for instance, between 9 P.M. and 7 A.M.). "You'll be surprised and pleased to rediscover the pleasures of being in control of your attention," Carr says.

26   One group of business people at The Boston Group, a consulting firm, discovered just that when they participated in an experiment run by Perlow.

27   As described in her book, *Sleeping with Your Smartphone*, the group found that taking regular "predictable time off" (PTO) from their PDAs resulted in increased efficiency and collaboration, heightened job satisfaction, and better work-life balance.

28   Four years after her initial experiment, Perlow reports, 86% of the consulting staff in the firm's Northeast offices—including Boston, New York, and Washington, D.C.—were on teams engaged in similar PTO experiments.

29   To manage my own smartphone well, more smartly, I **weaned** myself **away from** it.

30   I started by not checking it for 15 minutes at a time, then 30, then 60 (unless I was dealing with an urgent situation).

31   I decided to avoid using the web browser on the smartphone unless I truly needed information (such as an address or phone number).

32   And I swore off using social media on it entirely. I also made a firm commitment to not text, e-mail, or surf the web on my smartphone while driving.

33   The result? Even after a few days of this self-discipline, I found that I was concentrating better, more aware of my surroundings, and more relaxed—and I was more aware of when I was looking for something specific, as opposed to just looking for some kind of connection.

MAIN IDEAS

1 Look again at your ideas from the Preview on page 227. How did your answers to the questions help you understand the article?

2 Reading One is divided into four sections. Write one or two sentences that summarize each part of the article. Use your own words.

Part I: (*paragraphs 1–5*)
What are the signs of compulsive use of smartphones?

_____

_____

Part II: Hook or Habit? (*paragraphs 6–18*)
Is smartphone usage an addiction? Explain.

_____

_____

Part III: The Interrupted Life (*paragraphs 19–24*)
Explain how smartphones are a problem for our mental life.

_____

_____

Part IV: Managing Your Smartphone Use (*paragraphs 25–33*)
How can you control your usage?

_____

_____

DETAILS

Circle the best answer according to the reading.

1. People text while they are driving even though they know

    a. they might get a ticket.

    b. it is difficult to text and drive at the same time.

    c. they are putting their lives in danger.

(continued on next page)

2. Computer technologies can be considered addictive because

    a. they can change your mood and cause enjoyable feelings.

    b. they cause you to suffer withdrawal symptoms if you are not able to use them.

    c. they interfere with concentrating on more important activities.

3. Dr. Greenfield says that

    a. smartphone addiction is a reality because 44% of managers and professionals now experience anxiety about losing their smartphone.

    b. smartphone addiction is possible, but he hasn't seen it yet.

    c. there are currently many smartphone addicts.

4. Smartphone usage can be considered unhealthy if

    a. it is caused by "variable ratio reinforcement."

    b. you use it to work on the weekends.

    c. it disrupts your work or family life.

5. According to the journal *Personal and Ubiquitous Computing*, people aren't addicted to smartphones themselves, but rather to

    a. checking habits.

    b. social media.

    c. using them while listening to lectures.

6. According to the journal *Personal and Ubiquitous Computing*, checking habits include checking for all of the following <u>except</u>

    a. e-mails.

    b. GPS directions.

    c. news updates.

7. Nicholas Carr believes our relationship with smartphones is different from our relationship with computers, even laptops, for all the following reasons <u>except</u> that

    a. apps are free or cheap.

    b. we constantly have them with us.

    c. we can use them to access social media.

8. Carr believes that humans have a deep primitive desire to know everything that is going on around them. This instinct is/was especially helpful when

    a. checking social media.

    b. trying to survive in primitive situations.

    c. getting news updates.

9. In order to control smartphone use, experts suggest

   a. not always answering your phone and even turning it off.

   b. using your phone when you are with children, but not in a meeting.

   c. feeling anxious or bored when your phone doesn't ring.

10. Taking predictable time off (PTO) caused all of the following effects <u>except</u>

   a. more collaboration.

   b. getting a new job

   c. improved work-life balance.

MAKE INFERENCES

APPEAL TO AUTHORITY

To help make their ideas more believable, authors often refer to experts who support their point of view. Experts add importance and validity to the author's position. The author may quote an expert directly or either paraphrase or summarize the expert's ideas. Statistics can also help support an author's point of view.

   Look at the example and read the explanation.

In Reading One, Susan Davis uses statistics and quotations from many experts that support her ideas about smartphones.

Look at paragraphs 2 and 3. In paragraph 3, she includes statistics (underlined) from a survey done by the Pew Research Center and from a study done by Leslie Perlow, PhD. Why does Davis do this? What is the idea that she is trying to support?

   2 "In the orthodontist's office. Walking my kids to school. In meetings. Even while making breakfast. Sometimes it is in my hand before I even know what I'm searching for. Sometimes I tap the screen absent mindedly—looking at my e-mail, a local blogger, my calendar, and Twitter.

   3 I'm not the only one struggling with this very modern compulsion. <u>According to a 2012 survey by the Pew Research Center, 46% of all American adults now own a smartphone—up a whopping 25% from 2011</u>."

Davis shows us that excessive use of smartphones goes beyond her personal experience.

The statistics strengthen Davis's argument. She begins writing her opinion with a personal anecdote about her own compulsive smartphone habits. She then shares the survey information in order to show us that she is not alone and that many other professionals are struggling with this behavior.

For each quote from an expert, provide two kinds of information: the opinion of the author that the quote supports, and how the quote strengthens the author's argument.

1. David Greenfield, PhD *(paragraphs 12–13)*:

   "Smartphones, of course, allow us to seek rewards (including videos, Twitter feeds, and news updates, in addition to e-mail) anytime and anywhere. Is such behavior unhealthy?

   'That really depends on whether it's disrupting your work or family life,' Greenfield says."

   Author's opinion that the underlined part of the quote supports: _____

   _____

   How the quote strengthens the author's argument: _____

   _____

2. The journal, *Personal and Ubiquitous Computing (paragraph 17)*:

   "According to a 2011 study published in the journal *Personal and Ubiquitous Computing,* people aren't addicted to smartphones themselves as much as they are addicted to 'checking habits' that develop with phone use—including repeatedly (and very quickly) checking for news updates, e-mails, or social media connections."

   Author's opinion that the quote supports: _____

   _____

   How the quote strengthens the author's argument: _____

   _____

3. Nicholas Carr *(paragraph 21)*:

   "By design," he says, "it's an environment of almost constant interruptions and distractions. The smartphone, more than any other gadget, steals from us the opportunity to maintain our attention, to engage in contemplation and reflection, or even to be alone with our thoughts."

   Author's opinion that the quote supports: _____

   _____

   How the quote strengthens the author's argument: _____

   _____

4. Leslie Perlow, PhD *(paragraphs 27–28)*:

"As described in her book, *Sleeping with Your Smartphone*, the (experiment) group found that taking regular 'predictable time off' (PTO) from their PDAs resulted in increased efficiency and collaboration, heightened job satisfaction, and better work-life balance.

Four years after her initial experiment, Perlow reports, 86% of the consulting staff in the firm's Northeast offices—including Boston, New York, and Washington, D.C.—were on teams engaged in similar PTO experiments."

Author's opinion that the quote supports: _____

_____

How the quote strengthens the author's argument: _____

_____

EXPRESS OPINIONS

Work with a partner. Discuss your ideas about the questions. Then report your ideas to the class.

1. Which examples in the article describe your own behaviors? Do you think you have an addiction to smartphones or some other technology?

2. Go back to paragraph 25, page 230. Reread the advice for managing smartphone use. Are you likely to take this advice? Why or why not? Do you have any ideas of your own for managing smartphone use?

■■■■■■■■■■■■■■■■■■■■■■■■■■■ *GO TO* MyEnglishLab *TO GIVE YOUR OPINION ABOUT ANOTHER QUESTION.*

READ

1 Look at the boldfaced words in the reading and think about the questions.

1. Which words or phrases do you know the meanings of?

2. Can you use any of the words or phrases in a sentence?

2 Read the article about a technology-free vacation. As you read, notice the boldfaced vocabulary. Try to guess its meaning from the context.

Unplugging Wired Kids: A Vacation from Technology and Social Media
The Momoir Project

1   It's day one of our vacation on Cortes, a remote island in the BC wilderness[1] and my son is **literally** lying on the couch of our rustic[2] A-frame moaning, "iPhone. iPhone. iPhone." In front of him is a wall of windows facing a glistening ocean and coming in from the open deck doors—a warm, beautiful breeze. Clearly, he sees and feels none of it. He's too deep in his electronics withdrawal.

2   Back at home in Vancouver, after five minutes of listening to this kind of groveling, I'd normally **relent**. Instead of screaming "Shut up," I'd hand it over in defeat. He'd win.

3   Not here. We came here to get away from it all—our lives, technology, the constant pull of e-mail, Facebook, video games, and the never-ending ping of the iPhone.

4   Before we left, I told my 10-year-old son the rules: We were all going electronic-free for a week. There could be a few movies on the odd[3] night, but no TV, no video games, no e-mail. And here we are on day one and already, he can't stand it.

5   My 6-year-old daughter and my husband are doing just fine. They are outside on the deck carving pieces of driftwood and singing. Meanwhile, my son is inside blinded to the opportunities in front of him, complaining that he doesn't like the beach.

---

[1] **wilderness:** a large natural area of land that has never been farmed or built on

[2] **rustic:** simple and old-fashioned in a way that is attractive and typical of the countryside

[3] **odd:** different from what is expected

6   Confounded, I walk outside to let him suffer. I walk down the grassy pathway to the beach. It's so stunning, I can barely manage to read on my blanket. I just want to stare out at the islands and the glistening ocean. The eagles soar overhead. The seals pop their heads out of the water, and there isn't another soul in sight. My son can do whatever he wants. But he's not going to ruin the quiet and beauty of this trip for me.

7   Day 2. We spend the entire morning, and part of the afternoon, digging for clams and oysters and swimming in the lagoon. My son is one with his shovel, looking for the smallest clams and filling buckets with shellfish and other sea treasures. When we get back to our cabin, I give my son his book, put him in the shade on a lovely garden swing and it's almost dinner when he looks up.

8   The next few days pass in a blur of sun and sand. My husband **ensures** we do something every day to get out of the cabin and explore. One day, we all spend an afternoon swimming at the freshwater lake. Another day, my husband takes my son on a three-hour hike around the headland.

9   On day 6, he's lying beside me on the beach watching the sunset. We are wrapped together in a blanket and as I watch him play with the sand in his hands, the grains slipping through his fingers, I realize how much time has slowed down for both of us. It's exactly what I wanted. Finally, after just a few days, we are able to sit quietly without **twitching**, without thinking about screens, without the constant interruptions of phone calls and e-mail. Two hours pass, and, in that time, he happily throws rocks into the water, listens to a man play guitar down the beach, plays Frisbee in the grassy field behind us.

10   He's too young to see it, but it's clear to me. A week away from our dependence on electronics and we've slowed right down. We are breathing deeper and, literally, noticing the grains of sand. Life is good. If only we could live on vacation.

11   How do you handle the **influx** of technology in your house? How do your kids handle it? Do you ever feel the need for a vacation from technology?

COMPREHENSION

Work with a partner. Complete each statement according to the reading.

1. At the beginning of the vacation, the author's son couldn't enjoy himself because _____

_____.

2. This vacation was unusual because _____

_____.

3. One way the husband helped break the dependence on electronics was _____

_____.

4. The result of a week away from electronics was _____

_____.

▪▪▪ *GO TO* MyEnglishLab *FOR MORE VOCABULARY PRACTICE.*

READING SKILL

1 Go back to Reading Two. In the last sentence of paragraph 7, underline the pronouns "we," "I," and "he." What person does each pronoun refer to?

IDENTIFYING REFERENTS FOR THE PRONOUN *IT*

Pronouns usually clearly refer to a previously mentioned person or thing. In this passage from paragraph 5, "My 6-year-old daughter and my husband are doing just fine. **They** are outside on the deck carving pieces of driftwood and singing," *they* clearly refers to "my daughter and my husband."

The referent for the pronoun *it* is sometimes not as clear. *It* may refer to an idea, not a concrete person or thing.

In paragraph 1 the author writes:

"In front of him is a wall of windows facing a glistening ocean and coming in from the open deck doors—a warm, beautiful breeze. Clearly, he sees and feels none of **it**."

What does "it" refer to?

"It" = the beautiful environment: the glistening ocean and the beautiful weather.

At times, pronouns can also refer to information that follows the pronoun. In paragraph 3, the author writes:

"We came here to get away from **it** all—our lives, technology, the constant pull of e-mail, Facebook, video games, and the never-ending ping of the iPhone."

What does "it" refer to in this passage?

"It" = their everyday lives including all aspects of technology: e-mail, Facebook, video games, and iPhones.

2 Read the excerpts from Reading Two. Explain in your own words what the boldfaced pronouns refer to.

1. "We were all going electronic-free for a week. There could be a few movies on the odd night, but no TV, no video games, no e-mail. And here we are on day one and already, he can't stand **it**." *(paragraph 4)*

   Explanation: _____

   _____

2. "I realize how much time has slowed down for both of us. **It**'s exactly what I wanted." *(paragraph 9)*

   Explanation: _____

   _____

3. "He's too young to see **it**, but **it**'s clear to me. A week away from our dependence on electronics and we've slowed right down." *(paragraph 10)*

   Explanation: _____

   _____

▪▪▪▪▪▪▪▪▪▪▪▪▪▪▪▪▪▪▪▪▪▪▪▪▪▪▪▪▪▪▪▪▪▪▪▪▪▪ GO TO MyEnglishLab FOR MORE SKILL PRACTICE.

STEP 1: Organize

Reading One (R1) and Reading Two (R2) both address the problems caused by our growing dependence on smartphones and other electronic devices. They suggest some specific problems associated with this dependence. In R1, along with her personal experiences, Susan Davis also includes the opinions of experts regarding dependency issues. In R2, the writer uses her son as an example of some problems that overreliance on smartphones and other electronic devices *may* cause. Both readings also offer solutions for how to manage smartphone dependency.

Complete the graphic organizer by categorizing the items as either problems or solutions. According to the readings, each problem has specific solutions.

- ~~Slowly diminish use~~
- Make commitment not to use phone in certain situations
- ~~No texting and driving~~
- Self-discipline

- ~~Turn off alerts~~
- Use at inappropriate times
- Anxiety if lost or unavailable
- Predictable time off
- Avoid using web browsers

- Constant availability
- Make specific times smartphone-free
- ~~Continuous checking~~
- Wean yourself away

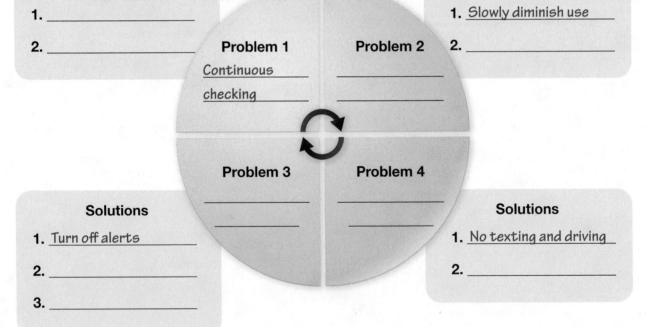

Solutions

1. _____

2. _____

Problem 1

Continuous _____

checking _____

Problem 2

_____

_____

Solutions

1. _Slowly diminish use_

2. _____

Problem 3

_____

_____

Problem 4

_____

_____

Solutions

1. _Turn off alerts_

2. _____

3. _____

Solutions

1. _No texting and driving_

2. _____

STEP 2: Synthesize

Go back to pages 226–227 and reread the letter that Sick and Tired Sadie wrote describing her husband's smartphone dependency. Using information from Step 1, work with a partner to complete the advice columnist's response to Sadie explaining how she can help her husband manage his dependency.

Dear Sick and Tired Sadie,

I applaud you for recognizing that your husband has a problem. You are definitely doing the right thing by trying to help him manage his smartphone dependency. It is not going to be easy for either of you, but there are definite strategies you can employ to make the smartphone a blessing again, and not a curse.

First of all, you need to help him to stop compulsively checking his smartphone. Tell

him to _____

_____

There are also things he can do to alleviate the anxiety he feels when he doesn't have

his phone nearby. For example, _____

_____

If one of his problems is that information is constantly available to him, I suggest _____

_____

_____

Finally, to help him stop using the phone at inappropriate times, you could tell him to

_____

_____

If your husband is able to implement these strategies, he (and you) will see a big change. He will feel more relaxed and more aware of his surroundings. His relationship with friends, family, and co-workers may also improve. I hope this advice helps, and I wish you and your husband good luck overcoming this problem.

Helpful Hannah

GO TO MyEnglishLab *TO CHECK WHAT YOU LEARNED.*

VOCABULARY

REVIEW

Complete the sentences with the words in the boxes.

diminish	relent	trigger	wean away from

1. For some people, boredom often can _____ the need to check their smartphone to see if they have any new e-mail or news updates.

2. Asking employees to make an effort to _____ the amount of time they spend on their smartphones is one strategy that businesses are employing.

3. Although it is difficult, these employees report that they have been able to slowly _____ themselves _____ their smartphones.

4. Despite the fact that I did not believe my son needed a smartphone, his constant begging for one caused me to _____ and buy him one.

anxiety	dependency	devices	twitching	urge

5. Some students report that sitting in class can trigger a(n) _____ to check their smartphones for news updates and e-mail.

6. In the past, people kept connected through their PC or laptop, but today there are many new _____, such as tablets, mini-laptops, and smartphones, that allow people to stay connected at all times.

7. Many professionals say they would experience "a great deal of _____" if they lost their smartphone and couldn't replace it for a week.

8. Scientists disagree on whether smartphone _____ can really be considered an addiction.

9. Some signs of heavy smartphone usage can be mental—loss of concentration, inability to focus on your surroundings—and others can be physical, such as _____ and headaches from eye strain.

compulsive	conscious	dysfunction	influx	literally	temptation

10. Although extreme smartphone usage may not actually be an addiction, there are signs, such as focusing on your phone at inappropriate times, that it may be a(n) _____.

11. In order to cut down on your smartphone dependency, you need to be able to resist the _____ to constantly check it for updates and e-mail.

12. You might not be _____ of it, but your constant checking behavior is not allowing you to concentrate on your work.

13. In the case of an emergency, your smartphone can _____ save your life.

14. _____ use of electronic devices can lead to physical ailments such as tendonitis, carpal tunnel syndrome, and eye strain.

15. The constant _____ of new information is one of the reasons that people compulsively check their phones.

EXPAND

Look at the boldfaced words and phrases in the following sentences. They have similar meanings but different degrees of intensity. In each sentence one of the words has a "stronger" meaning. Circle the word or phrase with the stronger meaning.

1. Many people feel the **urge / compulsion** to check their smartphones up to 35 times a day.

2. When I misplace my phone, I **search / look** for it until I find it.

3. His smartphone usage could be considered a(n) **addiction / dependency**.

4. For some people, being in class can **cause / trigger** a need to check their phone for news updates.

5. Because my wife is constantly checking her smartphone, I feel as if she is **ignoring me / tuning me out**.

6. Last night during dinner, my brother was **repeatedly / frequently** checking his email on his phone.

7. As a result of her continuous phone checking at the beach, I feel like my sister was **blinded to / not aware of** the beauty of our surroundings.

8. After I expressed my concerns to her, she made a **commitment / decision** to wean herself away from her phone.

(continued on next page)

9. The smartphone, more than any other gadget, **steals / takes** from us the opportunity to maintain our attention, to engage in **thought / contemplation** and reflection.

10. I **dislike / can't stand** when people interrupt a conversation to answer their smartphone.

11. If you know you are not strong enough to resist the temptation of constantly checking your e-mail, you should probably **shun / avoid** people who constantly text you.

CREATE

Imagine you are the person answering each question. How would you respond? On a separate piece of paper, write answers using the words given. Change the word form or tense if necessary.

1. **compulsion, influx, trigger, urge**

   To a manager or professional surveyed by Leslie Perlow, PhD (Reading One)
   Why are you constantly checking your smartphone from the moment you wake up until you go to bed, even when you are on vacation?

2. **commitment, conscious, diminishing, wean away from**

   To Susan Davis, author of Addicted to Your Smartphone? *(Reading One)*
   How are you able to manage your smartphone usage, and what effect did it have on your life?

3. **dependency, dysfunction, temptation, withdrawal**

   To David Greenfield PhD, author of Virtual Addiction: Help for Netheads, Cyber Freaks, and Those Who Love Them *(Reading One)*
   Why don't you consider extreme smartphone usage a true addiction?

4. **anxiety, contemplation, dependency, diminishing, ensure**

   To a businessman or businesswoman who participated in the Predictable Time Off (PTO) *experiment run by Dr. Perlow (Reading One)*
   What was the effect on your business and on your life of taking predictable time off (PTO)?

5. **can't stand, device, relent, repeatedly, twitching**

   To the ten-year-old boy who went electronic-free for a week (Reading Two)
   At the start of the week, what did you think of your mother's idea of going without electronics? How did the way you feel change as the week progressed?

■■■■■■■■■■■■■■■■■■■■■■■■■■■■■■■■■■■■■ *GO TO* MyEnglishLab *FOR MORE VOCABULARY PRACTICE.*

GRAMMAR

1 Examine these three sentences and answer the questions with a partner.

   a. <u>When we get back to our cabin</u>, I give my son his book.

   b. <u>You should turn off smartphone alert signals to avoid temptation</u>.

   c. <u>If you can't give up your phone altogether</u>, what should you do?

  1. What is the verb in the underlined section of each sentence?

  2. What is the difference between *get* and *get back*?

  3. What is the difference between *turn* and *turn off*?

  4. What is the difference between *give* and *give up*?

PHRASAL VERBS

  1. A **phrasal verb** consists of a verb and a particle (an adverb or preposition). The combination often has a meaning that is different from the meaning of the separate parts. Phrasal verbs are often used in everyday communication.

  2. Phrasal verbs (also called two-part or two-word verbs) combine a verb with a **particle**.

Verb	+	Particle	=	Meaning
go	+	back	=	return
tune	+	out	=	ignore
get	+	up	=	stand

  3. Some phrasal verbs (also called three-part or three-word verbs) combine with a **preposition**.

Phrasal Verb	+	Preposition	=	Meaning
come up	+	with	=	imagine or invent
think back	+	on	=	remember
wean away	+	from	=	stop (gradually)
look up	+	to	=	admire someone

  4. Some phrasal verbs are **transitive**. They take a direct object. Many (two-word) transitive phrasal verbs are **separable**. This means the verb and the particle can be separated by the direct object.

   She **tuned** **out** her husband.
      [verb] [particle] [object]

   She **tuned** her husband **out**.
      [verb] [object] [particle]

(continued on next page)

5. However, when the direct object is a pronoun, it must go between the verb and the particle.

She   **picked**   it   **up.**
        [verb]   [object]   [particle]

NOT

She   **picked**   up   **it.**
        [verb]   [particle]   [object]

6. Some phrasal verbs are **intransitive**. They do not take a direct object. Intransitive phrasal verbs are always **inseparable**. This means that the verb and particle are never separated.

I liked our vacation on Cortes Island. I want to   **go**   **back**   next year.
                                             [verb]   [particle]

7. The words in a phrasal verb are usually common, but their meanings change when the words are used together. Therefore, it can be difficult to guess the meaning of the verb from its individual parts.

call off	=	cancel
get together with	=	meet

8. Some phrasal verbs have more than one meaning.

She **took off** her jacket.	=	She **removed** her jacket.
She **took off** for work at 7:00 A.M.	=	She **departed** for work.
She **took** a day **off** from using her smartphone.	=	She **didn't** use her smartphone for a day.

9. Some verbs are combined with different particles or prepositions. Each combination creates a phrasal verb with a different meaning.

She **turned down** the volume on the phone.	=	She **lowered** the volume on the phone.
She **turned on** the phone.	=	She **started** the phone.
Smartphone technology has **turned up** in many new devices.	=	Smartphone technology has **appeared** in many new devices.
It **turned out** that the PTO method worked very well.	=	It **resulted** that the PTO method worked very well.
His smartphone use **turned into** a problem.	=	His smartphone use **became** a problem.
Using his smartphone, he **turned in** his application online.	=	Using his smartphone, he **submitted** his application online.

2 Work in a small group. Complete the sentences with the word or phrase from the box that has the same meaning as the underlined phrasal verb.

become popular	examine	~~ignore~~	persuade

1. Because my brothers are constantly checking their phones, they often <u>tune</u> me <u>out</u> when I am speaking to them. _ignore_____

2. The writer of *Unplugging Wired Kids* (Reading Two) had to <u>talk</u> her family <u>into</u> not using electronics for a week. _____

3. You should <u>check out</u> this new grammar app I downloaded to my smartphone.

   _____

4. Smartphones are starting to <u>catch on</u> all over the world. _____

conduct	discard	like	postpone

5. The Pew Research Center plans to <u>carry out</u> a new smartphone survey next year.

   _____

6. Although I know I should take an electronic-free week soon, I am going to <u>put</u> it <u>off</u> until next month. _____

7. Don't <u>throw</u> your phone <u>away</u> just because you are using it too much. Instead, be disciplined in your usage. _____

8. Although, at first, Americans were only moderately interested in smartphone technology, now they are starting to <u>take to</u> it. _____

(continued on next page)

cancel	invent	meet	return

9. Sometimes I think we need to get back to the old days before smartphones were invented. _____

10. I want to come up with new ways to entertain myself, so I am not so reliant on my smartphone. _____

11. We ought to actually get together with friends instead of just texting and e-mailing them. _____

12. I just received a text from Mr. Martin. He says he thinks they are going to call off the 3:00 meeting. _____

appear	become	extinguish/stop	start

13. Try using the predictable time off strategy, so your smartphone dependency doesn't turn into a problem. _____

14. Don't forget to turn off your phone when you are in class or in a meeting.

_____

15. I'm going to turn on the computer to see if there are any news updates.

_____

16. Although a few years ago they weren't so popular, smartphones are beginning to turn up all over the world. _____

3 Complete the paragraph with phrasal verbs from Exercise 2 on pages 247–248 and the grammar box on pages 245–246 in place of the verbs in parentheses. Be sure to use the correct verb tense.

When I _____ my first year in college, it is difficult for me to understand
　　　1. (remember)
how addicted I was to online gaming. At the time, I didn't know it would _____
　　　　　　　　　　　　　　　　　　　　　　　　　　　　　　　　2. (become)
such an enormous problem. I started online gaming in high school, and, in fact, I didn't

_____ it immediately. Slowly, the amount of time I spent online increased,
　　3. (like)
and gaming became my number one priority. I would _____ excuses not
　　　　　　　　　　　　　　　　　　　　　　　　　　4. (invent)
to go to social and sports events. I would say I was sick or had too much homework when,

in fact, I was gaming. When I did _____ friends, all I could think about
　　　　　　　　　　　　　　　　5. (meet)
was _____ to my computer. As soon as I got home, I would immediately
　　6. (returning)
_____ my computer and stay up all night playing with my cyber-friends.
　　7. (start)
Reality finally hit. I was not _____ assignments and was missing class
　　　　　　　　　　　　　　　8. (submitting)
because I couldn't wake up in the morning. My parents realized I had a problem and told

me I was _____ my life _____. Eventually, they were
　　　　　　9. (discarding)
able to _____ me _____ seeing an addiction therapist. I
　　　　10. (persuade)
_____ myself _____ my dependency, but it wasn't easy. One
　11. (slowly stopped)
thing that helped was that my friends did not abandon me. I am lucky that, because of my

therapist, family, and friends, everything _____ all right, and now I am doing
　　　　　　　　　　　　　　　　　　　　　　12. (resulted)
well in school.

■■■■■■■■■■■■■■■ GO TO MyEnglishLab FOR MORE GRAMMAR PRACTICE AND TO CHECK WHAT YOU LEARNED.

FINAL WRITING TASK

In this unit, you read about the negative consequences of smartphone dependency as well as the positive consequences of managing smartphone use.

You are going to **write a cause-and-effect essay focusing on the effects that another technology used today has had on its users and on society**, such as Tablets (iPad®, Galaxy®), e-readers (Kindle®, Nook®), MP3 players, and GPS. Use the vocabulary and grammar from the unit.*

PREPARE TO WRITE: Using a Flowchart

A **flowchart** shows how a series of actions, events, or parts of a system are related. Look at the flowchart showing the effects of smartphones. Which effects are positive? Which are negative? Some of the effects cause another effect and in some cases a further effect, like a chain.

1 In your opinion, are these effects positive, negative, or both? In a corner of each box, mark them as (**+**), (**–**), or (**+ –**). Then discuss with a partner. Did you agree with your partner?

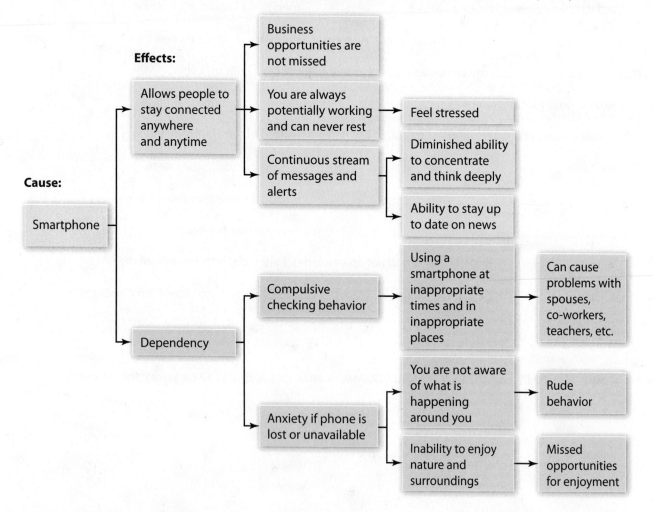

---

* For Alternative Writing Topics, see page 259. These topics can be used in place of the writing topic for this unit or as homework. The alternative topics relate to the theme of the unit but may not target the same grammar or rhetorical structures taught in the unit.

2 Create a flowchart of the effects of a technology you would like to discuss in your essay. Mark the effects as positive, negative, or both.

WRITE: A Cause and Effect Essay

A **cause-and-effect essay** discusses the causes (reasons) for something, the effects (results), or both causes and effects. Your essay will focus primarily on the effects a particular technology has had on the user and society, not the causes leading up to its creation.

1 Read the excerpt from Reading One. Then complete the cause-and-effect chart.

People keep their smartphones near them "from the moment they wake up until the moment they go to bed," and throughout that time the devices provide an almost continuous stream of messages and alerts as well as easy access to a myriad of compelling information sources.

"By design," [Carr] says, "it's an environment of almost constant interruptions and distractions. The smartphone, more than any other gadget, steals from us the opportunity to maintain our attention, to engage in contemplation and reflection, or even to be alone with our thoughts." Carr, who writes extensively in *The Shallows* about the way that computer technology, in general, may be diminishing our ability to concentrate and think deeply, does not have a smartphone.

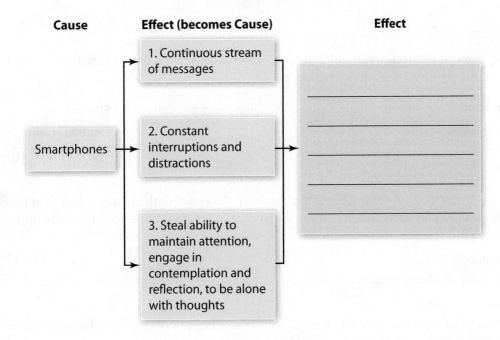

There are many ways to organize causes and effects and show how they are related. A cause may have only one effect, multiple effects, or cause a chain of effects.

A **simple** cause and effect:

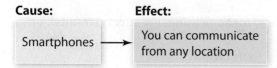

Cause:
Smartphones

Effect:
You can communicate from any location

One cause with **multiple effects**:

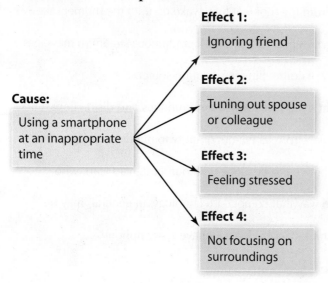

Cause:
Using a smartphone at an inappropriate time

Effect 1:
Ignoring friend

Effect 2:
Tuning out spouse or colleague

Effect 3:
Feeling stressed

Effect 4:
Not focusing on surroundings

A cause leads to an effect, which in turn can become a cause for a new effect. This is called a **causal chain**.

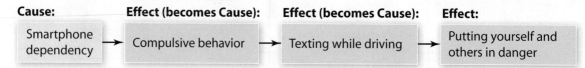

Cause:
Smartphone dependency

Effect (becomes Cause):
Compulsive behavior

Effect (becomes Cause):
Texting while driving

Effect:
Putting yourself and others in danger

If your essay has a causal chain, describe all steps of the chain so the reader can fully understand how the causes and effects relate. In other words, you cannot jump directly from the initial cause to the final effect.

Incorrect example

Because of smartphone dependency, you are putting yourself and others in danger.

Correct example

Smartphone dependency may lead to compulsive behavior. This behavior may include using your smartphone at inappropriate times. For example, some people feel compelled to text all the time, even when driving. This behavior may put you and others in danger.

2 Answer the questions with a partner.

1. Look at the flowchart from Prepare to Write, Exercise 1, on page 250. What are some examples of multiple effects of the technology that you chose?

2. What is an example of a causal chain?

3. Look at your flowchart from Prepare to Write, Exercise 2, on page 251. Are there examples of multiple effects and causal chains? Look at your partner's flowchart. Can you find examples of multiple effects and causal chains?

3 Use an outline to organize your cause-and-effect essay. Look at the outline of paragraphs 1–8 in Reading Two. Note that the author sometimes introduces a cause first and then writes about the effect. At other times, the author starts with the effect and then states the cause. In addition, a cause can have multiple effects.

CAUSE EFFECT	I. Writer wants her family to enjoy an electronic-free vacation.
	A. They go to a remote island in the wilderness of British Columbia, Canada.
CAUSE EFFECT	1. Writer's son is suffering iPhone withdrawal.
CAUSE	a. Son cannot enjoy the beauty of their surroundings.
EFFECT	2. Husband and daughter are doing fine because they have found things to do that don't rely on electronics.
CAUSE EFFECT (BECOMES CAUSE)	a. They are suffering no withdrawal symptoms.
	3. Time passes
MULTIPLE EFFECTS (1–3)	a. Son seems to have forgotten about iPhone.
	1. He spends an enjoyable day at the beach.
	2. He reads in the garden.
	3. He stays active swimming and hiking.

4 Complete the cause-and-effect outline for the Managing Your Smartphone Use section in Reading One (paragraphs 25–33). Use the information in the box.

Increased collaboration	More aware of surroundings	Slowly diminished time between checking	More relaxed
Stopped using phone for social media	Took Predictable Time Off	Stopped using phone for texting and e-mailing while driving	Better work—life balance

CAUSE
 	
EFFECT (BECOMES CAUSE)
MULTIPLE EFFECTS (1–3)
	I. The Boston Group participated in an experiment run by Leslie Perlow, PhD.
	
	A. _____
	   1. Increased efficiency
	
	   2. _____
	
	   3. _____

MULTIPLE CAUSES (A–D)
 	
MULTIPLE EFFECTS (A–D)
	II. Writer's plan to manage own smartphone use by using multiple strategies
	A. _____
	B. Stopped using phone for web browsing
	C. _____
	D. _____
	   1. Overall effects
	     a. Concentrating better
	
	     a. _____
	
	     b. _____
	     c. More focused use of smartphone

5 Make an outline about the effects the technology you have chosen has had on its users and on society. Think about how you will organize and order the causes and effects from your flowchart. Make sure to include background information, a thesis, and a conclusion. Your conclusion could be a prediction, a solution, or a summary of key points. Share your outline with a partner and suggest changes, if necessary.

6 Now write the first draft of your cause-and-effect essay. Use the information in Prepare to Write, your flowchart, and your outline to plan your essay. Be sure to use grammar and vocabulary from the unit.

REVISE: Signal Words: Subordinators, Prepositional Phrases, and Transitions

Certain words act as signals in sentences to show cause-and-effect relationships. Sentences in cause-and-effect essays have two clauses. The **cause clause** explains why something happened. The **effect clause** explains the result of what happened.

Cause: Because more and more people have smartphones today,

Effect: people have more and more interruptions in their lives.

SUBORDINATORS, PREPOSITIONAL PHRASES, AND TRANSITIONS

Subordinators, prepositional phrases, and transitions show the relationship between the two clauses.

Introducing the Cause		Introducing the Effect
SUBORDINATORS	PREPOSITIONAL PHRASES	TRANSITIONS
since	due to (the fact that)	as a result
because	due to + (noun)	consequently
as	as a consequence of + (noun)	so
	as a result of + (noun)	for this reason
	because of (the fact that)	therefore
	because of + (noun)	thus
		as a consequence

Stating Causes with Subordinators and Prepositional Phrases

- The **cause clause** is introduced by *because, since, as.* When the cause is at the beginning of the sentence, use a comma (,).

  Because you can receive a continuous stream of messages and alerts on a smartphone, you are able to stay up-to-date on news anytime and anyplace.

- When the cause is at the end of the sentence, do not use a comma.

  You are able to stay up-to-date on news anytime and anyplace **because you can receive a continuous stream of messages and alerts on a smartphone**.

Stating Effects with Transitions

- The **effect** is introduced by words such as *consequently, as a result, for this reason, therefore,* and *thus*. Cause and effect can be combined into one sentence by using a semicolon (;) and a comma (,).

  You can receive a continuous stream of messages and alerts on a smartphone; **consequently, you are able to stay up-to-date on news anytime and anyplace**.

- They can also be two separate sentences.

  You can receive a continuous stream of messages and alerts on a smartphone. **As a result, you are able to stay up-to-date on news anytime and anyplace.**

- Be careful. A sentence with *so* uses only a comma.

  You can receive a continuous stream of messages and alerts on a smartphone, **so you are able to stay up-to-date on news anytime and anyplace.**

1 Complete the paragraph based on the outline in Write, Exercise 3, page 253. Use appropriate subordinators and transitions.

The writer of the *Unplugging* article wanted her family to enjoy an electronic-free vacation;

_____, she took them to a remote island in the wilderness of British Columbia. On the

first day of the vacation, her son couldn't enjoy the beauty of their surroundings _____

he was suffering from acute iPhone withdrawal. On the other hand, her husband and daughter

were doing fine. They had found things to do that didn't rely on electronics, _____

they suffered no withdrawal symptoms. As time passed, her son forgot about his iPhone.

_____, he was able to have a good time at the beach and enjoy reading. He was also

able to have fun hiking and swimming _____ he was no longer thinking only about

his iPhone.

2 Write **C** (cause) or **E** (effect) for each set of sentences. Then combine the sentences two ways. Use commas and semicolons correctly.

1. __C__ Employees at usemyphone.com started taking predictable time off.

   __E__ There was increased efficiency and collaboration among employees at usemyphone.com.

   (as a result) _Employees at usemyphone.com started taking predictable time off; as_

   a result, there was increased efficiency and collaboration among employees.

   (because) _Because employees at usemyphone.com started taking predictable_

   time off, there was increased efficiency and collaboration among employees.

2. _____ It is easy to stay in contact with people even when they are not at home.
   _____ Many people have smartphones.

   (since) _____

   _____

   (therefore) _____

   _____

3. _____ People cannot concentrate or think deeply.

_____ Smartphones create an environment of constant interruptions and distractions.

(consequently) _____

_____

(due to the fact that) _____

_____

4. _____ There are approximately 40,000 medical apps available today for smartphones and tablets.

_____ It is like having a health expert at your fingertips.

(as a result) _____

_____

(thus) _____

_____

5. _____ Smartphone apps can remotely turn on and off the heat in your home when you are out.

_____ Homeowners can save money and help to cut down on the use of fossil fuels.

(because) _____

_____

(so) _____

_____

6. _____ The number of hardcover and paperback books being sold has declined.

_____ Many people use tablets and e-readers for most of their reading.

(for this reason) _____

_____

(because of the fact that) _____

_____

3 Look at your first draft. Add cause-and-effect signal words as needed.

GO TO MyEnglishLab *FOR MORE SKILL PRACTICE.*

EDIT: Writing the Final Draft

Go to MyEnglishLab and write the final draft of your essay. Carefully edit it for grammatical and mechanical errors, such as spelling, capitalization, and punctuation. Make sure you use some of the grammar and vocabulary from the unit. Use the checklist to help you write your final draft. Then submit your essay to your teacher.

FINAL DRAFT CHECKLIST

❏ Does the essay have a clear topic and controlling idea?

❏ Does the essay follow your outline?

❏ Does the essay have effective support and details or examples?

❏ Does the essay have appropriate cause-and-effect sentences?

❏ Does the essay have an effective or thought-provoking conclusion?

❏ Did you use phrasal verbs correctly?

❏ Have you used vocabulary from the unit?

UNIT PROJECT

Work with a partner to conduct a survey about the evolution of technological devices and then research them. Prepare a presentation for the class. Follow these steps:

STEP 1: Create a survey in which you ask participants about their observations concerning the evolution of (choose one) personal computers, laptops, tablets, or cell phones.

Here are a few questions you might ask. Add some of your own.

1. How long have you owned a _____?

2. What changes have taken place with this device?

3. Has the cost changed? How?

4. Has the size changed? How?

5. Have the features changed? How?

6. What do you think are the most significant technological advances for this device?

7. What technological advances of this device have affected you most?

8. Do you feel the need to keep buying the latest model of the device? Explain.

STEP 2: On the Internet, research the electronic devices the survey participants talk about. For example, if they discuss personal computers, find out what the earliest personal/desktop computers looked like and were capable of doing. Be sure to include information about cost, size, features, availability, etc.

STEP 3: Using the information you learned from the survey participants and what you learned from your Internet research, create a PowerPoint™ presentation for the class.

ALTERNATIVE WRITING TOPICS

Write an essay about one of the topics. Use the vocabulary and grammar from the unit.

1. Try to go smartphone-free (or do without another electronic device) for at least two days. Write about your experience. Did you suffer any withdrawal symptoms? What was hard about the experiment? Were there any benefits to being tech-free? Explain.

2. Computer technologies have both advantages and disadvantages for their users and for society in general. What do you think are the three biggest advantages and the three biggest disadvantages? Explain.

■■■■■■■■■■■■■■■■■■■■■■■■■■■■■■ *GO TO* MyEnglishLab *TO WRITE ABOUT ONE OF THE ALTERNATIVE TOPICS, WATCH A VIDEO ABOUT DISCONNECTING FROM WORK EMAIL AFTER HOURS, AND TAKE THE UNIT 8 ACHIEVEMENT TEST.* ■■■

GRAMMAR BOOK REFERENCES

NorthStar: Reading and Writing Level 4, Fourth Edition	Focus on Grammar Level 4, Fourth Edition	Azar's Understanding and Using English Grammar, Fourth Edition
Unit 1 Modals and Semi-Modals	**Unit 15** Modals and Similar Expressions: Review **Unit 16** Advisability in the Past **Unit 17** Speculations and Conclusions about the Past	**Chapter 11** The Passive: 11-1, 11-2, 11-3
Unit 2 Gerunds and Infinitives	**Unit 9** Gerunds and Infinitives: Review and Expansion	**Chapter 14** Gerunds and Infinitives, Part 1 **Chapter 15** Gerunds and Infinitives, Part 2
Unit 3 Past Unreal Conditionals	**Unit 24** Past Unreal Conditionals	**Chapter 20** Conditional Sentences and Wishes: 20-1, 20-4
Unit 4 Identifying Adjective Clauses	**Unit 13** Adjective Clauses with Subject Relative Pronouns **Unit 14** Adjective Clauses with Object Relative Pronouns or *When* and *Where*	**Chapter 13** Adjective Clauses
Unit 5 Contrasting the Simple Past, Present Perfect, and Present Perfect Continuous	**Unit 3** Simple Past, Present Perfect, and Present Perfect Progressive	**Chapter 1** Overview of Verb Tenses 1-1, 1-3, 1-4, 1-5 **Chapter 2** Present and Past; Simple and Progressive: 2-7, 2-8 **Chapter 3** Perfect and Perfect Progressive Tenses: 3-1, 3-4

NorthStar: Reading and Writing Level 4, Fourth Edition	Focus on Grammar Level 4, Fourth Edition	Azar's Understanding and Using English Grammar, Fourth Edition
Unit 6 Concessions	See *Focus on Grammar 5, Fourth Edition*, Unit 19: Adverb Clauses	**Chapter 19** Connectives that Express Cause and Effect, Contrast, and Condition: 19-6
Unit 7 Direct and Indirect Speech	**Unit 25** Direct and Indirect Speech	**Chapter 12** Noun Clauses: 12-6, 12-7
Unit 8 Phrasal Verbs	**Unit 11** Phrasal Verbs: Review **Unit 12** Phrasal Verbs: Separable and Inseparable	**Appendix** Unit E: Preposition Combinations See also Appendix B-1: Phrasal Verbs in Azar's *Fundamentals of English Grammar, Fourth Edition*

UNIT WORD LIST

The Unit Word List is a summary of key vocabulary from the Student Book. Words followed by an asterisk (*) are on the Academic Word List.

UNIT 1

anxious	image*
assimilate	interaction*
benefit*	persistence*
compensate*	predictable*
disabled	retain*
emerging*	savant
estimate*	sum*
expertise*	transforms*
flexible*	

UNIT 2

abandonment*	misery
accountable	poverty
defeated	self-reliance
dilapidated	shame
gives up	sordid
hopelessness	struggle
laborious	tormented
meager	yearned for

UNIT 3

advocate*	interaction*
alternative*	interpreting*
aspects*	linked*
consensus*	potential*
consulted*	reliable*
conventional*	revolutionized*
elicit	risk factor*
environment*	skeptical
impact*	

UNIT 4

achieve*	discern
acquired*	obvious*
apparently*	perception*
approach*	sensory
behavior	trait
category*	unconscious
cognition	unique*
confront	viable
controversy*	

UNIT 5

awesome
chilly
disparate
emphatic*
fond of
immeasurably
impetuous
inevitably*
insufferable

loveless
presumptuous
punctually
radically*
tolerable
ultimately*
utterly
vigorous
worrisome

UNIT 6

admiring
challenge*
determined
devote*
donate
fulfilling
indignation
inspired
manage

opposed
oxymoron
passion
proposal
proudly
resentful
satisfaction
thrilled

UNIT 7

adjusted*
analyzes*
anticipation*
assumption*
collaboration
crucial*
disappointed
dispute
diversity*

enhances*
issue*
overall*
sector*
significantly*
subsequent*
via*
virtual*

UNIT 8

anxiety
compulsive
conscious
dependency
devices*
diminishing*
dysfunction
ensures*
influx

literally
relent
temptation
trigger*
twitching
urge
wean away from
withdrawal

THE PHONETIC ALPHABET

Consonant Symbols			
/b/	be	/t/	to
/d/	do	/v/	van
/f/	father	/w/	will
/g/	get	/y/	yes
/h/	he	/z/	zoo, busy
/k/	keep, can	/θ/	thanks
/l/	let	/ð/	then
/m/	may	/ʃ/	she
/n/	no	/ʒ/	vision, Asia
/p/	pen	/tʃ/	child
/r/	rain	/dʒ/	join
/s/	so, circle	/ŋ/	long

Vowel Symbols			
/ɑ/	far, hot	/iy/	we, mean, feet
/ɛ/	met, said	/ey/	day, late, rain
/ɔ/	tall, bought	/ow/	go, low, coat
/ə/	son, under	/uw/	too, blue
/æ/	cat	/ay/	time, buy
/ɪ/	ship	/aw/	house, now
/ʊ/	good, could, put	/oy/	boy, coin

you don't
CRY
out loud
The Lily Isaacs story

LILY ISAACS with **SHAWN SMUCKER**

Praise for *You Don't Cry Out Loud*

Lily Isaacs book is one of the most incredible stories that I have ever read, and everyone now has an opportunity to share in this magnificent journey and testimony. From roots embedded in the ashes of the Holocaust to a triumphant life of music, Lily has lived a life of trials like no other and her unending faith in Jesus Christ has brought her through to unimaginable blessings. . . . and victories! Yes, I do LOVE the Isaacs. They are the finest singing group I have ever heard, and I just adore LILY! She is a constant blessing to ALL who are fortunate enough to know her. *You Don't Cry Out Loud* is an amazingly well-written story of one very special life. . . . Be prepared. . . . You will never read another book quite like this one! It just might change your life!

— Joseph S Bonsall, 40-year member of the
Oak Ridge Boys and author of *GI Joe and Lillie*

If ever there was a story that has all the elements, it is Lily Isaac's story: the Holocaust, ill-fated love, alcoholism, teenage angst, urban ethnic ghetto life, Greenwich Village folk-music scene in the sixties. It is the stuff of which movies are made. Amazingly, it is all the true-life story of the smooth-singing gospel-bluegrass matriarch who, with her three children, has endeared herself to audiences around the world. Lily's memoir will break your heart, make you laugh, inspire your soul. And it will explain why she looks so adoringly at her grandchildren, treasures every friendship, and savors every day she has to live.

— Gloria Gaither

How did a Jewish girl from the Bronx, the daughter of two Holocaust survivors, become a groundbreaking presence in gospel music? Lily Isaacs' story is both heart-wrenching and heartwarming. She holds nothing back as she reveals the laughter and tears, joys and sorrows of a journey that could have only been accomplished with the guidance of the loving hand of an almighty God. *You Don't Cry Out Loud* lets us know that every challenge can be overcome; every trial will yield to persistent faith; every foreboding valley will give way to the sunlit upland of a brighter tomorrow. You will be inspired, challenged, energized, and changed as she shares her life with you.

— Pastor Rod Parsley

We've known Lily Isaacs and her talented musical family, the Isaacs, for many years. We knew that Lily's parents were survivors of the Holocaust. And we have seen Lily face several personal trials (including breast cancer) with dignity, courage, and great faith. We did not know, however, what a wonderfully gifted writer she is! In her autobiography, *You Don't Cry Out Loud*, Lily pulled us into the story in a way that was totally captivating and very moving. Her life story is a testament to the love and mercy of GOD and the grace of our Lord Jesus Christ. We were inspired and encouraged, and we know you will be too!

— Sharon White and Ricky Skaggs

A story that people of all faiths, all walks of life, will enjoy! So inspiring and so uplifting — it will transform hearts. Anyone can see how God works in people's lives through this amazing story I just couldn't put down! We live in a world that is filled with immorality and godlessness . . . this is a book that is filled with hope to lift you out of that darkness. I love and admire the Isaacs, and this is a book you'll want to carry with you so that when you feel down or hopeless, reading it will lift your heart again!

— Terry Bradshaw, television sports analyst,
NFL Hall of Fame member

"Mama" Isaacs is my dear, sweet friend. I always sit with her backstage at the Gaither Gatherings. I always knock on the Isaacs' bus door at concerts, just hoping "Mama" is there. She is a very special spirit. She passed down her "talent DNA" to Becky, Sonya, and Benjie, her three incredibly talented kids. She always has a word of hope and good cheer. She is a mensch. (Google it, Christians.) And now she has written a book. She emailed a few pages to me and asked if I would say a few things about it. Well, here's what I have to say about *You Don't Cry Out Loud* — I can't wait for my autographed copy to arrive. I only had to read the first few pages in the email to know that she is a real wordsmith and a great storyteller . . . and she has a great story to tell. Speaking of stories, here's my story and I'm stickin' to it . . . I LOVE MAMA ISAACS!! After you read *You Don't Cry Out Loud*, you will love her too. KEEP THE FAITH,

— Larry Gatlin

P. S. Oops . . . almost forgot . . . she makes a mean fried bologna sandwich.

First printing: May 2014
Fourth printing: January 2018

New Leaf Press is a division of the New Leaf Publishing Group, Inc.

ISBN: 978-0-89221-724-3
ISBN: 978-1-61458-408-7 (digital)
Library of Congress Number: 2014938158

Cover by Diana Bogardus

Please consider requesting that a copy of this volume be purchased by your local library system.

Printed in the United States of America

Please visit our website for other great titles:
www.newleafpress.com

For information regarding author interviews,
please contact the publicity department at (870) 438-5288.

New Leaf Press
A Division of New Leaf Publishing Group
www.newleafpress.com

DEDICATION

This book is dedicated to my family who never survived WWII—My grandparents, aunts, uncles, and cousins who were killed before I ever had a chance to know them. I love you all.

To all the Holocaust victims who died or are still alive and still carry the scars of that nightmare.

To my dear father Oscar Fishman, who died in 1978 — Daddy, I will always love you. I'm so sorry I didn't understand your pain. I was young and self-absorbed in my own life's drama. I miss you always.

To my mother, still living and still a fighter at age 94 — Even with dementia you still have more energy and "chutzpah" than anyone I know! Mom, I love you very much and respect the decisions and sacrifices you have made in your life to give Hy and me a better life.

To my brother, Hy . . . my baby brother — We've been through so much together throughout our lives. I'm proud of the man you are today. You are an amazing husband, father, and soon-to-be grandpa! I love you.

To my wonderful children Ben, Sonya, and Becky — You three are my life! I admire and respect you. I am the most blessed mother in the world. Your talents are endless, and you have all become amazing human beings. I also want to thank Mindy (my daughter-in-law) and John and Jimmy (my sons-in-law) for being a part of my life. I couldn't ask for better spouses for my children, and you all have given me the joys of being a grandmother to some beautiful grandbabies! I couldn't ask for a more loving family. You have "loved me through the hardest times of my life." We've shared tears and laughter and worshiped God together. We've traveled many thousands of miles together, and you are MY ROCKS! I can't imagine life without any of you. Sonya, thank you for helping finish my book — you are a talented writer.

To my grandchildren, Levi, Jacob, Madeleine, Cameron, Kyra, Jakobi, and Ayden — you are truly a gift to me, and I am so proud of all of you. I love you.

To Joe — although we have been divorced for many years now, I'm grateful for the years we've had together. I probably would have never found the Lord if we hadn't met in NYC. And we wouldn't have had our three children that we both adore. We have shared many hard times and good times. Thanks for being a friend to my parents and Hy and for being a good father to our children. Thank you for sharing your family with me all these years. The Isaacs family are wonderful people, and I've been blessed to be a part of them all!

To Stacy — I'm grateful for you being a good stepmother to my kids and grandkids. I know this has been an overwhelming year, with the loss of your son, Jonas. My prayers are always with you and Jordan.

To Julie Beth and Little Joe — Thank you for being "my other kids!" I'm so thankful that you are a part of my life. I love you and your families, and I am proud of you and my other grandkids — Bradley & Ben, Daniel, Amanda, Megan, Dalton & Katie.

CONTENTS

FOREWORD BY ANDY ANDREWS

As an author, I am frequently asked to contribute things such as endorsements and forewords for friends of mine who have written books. I've come to learn that the old adage is true — everyone has a book in them.

This often puts me in an awkward position because, to be honest, many of the books I've been handed over the years should have stayed in the people who wrote them. Success in one field does not translate as seamlessly into publishing as many people think. Trust me — as someone who has seen his fair share of rejection letters from publishers (over 50 on my first book), I understand how difficult it is to break into this world.

So you can imagine the pleasant surprise I experienced upon reading the manuscript from my friend Lily Isaacs entitled *You Don't Cry Out Loud*.

Having seen Lily perform many times, I was no stranger to the immense amount of talent she possesses. I have seen her bring audiences to tears. She has the rare ability to open up the deepest wounds life has given us, only to heal them anew with a careful turn of phrase.

I knew she could do all these things on stage — but I had no idea she would be able to accomplish the same feat on paper.

I often like to remind folks that we're all either in a crisis, coming out of a crisis, or headed for a crisis. It's just part of being with us on this planet. *You Don't Cry Out Loud* is the rare book that is appropriate for all three of those seasons in life.

Lily Isaacs has experienced the full breadth of what life has to offer. Through the very best and the very worst, she has looked for — and found — opportunities of faith.

Regardless of the challenges you face in your life, you will never look at them the same after reading *You Don't Cry Out Loud*.

Andy Andrews is the *New York Times* best-selling author of *The Traveler's Gift* and *The Noticer*. He lives in Orange Beach, Alabama, with his wife, Polly, and their two sons.

Dear Dairy (Lenore),

This is my first day with you and I hope I will be able to confide in you the things I can't tell a single solitary sole.

There are some things I want to tell you and you should know.

I have an awful back. A crucked spin and one whole side sticks out and I hate it. I'm going to "many" doctors to get treatment and one doesn't know I'm going to the other. Dr Ludio is a very nice man. Ms. Cohen is a stinker.

I'm in love with

LOVE
MEMORANDUM

First entry of Lily's childhood diary.

CHAPTER ONE

I remember those Ohio winters: cold and biting with low gray skies and a harsh wind that swept over flat stretches of land. When the snow came, it stayed for weeks, white powder blowing around on the barren fields. At night the sky was crisp and clear, and you could see a million stars, each one lonely and still. More stars than I could ever see when I lived in the Bronx. The dark silhouettes of trees branched out against the moonlit sky, or storm clouds slipped from one end of the world to the other, drowning out the stars.

During those winters we all drew closer to the wood-burning stove in our Morrow, Ohio, home. Joe brought home scrap wood that he found where he worked at the Morrow Gravel Company, and when he opened the door and threw the wood inside the furnace, the flickering light would shine off the mirrors that lined one of our living room walls.

Evenings in that house bustled with life, filled with the sounds of children talking and arguing and plucking strings. Often our three children played with Joe's instruments. He left them lying around the house, cases open, knowing that curiosity would lead them to explore.

I made dinner. When Joe got home and opened the door, the cold winter air rushed in.

"Brrr," he said. "Cold out there today."

The kids crowded around him as he opened the furnace door and stoked the fire. Six-year-old Ben carried a piece of wood, happy to help. I held on to Sonya and Becky, four and three, so they wouldn't burn themselves. Air swept in on the coals and the flames glowed on the faces of the children, sparkling in their eyes.

The only sound on those evenings was the wind against the house, or the kids getting settled in for the night, or a quietly played instrument singing from the other room, one string at a time. When I finally caught up with the housework, I sat at one end of the couch and buried my toes in the tan, shag carpet. The dusk was so quiet and peaceful there, nothing like the Bronx where I grew up. But my mother would often call in the evenings, and her voice reminded me of the busy streets, the tiny apartment where I had grown up, and the bustling life of the city.

I remember one particular phone call in those early months of 1978.

The little phone on the end table beside the sofa rang. I answered quickly so it wouldn't wake the children.

"Hello?"

"Lily?"

"Hi, mom," I said, but there was something in the way she said my name that made me catch my breath. "Everything okay?"

"I'm not sure," she said in a hushed voice.

I pictured her there in her Bronx apartment. She was a small lady and so full of energy. It sounded like she was holding her hand over the phone, as if she tried to talk in secret.

"Mother, what's wrong?"

"It's your father. I don't think he's well."

"Why?" I asked. "What's going on?"

"This morning he got up, got dressed for work, and was about to walk out the door for work!"

"But he hasn't worked in five years!" I protested.

Silence from her end of the phone. I took a deep breath.

"What's wrong with him, Mother?"

"I don't know. He seems so out of it."

She sounded scared.

"What's he doing now?" I asked.

She paused.

"Well, he's sitting at the dining room table with his newspaper."

I could picture that, too, the way he sat there for hours every night looking through the Yiddish paper, not saying a word, just rustling from one page to the next.

"That seems normal enough to me," I said.

"No, Lily, he's not reading it. He's tearing it up into tiny, tiny pieces. He's shredding it. It's as if he's not even in the room."

I closed my eyes for a moment and sighed, wondering what was wrong.

"Mother, you have to get him to the doctor."

But both of us knew what a monumental task that might be. A recent hip surgery had him skittish about hospitals, and he had even quit smoking in an effort to avoid any further visits. I think his days in the concentration camps a half-century before led him to avoid any sort of confinement.

"I can't do it, Lily. He's too strong for me. I could barely keep him in the apartment this morning! He kept pushing toward the door."

She started crying quietly. I wished I was there with her. I could picture her tiny frame shoving with all her might as he tried to make it to a job he hadn't been at for five years. I wished someone could help her.

"What about Basha, Mother? Can't she help you?"

"I guess," she said.

"You have to get him to the hospital," I insisted. "Something is seriously wrong."

~ ~ ~ ~ ~

My father, born in Poland in 1912, spent his early years traveling with his father, a glazier. From town to town they went, working hard on tedious jobs. His own father drank, perhaps to ease the boredom of his life, perhaps to pass the time. I can picture my grandfather, at the end of a long day in a strange town, maybe sleeping outside or in a barn. I imagine him taking out a bottle and drinking to dull the pain of that life.

By the age of 14, my father also found solace in the bottle. I don't know if he had to sneak his drinks or if his own father gave them to him. I don't know if he, too, drank out of boredom or it was rebellion or that typical rushing to grow up. Whatever the case, his life consisted of traveling through the Polish countryside, working with glass during the day, then escaping with the bottle at night. My poor father. He never had much of a childhood.

What did he think, then, after the German invasion, when Jews began arriving from all over Europe to his hometown of Chenstechov, brought by the Nazis to six extermination camps established in Poland? My father rarely spoke of those long ago days. He kept his nightmares to himself. But when he occasionally told us stories, we grabbed on to them, desperate for some glimpse into our history.

I find great strength in the perseverance of my parents, a fortitude that wants to be told, that needs to be passed to my children and to their children. These are the things that are left to us, when our ancestors have already journeyed out of this life — memories and little stories and things to hold on to. Such things as these.

In September of 1942 the Nazis sent 39,000 Jews to Treblinka and killed the residents of Chenstochov's orphanage and its home for the elderly. My father's hometown was being disassembled, one human being at a time. Those who were not old or orphaned were taken as slaves to a munitions factory. Eventually, the ghetto would be emptied. Hitler's final solution.

Voices shouted through loudspeakers mounted on the back of the Nazi trucks.

"Everyone out! No one left behind! Out on the street! You may bring one small bag!"

The trucks stirred up dust as they rumbled through my father's neighborhood, and that dust floated through the open doors, settled on the abandoned furniture, and slipped down into the cracks in the floor.

"Everyone out!" the soldiers shouted in their foreign-sounding accents.

Soldiers ordered my father and his family to lie on the ground in the street, their hands on the back of their heads. They remained there at gunpoint for over ten hours, the hard ground making impressions in the sides of their faces. Tiny pebbles dug into their legs, their stomachs. They tried to hold their breath, afraid that even heavy breathing would gain unwanted attention. They willed their small children to lie still.

"Please, little one," I can imagine mothers pleading with their toddlers, tears in their eyes. "Please, little one, don't move."

They couldn't look around. They dared not move. Occasionally gunshots echoed through the ghetto — those who moved, those who grew restless or tired, were shot.

Finally the soldiers told them to get up. After that, they were separated from their families, some going here while others were told to go there. Other than one brother who he managed to stay with, my father never saw his family again. Not his siblings. Not his parents.

They were led to a train, endless chains of cattle cars sitting quietly on the iron tracks. I can imagine my father looking through the slats in the train car, watching the countryside roll away. The train took him away from Poland, away from his life, away from his family. He didn't know it at the time, but he was on his way into the heart of Germany, into the heart of the Nazi machine.

~ ~ ~ ~ ~

The telephone rang
"Hello?"
"Lily?"
"Mother! Did you get father to the hospital yet?"
It sounded quiet in the background. I could feel the emptiness in the apartment through the phone lines.

"Yes, yes, we did it. I tricked him, told him we were going downtown. When we got back to the hospital, I parked and your uncle and Aunt Basha helped me get him inside."

"He went in with you?"

"Not at first. He just sat there for a minute, stubborn as could be. But we pulled on him and told him he had to, so finally he came inside with us."

"So what did the doctor say?"

"His blood is poisoned, Lily. His kidneys are not working. They gave him a transfusion, Lily. Do you know what that is?"

"Yes, Mother."

"They gave him blood. Someone's clean blood."

"Is he okay now?" I asked. "What did they say?"

"He has to stay in the hospital for two or three days, and then he has to get dialysis three times a week."

"What does that mean, Mother? Every week? Will he get better?"

"I don't know," she whispered. "I don't know. I don't know what to do. He's too big for me. He still seems confused. How can I keep him inside? He's too big for me."

"I know, Mother."

"Lily," she began, then hesitated.

"Yes?"

"Lily, I think you should come here. I think we should look for a home for him to live in, somewhere safe. He's too big for me, Lily."

"Mother!" I said in surprise. Then I sighed. "That would kill him. He would hate it, you know that. He would think we didn't love him anymore."

"Please, Lily," she said. "Just come here and see him? Help me look. Maybe he will get better and we won't need a home for him. But I need your help."

~ ~ ~ ~ ~

For days my father stood on that train as it clicked and clacked across the Polish countryside. It was too full for anyone to sit or lie down. I can picture him, in his 20s, a young man whose quiet hope for some kind of future had evaporated in front of his eyes. I often wonder if he had a girlfriend or if he had his eye on someone before the soldiers came and took him away. I wonder what kind of friends he had, what they did for fun or how they spent what little leisure time they had.

But in a matter of hours, days, weeks, it all stopped: the games, the work, the courting, the marriages. Birth and death did not stop, but they were flipped upside-down: being pregnant, giving birth, was almost a curse in those days. And death, well, many would long for death.

My father was strong. All around him the weak and the sick and the old passed out or died, held up by the tightly packed bodies of those standing around them. They were not let off the train. There was no food. No toilets. The air in the car was filled with agonized moans and the stench of urine and feces. The smell of the dead.

It was the train to hell.

~ ~ ~ ~ ~

It was still dark when Joe, the kids, and I pulled out of our lane in Morrow, Ohio. The suitcases were packed, and the kids were excited to see their grandparents and the skyscrapers of New York City. But I felt nervous at the thought of returning home, as I always did in those days. I wanted my parents to accept my children, even though I had become a Christian, something which, in their minds, was an offense to their Jewish heritage. I wanted to be a source of pride to them, but in my mind I could only picture them shaking their finger at me.

We drove through Pennsylvania on roads with low-hanging branches and turned northeast toward New York. The sun was just beginning to soften the eastern sky when the city skyline appeared off in the distance. My heart warmed whenever I saw those buildings come into view, and I glanced at the back seat where all three kids slept, oblivious to everything. Their little mouths hung open, and their eyelids twitched as they dreamed.

The smells of the city greeted us as we pulled up to the corner of Waring Avenue and Bronx Park East: car exhaust and hot air blasting up from the subway mingled with the smell of fresh bread baking at the corner bakery. Even after all of those years, my parents lived in the same place, and so much about it was exactly the same as when I had left. Joe parked the car while I woke the kids, and we walked up through that old, familiar stairwell.

"Lily," my mother said in a relieved voice as she opened the door. She hugged each of the children. When Joe came to the door she smiled and started going through the list. He smiled back at her. It had become somewhat of a tradition for mother to give him a to-do list of things she wanted him to take care of while he was there. The apartment was old, and there were always knobs that needed fixing or hinges that needed tightening. He almost always gave their car a tune-up while we were there. I think Joe liked it, too. Somehow it made him feel like he fit in and was appreciated.

As our family filled the apartment with life and the kids swarmed my mother, pressing in for hugs and the chance to tell her their most recent stories, Joe made his way over to my father and sat down next to him. My father had recently returned from the hospital and was feeling a little better.

The two of them had always hit it off, even with such different backgrounds. Joe could talk to my father in ways that I had never been able to. They would have long conversations about serious topics and still be able to joke around with each other. Sometimes I wished that I could talk to my father that way.

It wasn't long before the real reason for our visit cut through the light banter. We had driven up to help Mother find a nursing home for my father. I glanced over at him where he sat talking to Joe. I hoped the situation wouldn't give him flashbacks to his days in the concentration camps. I hoped he wouldn't hate us for it.

~ ~ ~ ~ ~

The train took my father to Buchenwald, one of the largest concentration camps in Germany. It was originally established as a refugee tent camp for Polish nationals after the German invasion of 1939. The first 110 Polish prisoners had died in weeks from exposure and starvation. Two thousand more arrived in October, and an additional ten thousand arrived by the end of the year.

Initially, my father received a quart of soup and 12 ounces of bread each day, and that was meant to support him while he worked upwards of 15 hours each day. The rations were soon changed to a bowl of soup and bread crust, and my father's weight plummeted. Sickness ruled the camp. Additional clothing or shoes were not provided, so as the weeks wore on and the clothes wore out, some worked with no shoes. Their clothes disintegrated into rags.

Early on, his job involved carrying heavy bricks up a ladder. Balance, take a step up, balance again, another step. Do not move too fast or you will fall. Do not move too slow or you will be shot. Keep moving, keep balancing, keep living.

One day he paused, just a moment. Rest. The bricks were so heavy. He was so hungry. He closed his eyes. Just a moment.

When I was a child I would reach up to my father's face and feel the tiny scar on his forehead, that smooth gash of silent skin. I wouldn't ask him how he got it, but I would run my small finger along it, marvel at its smoothness, the way it dipped into his skin.

But all scars have a story.

A passing soldier, perhaps catching my father resting for just a moment, slammed a brick into his head. My father collapsed on the ground. Blood ran, life puddled among the stones. My own existence was in the balance in that moment, and the existence of my children and grandchildren. How fragile that small green shoot of life that brought me into being! How tenaciously it pushed toward the sun!

When my father finally stood, blood ran into his eyes, down his neck, on to his clothing. He had to keep moving. He had to work. He had to live.

Meanwhile, the commandant decided to have an indoor riding arena built for his wife, adding to the workload of the inmates. Elsewhere in the camp, doctors performed medical experiments on the prisoners. By the end of 1943, Buchenwald contained 37,000 people. Later, in 1944, inmates at forced labor camps in Chenstochov were also shipped to Buchenwald, swelling the numbers to 112,000. But when the Sixth Armored Division of the U.S. Army reached the camp on April 11, 1945, there were only 21,000 people left to be liberated. The missing 90,000 had been exterminated.

Yet my father survived it all. He survived the brick to the head and the years of malnutrition. He survived the cold and the heat, the sicknesses and the loneliness. He survived multiple concentration camps.

When he walked out of that hell in 1945, his 6 foot, 1 inch frame was wrapped tightly with just 100 pounds of flesh. Deteriorating muscle. He left the camp but had no idea where to go. He had no family. He was stunned by the state of the world, and initially his freedom was nearly as overwhelming as his captivity.

What did freedom have to offer? He still had no clothes, no food, no work. He found a relief camp and took refuge there among the thousands of other people who couldn't believe what they had been through, what they had just survived.

My father's brother, who had survived all those years in the camps, died shortly after they were liberated.

~ ~ ~ ~ ~

Joe and I took a second trip to New York City to see my father. He had contracted pneumonia during one of his trips for dialysis, and it seemed things were drawing to a close. We left the children home with a babysitter for that trip, hoping to get up to see my father and then return quickly. It was hard for us in those days to travel so much.

So for three short days in the spring of 1978 we ate breakfast at my parents' apartment, then went in to the hospital for the day with dad. We heard all the normal hospital sounds and smelled the hospital smells and talked in that hushed hospital tone. Quick meals in the cafeteria. Endless waiting while he slept or sat quietly staring at the wall. After three days we had to return to Morrow.

On the night we were to drive away, Joe and I went into my father's hospital room one last time. Something inside of me knew it was good-bye.

My father was so weak and frail, and all I wanted to do was pray for him, but I also didn't want to cause him grief as he lay there, dying. I didn't want our last memory together to be of me pushing my unwanted Christianity in his face. I didn't want to be rejected by him in that last moment.

Yet inside of me I knew that I had to pray with him or I'd drive back to Ohio and go on with my life and regret it forever. So when it came time for us to leave I looked nervously at Joe then edged closer to my father's hospital bed. The monitors beeped in the background and, outside the door, nurses and doctors walked down the hall.

I moved even closer, sitting on the side of his bed.

"Dad, can I pray with you?"

He couldn't speak, but his eyes looked deep inside of me, as if doing a final inventory. Then he nodded. Yes, I could pray with him.

I teared up but quickly grabbed his hand. I closed my eyes in order to pray, then opened them again and found that he was looking right at me, listening intently. I asked God that my father would feel peace, and that he would know that we loved him so much. I wanted to say so many things, I wanted to say everything, but those are the words that came out. And my father sat there quietly, squeezing my hand. If I think about it now I can still feel his leathery grip.

I kissed him on the forehead, and he managed a smile. I thought of the life that he had lived: the unspeakable horrors in the camps, the scary journey to America, the alcohol, his tenuous relationship with my mother, and now this, the last few moments of his life. I wanted so many things for him at that moment. I desperately wished that his life could have been different. Happier, perhaps, or more rewarding. Easier. As I sat there, I felt such sadness at what he had been through.

I walked away from him, but I stopped in the doorway. I turned around and blew him a kiss. It was the last time I would see him.

Goodbye.

CHAPTER TWO

*I*n 1934, my mother, Feigle, walked the Chenstechov streets with her younger brother, Mendel. She was 12 years old at the time. Papers littered the sidewalk, the remnants of a rally from the night before. They kicked at the pamphlets as they walked, then stopped and picked one up. They were too young to understand that they were reading Communist propaganda.

A police officer happened to walk by and saw them holding the pamphlets, so he arrested them on the spot. In those days it was illegal in Poland to distribute that kind of material. The officer took the children to the police station, and they spent the night in jail.

My grandmother bailed them out in the morning after what was certainly a restless night. She let them have it all the way home, her shouts echoing in the early morning streets.

"What were you doing?" she asked. (I imagine her smacking the back of Mendel's head in disgust.) "Why are you reading that trash? Why are you looking at things you shouldn't be looking at?"

The children felt more relief than anything else, finally arriving home after a dark night in a Polish jail cell. They probably welcomed her admonishments, glad to be hearing her voice again. My grandmother ended her tirade with one final command.

"Now, mind your own business!"

I wish that was it. I wish that was the worst thing that ever happened to my mother, that frightful one-night stay in prison. How that night would have grown in significance! I am sure that story would have been passed down and retold, over and over again: the scary inmates, the mean police officers.

But that night paled in comparison to that which was to come. It became a footnote, my mother's night in a polish prison.

~ ~ ~ ~ ~

Everything changed when the Germans invaded Poland on Friday, September 1, 1939. By Sunday, only two short days later, Nazi troops had reached Chenstochov. The next day, known as "Bloody Monday," the Nazis killed nearly 1,000 Poles, including 300 Jews, and began beating and humiliating anyone in their way. They confiscated Jewish property and took over Jewish businesses, seizing all possessions including bank accounts. They destroyed the city's historic synagogues, closed Jewish schools, and appointed a Council of the Elders to administer Jewish affairs under the thumb of the occupation. Poland was to be Germanized, and Hitler's Final Solution called for the eventual extermination of its Jews.

But in the beginning, my mother had hope that things might return to normal, or at least become bearable. She heard the triumphant Germans marching in the streets and the sound of their music and it frightened her. Yet even then a small glimmer of hope remained that things might change for the better. After all, a world power would be governing their country. Could this bring in more business? Make life better for everyone?

But their optimism would not last.

About one year after the invasion, in August of 1940, approximately one thousand Jews in their late teens and early 20s were sent to forced labor camps. Eight months after that, in April of 1941, the remaining Jews were pulled out of their homes and sent to a ghetto in the older eastern part of Chenstochov. The three million Jews throughout Poland were gathered into such ghettos in each of the larger cities.

Mother's oldest siblings, Moloch and Basha, escaped to Russia.

"They suffered there," my mother said. "They were hungry. But they weren't killed."

~ ~ ~ ~ ~

"Feigle," my grandmother said one day, putting money into her hand, "take Zlotta and Mendel to buy groceries."

She sent my mother to a neighboring town. My mother always felt a foreboding when she left the house and left her mother, but on that particular morning, she walked away with her two younger siblings feeling very certain that something bad was going to happen, certain that she would not see her mother again.

Several hours later, when they returned, her mother and her crippled sister, Tsurah, were gone.

My mother soon discovered they had been taken out and shot.

I wonder if my grandmother had a feeling that day, a premonition that the children needed to leave the house. Is that why she sent them to a neighboring town for groceries, instead of to their own market? Would my mother have survived that morning if she had been at home? She was 19 years old, now the matriarch of the family, with Mendel and Zlotta to look after.

~ ~ ~ ~ ~

It wasn't long before the thudding boots of German soldiers arrived on their street, their harsh voices shouting cruel orders, demanding that my mother and her brother and sister, along with everyone else on their street, leave their homes with nothing more than the clothes they had on their backs. She still refused to believe that her mother and sister had been killed — she desperately looked through the crowds. Maybe everyone was mistaken. Maybe her mother wasn't dead. Maybe she would come back.

Complete chaos set in as soldiers stormed houses and beat those who did not move fast enough. Belongings were thrown out into the street. My mother, her sister, Zlotta, and her brother, Mendel, were led to a room in a church before being separated. The girls went one way; Mendel was taken to another room, along with the rest of the men.

My mother witnessed thousands of Jews stream into the city from other areas in Poland, and once they arrived they mostly fled to the ghetto. Soon, 48,000 Jews lived in their ghetto, scrambling for rations, terrified for their families. By the end of the summer, they were completely sealed off from the outside by guards and barricades lining the streets, hemming them in. My mother watched helplessly as neighbors who complained about the conditions were taken away. No one knew for sure what happened to them, but there were horrible rumors.

Soon the fate of anyone who complained or didn't follow orders became obvious and straightforward: instead of being taken to a separate room and never being seen again, they were simply shot in the street.

My mother struggled to care for her younger sister. If she became sick, there was no medicine and not nearly enough food to get well on. More than once my mother had to sneak out of the barracks to find milk, or bread, or some other food for Zlotta. When the soldiers celebrated a holiday, the residents of the ghetto searched the trash after their parties, hoping to find potato skins or coffee grounds.

My father never stopped eating the skins of potatoes his entire life. I wonder now what went through his mind when he did something as simple as eat a potato or drink the broth from his soup. I wonder if his body ever forgot those things or if, like muscle-memory, his mind would always flash back to the days he hungrily ate a cold potato the way I eat an apple.

My mother must have had difficulty keeping track of Mendel once he was put in the separate area with the men. The last word she had of him was that he and perhaps ten other teenage boys, wanting to join the sporadic resistance springing up around the ghetto, or perhaps simply wanting to escape, got hold of some guns and ammunition and decided in desperation to fight back. I picture him as a brave and gangly teenager joining a group of scared but determined comrades, aiming their weapons at the Germans and having their futures snuffed out in a loud and furious round of gunfire.

"They killed them all," my mother told me, shaking her head slowly. "They killed them all."

He was only a boy.

~ ~ ~ ~ ~

When the roundup of Jews began in the ghetto of Chenstochov, my mother fought to stay with Zlotta. They clung to one another against the chaos sweeping through the neighborhood. First they went to a work camp in Poland. But soon they were herded together yet again, for another purpose. This time they were loaded onto a train's crowded cattle cars.

Rolling over those endless miles of track, the train sounded ominous to the passengers. Would they be tortured? Killed? Wherever they were going, they knew it wasn't good, and the train was taking them there. For hours it moved, stopping only to take on more Jews. There was no food. Sometimes a German soldier doused the windowless cars in water and the passengers looked toward the sky, mouths open, trying to capture the drops that dripped from the dirty ceiling. Anything to quench their thirst.

"Every time the train stopped," my mother said, "we thought everybody was going to get killed. They could have done it just like that. They often did."

The train came to a stop, and for the first time, the passengers were allowed to walk around. My mother looked through the door and saw a small town. Standing at the edge of the town was someone selling bread. Her stomach rumbled at the thought of food, real food, so she and a friend wandered close to a guard. The two young girls flirted with the Nazi soldier. He smiled. He let them buy bread. My mother and her four friends broke it into five pieces, devouring it in a matter of seconds before getting back onto the train.

For over a week they rode that train, a few bites of bread their only meal. I have never gone that long without food. I can only imagine how weak they must have felt, how they dreamed of eating and of a comfortable place to rest. But the only relief they received came in a series of shouts.

"Get out!" soldiers shouted, banging on the train with their hands and their guns. "Get out! Get out!"

As they got out of the train cars, they left many dead or nearly dead lying on the floor behind them.

They had arrived. They were at the camp of Bergen-Belsen.

The Nazis established Bergen-Belsen in 1940, originally for the French and Belgian prisoners of war. But, like many camps, it quickly filled with Jews the Nazis either wanted to exterminate or exchange with the Allied forces for captured German soldiers.

My mother arrived at Bergen-Belsen in January. The ground was hard, covered in snow, and the air was cold. The Nazis stripped her, and soon she was numb, standing there in the winter air. The women all stood around, naked in that January day, crossing their arms, trying to stay decent, trying to stay warm. Guards shaved her entire body, and then she was driven, along with the others, into a large building.

She thought she was about to die.

Instead, they were given showers and a camp outfit and then led to the barracks. The building was designed for 100 people, but each barrack would eventually house 500 to 1,000. My mother's unheated building contained girls in their teens and 20s. The guards gave them burlap sacks to use as blankets and chamber pots to use as toilets. The smell inside the barracks was overwhelming.

My mother's schedule was basic and, for the most part, unchanging. Sleep as well as she could, on a bed if she could find an empty space, or on the wooden floor among the chamber pots. Guards woke them at 5 a.m., and a roll call was given, out in the cold. Some days it went on for hours. Some days they stood there in sleet or snow or a cold rain while the Germans called out their names. Feet grew numb. Muscles shouted with pain. Those who fell over were usually shot where they lay.

As poor as the conditions were inside the wooden barracks, my mother still chose to stay inside as much as possible. Outside of its walls, predatory Nazi guards looked to rape or kill, based on their mood. Get too close to the gate? They would shoot you. Of course, you could also be shot for absolutely no reason at all.

"Everybody was just scared," my mother said. "Scared they're gonna get killed."

Nourishment came at the front of the food line: a roll of bread that had to last for several days, one cup of black coffee, and one cup of watery soup, sometimes with nothing in it but grass. Later in the war, as German stores depleted, the daily ration dwindled to even less than that.

It seemed they were always being put in lines and separated, either to do jobs or to get food or to simply turn around and go back to the barracks. Yet lines often led to worse things than a cup of grass-filled soup and watered-down coffee.

One day, as my mother waited in line with her sister Zlotta and her friend Sabrina, a soldier began separating the women.

"You! This way. You! That way."

Initially, the girls were separated, my mother directed to the left while Sabrina and Zlotta remained in line. Suddenly, as the line began to move forward, Sabrina grabbed my mom's arm.

"She's coming with me," Sabrina said, and the guard ignored her, allowing my mother to change lines.

The line my mother had been in at first went to the gas chamber. Everyone in that line was killed that day. The line that Sabrina pulled my mother into received their normal ration and went back to their barracks.

Day after day, week after week, year after year, the difference between life and death could be something as simple as a guard separating people into lines, or a prisoner taking one step too close to a fence. Or the random tug of a soldier's trigger finger.

Or the angelic action of a friend named Sabrina.

More and more people in Mother's barracks began to die as illness and malnutrition took over.

"What can you do?" my mother asked while reflecting on those nightmare days. "Tell me, what can you do? In a situation like that the only thing you think is, *I hope I survive*. I want to see where my family is. That's what I was thinking. Nothing else. Sure, you cry inside, but you don't cry out loud."

Thinking about her words, I cry inside, too. Thinking of her in that camp, her hope and life slowly draining from her body, causes sorrow to flood over me. I try to picture myself in that camp and find it hard to breathe. A heaviness sits on my heart until I cannot allow myself to think of it.

The work was relentless and mind-numbingly dull. Carry rocks from here and pile them there. Now that all of the rocks have been moved, bring them back. In the meantime, she grew thinner and thinner. Her beautiful, young body, so feminine and lively, began to disappear. Her breasts all but vanished. Her periods stopped coming. Her bones protruded. There was nothing left, only a brittle frame wrapped in fragile skin, constantly pounded by more work and cold and illness.

Meanwhile, her camp continued to fill, and by the end of the war 125,000 prisoners were crammed inside. Anne Frank arrived in October of 1944, eventually dying of typhus as disease swept the camp. Every morning someone from each barracks would report to the guard how many had died in the night. It was at night when most would give up, their souls striving for some sort of peace no longer available in the world. In the morning, all that was left was a thin body no longer breathing, eyes open but still. Early in the war the bodies were taken out and burned, thrown into a large bonfire like lumber. Later, the Nazis did not even do that.

"Some bodies remained in the barracks until we were liberated," my mother recalls. "And it smelled like hell. We stepped on the bodies — you couldn't help it. When you walked you would have to step on them. You just went on. You couldn't help yourself. You didn't look at death if you wanted to survive."

Soldiers from the British army reached my mother's camp on the afternoon of Sunday, April 15, 1945. The German Commandant Kramer put on a crisp, fresh uniform and met the soldiers at the gate. Although the world, in general terms, knew what the Nazis were doing to the Jews and the others in the concentration camps, the British troops were horrified at what they found in Bergen-Belsen.

At least 13,000 corpses remained unburied. Mass graves lay hidden, waiting to be discovered. At least 40,000 people lost their lives in that particular camp, many from starvation despite the fact that warehouses full of food from the World Jewish Congress sat nearby. The Nazis had refused to distribute it.

Many of the 60,000 prisoners remaining were so weak and lethargic that the idea of liberation didn't sink in for days, and there was little joy in the camp at their release. Most believed their survival had been a matter of luck and timing.

"I don't know how I survived," my mother said. "I came out at the end weighing only 80 pounds. I was like a skeleton."

But she was a survivor. When the British came, she made her way to the camp's kitchen as quickly as possible.

"I grabbed potatoes and grabbed everything that I should not be hungry anymore," she said. "There were people working there but I went in to get food for people in the barracks. I brought out bunches of everything because the other people couldn't walk. A lot of them were sick. They couldn't do nothing."

The prison population was so weakened that 9,000 people died in the two weeks after liberation. My mother saw many people she had grown to know, people who had lived through such horror, die before her eyes after they were free. Another 4,000 would die in the following month.

For over four years my parents lived either in the ghettos or the concentration camps. A four-year nightmare, carried on 24 hours a day, and I know those experiences went to the core of who they were, who they would become.

~ ~ ~ ~ ~

Freedom. Liberation. I thought that must have been the most exciting day of my mother's life, but after she was released, she didn't know what to do. In fact, she feared what she would find.

"I didn't know where anybody was. I didn't know if anybody was alive," she said.

It was the spring of 1945, and my mother was just one individual of the ten million displaced people traveling through a shattered Germany.

The Allies, along with various international aid organizations, transported the Jews to relief camps. My mother watched desperately as her train traveled over the countryside. Unaccustomed to such freedom, she stared into the passing villages and towns and cities, wondering what the world was like. What had changed? I am sure her nights were filled with flashbacks to other, more terror-filled train rides, but each morning she woke to the clack-clacking of the train taking her farther and farther away from Bergen-Belsen.

But then the ride stopped, and she had to figure out what to do. As she walked away from the train, toward the relief camp in Feldafing, Germany, she tallied up the dead: her widowed mother who had worked so tirelessly all those years, only to be shot; Tsurah, the sister she had bathed and fed and told stories to, helpless Tsurah, never given a chance; little Mendel, her younger brother, filled with that youthful fire, overwhelmed by the Nazi soldiers.

Yet there were others whose fates she did not know. Her younger sister, Zlotta. Basha, her second mother and older sister. Her older half-sister, Mania, who moved to Israel before the war. Moloch, her gentle older brother who had already left the house when she was very young. They might be out there. They must be. Her loving family. Their pet name for her had always been Feigle — Yiddish for little bird. How she longed to hear that name again!

"I thought maybe Basha was somewhere alive, but I didn't know which way to go. I didn't know what to do."

So she wandered the streets of that small town in ill-fitting shoes and clothes that hung loosely from her bony frame. She sometimes stopped to sit and rest, sometimes wept at what life had become, but she always stood up again, shook off the fear that everyone had died, and continued on.

Finally, one beautiful day, she walked down a street full of shops and little businesses. The sunlight reflected off the glass and the blue sky filled her with hope. And she heard it.

"Feigle?"

Standing in front of her was an old friend from home. They hugged each other and wept in the middle of the street, my mother feeling that her life was finally turning. It was her first bit of hope, of home, and she held tightly to that friend.

Her friend had a little money, so the two of them hung out together, telling stories of what they had seen. They talked late into the night until my mother, exhausted, fell asleep. The next morning she hugged her friend goodbye and continued looking for anyone else she might know. It didn't take long.

"Feigle! Feigle! Come here!" a woman called out. She was from my mother's old neighborhood. Before my mother could even run to her, the woman shouted something else.

"I know where your sister Basha is!"

For a moment the news overwhelmed my mother, and she couldn't move. She started to shake. Then, holding both of her hands to her head and weeping the entire way, she followed the woman to a house.

They both knocked on the door and waited. My mother looked again at the woman. Could it be true? Silence. Then the door swung open.

It was Moloch, her older brother.

He was thinner and older, and for a moment his eyes slowly studied the tiny woman in front of him. My mother must have looked like a little girl, even though she was over 20 years old by then. Then he recognized her, and in that moment was perfect joy.

They held each other close for a long time.

"Basha is out," he said. "She will be home soon. Feigle! She will be home so soon. Please sit down."

My mother, exhausted, fell asleep. A joyful screaming woke her up.

"My God, my God!" Basha cried out. "This is my Feigle! Oh, this is my Feigle!"

~ ~ ~ ~ ~

In the late spring sun, Feldafing's stone and wooden barracks were welcoming. Accommodations were simple, but the comforts were so much greater than those of the camps. The flowers and the green countryside were like food to my mother after seeing so much violence and death. For a moment she allowed herself to dream of happiness and a new life in Germany.

Then their paths finally crossed: my 22-year-old mother now known by everyone as Feigle Jakobowitz and my father, the 32-year-old Uszer Fiszman. In the camp, she was known as an attractive and vivacious young woman. She slowly put on weight and regained her girlish curves. When she met the older man, her future husband, she was hardly impressed.

"I didn't like him," she said. "He was older."

Feigle had always dreamed of glamour and beauty. As a young girl she had crept into her older sister's closet and put on one of her beautiful dresses, then paraded up and down the street. When Basha saw her she was furious and gave her a beating, the type of beating only a sister can give. Mom always said it had been worth it though, just to experience that feeling of walking up and down the street in beautiful clothing.

So the thought of marrying this staid man ten years her senior did not fit the image she had for her life. So many years had been lost in the terror of the camps, and she had no time for practicality.

But Basha spoke to her.

"He'll make a living for you," she urged my mother. "He's not going to run around on you. These other youngsters are just flying wild."

My mother was young, and she let her sister talk her into it.

My father, on the other hand, fell madly in love with that attractive, high-spirited woman, and he did his best to win her. She heard rumors of his drinking, but she wasn't going to let those rumors influence her decision.

They married in the summer of 1946. Old friends from their apartment and the ghetto in Chenstochov joined with new friends from Feldafing to celebrate. Ceremonies in those days took on added meaning, symbolizing a return to life, a return to hope. There was this fragile belief that perhaps they could gather the scraps that were left and create a beautiful life.

And then I was born on September 20, 1947, another confirmation of hope: Leia Cirla Fiszman, after my grandmother and my mother's beloved sister Tsura (Cirla). After my birth, my parents became determined to leave Europe. They made plans to move to Israel to join Mania, packed their meager belongings, and prepared for the trip.

But a letter arrived from my mother's uncle Lou Ultmann. He lived in the United States. He was a baker. He would sponsor our family if we wanted to come.

"Feigle, don't go nowhere. I'm sending you visas to America," is how my mother recalls the letter.

So it was decided. America would be our new home.

CHAPTER THREE

City sounds came through the open door that led to the fire escape. I could feel the cold kitchen floor under my feet as I walked slowly across the smooth surface. My mom worked at the sink, silverware clinking together, cabinets closing. The summer air was all around us, gently moving through our Bronx apartment. I looked at a small mouse in the corner of the kitchen — its tail twitched, but apart from that it stayed completely still.

I was four years old.

Then Mother scooped me up in her sweet-smelling arms, humming a Yiddish song in my ear, placing me gently through the window and onto the first-floor fire escape — because it was on the first floor and was completely closed in, Mother let me play around out there. I cradled my doll, dressed her, and put her to sleep as the cars moved past the house. The rusty, wrought iron was warm and gritty under my feet. The city air was hot and relaxing.

Children's voices rose up like music to where I sat. I peered through the bars, gripped them with both hands and pushed my forehead up against them, trying to see down to the street. I leaned against the iron and caught a glimpse of them playing on the sidewalk, colorful and dancing. Then, the gentlest easing, and my head slipped through the gap in the rails. I was stuck.

Screaming, Mother panicked, greasing my ears and head with butter and Crisco and anything slick. But the iron bars would not let me go. Pushing for a glimpse of what went on beyond that small metal platform, I had trapped myself.

Sirens screamed down the city streets, then I saw the fire engine move through, cars slowly pulling to the side. Beneath me the children stopped and stared. A fireman came through the window behind me — I couldn't see him but the weight of him on the fire escape made it creak and sway. He forced the bars apart, freeing me.

My eyes were swollen from crying. I clung to my mother's neck.

~ ~ ~ ~ ~

I grew older, and the city became a part of me. That old apartment formed the backdrop for my life, a backdrop that wouldn't change.

Sometimes I fell asleep in the evening before father left for work. He was a baker and worked the night shift. Sometimes, in the dark, I heard him whisper into the room.

"Leiala? Leiala?"

Sometimes I woke up slightly at the sound of his voice, warm and kind. I pictured him squinting into the darkness.

But I was still half asleep, and I didn't move. I felt him kiss my forehead, press back my hair. After he left, and the room was silent again, I rolled over and put my hand under the pillow, clutching the dollar bill he had left behind.

One day Father came home from work holding a stray cat at arm's length, wrapped up in his coat, the answer to our mice problem. The roaches we had given up on. So on his way home that morning he had tempted the stray with his lunch, then snatched the cat and wrapped it in his jacket. But when he released it into the apartment, it hissed and swiped at us with its claws. It scratched us and clung to our clothes.

My brother Hymie and I avoided that mangy animal and crept around the apartment like stalked prey. Those were long, scary nights, and my brother and I slept in the same bed because we thought that cat would jump on us in the night and attack us. Before father left for work, he checked in on us. After seeing how jumpy we had become due to that cat, he took it out with him and we never saw it again.

This was my family's existence in the city. Out of nothing, my parents had created a life for us. We made the best of things, and if they didn't work out we did something different. Whether it was a cat or a job or an apartment, we worked for what we had, and sometimes we got lucky, and sometimes we got unlucky, but there was always a feeling that we were forging our way, and that in America anything was possible.

Lillian Fishman.

Lillian Fishman.

Lillian Fishman.

Someone important to me had suggested "Lillian" as my official name, so I wrote it over and over again in cursive, trying to prepare myself for the big day. I would show it to my mother and she would critique my writing, and then I would go back to the table and keep writing it over and over again, the curving letters etching their form into my mind.

Lillian Fishman.

Then, finally, the day came. April 15, 1955. That morning when I woke up, the importance of what was about to happen overwhelmed me. The night before, I hadn't slept a bit. Mother helped me get dressed, and everything had to be perfect: my blouse, unwrinkled, my skirt, just so. I felt very grown up as we boarded the subway to Ellis Island.

The four of us stood close together as the train carried us under the city. My brother was already a citizen because he had been born in the States, but for my mother, my father, and me, this was a huge day. The beginning of something wonderful. I would finally belong here.

We traveled to the tip of Manhattan, joined a long line, and were eventually taken into a large, open area. I remember how all of us stood together, expectation reverberating around us. I raised my right hand, along with everyone else, and said the oath of citizenship.

The certificate I received nearly one year later lists only the facts: Lillian Fishman, 4 feet 6 inches, 70 pounds. But I remember how exhilarating it was to be part of that. America was a place where anything could happen. It was a place where anything would happen.

Most of all, I remember how tall I felt, signing my name on that certificate in perfect, curving script:

Lillian Fishman.

~ ~ ~ ~ ~

"Why do we celebrate Rosh Hashana?" I asked my father as we left the house.

"Because it's the Law," he said without emotion, as if that was the answer for everything. The Law. I knew by the way he said it that it was all very serious and somber and important, but I didn't understand it at all.

Yet it felt good to be together as a family, something we rarely experienced with my father working the night shift and my mother always out with her friends. It was a slow, meditative walk to the synagogue on Astor Avenue twice a year, once for Rosh Hashana and then again nine days later for Yom Kippur. We were not a religious family, but our Jewish roots were deep, and my parents made sure that we were in attendance for these festivals.

The inside of the synagogue was very plain with long wooden pews, and I tried to walk quietly with my mother and Hymie (because he was a young boy) to the women's side, keeping my gaze respectfully on the floor. All of the women wore prayer scarves to cover their heads. I liked wearing mine — it was different, and it made me feel like I belonged in the community with these people, many of whom were our neighbors in the apartment building.

On the other side of the aisle the men stood looking large and serious, their broad backs covered by prayer shawls. Perched on the top of their heads were small, round yarmulkes. I spotted my father through the crowd, his prayer shawl long and white with the Star of David in the middle and tassels hanging from the edges. I remembered him taking it out of its small case that morning, unrolling it slowly and sweeping it around behind him so that it came to rest on his back like a cape with special powers.

A feeling of mystery and reverence filled the silence as the rabbi went to stand at the front. Two younger boys took the scrolls wrapped in beautiful blue velvet and walked through the congregation. Then it seemed there were reaching hands everywhere, all of us wanting to touch the Torah. I loved the feel of the soft velvet, the idea of its holiness. I kissed my hand after I touched it, feeling a certain sense of awe.

Then the rabbi read in Hebrew, the words sounding like an ancient incantation I didn't understand. We repeated after him, standing, our voices sounding out together in a sing-song manner.

It was all very comforting, but I had no idea about God. Who was He? Where was He? Sometimes, if I had a big test, or mother and father were fighting, I would touch the mezuzah on the doorframe leading into our apartment, then kiss my hand and pray to God. The mezuzah is a small case affixed to the outside of the front door, in which is held a parchment with a Hebrew prayer. The prayer was one of protection over the home. If I asked my father why we had a mezuzah, I'm sure he would have said the same thing he always said.

"Leiala, it is the Law."

But again I wondered, *Who is this God? Does He even exist?*

Why were these things that we did so important to God? Eventually, on Rosh Hoshana, we walked out of the synagogue, the parents mingling together while the smaller children ran up and down the sidewalk. I felt pure after those days in the synagogue, as if I had done something right and noble, even though I wasn't sure exactly what.

~ ~ ~ ~ ~

My flip-flops slapped on the concrete steps, all the way down the stairwell of our six-story apartment building on the corner of Waring Avenue and Bronx Park East. They felt familiar in between my toes, cool against the bottoms of my feet, and their sound echoed back at me. It was a lazy summer morning in 1959, and I made my way to the lobby of our building.

I hung out there for a little while, watched people come and go, hoping to spot the cute high school boy from the floor below us. When the front doors opened, a wave of stuffy heat and city noise billowed in like a cloud. I adjusted the strap on my bathing suit and hugged my towel, leaned back against the wall and looked around. My 12-year-old body felt foreign to me, too tall and skinny. One girl at school, a mean, spiteful girl, took to calling me Olive Oyl because of my long legs and the way I walked.

I pretended to wait for my friend Gloria Feldman, but I didn't stay in the lobby very long. I was only hoping for a glimpse of the boy and had no idea what to do if I did see him. When he didn't show, I went through the doors and onto the Bronx sidewalk. I didn't want to be the last one of our group to the pool. Otherwise they would probably all start talking about me before I got there.

Through those doors were the sounds of my adolescent summers: car horns and kids playing with one another and shop owners' voices shouting from their storefronts. A group of boys threw a ball in the empty lot across the street, hollering back and forth to each other. I showed my pool pass from the sidewalk and they let me through the rusty iron gate, into the pool area. Two six-story apartment blocks rose on either side of the pool, and our own personal square patch of blue sky looked down on the shimmering liquid. I could smell the water roasting on the cement slab. I started to sweat almost as soon as I walked into the sunlight.

The pool was full of people, and all the chairs and small squares of grass around the outside edge were filled. Children's delighted screams were punctuated by plunging splashes. I looked around and happiness overwhelmed me — we had recently moved from a rough area of town, and those buildings, that pool, even those people, represented a better life. Our family was moving up. No more worrying about being mugged as soon as we walked out of the building. No more worrying about what might happen to us in the dark stairwells. We could even cross the street to play ball, and our parents didn't care.

The families in our new building were hardworking, blue-collar families living the American dream: African American families and

Italian families and Jewish families. And we were all different, which made us all the same. That's all I wanted in those days — to be the same as everyone else. I walked toward the pool, unable to stop the smile rising.

Then I saw my friends: Gloria, Elana, Lauren, and Barbie. They sat on the edge of the pool, dangling their thin legs into the coolness. Kids played all around them, and they leaned back to avoid the larger splashes, shielding themselves with their arms, talking all the while. I suppose we were a typical group of adolescent girlfriends, with constantly ebbing levels of affection, constantly changing alliances. One day, four of us would despise the loner; the next day, three would have disdain for two; and then suddenly, without warning, I would be the one on the outside. Then I would be back in, complaining about one of the other four. Our spats were silly and numerous. But they were my friends, and their friendship, no matter how fickle, meant I was not alone.

I kicked off my flip-flops and sat down on the end beside Gloria. My legs sank softly into the cold water.

"Hi, Gloria," I said.

She smiled widely. She was my favorite.

"Hi, Lily. Did you see Joel over there?" she asked, looking out of the corner of her eye.

I glanced across the pool in his direction. Then, when he looked toward us, I looked away.

"He's so cute!" she said, laughing, reaching forward and splashing me.

I laughed, then glanced over at the other three girls.

"Hi, Lauren," I said nonchalantly.

She just looked at me then whispered something to Barbie and Elana.

I looked at Gloria and raised my eyebrows in an unspoken question.

She rolled her eyes.

"I'll tell you later," she hissed.

I closed my eyes and faced the sky, my weightless legs floating in the water, the sandpaper cement under my thighs, the warmth of the sun glowing deep red through my eyelids. We all wanted to be tan in those days, like the movie stars. And we all wanted to be blonde, so Gloria would bring lemon juice for us to put in our hair, and the sun would lighten it. The sun seemed to provide a solution for nearly everything.

"Barbie stuffed her bra yesterday," Gloria said, whispering again and giggling. I snickered, trying hard not to blush because I had tried the same thing, with very lumpy results. But we laughed and laughed.

Yet on that afternoon, in the midst of a long-sought feeling of security and belonging, one of the most terrible things that could possibly have taken place came to pass. As I sat there on the edge of the pool with my four friends feeling the sun and the water and the sounds of a community, it happened.

My father arrived back from work.

He still worked at night in a bakery that he co-owned — my father made the bread and his partner made the cakes. His trips home consisted of a 45-minute ride on the subway and then a five-block walk from the train to the apartment building. He usually got home late in the morning, any time from nine until noon. Part of that was due to the nature of his job, having so much to do to keep the business going. But his widely fluctuating return times were also a result of the couch he kept in the back room of his bakery where he drowned his sorrows early every morning in a bottle of whiskey.

My father drank nearly all the time, but he never laid a hand on us. He was, for the most part, a peaceful drunk. He was also a loner and never listened to the radio or had a social life. He suffered from having a wife ten years his junior, with more exuberance and spunk and desire for fun than his hardworking life could ever allow or contain. He would eat, sleep, work, and occasionally sit at the dining table reading the Jewish paper.

I saw his kind face as soon as he walked up to the gate outside the pool. He often rubbed his long, arthritic legs while he walked, his green eyes wrinkled in a sweet smile, his long Jewish nose and bald head shining red in the sun. At six feet tall he rose above most others in the pool area. His big hands clutched a brown paper bag full of rolls.

He always brought home rolls, always asked if we wanted something to eat, as if he was back in the concentration camp, finally able to slip bits of food to the skeletal children he had, in reality, been forced to watch die of starvation.

When he came through that iron gate, every bit of my happiness and newfound confidence evaporated. I knew he was drunk by the way he walked, his toes stubbing the ground, his steps short and sliding. It took my breath away, and I didn't want my friends to see him.

"Leiala," he called out, loud and slow, his voice full of alcohol and fatherly love, the -la at the end of my name exaggerating his affection.

I could hear a rush of blood in my ears. Panic. I wanted to run.

"Leiala?" he shouted again, and to me it seemed the pool grew silent, the splashing dimmed, and folks stopped what they were doing to find out whom this drunk man called for.

"Leiala!" he called with relief, having seen me across the pool.

I grabbed my little brother and my towel and, hunching over, ran toward him, hoping none of my friends had seen him. But the four of them just sat there on the edge of the pool, staring. I grabbed my father's arm and practically drug him from the pool area.

"My Leiala," he said slowly, his bloodshot eyes tearing up, as if he had found me after years of searching. "I just wanted to say hello."

I hope he couldn't see it at the time, but I didn't want him around. He worked all night and slept during the day. His drinking was an embarrassment to me — I didn't want to be different anymore. I wanted to be just like my friends with their normal families, their normal fathers who worked normal jobs and didn't carry bags of rolls wherever they went. We took the elevator up to the apartment, and I felt so alone. So different.

My little brother and I got him into bed.

"Are you hungry?" my father asked again, trying to sit up, his voice slurred and his eyes watery.

"Go to sleep, Papa," I begged him, turning out his light.

~ ~ ~ ~ ~

"Next!" the school nurse shouted from behind the curtain.

I walked slowly around to the other side.

"Lean forward," she said, running two of her fingers down the sides of my spine.

"Stand up straight," she said, doing the same thing again.

"Next!" she shouted, pushing me away.

The following day my mother was called into school.

"Lily has scoliosis," they told her. "Curvature of the spine. Here's the information for a specialist she'll need to go to."

At first when I found out about it, I didn't know what to think. Scoliosis? Sounded serious enough. But as I discovered more about it, the life slipped out of me — wasn't it enough that our entire apartment building knew that my father was a drunk? That my mother stayed out late at night with her "friends"? Hadn't God given me enough hardships? Now there was yet another way I would be different.

We traveled to Manhattan, to the Hospital of Special Surgeries. They had a wing dedicated to the treatment of scoliosis. We walked down the long hall and through the door to the waiting room. I couldn't believe what I saw.

Children everywhere, some unable to walk, disfigured by their curving spines. I specifically remember a little boy whose back was so bent over by the disease that he could only shuffle around on his hands and knees. What would become of me? Would I end up an old lady in a wheelchair, crippled by my own back?

"Lily Fishman?" the nurse called out, and my mother and I stood and walked into the examination room. I was sweating. My mother was nervous. They took some x-rays, and then the doctor came in.

"You are still in the early stages of scoliosis," he said quietly. "We are going to create a back brace for you that will keep your back growing straight. You must wear it all the time, okay?"

I nodded slowly, my eyes wide open. I would do anything not to end up like the people in the waiting room.

Two weeks later we took the train to Manhattan again, and I saw the crippling effects of the disease and swore I would do anything to keep my body from ending up that way.

Then I saw the back brace.

A heavy iron contraption with horizontal slats across the top, the brace laced down the front like a corset and was very tight and uncomfortable. I tried it on and some of the metal pieces dug into my back. I found it hard to take deep breaths.

"You need to wear this throughout your formative years," the doctor said again, probably sensing my distaste with the metal cage. "Probably until you're 18. If you wear it all the time, your back will grow straighter and you might even avoid surgery."

Then the doctor looked at my mother. "Bring her in every six months for measurements and tests. We'll monitor her progress."

For those first few days I was home, the image of those poor children bent over with untreated scoliosis was enough to get me to strap that brace on. At first, I tried buying my clothes in larger sizes, hoping that would disguise the brace. I would stand by the mirror and adjust my dress or my shirt, trying to get it to cover the little bit that stuck out the top. I was so tall and thin that I thought I could hide it.

But once in class things went bad, as I had expected them to. If I bent over, the vertical braces stuck out through my neckline and the back of my shirt. A few days into it I was bending over my desk, doing some class work, when one of the boys behind me laughed.

"Hey, it's the Hunchback of Notre Dame!"

With that one sentence, my determination to wear the contraption and fight off the effects of scoliosis crumbled. I felt so imperfect, so broken, and I carried that feeling around for the rest of my life. It would become difficult for me to let myself be defined by that deformity.

Not only that, but I was just starting to like boys, beginning to hope they would find me attractive, and I did not need a metal birdcage strapped to my body under clothes that didn't fit. The prospect of living in a wheelchair, or even undergoing a painful surgery, was too far in the future. So I hid the back brace deep in my closet under my clothes so that Mother wouldn't find it and make me wear it to school.

On those days when the inside of the apartment felt like a trap, my friends and I met in the stairwell. We sat there on the cool concrete, talking about school and boys and music, and when an adult would pass by our voices collapsed to a whisper, or silence. Sometimes one of the girls would sneak a cigarette from her parents and we would take tiny sips of the smoke, trying to look like the movie stars, trying not to cough.

"Who is smoking out there?" someone shouted, and we scampered around trying to rid ourselves of the smell.

Then, "Time for dinner, Lily."

I knew it must be around 5:00 or 5:30; we ate dinner every night at the same time. Mother never missed it. She loved her routines, and our days passed in a gentle wave of schedules.

I said goodbye to my friends and walked back into the apartment, pulling the heavy door closed behind me. Wednesday night: that meant veal cutlets. Every night of the week Mother made a particular dish: chicken, lamb chops, beef liver, and so on. She mixed up the sides, but the mains were almost always the same on their night. She was a great cook. We loved to eat her food.

We sat down, and father was there that night, a rarity. Almost always at work or sleeping in preparation for his night shift, he wasn't a regular fixture at our evening meals. But that night he was there. He sat quietly, casting small looks of longing and love at my mother. Sometimes I wonder why he didn't fight harder for her. He was so in love with my mother — why didn't he react to her increasing absences with a determination to win her over? Maybe he thought he never would. Whatever he thought, I never saw him attempt to get her to love him the way he loved her. He just seemed to drink more and more.

He mumbled while he ate, little anecdotes or jokes. But if you didn't catch it the first time, he just went on eating.

My father would have drunk liquor from a slop bucket, but one thing he did his entire life was to try to observe the Jewish dietary laws. He always ate kosher. Among other things, that meant you never had milk at a meal with meat, and you never ate pork. The food had to be blessed by a rabbi, and all the meat came from animals killed in a prescribed way by kosher butchers.

Mother, however, was not as strict, and sometimes her kosher diet fluctuated along with her grocery budget. As I went to the kitchen that night with my empty plate, I saw the meat package on the counter. Pork chops. Not veal cutlets. I sighed and threw the butcher paper in the trash so father wouldn't see it.

~ ~ ~ ~ ~

I sat quietly in the synagogue. We prayed many times on the tenth day of the festival of Yom Kippur. It was the Day of Atonement, when all of our sins were paid for. We stood and repeated the words of the rabbi. Then we sat down and prayed the liturgical, Hebrew prayers. In between prayers, when the rabbi's voice was silent, the air felt holy and alive.

In the afternoon we walked to a park that was close to our apartment. My brother and I went slowly behind my parents. I wondered about them. I wondered about their past, if they were happy. My father always seemed subdued and brooding, while my mother had this constrained feeling about her, like a bird with clipped wings.

Some nights my mother disappeared and ran off with her friends. Sometimes when I came home I found her whispering into the phone in the bathroom. She quickly hung up when she noticed me. Sometimes I answered the phone late at night but the person would just hang up. Sometimes Mother stopped to speak with people on the street, complete strangers.

Occasionally my father came home early from work to find out that she was away — her absence brought about a rare show of emotion, and he fumed around the house, bumping into things and threatening to break furniture. My brother and I tried to calm him, tried to assure him that she would be back soon. Usually we managed to usher him to his bedroom and under the blankets, and soon he fell asleep.

Yet in spite of those angry nights, my father still worshiped the ground she walked on. You could see it in his eyes when he watched her from the table while reading his paper. There was pride there that she was his wife, and there was adoration. But they were separated by over ten years and had been married under a veil of haste and convenience, so there was little relationship there.

But still we had the peaceful days of Yom Kippur, and we stopped beside a stream running through the park. The wind blew

APRIL 3

Dear Lenny,

I feel awful. Mom and Pop had an argument this morning. Dad was crying cause he was drunk. I went to him + talked mean & started crying and said he had something in his eye. I hate him. He's not a good father at all. He drinks, he's stupid + oh dear how I wish I had a decent father like everyone else — Gloria Tay so even Lauren but a decent one. I wish they don't fight anymore. I feel like running away but that the way LIFE goes or live I got to live up to it. He gonna sleep on the chair + no in his bed. Ma I love Ma so so much. Poor thing having to be married to Pa.

Love,
Kellie

my dress against my legs. My father's prayer shawl fluttered in the breeze, the tassels dancing. He turned his trouser pockets inside out and threw everything into the water, as was the Jewish custom of that holiday, and all the bits of lint and crumbs from the rolls he always carried washed away. It was symbolic, throwing off all that was old, starting fresh.

I watched as those pieces of old things caught in the current. Some of the breadcrumbs sank to the bottom while the lint was carried away, bouncing on top of the small ripples like water bugs. Then the debris floated out of the park, vanishing around the bend.

We all followed suit, emptying our pockets, watching our sins float away. My mother became glassy-eyed and reflective. I wondered what she was thinking about, or who she was thinking of. Now that I'm older, sometimes I wonder what past sins she envisioned were floating out of her life.

It was the Day of Atonement, the day that all of our sins from the previous year were washed away.

~ ~ ~ ~ ~

"Where's your mother?" my father asked us.

Hymie and I stared at the floor. Outside we could hear the city traffic moving slowly along the street. The city always felt so alive, even at night when everything was dark and waiting.

"I don't know," I mumbled. And I didn't know where she was. But my brother and I both knew what was coming.

On that night he stormed into the bathroom and slammed the door. The apartment rattled. Hymie and I sat down on the couch, hoping that would be the end of it. The plastic cover my mother kept on the sofa squeaked underneath us. Then suddenly my father was coming out of the bathroom, drunk and wobbling from side to side, vanishing into their bedroom and slamming the door once again, like a child throwing a tantrum.

It wasn't long before he walked quickly into the dining room and sat at the table. He pulled a pack of cigarettes out and began smoking furiously, his eyes staring straight in front of him, A haze filled the room and still he continued smoking, going through one pack and starting another. That's when the coughing started. I thought he would cough his head off.

Then, still coughing, he fled into the kitchen and started throwing dishes out of the kitchen cabinet. Some of them hit the floor and just bounced toward us. Others shattered into a hundred pieces, each small shard sharp as a knife. That's when Hymie and I started shouting.

"Stop it!"

"Dad, please!"

He picked up one of the dining room chairs and shuffled clumsily over to one of the windows. I could hear the traffic four stories beneath us clearly as he wrenched the window up. He picked up the chair and started throwing it out, but my brother and I ran over to him.

"No! You can't do that! Stop!"

I don't know how we did it, but we convinced him not to throw the chair. He put it down and sat in it for a moment, putting his hands on his head, broken shards of china under his feet. We didn't know if he would start screaming again, or weeping, or just sit there for the rest of the night staring at the floor and the broken pieces.

When he finally disappeared back into his room and went to bed, the house felt empty and sad. Hymie and I would pick up the china, then go back to the room that we shared, he in his bed and me in mine. It was late, and the sun had set a long time ago behind the high rises. I would lie in bed and wonder when Mother would get home. I wondered where she was and what she was doing out there.

~ ~ ~ ~ ~

I was 13 years old when I came home one day and found three suitcases in the living room flanked by a few packed boxes, bulging with stuff. The apartment door closed slowly behind me, and I stood there, not moving, seeing the suitcases but wondering if I was in the right apartment.

Everything else looked like our place — when you walked in the first thing you saw was the dining room table with the chandelier above and the six empty chairs. Straight ahead you could see the living room with lots of natural light spilling in through the windows. On the right-hand side of the living room was an off-white colored couch with gold embroidery and that plastic cover to keep us kids from getting it dirty. There was a table in the corner with a lamp on it and a couple of off-white chairs with the same gold embroidery. The blue shag carpet had a plastic runner where we walked. The coffee table sat against the left-hand wall and held the television. It wasn't a warm living room — we weren't allowed to eat in there, and Mom was so particular about us keeping our feet off the couch and not messing stuff up that we spent most of our time in our room.

But the suitcases were out of place.

Mom came toward me from the kitchen.

"Why are you packing?" I asked her, a strange feeling gathering in my stomach when I saw her face. She looked determined, and scared.

"Come sit down," she said, and I followed her into the living room still holding my bag from school. I sat down on the plastic couch. Hymie was standing there, too, little Hymie only seven years old and as confused as I was.

"We're leaving your father," she said, her voice unwavering.

"Where are we going?" I asked, my breath coming fast and short.

"We're moving to California, with Felix."

"California? Felix? Who's Felix? I'm not leaving," I said, panic rising inside of me.

"You'll go if I want you to go," she said, taking the same tone she always took with me when I was being rebellious or stubborn.

"I'm not leaving my father!" I screamed.

I dropped my bag and ran out, dodging the dining room table and slipping through the door, into the hall. I escaped down those four flights of stairs, tears streaming down my face, the sound of my crying echoing through the stairwell.

Soon after my fight with Mother I was in the street outside our building. It was four in the afternoon, and I didn't know where to go, so I just ran and cried, and when I got tired I slowed to a walk, staring at the cracks in the sidewalk. I couldn't stop thinking of my father, always drinking, always working. Always upset about Mother. What would he do without us? Would he still carry that bag of rolls around, giving them to strange children if we weren't there to take them? Would he

Dear Diary,

It's all over.

We're running away
from my father. We can't
stand it any more. But to
mother is ...

... Kate ...

We're leaving Friday &
going to my father's & you
even though he drinks & you
mean to my mother & he can't
my father & mother he can't
We're going to his finger's
California & finger's
want to ...

who'll take care of my father? Who? Whose going to wash his clothes & make his meals. My mom said I could stay with Basha & help my father, but its my brother, who I'll miss because I love him so. He's the only thing I love (really love) in the whole wide world. Oh Diary I would like to know why all of this is happening to me? Why? Why? Why?

Oh S***, I hope everything turns out al-right.

Please! Dear God, let everything be O.K.

still sit at the dining room table reading the newspaper?

Could he live without us? Who would be there to keep him from throwing chairs out the window?

I ended up at my girlfriend Goldie's house, trying to hide the tears. I didn't say much, and it felt good not to be at home, trying to forget those three suitcases, those already-packed boxes. Two or three hours later I decided I had to go home. I couldn't circle the block forever, or move in with Goldie. But I was determined not to leave my father.

The elevator ride seemed to take forever, like walking to your own execution. I didn't want to see my mother again. I was scared. But when I opened the door, the suitcases and boxes were gone. Mother raced across the room and hugged me, squeezed me tightly against her.

"Oh, I am so glad to see you," she whispered. "I was so worried, Lily!"

"Mother," I began, but she interrupted me.

"I wanted to kill you!" she said. "But I thought you were never coming back. I thought you were never coming back. I didn't realize it meant that much to you."

I could feel my mother's heart beating through her blouse.

"We won't go," she said quietly, whispering into my hair. "We won't go."

~ ~ ~ ~ ~

"Baruch Atah Adonai," my father began, the prayer filling his voice with an ancient holiness.

We held on to those traditions as if we were holding to life itself. It hadn't been very long before that Hitler and the Nazis had tried to destroy our heritage, and I think that made anyone of Jewish ancestry determined to preserve this way of life. Even those of us who didn't understand what those traditions meant, or know the God they pointed to, were bound together by that common resistance against extinction, the desire to survive.

My father repeated the traditional prayers. My brother asked the questions. We ate hard-boiled eggs and matzoh and bitter herbs in remembrance of the deliverance of the Hebrews from bondage in Egypt, and my father hid a piece of matzoh someplace in the house and whoever found it would get a dollar.

"Why is this night different from other nights?" my brother Hymie asked.

I remember the years when he was first old enough to ask the questions. His large eyes reflected the light, and the air in the dining room was as still as the air inside a temple. The dishes shone, and the glasses of red wine gave the room a solemn feel. Everything about life seemed good, then, when we were together as a family, living out our traditions.

~ ~ ~ ~ ~

In the days that followed I finally got the nerve to ask my father to stop drinking, and he agreed. I wrote up a small contract on lined notebook paper, and he signed it.

I happened to find this slip of paper as I went back through my old things. Unfortunately, he didn't follow through on the promise, but I remember how excited and hopeful I felt when I watched him sign the lined paper and date it, 1962.

But nothing changed.

CHAPTER FOUR

I was 16 years old and I laid my hair across the ironing board. Gloria flattened a cloth diaper over it, then ran the hot iron slowly back and forth. I closed my eyes, imagining the straightest hair possible. I pictured Mary Travers from Peter, Paul, and Mary, and I smiled. In high school we all wanted to be her.

Lying there, my eyes closed, the heat radiating from the iron, I also thought of that last visit to the doctor, trying to sit up very straight in a thin hospital gown while the doctor reviewed my record.

"You're full-grown now," he said to me. "Your bones are not going to grow anymore, so your scoliosis is probably not going to get any worse. The curvature is something you can live with."

"But my shoulder blade still sticks out a little," I mumbled.

"Just let your hair grow long and cover it up," he said matter-of-factly, and that's exactly what I did.

When it was Gloria's turn, I stood slowly and ran my fingers through my straightened hair, reached back and felt to where it lay

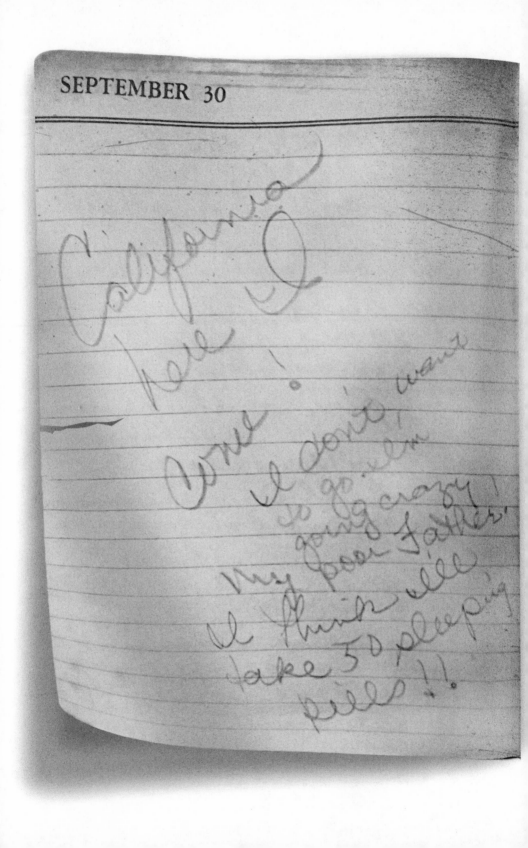

California
here I
come!
I don't want
to go...I'm
going crazy!
My poor Father!
I think I'll
take 50 sleeping
pills!!

over my shoulder blades. Gloria settled into a position so that her hair was on the ironing board. I looked at that bush of curls and shook my head at the impossible task ahead, then tried to lay the cloth diaper flat. She closed her eyes and I went to work.

Those high school years were so intense. One moment Gloria and I would be shopping downtown, my brother Hymie tagging along for the ice cream treats. The next day we'd be talking with our other friends in the apartment building, or arguing with them. Then we'd be making out with our boyfriends in my room on a warm summer day, my father asleep and my mother out grocery shopping. (Gloria's parents watched too closely for anything like that to happen in her apartment.)

Mother encouraged me in the arts from an early age — whether it was the ballet lessons I took at age 5 or the voice lessons at age 12. This love of music and acting was in my blood, too — Mother loved to sing along with the records she put on, and sometimes, while we were watching television, she would get up and dance to the music that came on.

Hymie and I would always protest.

"Mom, what are you doing? Sit down!"

She would laugh and keep dancing, and we would roll our eyes, squirming uncomfortably on the plastic sofa covers. If Gloria was there she would laugh and laugh.

In high school I tried out for anything musical. Christopher Columbus High School had an a capella choir called the Melody Singers, and I became a member. We sang at school functions and rehearsed twice a week. Soon I was addicted to the feelings that came along with performing.

When I sang I felt like my soul was escaping my body, and that's what I wanted — escape. I wanted out of that body that kept letting me down with its blemishes and its scoliosis and its imperfections. Tension in the house between my parents never ceased, and my father continued to drink. My mother continued to run around. At home, I felt the constant pressure to make everything work, to negotiate a tenuous peace between everyone. I went out of my way to arrange happiness for everyone around me. Everyone that is, except myself.

Soon I realized that acting gave me the same opportunity for escape that singing did. I took the lead in all the school plays: *Oklahoma* and *The Glass Menagerie*. It was a new, exciting life, and I went after it.

I remember many times, after the shows were over and the audience was going wild, I felt so important and loved. I scanned the crowd and usually found my mother, beaming with pride, clapping and smiling. I knew she would love nothing better than for me to go into the Jewish theater in New York City — I spoke Yiddish and could act and sing. Why not? I wanted to make her happy.

But my father never came with her. My very first boyfriend, Ronnie Nahoum, had just gotten his driver's license and would sometimes bring her to my shows if she needed a ride.

My senior year finally ended. Being popular at school, doing the things I loved to do with my mother's enthusiastic backing — it was one of the best times of my life. In my graduating class of 600 I won the theater arts award. The caption with my senior yearbook photo said that I was planning on attending Hunter College and becoming an actress, and as I came to the end of high school I felt that I could accomplish anything that I wanted. Forget the scoliosis and the alcoholic father. Forget my parents' deteriorating marriage. I was confident and ready for anything.

But all the action would slow when I found myself in bed at night, the darkness pressing on my eyes. Hymie's slow breathing sounded quietly from the bed across the room. The train click-clacked through the city, and through my window I heard the traffic ease along. I loved the city with its comforting sounds. I loved how it wrapped around me.

I could feel the big world pulling on me. I knew the life I lived in the apartment with my family would not be enough for very much longer. I rolled over and closed my eyes, listening to the city, smiling to myself.

~ ~ ~ ~ ~

I sat on the edge of my bed and stared at my trunk, packed and ready to go. High school had ended only a few weeks before, and I

Now its June 21, 1963

I love the Dear Lord
a miracle must have
happened ——→
We did not go to
Cali. — we stayed
one, all of us-

me
Mom
Sis
Dad

Fishman

stood on the edge of this huge chasm of opportunity — sometimes it took my breath away. My parents agreed to pay my way through a summer course at the Carnegie Institute of Technology in Pittsburgh, which in those days was known for its acting program. George Kennedy and Jack Klugman had graduated there, and in the coming years many of the Hill Street Blues cast would come from that school. In the fall I planned to attend Queens College in New York and major in theater arts. It seemed like the perfect next step after all of my previous acting experience in high school — the fact that I had been accepted into these programs gave me a measure of confidence that I could do it and that I was on the right path.

The taxicab picked me up in front of our building, and as I sat in the seat waiting to pull away I couldn't help but stare. Nearly every night of my life that I could remember had been spent in that building. The swimming pool was there in the empty space between two apartment complexes, and for a moment I remembered my father stumbling in through the gate, drunk and looking for me. I looked away, at the empty lot across the street. As the cab pulled away I resisted the urge to look back through the rear window, instead staring straight ahead, watching as each of the city blocks moved toward me.

The cab arrived in Times Square, where I boarded a bus for Pittsburgh. It all felt so grown up and exciting and full of promise. Was there any goal I couldn't accomplish? Was there any dream that would not come true? But should I forget who I really was, there was always my packed lunch to remind me: a brown paper bag with a tuna sandwich on a Kaiser roll with a dill pickle, a bottle of juice, and a Hershey bar. Carrying it was a little embarrassing, so I hid it in my shoulder bag.

The bus groaned and pulled away, navigating the streets like an elephant. We traveled west, out of the city, and it wasn't long before the high-rises were replaced by vast, empty fields and forests stretching out over rolling hills. The bus picked up speed, and the Pennsylvania countryside flew by in a blur.

When I wasn't dozing or staring out the window, I was surveying the other passengers and creating lives for them. The older couple was headed to a far-off small town to visit their grown kids. They couldn't wait to see their grandchildren. A pair of young lovers was traveling for pure adventure, having no idea where they might end up. See that woman sitting by herself? She was on a cross-country journey to see an old flame. Others were on their way to funerals, or weddings, or reunions. And mine was the most exciting journey of all.

Finally the bus wheezed to a stop in the center of Pittsburgh. I felt at home there calling a cab and loading all my things into the trunk then once again riding through the city. We drove down bustling Forbes Avenue onto the Carnegie campus and stopped in front of a large, brick dorm: Margaret Morrison Hall. My home for the summer.

I hauled my trunk and bag upstairs to my room and pushed open the door. There were two small beds in the main area, and the bathroom had one mirror above the sink. There were two chests of drawers, one on each side of the room, and a window in the center that overlooked a busy side street. I picked a bed, a side of the room, and began transferring my clothes from my trunk into the drawers. Then my roommate walked in.

~ ~ ~ ~ ~

She was tall and thin and very pretty, with long, dark hair. She carried herself very straight and sure, and the look on her face was part sophisticated, part aloof.

"Hi," I said, only because I had to. We were roommates, after all, and would have to speak to one another occasionally, but I couldn't imagine having fun with someone like her. She was so different from my high school friends, so grown-up and professional looking.

"Hello," she said. "I'm Maria Neumann. I'm here from Manhattan."

"I'm Lily," I said. "Lily Fishman." But inside I was thinking, *Oh my God, how can I room with this girl?* I should have guessed she was from Manhattan with that perfect look and that straight hair and those appropriately disinterested eyes. Girls from the Bronx did not mix well with girls from Manhattan. We were in-your-face and direct — they were completely cool and unapproachable.

We chatted while we put our clothes away. Her parents had show business backgrounds, and her knowledge of all the important people and places intimidated me. I couldn't help but feel disappointed that I didn't have a roommate more like me, but on the other hand it was just for a few weeks and then I'd be busy making new friends at college. I sighed and pushed my empty trunk into the corner.

We settled into our daily schedule of classes and acting workshops, and in between sessions I found myself talking to Maria more and more.

"I just want to act," she would say with a sigh, and even though our backgrounds were diverse, that common longing began to unite us. She told me about the lessons she took on Saturdays at Manhattan's "Neighborhood Playhouse," a theater that had churned out Paul Newman and Joanne Woodward, among others. She would tell me about the things she learned there, and I listened, taking it all in.

Outside of our school, a cultural revolution was in full force: the civil rights movement was at its height as Martin Luther King Jr. was preaching civil disobedience and the Black Panthers were promoting black power. The hippy culture petitioned for peace and love, and protests against the Vienam War appeared on nearly every campus.

Perhaps nothing mirrored these movements more than the music sweeping the country: Bob Dylan, Judy Collins, and Joan Baez. The harmonic duo of Simon and Garfunkel were singing about Bleecker Street and the Sound of Silence. If you were young and had a radio, you were listening to either this new brand of powerful music or to the news bulletins barking out the latest changes taking place: protests and sit-ins and Vietnam casualties.

Maria was one of several students who brought guitars to Pittsburgh, and some of us sat around in our rooms and dorm lobbies and stairwells playing music and singing these new songs and talking about our world, balancing on the edge of a revolution. Sometimes Maria would break out something she had written, and I would sit there listening. Then, spontaneously, I would harmonize with her. We both loved how we sounded, our voices ringing out through the stairwell or the dorm rooms. When we finished a song we would both sit there, not saying a word, letting the sound of our singing trail off into silence.

My weeks at the Carnegie Institute went by too fast. Before I knew it I was back on the bus, rumbling through the Pennsylvania countryside. Then we coasted through the New Jersey suburbs and the New York City skyline rose up out of the horizon. Every Simon and Garfunkel song I knew about New York danced through my mind. I pressed my forehead against the glass and smiled.

As soon as I got back to New York City, I hit the street, looking for a good guitar. I visited every instrument store I could find, eventually settling on a beautiful little Favilla with nylon strings for $100. I practiced chords, and for a time all that I wanted to do was play my guitar. In my room, in the stairwell, at the park — in those days you could find me just by listening for the sound of strumming.

Maria and I stayed in touch after returning to New York. We would meet downtown and talk about music and school and the future. My old life, my life in high school and with Gloria, wasn't receding, but my new life with Maria and my dreams of music and acting were merging with it. It seemed everything was evolving, changing: the Beatles and the Rolling Stones, whose sound affected the way everyone viewed folk music, had helped Bob Dylan commit the heresy of playing electrically amplified folk rock. The Byrds were also moving forward, and the genres were melding together before our eyes.

Just like my life.

"Hello?"

"Lily, it's me, Gloria."

"Hey, Gloria. What are you doing?"

"Come with me to Montreal." Her voice was giddy.

"What?"

"Come with me to Montreal, Lily," she said again, laughing. "I'm going to visit my grandparents."

"I don't know if my mom will be okay with that."

"Well, *my* mom wants you to go with me," Gloria protested. "She doesn't want me to go alone. You have to come. Imagine it! Just me and you in Montreal with all those French boys!"

I laughed out loud. It did sound like fun.

"Aren't your grandparents kind of, well, old?"

"Who, Bubby and Zadey?" Gloria said. "We'll behave at the

house, but we've got the whole city at our fingertips!"

That night Gloria's mother called my mother, and we got the okay.

A couple days later we packed and boarded the bus. The ride took six or seven hours. When we arrived in the city everything felt exciting and foreign. Everyone spoke French and almost all the signs were in French and I wondered what it would be like to travel through Europe. Gloria and I took a cab to her grandparents' house, and everything was exactly as I had imagined: quiet and peaceful and slightly dull. But when we got out on our own, in the city, the whole world opened up for us.

One day we walked the streets together. The late summer sun beat down on the sidewalks and the cars raced by us.

"Are you ready for this fall?" Gloria asked me. "Are you ready for college?"

"I can't wait," I said, taking everything in around me. "I really can't wait. It's going to be so exciting."

"I know," she said. "Did you get your paperwork back from Queen's College yet?"

I nodded. During the summer I had changed my mind, deciding instead to attend Queen's College in New York City. It seemed more of a fit for me after my summer experience in Pittsburgh.

Just as we were starting to chatter about the autumn that was only a few weeks away, two motorcycles roared to a stop along the curb beside us. Each was driven by a cute college boy, and they smiled at us and waved us over. Gloria and I looked at each other, our eyes huge. Then we walked over to the curb.

"Where are you guys going?" I asked coyly.

But the two boys just looked back and forth at each other and shrugged. Then one of them starting speaking in French. Gloria and I both groaned. We couldn't even talk with them! Yet once again they motioned for us to get on the back of their motorcycles, sliding forward to make room. We hesitated for a moment. Was it safe? Where would they take us?

But then, without discussing it, we both climbed on.

Her driver moved out into traffic first, dodging a car and quickly getting up to speed. It didn't take long for me and my French-speaking boy to catch up. The wind blew my long hair all over the place, and in front of me Gloria's curly locks flew up behind her. My bell-bottom jeans flapped wildly against my legs. Under my sandals the gravel raced by. I leaned forward and held on tight as we drew up alongside Gloria and her driver.

"Let me off!" I could see Gloria screaming, but either the boy couldn't hear her or he was ignoring her, because both of our motorcycles only went faster. I could see Gloria close her eyes and bite into the guy's jacket. I couldn't stop laughing, and the wind blew into my eyes and made my breaths come in guarded gasps.

The longer the ride went on, the more worried I got. Why did we do this? We could end up anywhere.

But then, as suddenly as it began, it was over. They pulled to a quick stop along the curb in front of Gloria's grandparents' house, right where they had picked us up. We climbed gingerly off the bikes and the boys yelled something at us in French, both of them laughing. Then they zoomed off. Gloria and I sat down on the sidewalk and put our heads back, the sun shining warm on our closed eyes. We were still catching our breath from the excitement. I could still feel the motorcycle humming on the inside of my legs.

The rest of the summer would race away with us, much the same way those boys did on that Montreal day. During August of 1965 the Watts Riots began in Los Angeles and news bulletins about the Vietnam War seared into our minds.

~ ~ ~ ~ ~

The Beatles performed the first stadium rock concert in New York City, and it seemed like the biggest thing ever — somehow Maria got tickets through her mom. We took the bus to Shea Stadium and found our seats, way up in the bleachers. The Beatles looked like tiny ants. All I remember is screaming the entire time, at the top of my lungs.

Late that night we got on the bus, exhausted and barely able to keep our eyes open. Maria spent the night at my house, but we could barely speak from losing our voices at the concert.

From that point on, I was a Beatle-maniac. I bought all their albums and t-shirts and dreamed of meeting them in person, perhaps having a love affair with John Lennon or Paul McCartney (I went back and forth regarding that on a weekly basis). I dressed like them and learned every song.

It was a monumental time in the musical history of our nation, and I was somehow a part of it.

~ ~ ~ ~ ~

I walked toward the bus station through the winter morning, pulling the scarf up higher over my mouth and trying to draw deeper into my winter coat. The cold air made my face tingle, and I wrapped my arms around myself, trying to stay warm. The streets were freezing and hard, yet somehow the cold made everything feel alive. This was the city in the winter.

Finally I climbed into the first of three buses I had to take to get to college, and the warm air melted me. I leaned my head against the cold glass window, the heat bursting out from under the seat. Soon the bus rolled out onto the street and, just as I was about to doze off, it arrived at my stop, so I pried myself out of the warmth and stood in the freezing cold again, waiting. The next bus came, and the whole process was repeated.

That entire first semester I took all the classes I really wanted to take, none of the required general education courses, just acting courses and theater courses on technique and improvisation. They could not teach me enough — I wanted to learn it all. Class after class, hour after hour, and I loved it, breathed it in, consumed it. On the bus, I imagined that I was on stage. At home, I locked the door to my room and pretended I was on a Broadway stage.

Then came the end of the day and the cold waiting, the warm buses, all the way home again. Some of the time, most of the time, I would get home after dark, take the elevator up to my parents' apartment, go into my room, and look out on the city lighting up the snow-covered sidewalks. The cold went right to my bones, but I loved every minute of it.

~ ~ ~ ~ ~

At the end of my first semester in college, my brother Hymie and I boarded the subway and took a one-hour journey into Manhattan, through the snow. It was Christmas Eve, and when we came up from under the streets the city was alive with the holidays: there were Christmas trees and lights everywhere, bells were ringing and Christmas music burst out through every door.

It was the first time we had ever celebrated Christmas.

When we arrived at Maria's house everything was bright and smelled incredible: spices and cider and red wine. The house was full of people, all there for Christmas Eve dinner, and loud voices seemed to come from every room, voices full of happiness and friendship. Loud music played from somewhere in the house and everyone had a cocktail in one hand and an hors d'oeuvres in the other. Hymie's eyes opened wide, as if his sense of sight just couldn't take it all in.

Maria's cheeks were flushed from the warmth and the party, and her parents welcomed us. Her mother walked from room to room, elegant, the perfect hostess, and her father was appropriately removed from the entertaining, chatting intellectually with the other men. Neither of them seemed very religious, but they were Catholic and filled their house with all the traditional decorations. Mistletoe hung from a doorway and there was a Santa Claus in every room. The Christmas tree reached to the ceiling and was covered with tinsel and lights and ornaments.

Then came the meal, with everyone gathered around their huge table. Turkey, ham, all the trimmings, shimmering wine, and then Christmas cookies and spiced cakes for dessert. By the end I was so full I didn't think I would be able to move.

Hymie and I stayed overnight, each of us placed in a plush bed with warm comforters. I fell asleep so filled with Christmas that I nearly believed in Santa Claus. When we woke up on Christmas morning I could smell cinnamon rolls baking in the oven, and the aroma of fresh coffee sifting through the house. We exchanged our gifts with Maria and her parents.

When I close my eyes and think about that morning, I can still smell it. Whenever I think of Christmas, I think of that day.

~ ~ ~ ~ ~

For a moment I looked through the open classroom window — a spring day fell down through the buildings and bright sunlight bounced off the budding trees. Spring in the city lets people breathe again — everyone is relieved to be outside and feeling the air on their skin. Cars cruise the avenues, windows rolled down. Just as I began to daydream, the professor's voice caught my attention and I remembered I was in class, sitting front and center.

I adjusted in my seat, pulled my miniskirt down, but it didn't help to cover my legs. I leaned forward and stared into my professor's eyes, intent, wanting him to know that I cared about French more than any of his other students. Even though I probably didn't. For the most part, I only cared that he saw me — I couldn't stop thinking about him: at night, during the day, on the bus, walking to my classes. Maria and Gloria probably got tired of hearing me talk about him.

He was gorgeous, and I was young and in love and he spoke French.

He paid me a lot of attention, this European-looking, first-year teacher. He was 22 or 23 years old, medium height, with jet black hair. He had olive skin and dark eyes, and I wanted him to look at me, just me, so I flirted shamelessly. But he was courteous and a good teacher and while I imagined that he occasionally sent me a special look, I suppose he was mostly professional and appropriate.

Then, as the semester reached its end, he started to respond. Soon he was flirting back with me, making little comments that teachers probably shouldn't make, talking to me after class. On the last day of the semester I gave him my phone number on a slip of paper.

"Now that I'm not your student anymore, you can call me, right?" I asked.

He just smiled.

"I'll give you a call," he said.

Every night I waited, waited, waited for him to call.

"Mom, any messages for me?" I would ask when I came into the apartment late.

Nothing.

Dear Lenny

Today's the day of the
show and I'm as shaky as
can be. But I'm going to be
the best one on stage. I've
got to. —

The Show was
Terrific & so was
I!

Love
Lillie

Then, two weeks after school ended, he called.

"Hi, Lily," he said, and just the sound of his voice doubled my heart rate. "You want to go to a party with me?"

All the excitement building up made me want to scream, but I very politely said "Yes, of course," and got the details from him. All week I imagined the romantic relationship we would have, the way we would look at each other, what it would be like to kiss him, to be close to him. I imagined this relationship developing into something serious, something worthwhile.

He picked me up, and we went to this party that some friends of his were having in Queens, not far from the school. We were having a good time, dancing and drinking. The music was loud and it was a typical party in the 1960s — lots of joints making the rounds, lots of beer and whisky and clouded conversations that felt cosmopolitan and important.

But this professor of mine just kept drinking shot after shot until his eyes were glazed and his words stumbled over each other.

"Come dance with me," he blurted out.

My knees felt weak, but I stood up and walked with him. The music beat against my skin and pounded inside my head. The lights seemed brighter, and I could hear voices in the shadows talking and laughing and having fun. Cool night air rushed in through windows left barely open.

We slid out onto the dance floor, but he looked confused, head cocked to the side, and suddenly he was throwing up all over the dance floor, right there beside me. For a moment I was a teenager again on a hot summer day and my father was stumbling into the community swimming pool, shouting my name in his drunken voice.

"My Leiala! Where are you? My little Leiala?"

And I wanted to cry and punch this French professor in the face because in his drunkenness he had taken this whole fantasy I had crafted, this whole idea of what my life would be like with him, and he shattered it. He took the feeling I had of being grown-up and dashed it to pieces, and replaced it with the same old feelings of childish embarrassment and being forced to help people out of difficult situations they had gotten themselves into. All of the beautiful nights out, the suave restaurants, the romantic walks, everything I had hoped for suddenly closed in and vanished like a movie screen going black.

I looked around the crowded party for a friend I knew, someone I had recognized earlier in the evening.

"Can you give me a ride home tonight?" I asked them, trying not to let the tears of humiliation fall.

~ ~ ~ ~ ~

During that summer after my first year in college, Maria and I continued our Actor's Guild lessons, and part of it was apprenticing to an off-broadway production. We spent long nights together, rehearsing, going over all these new acting techniques, and studying. We both decided to audition for bit parts in a Greek play, *Antigone*, at the Sheridan Square Playhouse. Maybe this would lead to our big break. Maybe we would meet a director that would pick us out from the crowd. At the least, it would look good on a résumé.

We both tried out, and I got a part, but it was all bittersweet because Maria didn't. For the first time, I would be on my own, but it was important for me. I wanted to prove I had the guts to do it, to go out in the acting world and succeed on my own.

I don't think I was that good in my little part, speaking with the chorus, but it made me feel important because I was able to make friends with some of the other actors. Riding the subway from the Bronx to Greenwich Village on Fridays and Saturdays, dressed in my wide-leg bellbottom jeans, Jesus sandals, and flower-child shirt, I felt like I had what it would take. I could really do it.

I would hop off the subway train and emerge into the world, my hair ironed, briefcase in hand, headed to my off-broadway gig. Carrying that script felt prestigious. I, a Jewish kid from the Bronx, had made it that close to Broadway.

What couldn't I do?

~ ~ ~ ~ ~

"Mom, you should come up and see Maria and me. We've got parts in *Oklahoma!*"

Maria and I both went to summer stock at Woodstock, about 80 miles north of the city, and worked backstage: we built sets, did bit parts, and experienced the backstage chaos and processes that can turn a normal play into a great performance. It was mostly all behind-the-scenes type stuff, but we loved the environment and being away from the city on our own.

I made friends with all the actors, and there was this little Italian place where we would go eat when we could scrape together enough money. One night we sat there eating when I noticed someone resembling Bob Dylan. I just kept looking at him over and over. Then I realized — it was him! It was Bob Dylan! I freaked out. But I was far too nervous to go over and ask him for his autograph, so I just sat there fidgeting at my table, wishing I had the nerve.

Mother eventually came up to see us act. It was so important to me that she was proud of what I was doing. I just wanted to make her happy, and whenever I saw her smiling and clapping in the audience I felt like I was doing something important. Something worthwhile.

I still have a photograph from those days of Maria and I leaning close together in our gingham dresses. I was feeling so good about myself in those days, happy with who I was and who I was becoming. When I got home from Woodstock, my father was still working nights and drinking, my mother still running around with her own friends. But family life was beginning to fade as my own identity began to develop, like one of those Polaroid pictures coming into view.

Even with all the things going on in 1966, I don't think I realized I was in the middle of some kind of cultural or musical revolution. There are things about our lives that we cannot see properly without the perspective of years, decades even. The only things I knew for sure had to do with how much I loved music and acting, how much I loved my life in the city and my wonderful friends, Maria and Gloria.

Maria and I would walk through the Village in 1966, just wandering through the park and hearing a little jam session here, a jam session there. I would go through the park with my guitar in a gig bag, feeling so in touch with life. Maria and I would sit down under a tree and start playing, and before we knew it a small group had gathered around us, singing along to the songs they knew, just listening with their eyes closed to the ones they didn't know. This was life in Greenwich Village in 1966 — peaceful and musical and fantastic.

Like a fairy tale.

I can still feel the air. I can hear the breeze rustling the branches in between songs, I can still feel the way my heart would jump a little when a few new strangers would sit down to listen to us sing. The guys' beards were long and bushy and the girls' hair straight and even. I wasn't famous at all, and neither was Maria, but that's what the park was about — you could be listening to a nobody with a great voice, or you could be listening to Judy Collins or Steve Crider or Sam Bush. Richard Greene or Gene Yellin.

The Village wasn't as pretty back then as it is now — there were still a lot of shops, but it was rough around the edges. Yet it was a place for anybody who wanted to sing or play their guitar, harmonica, banjo, anything. It was a summertime sort of place, and we'd stay there until the sun went down, then head to a bar or a coffee shop to listen some more.

I don't remember the first time it happened, but Maria and I started getting calls from people who heard us singing in the Village, asking us to perform at parties or open nights at their bars and shops. It was a gradual transition, but it would lead to bigger things, both professionally and personally.

Things I couldn't even imagine.

CHAPTER FIVE

Maria and I looked at each other, nodded our heads, and started playing. We leaned forward on the sofa, and our voices combined and swirled in the air, sounding out through the small flat. Just the thought of singing with Maria back then makes me want to close my eyes and start humming. We really had something special.

The talking at the party began to quiet as everyone turned and watched us. Some people leaned against the wall, holding their drinks and snacks; others sat down on the other sofas and chairs, or cross-legged on the floor. The environment was very relaxed, and we felt completely at home. We had been performing together for over a year at that point, starting in the isolated stairwells of Carnegie Mellon, then for our friends, then in front of impromptu crowds in the Village. Now there were people calling us, asking if we would sing at their parties or bars.

We played long into the night, and sometimes the crowd listened the entire time. At other times they mingled and talked quietly, but it didn't bother us. We were so focused on our music. We'd go from song to song, some popular favorites, others that we had written. As the night came to a close we began putting our guitars away, feeling tired and exhilarated.

Many times, at the end of those parties, folks came up to us, wanting to talk or find out more about our music or ask us to play for them somewhere. Sometimes another musician would sit down beside us and we'd talk shop — those were my favorite conversations, discussing music and songwriting and the sounds of other bands.

I suppose we weren't that surprised when this small man approached — he had dark hair and was very charismatic.

"Hi! Maria? Lily? Nice to meet you. I'm Stu Crane."

We both smiled and shook his hand.

"I think you've got something going on here, a very interesting sound. You both just sound so beautiful."

We smiled again. He was very nice, and he had this aura of excitement about him that, for a moment, made you believe everything he said was possible.

"Do you know Jay and the Americans? We've had some radio hits. A great band. Anyway, I'm their manager."

I looked at Maria. We had heard Jay and the Americans on the radio.

"I think I might be able to get you an audition with Columbia Records," the man continued.

As soon as he said Columbia Records, this voice of reason came into my head. It seemed almost silly, that this man might think that Columbia Records would be interested in us. It all felt like a harmless joke — after all, Dylan recorded with Columbia Records. Bob Dylan. THE Bob Dylan.

"Yeah, sure," I said. "We'd love to."

As he walked away with our phone numbers, Maria and I looked at each other and rolled our eyes. I guess both of us felt excited to talk to someone like that, but we couldn't imagine it was possible. I figured he was just an excitable little man blowing smoke, or flirting with us. There we were, two young girls who didn't have a clue about what we were doing. Neither of us gave that conversation a second thought — we figured we'd never hear from him again.

About a week later, though, he did call, and he gave us the phone number for an entertainment attorney. She had written some of her own songs and knew the industry well. She felt our image had potential, with Simon and Garfunkel popularizing the folk scene and people really going for the harmonizing duet sound. She worked with some major acts and got us an appointment for an audition with John Hammond at Columbia Records.

Suddenly it was real.

John Hammond had discovered Billie Holiday, Benny Goodman, Bob Dylan, and Joni Mitchell. Now it would be us playing for him, Lily and Maria. We just about freaked out.

~ ~ ~ ~ ~

I spent two or three hours picking out something to wear, my hands shaking. Everything I put on felt funny or uncomfortable, or looked weird, and we had to look the perfect part. I took some time out from choosing a wardrobe to iron my hair, and eventually I chose a short skirt with a loose top and boots. I was living in two places those days, sometimes with my parents and sometimes with Maria, so a lot of my stuff was divided up between houses.

When I met up with Maria I thought she looked just gorgeous — she wore a dress, too, with a jacket, and her long, dark hair was straight, hanging down her back. She had such a nice figure, and her deep-set, dark eyes were striking. We both wore long, beaded necklaces, and I had my Star of David around my neck, something I had worn for years. I guess maybe I wore it for luck.

"Are you ready?" she asked me.

I nodded, the biggest smile on my face, the most enormous butterflies in my stomach nearly lifting me off the ground.

We got onto the subway at Maria's parents' apartment to ride the 23 blocks to West 57th Street, where the Columbia offices and recording studios were located. When we walked up in front of that massive building, we had to stop for a moment — I was out of breath and nervous beyond belief. Neither one of us knew what to expect. Would we play in a recording studio or an office or on a stage somewhere? How many people would be there — 3, 10, 15? Who would be there? I was very nervous about somehow being embarrassed or humiliated by these professionals. Would they laugh when they heard us, apologize, insist it was some kind of mistake? We stood there outside the building, just killing time.

Maria looked over at me. "Are you ready to go in, Lily?"

I nodded, took a deep breath, and then we went inside.

One of the women from the front desk escorted us to a side office and led us to two chairs on one side of the room. We pulled our guitars out and started tuning them, not really saying anything. I don't know what Maria was thinking, but I was trying to decide what songs would be best for us to play. Then we sat there, waiting, whispering to one another.

A group of men came in and they all sat down. One of the gentlemen spoke up. "Thanks for coming, girls. Can you play something for us?"

I have no idea what we sang. I only remember that my mouth was so dry I couldn't believe words were coming out. The strings vanished from under my fingers — all feeling was completely gone. Numb. It was as if I were somewhere outside of my body, watching these two 19-year-old girls auditioning for Columbia Records, and I couldn't believe they had the nerve to do it. And I couldn't believe they were us.

There was nothing between us and the businessmen, just our voices and the sound of our guitars. No microphones or speakers. And they all sat there very politely, very quietly, just listening — I don't remember if they moved at all to the music, or what their faces looked like as we played. I was in another time and place. I was there, yet I wasn't there.

As we packed up our things, the gentlemen spoke in hushed tones. At some point one of them spoke up.

"We definitely like your sound and would like to make an album with you. We're offering a $10,000 advance that you can use for recording, and you can do your own songs."

I wanted to scream, but I didn't. We knew that Stu would handle all the details. I don't even remember saying anything, but I know that somehow we got our things together and walked out of that office. How did I walk? My legs were weak, and I could barely breathe. When we got out onto 57th street we just looked at each other in disbelief, then started jumping up and down and going crazy. We had a recording contract. We would have our own album. Would we be the next big thing? Would Lily and Maria become a household name?

~ ~ ~ ~ ~

I think in those days I found a lot of value in throwing myself into things — it helped give me an identity and avoid the unpleasant parts of my life, like my father's problems with alcohol, my insecurities regarding my scoliosis, or my parents' relationship. When something came along that I could throw all of my energy into, I did it whole-heartedly, without reservation. That was how I escaped: in high school it was acting; then, in college, it became playing music with Maria. Later it would be other things.

I could tell the recording process was going to take a lot of time and energy, and I just couldn't imagine myself going into it with everything I had if I was still riding three buses to college and back every day of the week. It didn't seem possible. The only option I could see was dropping out of Queen's, but at first I couldn't gather the courage to tell Mother, even though I knew that was the decision I was making.

For a few days I walked around, pinching myself, unable to believe this recording contract was real, unable to face Mother with the news. I felt so conflicted — one moment I was on a complete high, thinking about the contract, but the next moment I would plunge into these miniature bouts with depression, scared to death of telling mother I was dropping out of college.

One night I decided the time had come.

She was lying in her bed, in that little bedroom off of the kitchen. My father was still at work, and there really wasn't any point in going around Mother on this one anyway — she would find out one way or the other, and I was pretty sure I would have to face her wrath in either case. So I eased open their accordion door and peeked inside.

"Mom," I said, standing in the doorway. "We've got to talk about something. And I don't want you to say anything until you hear me out."

She sat up in bed and looked me straight in the eye, which intimidated me way more than those executives in the Columbia Records office.

I started again, reluctantly. "This record contract is a big, really big, deal, and I want to be able to go for it. The recording could take weeks, even months, and when it comes out we might have to go on tour. I want to take a leave of absence from college."

"No," she said, interrupting me. "If you leave now, you'll never go back. You'll never finish your education."

I knew that for her to interrupt me she must be upset. I looked at her sitting there, and I already knew what I was going to do, and it hurt me to see that no matter what I said we would be at odds about it. I was old enough to make my own decisions, but I so desperately wanted her blessing. I wanted her to see what a big deal this was.

But inside she was still a little Jewish girl who hadn't gone past the fifth grade, and she wanted so much more for her children. She wanted us to get ahead, to progress, and she knew that getting an education played a huge part in that. They could take away your livelihood, they could take away your liberty — she had seen all of these things happen. But they could never take away what you learned. Those things were embedded in your mind forever.

"But, Mom, I will go back! I know what I'm doing! You don't understand what a big opportunity this is — this is one in a million! People dream about getting chances like this for their whole lives and it never happens. Maria and I, we've got it, right here in our hands! I want to make the most of it. Please, Mom, try to understand."

"It's not bigger than an education," she said from there in her bed, her voice even and unyielding. "You'd be making a big, big mistake. The biggest mistake of your life."

I could feel the tears pushing up into my eyes.

"Well, I have to try it. I just have to."

I walked out of the bedroom crying and torn between what I knew I had to do and what I knew my mother desperately wanted. I stopped in the kitchen. I knew what I was going to do and didn't want to drag it out any further, so I turned around and stood back in the doorway again.

"Well, I'm sorry, Mom. I just have to do this. I have to try."

The next day I filed for a leave of absence from Queens College. Mother and I didn't talk for a long time, and the tension in the house was thick. I probably stayed at Maria's house more often in those days, especially once the recording started. I felt sad that Mother couldn't come around to my way of thinking, but I still knew it was the right thing to do.

I guess Mother was right in one respect — I never did go back to Queen's. But it was an opportunity for a life-changing experience, and I took it. After all, my dad was doing his own thing, and Mom was, too. Everyone in our family lived their own life. Even Hymie seemed to fly under my radar — soon he'd be on his own at college. There seemed to be so little holding us together.

~ ~ ~ ~ ~

Maria and I began selecting songs and working up arrangements in the spring and summer of 1967. An 18-year-old guitar player from Indiana named Steve Kreider helped us arrange and rehearse songs and worked up guitar parts. At first we practiced in Maria's living room, then in an old loft near Chambers Street that was a crash pad for a Texas band. It seemed like every waking moment was spent practicing — our lives were consumed with making music, our music, and I couldn't imagine trying to do school at the same time.

Our practice times leading up to recording in the studio were so intense that Maria beat her leg black and blue with the tambourine. We wanted to be ready.

Finally the recording began. Walking into the studio, with its huge recording console and professional microphones and headsets, felt like an out-of-body experience. Our producer was Gary Sherman — he had arranged music for the Drifters and produced Freddie Scott. Our engineer was Roy Halee — he engineered Dylan's "Like a Rolling Stone," as well as everything that Simon and Garfunkel and the Byrds had done.

Sometimes we would sing the same song over and over and over again. When we would finish a song, or part of a song, we'd look up, hoping it was good enough.

"Let's try that one more time, girls," they'd say, and we'd start over.

We worked on that album for three months, two to three days a week. It didn't take Maria and I long to find out that, even though we were doing our own material, the album wasn't going to sound anything like what we had expected. And we were too young and inexperienced to jump in and say, "Wait, this isn't what we want," or, "Hold on, we don't like how that sounds." Are you kidding? We were 19, maybe 20 by then, and we were working with professionals. We trusted them to create the right product.

It would be our biggest mistake.

Our strength, prior to the recording, was in our harmonies. That's what caught people's attention in the park or at the parties we played — the combination of our voices somehow created this unique sound, something that made people stop and listen. Our harmonies were pure and clean and crisp, something special, especially when it was just our guitars and us.

That's one reason Maria's parents thought Columbia Records, and especially John Hammond, would be the perfect fit for us. He had recorded Dylan's pining tones and included only his guitar and harmonica — a powerful combination, especially in its simplicity. But Gary thought we needed orchestration, and lots of it, adding string arrangements and rock effects.

We didn't like the first playbacks and re-recorded some of it, but it didn't get much closer to what we liked or expected. Lots of people around us complained that the album was overproduced and needed less of Gary's production and more of just our voices and guitars. We started out as a folk duo, but the album sounded more like folk rock, even acid rock. I'm not even sure what you would call it — you'd have to hear it for yourself.

I guess everyone always has different opinions about how any album is put together. Even the name drew some controversial discussions

— we had chosen Lily and Maria, and even though it had a nice sound to it, Maria's parents made it clear they would have preferred Maria and Lily.

But the album was finally finished, and it was time to promote it. Columbia Records released the first single, "Everybody Knows," and we all waited to see what would happen next.

We worked hard promoting the album, playing wherever we could. Most of our nights, especially on the weekends, were booked. We started playing gigs in the Village at places like the Village Cafe, and even auditioned at the Bitter End for the chance to play some shows on the college circuit. We met Linda Ronstadt and the Stone Poneys there — soon they would be opening for bands like the Doors, and later that year they released a single that would launch Linda's career.

We didn't go on tour, but we did earn a few college gigs from the Bitter End audition, and when our single took off in Cleveland we went there and did a live television show.

Meanwhile, we kept pushing our sound around New York City. We visited the Upper East side apartment of *Tonight Show* band leader Skitch Henderson a few times — there was a studio on one floor at a party attended by Steve Lawrence and Eydie Gorme. I remember playing in dresses we had made especially for that occasion.

All of this was going on in the larger context of America in the '60s, yet somehow Maria and I managed to avoid the drug scene. If there was anything we did in excess, it was devouring Haagen-Daas rum raisin ice cream on Maria's couch after a long night of playing. Don't get me wrong, we smoked marijuana from time to time, and drank on occasion, but neither of us ever got swept away by it.

Very little about those years feels real to me — it happened fast, and we were so young that it felt like a game, a huge party, and we were just along for the ride. The parties, the fans, the music — all of it came in a whirlwind. Yet with all we were doing, none of it ever translated financially. We never saw a dime of the $10,000 advance from the label — that all went straight into the costs of recording, which had mounted for no good reason. That meant Maria and I were both living off of our parents' money, and that couldn't last forever.

We both decided that while the album was being distributed we should get part-time jobs. Soon, both of us were working at Bellevue hospital, handling files, arranging records, taking the occasional phone call. It wasn't the glorious rock star life we had hoped for, but there was something nice about earning my own money, working my way through life at a job I didn't necessarily like while still working hard on our music.

Maria decided to move into her own place, a little walk-up on Avenue A in the East Village. Her parents had moved to Los Angeles, where her mother was teaching ballet at UCLA. Maria didn't want to move — we both wanted to see what would happen with our album. We both believed so much in what we were doing that we would do anything to pursue it, whether that meant dropping out of college or moving out on our own.

I still lived with my parents, but I stayed with Maria a lot. The apartment was basically one room with a bed behind a partition and a toilet in a little closet. The bathtub sat right in the middle of the room, and there was an old gas heater that had to be turned off at night so the gas fumes wouldn't overcome you. We'd wake up on those cold winter mornings to a fine layer of ice on the inside of the windows.

It felt like we were playing house. I sat at the window and watched all the commotion in the Village, and in that same room we had the kitchen table, the bathtub, and the bed! The bathtub was one of those old claw foot bathtubs with a curtain that hung from the ceiling on a runner, and you could pull it around the tub for privacy. We fixed that place up with anything we could find on the street: old armchairs or throwaway rugs and lamps, and eventually it became this getaway, a perfect little flat. I preferred it to my own house, in a way.

There were only two things we didn't like about the place. One was carrying the groceries, or anything really, up all those flights of steps. I could have done without all those steps. The second thing was an old lady downstairs, a self-appointed concierge, who screamed at Maria whenever she brought a guy into the building.

After a few months, Maria decided she wanted a place farther uptown. We talked about me possibly moving in with her, and I decided I would. It was a huge decision for me to move out of my mom and dad's house, but Maria and I spent a lot of time together. And if we lived together, we could play our music nonstop.

We got a small, 10th-floor apartment on 84th between Riverside and Columbus. The living room and bedroom were one area, but there was a small kitchen and bathroom that were separate. The main area was large enough that we could put two couches on either side of the room, one of which opened up into a bed, and during the day we would use both of them as couches. But the thing I remember most about that apartment was the rocking chair.

Maria had always had a rocking chair, wherever she lived, and she had this habit of rocking. She would sit there, rocking back and forth, back and forth, holding a cigarette, thinking about a song. She called it conkling, rocking back and forth like Ray Charles, and when I saw her doing it I knew she was thinking up some fantastic song or new theory to share with the world.

I can still picture her with her eyes closed, slowly smoking a cigarette, her whole body swaying front and back.

That was where we were living when, in the cold early months of 1968, we were booked into a legendary little spot in Greenwich Village called Gerde's Folk City. What happened in that tiny club would change my life.

CHAPTER SIX

Maria and I had just finished a Monday night show at Gerde's, a small coffeehouse on 4th Street that had promoted folk music since the late 1950s. Their Monday nights started off as amateur nights, but after spawning folk legends like Bob Dylan, Tom Paxton, Judy Collins, and Arlo Guthrie, the place became a big hangout and was seen as an important launching point for the careers of folk musicians.

Anyway, Maria and I were cleaning up in the dressing room with barely enough room to turn around. It smelled damp and moldy and reeked of old cigarette smoke and dill pickles, yet something about the bustle and environment of those changing rooms made me feel like I had really made it. Bob Dylan had probably smoked cigarettes in that room, and that turned what would normally be a sour odor into the smell of hope and success.

Through the door I could hear the band we were sharing the bill with: the Greenbriar Boys. They picked away on their bluegrass banjos, and the guitar twanged in a way it wouldn't for us folk singers. I didn't understand their kind of music, but the skill it took to interweave and play the way they did blew both Maria and I away. Folk music came from the English ballads, and seemed to carry a weight and depth to it that sometimes made me ache. But bluegrass music was primal and authentic — everything that needed to be said was right there for everyone to see. It fascinated me.

Maria and I came up out of the dressing room into the main area of Gerde's — it was a small, eccentric place with a tiny stage. The whole bar probably couldn't hold one hundred people. We grabbed a table and ordered the tuna fish sandwiches on rye bread (they had the best rye bread in the world) with dill pickles, and I got a Brandy Alexander. I felt so liberated in that place, having a drink, smelling the cigarette smoke and the freedom, people coming up and telling us how much they enjoyed the show.

"What's the banjo player's name?" I asked someone.

"Joe Isaacs."

"Joe," I said to myself. He was adorable.

After the show Maria and I hung around, and we ended up talking to the Greenbriar Boys. We got to meet some of the members of the band — Frank Wakefield was the leader, a vocalist and mandolin player. Their lead guitar player was called Buck. He asked me out later, but I turned him down — I was kind of stuck on Joe.

Joe was 21 years old, just a Kentucky hillbilly all the way, with jet-black hair and dark eyes and one of those Kentucky accents that caught me off guard. I really loved the way he talked. He was Mr. Personality on the stage, just bouncing around, and he was charismatic off stage, too, friendly with everyone and flirting nonstop. Frank would often introduce Joe as "Joe Isaacs, the only Jewboy in the group," and that got my attention right away. I assumed that with the last name of Isaacs he must be Jewish — when I found out he wasn't, it only made me want to date him more.

"Hey, Lily," Joe asked me one night after the show. "You want to have dinner sometime?"

Then one night, down in that dark, musty-smelling dressing room, he came to talk. I asked him where he was from. He asked me about New York. We moved closer, and he flirted with me. Before he left we had kissed, and I thought I might just fly up those steps.

We started going out a lot. I was infatuated with him right away. He came up to our apartment now and then — from the beginning our relationship was passionate. He was romantic, and I loved being in his arms. He never seemed afraid of anything, and I felt safe with him.

"Will you marry me, Lily?" he asked playfully one day.

I laughed it off, but his playful self-confidence disarmed me. I knew it was going to be an intense relationship. I couldn't picture how things would ever work out between a Jewish girl from the Bronx and a bluegrass singer from Kentucky, but that didn't stop my mind from trying to figure it out.

Soon we were together every day. But then, seemingly out of nowhere, the Greenbriar Boys' six-week engagement at Gerde's came to an end, and Joe went back to Ohio where he was living at the time.

"Don't worry, Lily," he said with that trademark smile. "I'll come back and visit you as soon as I can."

I wondered if he would, or if that was just as off the cuff as his proposal. But as soon as he was gone, there was one thing that I knew — I was very deeply involved with Joe emotionally, and there would be no forgetting him. What had started as flirtation and enchantment had quickly moved to abandoning myself to that great physical attraction — I was young and hormonal and foolish, and things like consequences bore no weight in the way I thought.

There was nothing at all rational about it — when Joe was in the city, everything was light and airy and fun, but as soon as he left the balloon was deflated. I spent my evenings at home, waiting for him to call. Depression pushed in around the edges of my mind. New York by itself just wasn't enough anymore.

~ ~ ~ ~ ~

I picked up a few more odd jobs like the one I had at Bellevue Hospital, trying to make a little money, and my days gathered pace and a certain routine. I took the bus across the city to my various jobs, my eyes occasionally heavy from the previous night's show. I wouldn't be surprised if my mother walked around the house those days with that

"I told you so" look in her eyes — the album wasn't really taking off, and now I wasn't in school, just working part-time jobs and playing a few gigs here and there.

But if she did have that look in her eyes, I didn't notice. I just sat around, either at my apartment or at my parents' house, waiting for the phone to ring.

Finally, a few weeks later, Joe called.

"Hey, Lily," he said, and the sound of his voice was so fresh. No one I knew had that accent, so when I heard him talk it was instant flashback to the times we had together in the city.

"Hey, Joe. Where've you been?"

"Oh, just here and there. I'm coming to the city for a visit next week. Can you pick me up?"

I didn't drive at the time, so I took a cab out and picked him up, and everything was the same again, as if he had never left New York. The more time we spent together, the more I realized there was no one like him — a southern hillbilly, comfortable in his own skin and a self-taught mechanic and musician. Most of our conversations revolved around his background and what it was like growing up in Kentucky.

He stayed with Maria and me for a week in that cramped little apartment, and it was the time of my life. We fell into our old habits of talking late into the night, making out, and doing things around town. I didn't want him to leave. But he did.

Joe flew back to Ohio, and we kept in touch by phone pretty often. About this time I had to move out of the apartment with Maria and back in with my parents. I didn't have the money to stay on my own, and my parents couldn't afford to support me. I kept working my part-time jobs and stayed with Maria in Manhattan when we had shows.

But my focus was changing — I cared less and less about our album, and more and more about my conversations with Joe. I lived for the next call or hints that he'd drop about coming to visit again. Then, out of the blue, he stopped calling. No word, no reason, just silence. My subway ride home from work was filled with questions about whether or not he had called, and when I got into my parents' apartment I asked the same thing.

"Anyone call?"

Week after week went by without any word. Sometimes I would just sit, on the bus or at work or backstage, crying my eyes out, not able to function because of that weight of rejection. The weeks turned into months, and I could tell mother worried about me. I worried about myself. But there was nothing I could do to get out of that downward spiral.

~ ~ ~ ~ ~

"Joe? Joe, is this you?"

"Yeah, yeah, it's me. What's up, Lily? How are you?"

I had to sit down. I don't know why I kept trying to get in touch with him all those months, why I didn't just give up. I guess I just couldn't believe that all those good times we had in the Village were for nothing, especially after he came and visited and we had such a good time.

"What's up? How am I? Joe, we haven't spoken in months! Where have you been? I've been worried sick about you! What's wrong? Why don't you call me anymore?"

Just silence. Then he finally told me — there was someone else. I could feel myself falling into this bottomless pit.

"Lily? I have to go. I'm glad to hear from you."

Perhaps that phone call allowed me to hit bottom, to reach a point where I could take inventory of my existence and start again. I got busy with life, writing songs and playing gigs with Maria, working longer hours at the hospital. I tried to fill my life with activities, anything that would help me not to think about him, if even for just a few minutes at a time.

Then, just as I began to settle back into life, Joe started calling again.

"Hey, Lily, it's Joe."

"Hi, Joe," I said, trying not to go back to how I had felt before, but an old ache couldn't help but rise to the surface. "What are you doing?"

"I just wanted to say hi. How are you?"

"Oh, I'm doing okay, I guess. How are things in Ohio?"

Joe grew quiet for a moment.

"That's kind of why I'm calling. Things aren't working out for me here. I can understand if you don't want anything to do with me. But I wanted to let you know I'm coming back to New York, regardless. I really liked it there, and I want to play music."

And again I let him back in — not quickly at first, but the red flags were coming down. I was so attracted to him and what he brought to my life that I was willing to overlook these other issues. Since he was coming to New York whether or not I wanted him to made it easier for me to spend time with him. We talked things over and eventually decided to pick up where we'd left off.

Then he was back in New York and it felt like nothing had ever changed. Joe got an apartment in the Village with some friends he'd met on his earlier visits — one of them was Charlie Blake, a bluegrass musician, and the two of them put together a band and began singing around town. He also got a job working in a leather factory, just to pay the bills.

Those six months in New York, when Joe came back, were some of the best in our time together. The city felt more alive than ever, and we would roam the streets listening to new bands and fresh sounds. In the evenings, if Maria and I or Joe weren't at a show, we'd hang out in Maria's apartment playing music and harmonizing. The three of us sounded really good together, and we enjoyed each other's company.

Joe taught us all the old bluegrass favorites — he was a walking encyclopedia of the genre, having sung lead and played guitar for Ralph Stanley before teaming up with Frank Wakefield. When he picked at the banjo Maria and I would try to watch his fingers and learn the rhythms, but mostly we were mesmerized.

I learned so much about him during that time. He had a mind for anything mechanical, more than anyone I had ever met: he was great with his hands and had learned to take apart a car engine and put it back together when he was five or six years old. He could play any number of instruments.

And all of this he had learned back in the holler where he grew up in Kentucky, and the more I learned about that remote place, the more it took on some sort of fantastical trait. I could hardly believe he was the youngest of 17 children, or that he grew up in a log cabin his father built in the woods, with an outhouse and wood stoves and no electricity or running water. It sounded to me like some third-world country the Peace Corps might send you to. He promised to take me there someday.

As I saw him adjusting to life in the big city, a maternal part of me came out. I wanted to help, to give him some of the skills we took for granted. I guess I thought I could make him more of a city slicker — that I could help him become what I wanted him to be, instead of letting him be who he really was.

I taught him about riding on the subway and explained why you couldn't be friendly with everyone you saw. I showed him how to be wary in different circumstances on the streets of New York. His generosity and bravery would have him walking the Harlem streets at night, talking to anyone that crossed his path, and his accent was a dead giveaway to his innocence and naiveté.

Just as I thought I was changing him, he was changing me. When he talked about his parents and extended family in Kentucky, I felt a longing rise up in me for this kind of community, the kind of family feeling I just didn't get with my parents. When he talked about hog killing and making lye soap and bathing in the creek and riding a horse, hoeing corn, or gathering tobacco, I became very enamored with that backwoods life.

"We have a kerosene lantern in the living room," he told me, "that glows off the cabin beams, and a wood stove to cook on — the smell of wood smoke is always lingering about the house."

My fascination with the mountain folks and their way of life fostered this seed of an idea in me — I began to see those beautiful faraway places in a different way. I began to fantasize about going south, educating the children and Kentucky folk about life outside the mountains, helping them follow in Joe's footsteps and make their way in the big world. I suddenly thought I might have a lot to offer.

As Joe and I grew closer, Maria and I began to pull apart. Maria liked Joe, but she definitely had her concerns about how stormy our relationship was. Joe and I loved each other fiercely, but that passion could just as easily swing into angry, tearful scenes. Maria knew Joe didn't have a mean streak, but she sometimes commented on how much he drank.

I found out later that Maria had also commented on our relationship to a friend.

"I know she is gone," Maria said of me. "And I know there is nothing I can say or do. It's just her fate."

It didn't help that Maria's and my recording career was going nowhere. Maria always seemed slightly bothered by how quickly we got our first deal. I think she would have preferred to slog away for years, singing in little cafes, developing our musical sound. But we hit it big, perhaps too fast, after writing a few songs and singing in front of the right people and suddenly we were on Dylan's label. And just as suddenly we were stalled.

Then there were some strange rumors that there were Mafia connections among some of the people helping us along, and Maria became downright terrified. It was like we were on the edge of this precipice, looking over into a part of the city with which we'd rather not get involved.

"Lily," she said one day. "We're not making a lot of money for anybody yet. We haven't got any hits. Columbia still has an option on a second album and they're not beating the door down — let's just vanish and get out of this."

We decided to abort the record deal and split up. Perhaps we'd get together later on (which, like my returning to school, never happened). Maria moved to Los Angeles with her parents, and I settled in with mine. All of this would have been devastating for me if I didn't have Joe to lean on and put my hope in. It was another shift for me, another thing to take up my energy.

A relationship with Joe seemed the answer to everything back then. He had the musical interest and talent of Maria, but the masculinity and attractiveness I was looking for in a man. Even though we had a rocky courtship, we moved ahead into what I thought could quite possibly be the perfect relationship.

~ ~ ~ ~ ~

There was an engagement ring on my finger before I knew it, although there was no official proposal. Everything just happened naturally, and I took it as it came, falling more and more in love with Joe. I didn't care about a wedding or where we would live or any of that practical stuff. All I cared about was living with Joe for the rest of my life.

Meanwhile, my musical career was on hold. After Maria left town I stopped playing gigs or writing much material. But Joe's music was moving. He recorded an album for Decca Records, and among his stellar sidemen were fiddler Richard Greene, guitarist Gene Yellin, bassist Kevin Smith, Fred Bartenstein, and Frank Wakefield on mandolin. Somehow, though, Joe became moody and depressed in New York.

I tried to imagine what it would have been like for me, far from my family and the only home I'd known, being thrown into a completely different lifestyle. I thought I could relate with how he felt. He started drinking even more than usual and grumbling about New York, occasionally talking about how much he wanted to move back to Ohio or Kentucky.

Knowing what I know now, I sometimes wonder if Joe's restlessness wasn't the result of some internal conflict. His father was a preacher, solidly opinionated about the Bible and how a believer should live. Joe had never dedicated his life to Christianity, and he was certainly no saint, but he believed much of what his father preached. His drinking and the music he played went against everything his father taught.

I think this feeling of miserable conviction drew him in some strange way back to his roots. My family's Jewishness was cultural and had little effect on how I lived my life — there were some traditions and beliefs I felt were important, but for the most part it didn't impact my day-to-day choices. This wasn't the case for Joe, where his father's teachings demanded a certain lifestyle. Occasionally, this difference in how we viewed the world would cause arguments — I don't know, maybe we should have seen this as a warning sign about our being together, but we were in love and it didn't really matter to us at the time.

Soon he had a chance to go back to his roots.

"Lily, something's come up," he told me. "My friend Larry Sparks is forming his own group back in Ohio. We'll be the Lonesome Ramblers."

I felt okay with it. After all, I had a ring on my finger and could see how unhappy Joe was in New York. So late in 1969 he moved back to Ohio where the new group would be headquartered.

A few weeks passed, and Joe called with the invitation I had been waiting for. "Why don't you come out and visit?" he asked. "I'll show you where I live and take you down to the holler in Kentucky where I grew up."

I was really excited — apart from visits to the resorts in Pennsylvania, my time at Carnegie Melon, and that short trip to Montreal with Gloria, I hadn't traveled outside of New York. I took a week's worth of vacation from my job at the hospital and arranged a flight to Lexington to meet up with Joe.

One problem, though: I had never been in an airplane before, and the thought of leaving the ground petrified me. I didn't sleep at all on the night leading up to my departure, and when I kissed my parents goodbye as I got into the cab, I thought I'd probably never see them again — not because I wouldn't come back if I could, but because I thought I probably wouldn't survive the flight.

I boarded my plane in LaGuardia, more nervous than I had ever felt playing a gig or even auditioning in front of those men at Columbia Records. My hands shook when I held out my ticket for the attendant to take. I sat down in the middle of three seats – on one side of me was an 80-year-old Spanish woman in the United States for the first time, and she barely knew three words of English. To the other side was a 9-year-old girl flying alone for the first time, and she looked just about as nervous as I felt. She was flying out to see her grandparents.

Then, miracle of all miracles, that huge plane lifted off the ground and began to soar. We rose up and flew over the countryside, leaving the city behind.

Before I knew it we were flying over Pennsylvania, almost the same path I had taken on that bus to Pittsburgh only a few years before. How many things had changed since then! I had gone from a high school kid full of hope and determination to a recorded artist playing gigs all over New York City, to a young woman in love, flying across the country to see the man I was engaged to.

With every shimmy and shake of that plane, I thought we were going down. But it's in my nature to be a protector, so I started focusing on making the little girl beside me comfortable. We played little games and became friends, laughing and joking. I dug some of my high school Spanish from the recesses of my mind so that I could have at least a basic conversation with the Spanish lady. She was so brave to come to this country without knowing the language.

From then on I didn't even think about the flight until I felt that slightest of drops, and the plane began its descent. It dawned on me that when I tried to help others, I forgot about myself and my problems seemed a lot smaller.

Joe met me at the airport, and we hugged and kissed and I was so happy to see him. Seeing him there with his dark hair and relaxed smile I fell more and more in love with him. I realized that no matter how much I loved the city, I would leave it in a second if it meant spending my life with Joe.

As we drove away from the Lexington airport, I was amazed at the majestic surroundings. Those East Kentucky hills rose up and up into the clouds, and everything was so green and lush. Here was a place that seemed far removed from the turmoil and cultural changes going on in the rest of the country. The university protests and Vietnam War and racial strife felt a million miles away while we drove the back country highways.

I'll never forget the huge yards of those rural houses, stretching up to the base of the hills. Clotheslines hung from house to tree with colorful garments flapping in the breeze that swept through the valleys. The gardens looked like something out of Eden, with barefoot children chasing their dogs and cats around the houses. It was peaceful — a mountain version of *Little House on the Prairie*.

There was no traffic, and I sat right up against Joe. I felt part of something unique and wonderful — I was this city-born hippie wearing a flower-child blouse and bell-bottom jeans, my straight hair halfway down my back, and beside me sat this handsome and talented backwoods banjo picker. Joe's arm was around me, and the smell of leaves and grass and fields flooded in through the open car windows. I smoked a cigarette, and he drank a beer. Perfection.

Soon the roads wound up into the mountains toward Berea, the town closest to where he grew up. Small tractors raised clouds of dust in the fields, and women with babies in their arms were picking vegetables from their gardens. The animals, mostly cattle or pigs or horses, ate slowly or rested in the shade.

Soon Joe was telling me who lived in each house, how many kids they had, and how their kids had married this particular neighbor's kids.

"See those houses with the smoke coming out the chimney?" he asked.

I nodded — seemed strange for a fireplace to be going on a summer day.

"That's how you know they are cooking on wood stoves."

For a girl like me, who had spent 99 percent of her life in the city in an apartment or at college or at bars in the Village, this was a fairyland.

Some of the farmers, if they were close to the road, would wave at us as we passed, and Joe kept his arm out the window so he could raise his hand in greeting.

"Hey there, Joe," some of them would call out as we drove slowly past.

People seemed much friendlier than in New York. The warmth of those southern mountain folks just pulled me right in.

His parents lived outside a little community called Red Lick, and even though I didn't think it was possible for things to get more backwoods than what I was seeing, they did. The road gradually went from humming blacktop to a gravel that spit rocks up on the underside of the car, to dirt roads full of deep gullies. At one point we actually drove through a creek for about a quarter mile, then up the mountain on another dirt road. The isolation of where we were somehow made me feel safe and far away from all my troubles.

Soon we were on another small dirt road and the branches and tall grass alongside reached up into the window, scraping the side of the car as we drove. A few times I thought we were going to end up in the ditch, but Joe would turn the car at the last moment. At other times we had to go up a steep hill and he'd gun the engine without even being able to see the top of the small ridge, but we'd fire up over the top and just keep going. I was nervous and scared and let him know it, but he just laughed and drove a little faster. Joe knew those roads as well as anyone, having memorized every turn or low-hanging branch or outcropping rock.

Eventually, after a few hours, we pulled up to a log cabin, parked in the barn, then walked up to the house. Around us there were two-foot high corn stalks and a tobacco field where the leaves were sprouting up out of the dirt. I could hear hogs snorting (and I could smell them), and just past the hog lot was a huge barn where they dried their tobacco in the late fall.

Then we got to the gate, held closed with a horseshoe latch. We walked through and approached the house and I felt like I was going back in time — the dirt path, the log cabin, the wood smoke easing up out of the chimney. Everything took me back a hundred years or more.

"Now this place doesn't have electricity," Joe said with a straight face, but I could tell a punch line was coming. "But it does have running water."

He pointed to the little creeks running on both sides of the house, and we both laughed.

There was something so earthy and genuine about this way of life, and it amazed me that people could live their lives in a place like this, so far removed from the rest of the world, and raise their families. It was all so beautiful and fascinating.

"I hope they'll like me, Joe," I said, feeling nervous about meeting his parents.

He just smiled and put his arm around me.

I felt very bashful, but as we said our hellos and made small talk about my journey and their valley, I was completely taken by their humility and simplicity. His mother was shy, holding back at first, but his father asked all kinds of questions about me and my background. They were genuine and curious in a nice sort of way. Soon I felt right at home, comfortable around them, because I knew they accepted me without reservation.

We walked around to the back porch and stepped into the kitchen — there were two wood stoves, one on either side, and an old sink with two wash basins. They would bring water in from rain barrels right outside the kitchen window, heat it on the stove, and then pour it into a big aluminum container to wash dishes. Rainwater was used for bathing, too, and their drinking water came from a well.

There was a large picnic-style table that seated 12 people easily, and another that seated 6 or so. Yellow wallpaper blended in with the throw rugs in brown and tan and green. The floor was a linoleum, very modest.

In the living room, an old grandfather clock hung on the wall, the pendulum slowly swinging, and it chimed out the hours in a way that made you think it had been there since the beginning of time. Two kerosene lanterns sat on a white doily on top of a beautiful old wooden chest under the window, and an enormous black Bible sat on a chest of drawers.

The wooden slats moaned under my feet. There was a pot-bellied stove for heating in the winter, and more throw rugs covered the wooden floor. Everything had its place and was tidy and clean. Off to one side was a little bedroom where Joe's mom and dad slept, and up at the top of an open set of stairs were two big bedrooms on the second floor. The entire roof was tin.

Did I remember the city while I was there? Did I wonder what my parents would have thought of a house like that, a place like the holler? I don't think I did. Everything about my life outside of that valley suddenly seemed like a dream, and as I feel asleep that night the only thing that seemed real was the rain pinging down on the tin roof, or the lightning flashing bright white through the trees.

In fact, the storm got so bad on that first night that I was up and down and restless in my bed. The lightning got louder and louder and the rain came down in sheets of sound — I was sure the roof was going to collapse in on all of us, and that lightning would strike the house and burn it to the ground on top of our heads.

I slept in the downstairs bedroom with Bessie, Joe's mother, and she must have heard me getting up and down and pacing around. I couldn't sleep. I was terrified.

"Lily," she whispered from her bed on the other side of the room. "The storm is pretty bad tonight. You can sleep in my bed with me if you'd like."

Like a little girl (and very unlike the sophisticated, city musician I thought I had become), I quickly took her up on the offer and slipped in beside her.

~ ~ ~ ~ ~

I woke up the next morning, and a shadow of light was creeping in through the forest. At first I wasn't sure what woke me up, but when I moved around in the bed I realized Bessie was already up, and then I smelled the most incredible smell — fresh bacon frying on the stove. I didn't get up for a few minutes, just stayed there listening to the crackle of the bacon, the singing of the birds outside. The floorboards started creaking. Folks were waking up.

I made my way toward the main area of the cabin and stood in the doorway for a moment. Bessie was busy in the kitchen, making a breakfast of fresh eggs from their chickens outside, fresh ham from one of their hogs, fresh milk from their cow. When I ate that breakfast I thought it was the first real meal I had ever eaten. It was certainly the first time I had ever had gravy — all of my kosher upbringing never even entered my mind.

I would steal glances at Joe and think over and over again how handsome he was, how lucky he was to have grown up in this environment, with this close-knit family. Sometimes he would catch my eye and smile at me, or wink, and it filled me up with all kinds of warmth and good feelings.

The rest of that week was a lesson in backwoods farm life, and I soaked it all in. Bessie was wonderful to me, so accepting and lovely and never treated me any different from her own children, except in the way she explained everything to me step by step. I started following her around, and she talked softly, helping me understand everything she did.

I washed the breakfast dishes in a tin pan with heated rainwater while she made lye soap out of pig fat on the wood-burning stove. It had a greasy feel to it, and they used that soap to bathe and wash their clothes.

Later in the morning we went out to the garden and picked tomatoes and cucumbers and green beans, and the whole time I couldn't stop thinking how crazy this was, that a New York City girl from the Bronx was on her knees in this garden in the middle of the Kentucky backwoods, picking vegetables. I chewed the green beans, feeling their texture for the first time. And suddenly I had this respect for farmers, for people who grew their own food and lived on it and didn't go to grocery stores but took care of themselves. I was amazed.

In the afternoon I helped churn the butter. The cream was kept in a big jar overnight, near the stove, so that it got a little warm. We would shake that jar back and forth and back and forth until little clumps of butter formed in the milk. We pulled out the butter and Bessie washed it and put it in tubs in the cellar so it would harden. It makes me hungry, the thought of slathering that fresh butter on cornbread made from freshly ground corn.

That evening we sat down for dinner and I couldn't believe that it could get any better than breakfast, but it did: fresh green beans with a piece of pork fat, a pot of pinto beans, potatoes with homemade butter, a piece of tenderloin or canned beef. This was food that I tasted for the first time in my life.

I kept the same routine for the rest of the week: up at 5:00 for a fresh breakfast, then gardening or making butter or cornbread, then an afternoon of chores and work around the house, a huge meal in the evening, and finally bed at 9:00, when I didn't think I could move another inch.

Some evenings neighbors would swing by for dinner, and Joe's parents were fine with it. Everyone in the neighborhood knew that their house was always open. This blew my mind, that you would work so hard and then just give away this amazing food to whoever came knocking, but this was the culture of Kentucky. This was how they lived.

At some point that week I had a dream about moving to Kentucky and helping change the lives of the people who lived there. In my dream I was a schoolteacher and helped educate the kids who couldn't go to school; I was a mentor to the adults who wanted to expand their horizons. For the rest of the week, I couldn't stop thinking about that dream, and I started thinking of ways I could improve life for them.

I didn't see that it was just an idealistic dream that for the most part they didn't want to be changed, that they enjoyed their lives and their community just as it was. Maybe I was trying to dream up an identity that would place me in that setting, with Joe. Maybe it was just another example of me trying to come up with a mission on which to focus my life so I wouldn't have to address the areas of my own life that made me unhappy.

I was searching for something, but at that point I was fairly certain that marrying Joe and being with him would solve all of my problems, assuage all the unhappiness just below the surface. For the next few months, I traveled back and forth from New York City to Joe in Kentucky.

I became two different people: Lily from the Village, the musician and flower child; and Lily from backwoods Kentucky, canning vegetables and waking up at 5:00 a.m. to help with breakfast. I lived in that tension, taking all that I could from both worlds.

~ ~ ~ ~ ~

Joe was going back and forth between Ohio and Kentucky a lot. During one of my visits, he went off with Larry Sparks to do a show at one of the local bars and left me with Larry's wife.

"But why can't I go with you, Joe? I want to see you guys play. It would be fun."

"These bars aren't like your Village clubs, Lily. These places are rough, no place for a city girl like you," he said, trying to charm me with one of his smiles.

I pouted though, turned away when he tried to kiss me good-night. He just shrugged, laughed, and walked out.

"See you girls in the morning," he said.

All night I sat around feeling glum, picturing him picking away on his banjo and having a great time while I sat there in that quiet little house having polite conversation.

"I think I'm going to go to that bar," I told Larry's wife.

"I don't know if that's a good idea, Lily."

I stewed, getting annoyed with her for not going with me, or at least encouraging me to go. I decided I would go anyway — forget all these people trying to tell me what to do! But showing up at this strange bar, knowing Joe didn't want me there, made me real nervous, so I went out and bought a pint of vodka and drank about half of it. By the time I got a cab and arrived at the bar, I was smashed.

It was one of those little country bars, just like what you'd see on the *Dukes of Hazard*. Inside it was pretty dark, and it took my eyes a little while to adjust. It must have been pretty late when I got there, because no one was playing music anymore but there were still a lot of people talking and milling around. I scanned the crowd. That's when I saw Joe. He was dancing with this little blonde-haired girl.

I had never hurt anyone before in my life, at least not physically. But something rose up in me that I had never felt, and I wanted to punch someone. I walked straight over to the two of them and pulled her away from him, my eyes staring hard at her. Then I grabbed Joe by the collar before turning back to the girl.

"You'd better sit down if you know what's good for you," I told that girl. I think she could tell I wasn't messing around. Maybe she walked off, I'm not sure, but at that point I turned to Joe and told him off with every foul word I knew. It was a big scene. I ripped off my en-gagement ring and threw it on the floor, stomping back out of the bar. The next morning I made flight arrangements and returned to New York, crying the entire way, convinced I never wanted to see him again.

Two weeks later I got a phone call at my parents' house from Joe.

"There was nothing going on," he told me. "It was innocent, just somebody I was dancing with. Honest Lily, it was nothing."

Somehow I let him talk me back. Weeks passed, and I decided to ignore what had happened. I took responsibility for it, convincing myself that in a fit of drunken jealousy I had overreacted. Besides, New York began to mean less and less to me without Joe there, and the thought of moving to Kentucky filled me with excitement and a sense of purpose. My parents didn't say much to me about Joe during those days — I think they knew I was way too headstrong to be talked out of my love for him.

We decided to get married that coming May.

~ ~ ~ ~ ~

May 28, 1970, was the beginning of a new decade and a new life for me. I was Lily Fishman, but on that day I became Lily Isaacs. Joe and I were married in the Madison County Courthouse in Richmond, Kentucky. His brother Herman was the best man and his sister Faye was my maid-of-honor. The ceremony was nothing like what I had always imagined my wedding would be, but Joe and I were happy.

My parents weren't there. We decided to have two ceremonies, since Joe's family couldn't make the trip to New York and I couldn't imagine my parents walking around a Kentucky holler. So the wedding was there in Kentucky, and Joe's parents had a reception for us at their cabin.

The meal was what I had come to expect from Bessie, and there was even a beautiful wedding cake. We ate and laughed and when I stepped outside I could hear the hogs and the chickens and for a moment I was yet again overwhelmed by how my life was going in this direction I had never expected. Inside I could hear the family talking and singing and feasting and I felt comfortable with the decision I had made to leave New York.

But, when I went back inside, there was always this nagging fear that things wouldn't turn out as happy as I would like. We came from such different backgrounds, and each of us had a lot of baggage. It concerned me. On our wedding night another worry cropped up: Joe's drinking, and by the time we got to Faye's house he was drunk. I was a little tipsy myself, but it wasn't what I had in mind for a wedding night.

We didn't have any money for a big honeymoon trip, so Joe's sister, Martha and her husband, Eugene, offered us their house in Ohio for the weekend, since they would be gone. They were really nice about it, stocking their fridge for us and even leaving some T-bone steaks, but I didn't have my driver's license so I felt kind of stranded, and there was a lot of drinking going on. It wasn't my ideal honeymoon. Things weren't off to the best start.

That next week I flew to New York to get ready for the big reception my family was throwing for us in the Bronx. Joe drove up later with his sister Martha and her husband. Mother welcomed me with open arms when I arrived at the apartment, and we started making the final preparations.

Why was I so eager to leave New York? What was it about me that so easily walked away from everything I had worked so hard to achieve? I grew up there, had all kinds of opportunities to play music or get involved in the theater, and had even signed a record deal there. I think I was missing out on some kind of connection, some sense of family, and Joe's family and culture were so accepting of me, and drew me in so quickly.

My parents weren't thrilled about my choice to leave, but they put on a good face that weekend for the reception. I think they were worried that I would walk away from everything — not just the city, but their values and family and culture. They weren't crazy about my decision to marry Joe; after all, he wasn't Jewish, and he had been married before. They would have preferred a Jewish professional who would keep me in the city and give me a better life than the one they had lived. But after dropping a few hints, I guess they picked up on the fact that I wasn't changing my mind, and they wished me well.

My mother let my father know, in no uncertain terms, that he was not to drink at the reception. These little exchanges between the two of them always made me cringe, and stirred up all those old

Dad's Buchenwald Concentration Camp release papers, 1945.

Datenbank: Häftlingsnummernkartei Buchenwald

Haft-Nr.: 114552
Name: Fiszman
Vorname: Uszer
geboren: 28.10.1909
in: Tschenstochau
Beruf: Glaser
eingeliefert: 18.01.1945
aus:
Verbleib:

Kategorie: Pole Jude

Quelle:
Thüringisches Hauptstaatsarchiv Weimar
NS 4 Bu Häftlingsnummernkartei

114552

Fiszman, Uszer
geb.28.10.09 Tschenstochau   Pole
Glaser   Jude

18. Jan. 1945

Mund: Bart: Gesicht: Ohren:
Sprache: Augen: Zähne:

poln. Jude

Konzentrationslager   Art der Haft: , Gef.-Nr.: 114552

Name und Vorname: FISZMAN USZER
geb. 28.10.1909 zu: Tschenstochau
Wohnort: C.o. ul. Stary Rynek 14
Beruf: Gläser   Rel.:
Staatsangehörigkeit: Polen   Stand:
Name der Eltern: Keine Angehörigen   Rasse:
Wohnort:
Name der Ehefrau: Rasse:
Wohnort:
Kinder: Alleiniger Ernährer der Familie oder der Eltern:
Vorbildung:
Militärdienstzeit: von bis
Kriegsdienstzeit: von bis   17.1.45 RSHA
Größe: Nase: Haare: Gestalt:
Mund: Bart: Gesicht: Ohren:
Augen: Zähne:

In Poland, pre-World War II.
Left to right: Mom, Mendel,
my Grandmother Lea, and Aunt Zlotta.

Mom pregnant with me, 1947.

Aunt Esther, Mom,
Aunt Beatrice, Aunt Basha.

Lenny, Pearl, me and Sammy.

Around 1952. Left to right, front row:
Sammy, me, Lenny, Hy, Pearl.
L-R Back Row: Aunt Basha,
Aunt Esther, Mom.

Me, age 6.

Me - 12 years old.

Cousin Sammy and me, 1953.

My 5th grade school photo.

Dad, me, Mom and Hy
at my Sweet 16 party, 1963.

Dad and Mom at my Sweet 16 party.

Hy and me at my Sweet 16 party.

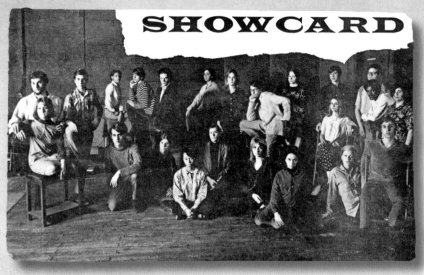

Off Broadway show "Antigone"- I'm seated 4th from the right on floor.

Performing in "Oklahoma" at the Woodstock Playhouse.
Maria is 3rd from left, I'm the far right.

Lily & Maria album cover, 1967.

Lily & Maria Columbia LP cover.

Maria and I writing for our album.

Maria and I performing at Gerde's Folk City, 1967.

Lily & Maria photo shoots
(I'm on the right).

Pictures from my acting portfolio.

My first guitar; I'm 17 years old.

My high school graduation
picture in 1965.

Dad blessing the bread
at my wedding, 1970.

Our wedding day: May 28, 1970.

Joe's parent's home in McKee, KY.

Joe's Parents: Godfrey and Bessie Isaacs.

Joe holding our first born, Benjie, 1972.

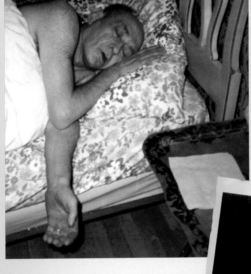

Dad sleeping; he worked very hard to provide for us.

Left to right: Sonya, Grandpa Godfrey, Benjie, Becky and Grandma Bessie, 1976.

Benjie, age 3.   Becky, age 6.   Sonya, age 7.

Clockwise from top: Becky, Ben, Mom and Sonya.

Mom's 87th birthday.

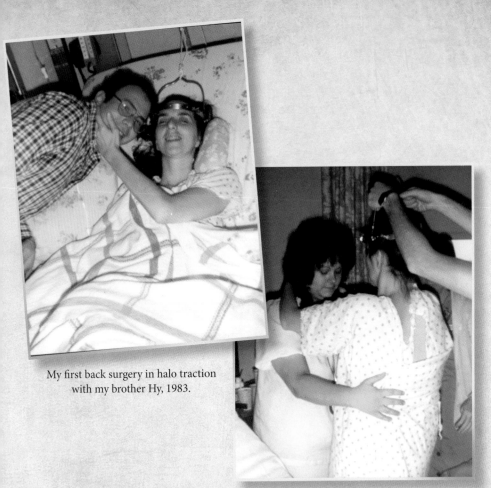

My first back surgery in halo traction
with my brother Hy, 1983.

Learning how to
walk again
after my first
back surgery.

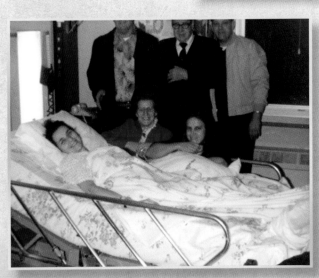

Second back surgery.
My dear friends Tom and Janice Roach at far right.

Carnegie Hall 2001- Bill Gaither introducing Mom.

"The Isaacs"- present day.
Left to right: Sonya, Ben, Becky, Lily seated.

memories of my father's drinking and how it affected me as a child. I tried to stay out of it.

But during the reception I saw Joe slip my father a few drinks. Part of me wanted to yell at him, tell him to stop, but another part of me was happy to see him bonding with one of my parents, so I let it go. The two of them actually became great friends over the years. Perhaps it all began there at the reception.

My friends and family had none of the reservations my parents had, seeing only a happy couple, two musicians so obviously in love, and they lavished us with wonderful gifts. They celebrated with us, toasted us, and wished us well. Joe and I were caught up in the atmosphere of love and support. It seemed an appropriate send off — I knew it was the end of my life in New York, and I was fine with that.

When we left the city I could tell my parents were still worried that I was walking away from my Jewish heritage, that I would forget everything. I can understand that, especially after all that they had been through to preserve their way of life. But I didn't want them to worry. I thought everything would be fine.

I had no intention of walking away from Judaism.

CHAPTER SEVEN

I looked at the clock — 2:00 a.m. My eyes were heavy, but I stayed awake waiting for Joe to get back from his show. After we got married, I started a job as a secretary there in Ohio, and Joe was playing five or six nights a week, mostly in a place called the Old Crow Bar in Middletown, Ohio, a tiny little town about ten miles away from our house.

Joe still didn't want me in the bars so I stayed home, reluctantly. I felt a growing resentment toward him, that he was out playing music and having fun and I was home. When he got home I could tell he had been drinking, and I started to worry that maybe he was doing some other things he shouldn't be doing. All of my insecurities consumed my mind.

I remember one night in particular. Usually he got home around 2:00 a.m., but on that night two came and went and no Joe. Then 3:00 a.m. Then 4:00 a.m. I started to toss and turn, getting up out of bed and pacing around the room. He had never been out that late before. Finally I got so worried that I called his sister Alice.

"Hello?" she said, her voice groggy yet anxious — a 4:00 a.m. voice.

"Alice? It's me, Lily."

"Lily! What's wrong? Are you okay?"

"Joe's not home. I think he might have been in a car accident or something. He's never out past two."

Alice was a very committed Christian, a prayer warrior, and I respected her. When I told her I was worried her voice took on a soothing tone, and she really calmed me down.

"Let's say a prayer, Lily."

"Okay," I said, kind of caught off guard. I guess I expected her to wake her husband and go out looking for Joe, or something along those lines. But when she suggested we pray it seemed the right thing to do, even though I had very little belief in God at the time.

She said the most wonderful prayer, asking that Joe would be safe and get home soon and that I would feel peace. As we were praying I heard the key slip into the lock. Joe was home.

This prayer thing really works, I thought to myself.

I had never experienced anything like that before. I had never even considered going directly to God with my problems or requests — the Judaism that I knew always involved going through the rabbi. There wasn't anything one-on-one about going to God, or at least there never had been for me. Yet during that phone call with Alice I heard her, almost out of nowhere, start a dialogue with God, the God of the universe.

That prayer may have brought Joe back, but I began to doubt if any prayer in the world could bring our relationship off the rocks. The late nights, the lonely evenings, the fact that I didn't know anyone and was young and ready to start a family of my own: all of these things started weighing on me. But I kept working my day jobs, just getting by.

A few weeks later, an argument between Joe and I took me past the tipping point. So I packed my bags and got ready to head back to New York. *I can return to music*, I reasoned with myself, *and I'm sure Mom and Dad would be happy to have me home.* I slammed each article of clothing into the suitcase. *Or I could pursue acting. That's what I'll do*, I thought to myself. *I'll track down all my old contacts and become an actress, make it on Broadway.*

There were three different times that I packed my bags for New York, but each incident ended the same way — with me unpacking them. Going back to the city wasn't what I wanted to do. I wanted to make my marriage work. I wanted to have a family. I was still in love with Joe and didn't want to leave him.

So I stayed, and very little changed. Except that I landed a job I loved doing secretarial work for a place called Mulford's Greenhouse in Lebanon, Ohio, where we lived. I still hadn't found what I was looking for, wasn't even sure what I was looking for, but that job gave me something to look forward to every day. The people were nice, and I felt good about what I did and I was appreciated.

That was enough, for the time being.

~ ~ ~ ~ ~

All of this happened in the first few months of our marriage. Sometimes I can hardly believe that Joe came home every night, with the life he was living, or that I didn't leave for the city. But we did make it, and there were still good times, plenty of them, and we were still in love, just trying to find our way.

It was 1970, and Christmas was approaching, our first Christmas together as a married couple. I decorated the house as best I could on limited funds. I didn't have any experience decorating for Christmas, having never celebrated it in my house growing up, but somehow it felt like a Christmas holiday. I can't remember if we had gotten any snow yet, but everything felt like Christmas, and I walked around the house humming to myself.

On December 22, Joe got back from playing at one of his shows. We had just fallen asleep when the phone rang, and Joe answered it.

"Hello?"

He sat down, asked a few questions very quietly, then hung up the phone. He looked devastated.

"What?" I asked, walking over and sitting beside him. "What's wrong?"

"It was the sheriff's office," he said, and I could tell he was fighting back emotion. "Delmer's dead."

At first that was all he could get out.

"What?" This feeling of shock spread through my body.

"Delmer's dead," he said again, his voice shaking. "I have to go identify the body and pick up his stuff."

Delmer, Joe's brother, was 27 years old at the time, four years older than Joe. His car had slid off a rainy road, and Joe, along with the entire family, was devastated. I had never experienced anything like that before in my life. I knew Delmer and his wife and kids. How could this have happened to them? During the next 24 hours, all of their brothers and sisters and relatives poured in from Indiana and Kentucky for the funeral — I had never seen anything like it.

I hadn't been inside a church before, let alone attended a funeral. The place was packed, standing room only. The preaching and singing was so full of emotion, and I found myself being drawn into the feelings of love and community that everyone had for Delmer and for each other. There was this atmosphere of commonality — whatever anyone possessed was shared by everyone, and what was lost was also lost by everyone. I thought that, no matter what happened, in that environment it was impossible to be alone.

The service ended with all of Joe's aunts and uncles standing around the casket singing.

I will meet you in the morning at the end of the way
On the streets of that city of gold
Where we all can be together and be happy always
While the years and the ages shall roll.

Delmer's funeral gave me my first glimpse of Christian love and togetherness. It had a huge impact on my life.

Later, Joe's sisters wanted to go to the church where Delmer and his wife had attended — they wanted the family to get together one more time before they separated and went back to their homes. In spite of the feeling of community at the funeral, I didn't really want to go to another service — it was emotionally and mentally exhausting, and I thought I'd rather just stay home. Joe didn't want to go either.

But Alice, Joe's sister who had prayed with me for his return on that early morning, appealed to both of us. "C'mon, Lily. If you'll go I'll buy you a steak dinner afterward."

What's it going to hurt? I thought to myself. Joe was having trouble holding it together — he was so distraught over Delmer's passing. Maybe it would help him to attend church with the family.

So we went. The church was called Shawhan Road Pentecostal, and it was nothing more than a converted garage attached to someone's house. We drove down a country road, about six miles from where Joe and I lived. At first, when we got out of the car, I couldn't even figure out where the church was.

Once inside, I looked around. It didn't look anything like the synagogue I had gone to as a child, although it did have wooden pews and a tiny pulpit. About 100 people could fit into that garage, and by the time Joe and I got there the place was packed, which was fine with us. We nestled into a seat in the back row, content to just take it all in, put in our time, and leave.

Delmer's widow sat at the front with their little children, and I felt so sad for her. But she was surrounded by family members, many of them sitting close and looking after the kids. The stage was empty for a moment, and I wondered who would be speaking. Then someone from the crowd got up and walked to the front and began singing another song I hadn't heard before, one about heaven.

Even though I didn't believe in heaven, the words brought something alive in me. The sound of the voices, the sense that everyone was striving through life together: all of these things combined to make me wonder, *What if it's true?*

It didn't take long before everyone joined in and sang through every verse. I didn't know the song, but the words were soothing at a very deep level. As soon as that hymn ended, someone else walked up and started singing, and the crowd joined in every time. During the singing, different people would go up front and give Delmer's widow a hug, lift the children up and kiss their cheeks. Even in the midst of the congregation people put their arms around one another and wept on each other's shoulders.

The singing went on for about 30 minutes and ended naturally, without an announcement or anything. After that, various folks would take turns standing up at their seat and talk about God, how good He had been to them and what He meant in their lives. It didn't seem out of place, even in the midst of such sadness — in fact, it made perfect sense to me, but I wasn't sure why.

That's not to say I wasn't uncomfortable, especially when they would talk about their lives in a very personal way. I felt kind of ashamed to be listening, like I wasn't one of them. Would they want me hearing all of these things if they knew I wasn't a Christian?

There was also this name that kept coming up in the songs and the testimonies: Jesus. I didn't believe in Him and had been taught my whole life not to believe in Him. There was something about hearing that name that, at first, made me cringe and feel uncomfortable, but as the service went on this feeling of awkwardness began to be transformed by the togetherness and the singing and the bonds between the people in that little garage.

The service started drawing toward its conclusion, and still no one had preached or lectured. It wasn't what I had expected from a church service. Then the pastor, Dewey Hisel, an older man with a silver guitar, walked up to the front.

"Anybody who wants to can just come on down front and pray, if you'd like. We're going to leave this place open for anyone who needs it."

A flood of people walked toward the front. Joe got down on his knees to pray. Before I knew it, I was weeping, and I couldn't stop — I was overwhelmed by emotion. Maybe it was because of Delmer's death, or maybe it was because I was homesick.

At that moment I knew I wanted to be part of that community, but I didn't know what to do about it. I didn't know what to say, or how to pray to God. I didn't know enough to say, "God, save me," because I didn't know I was lost. I didn't say, "God, forgive me," because I didn't know anything about sin. But I just knelt there and cried and cried.

I do believe that on that day God looked into my heart and saw my willingness, my openness to him. I think at that moment, in that little church, all the longings and confusion and emptiness surfaced and were swept aside. I cried my way to salvation. I didn't know what had happened, but I knew I would never be the same.

~ ~ ~ ~ ~

Delmer's death gave Joe and I a chance to start over, and we both took that opportunity. Joe stopped drinking, and we spent evenings together. I remembered how it had been to walk the city streets with him and laugh together in Maria's apartment. I felt like the woman he had fallen in love with in Gerde's Folk City in the Village.

But as far as Christianity went, I knew nothing. My heart had needed a change, needed something, and I found it that night in the church — now it was time to learn more about what I had experienced. I didn't have a lot of trouble believing in God, even though I had often thought of myself as an atheist. Deep down I had always believed in a supernatural power, probably due to my Jewish upbringing, so it wasn't much of a leap to believe in a Christian God.

Dealing with Jesus, though, was another matter. I could say the word "God." I could say "Lord." But Jesus? Just thinking of that name brought images of my parents into my mind, shaking their fingers at me, rebuking me. It had been their greatest worry when I left New York for, in their words, "the backwoods country," that I would leave my Jewish roots, and suddenly it had come about. Their worst fear had happened.

Yet, as I read more and more about Jesus, some of this confusion began to melt away. When Joe and I sat and read the New Testament, one thing that impressed me early on was the simple fact that Jesus was Jewish, like me. He attended synagogue, just like I had when I was growing up. He was taught the same Scriptures I had been taught.

But while reading the Scriptures seemed to simplify my understanding of Christ, some of the things about church complicated it. Because I knew so little about Christianity, it became easy for me to get caught up in the surface-level expectations of the church we attended.

For example, there was a strict dress code, and it was pretty clear that if you didn't adhere to it you weren't living "the holiness life": women were expected not to cut their hair or wear makeup, and pants were definitely not allowed. I did my best to follow all of the rules.

In spite of these rules, there were deeper, more meaningful changes that took place in our lives. Our marriage calmed down, and we weren't fighting all the time. I felt peace. And being in the church gave me such a sense of belonging, unlike anything I had ever experienced before. Joe was a completely different person — he gave up playing in the bars, quit Larry Sparks' band, and got a job as a logger, cutting timber and selling logs to local paper mills.

My Christian education continued during our occasional visits to Joe's family in Kentucky — his father was a sort of community pastor. Folks would come by car or horse or wagon, at all hours of the day or night, just to ask him to pray for them. Family members of those who died came to Joe's father, and he made the coffin, preached the funeral, and never charged a dime. On Friday or Saturday nights, the neighbors gathered in their house for prayer meetings, their voices crying out to God long into the night.

Joe's father Godfrey's strong beliefs are what led him into the mountains in the first place — when the Social Security system was instituted in the 1930s, workers had to take government-issued numbers. For young Godfrey Isaacs, this was too much like the Mark of the Beast discussed in Revelation for his liking, so he went off into the mountains and farmed.

Someone in the family told me a story about how one night when Joe was a kid, Godfrey went outside to pray and reflect on God — that particular night the Northern Lights were in full display, and Mr. Isaacs was sure God was coming back, so he ran inside and told everyone to come out.

"The Lord is coming back!" he shouted.

To his dismay, when he entered the cabin he found his boys playing cards and his girls curling their hair, neither of which were allowed in the Isaacs home. Joe said there were cards and bobby pins flying everywhere in the scramble to get presentable and get outside in time to see God return. They wept and prayed and cried for hours, but it turned out that wasn't the night.

I tried hard to conform to their standards, but Joe found it even more difficult, seeing that his father didn't allow musical instruments in church services. Joe loved music — it was literally part of his soul, and he would have long arguments with his father about playing music for God. Sometimes Joe would walk away from his father in frustration, giving in to that way of thinking.

"I guess I'll never play that instrument again," he would say of his guitar.

But he'd always pick it up again, something I was happy about.

~ ~ ~ ~ ~

I sat in the living room of our little apartment one night, putting the dishes away after supper. Joe walked toward the front door, putting on his jacket.

"Where are you going?" I asked.

"My friends are going out. I'm going with them," he said.

I stopped in my tracks.

"What?"

"I said, I'm going out with my friends. We haven't gone out for a while."

"Where are you going?"

"Just out."

His friends had enticed him to go, and it upset me. All of the hope, all of the peace that had found a spot in me since Delmer's passing vanished like the mist in a breeze. I was worried about his friends influencing him.

"Why? What do you want to go getting into that stuff for? Things have been so good, Joe! Don't do it. Don't start that up again."

He just turned and walked out the door.

I was devastated, and I could feel this thick haze of depression settling in over me. I sat there for a long time, willing him to walk back in that door, apologize, and say how wrong he had been, but he didn't. At some point I remembered it was a church night, but for a while I didn't want to see anyone else. I guess I just wanted to wallow in my own sorrow.

But then a feeling grew inside of me, this insistent voice saying, "You've got to go to church. Church is where you need to be tonight." So I got my things together and headed out.

Sitting in that little church, I began to sob. So much had changed for the better during those months. I had found something that gave me hope and peace, but now it was all falling apart because Joe was going out and maybe drinking again. A realization hit me: even if Joe went back to his old lifestyle, I couldn't let myself go back. I couldn't return to the fear and anger from before. I decided to do it for me and try to live this Christian life, with or without Joe.

As I sat in the church worried about our marriage and our future, I began to feel confused about some of the legalistic areas that I hadn't conformed to. One of those areas was shaving my legs. During Joe's upbringing he was taught a woman should look the way God created them: natural, without artificial changes. This included not shaving her legs. To be honest, shaving my legs wasn't something I had even thought of — it was just something I had always done, since I was 14.

On that night, feeling confused and overwhelmed by religion and all of these rules, I made a bargain with God. "God, if you bring Joe back and he stops drinking then I won't shave my legs again."

I thought that maybe Joe's drinking was a punishment to me for not following all the right rules, and I hoped that if I got in line then maybe God would change Joe's heart. It was such a childish way to think, but I was still new to these ideas, and I thought that's how it worked.

Joe was drunk when he came home that night, but the next night he went to church with me and apologized for the mistake he made. I felt like the vow I had made was what brought him back, so I followed through with my end of the deal. I didn't shave my legs for 12 years, and it was a huge sacrifice for me. Even though in hindsight it seems kind of silly, I believe God honored the sincerity in my heart regarding that vow.

From that point on, Joe and I entered the best years of our married lives, both of us staying on track, making good choices, treating each other with love and respect. But it was also during this time that my parents found out about my new life, my decision to follow Jesus, and their reaction would bring me a lot of pain.

~ ~ ~ ~ ~

"Lenny!" I said, walking out the front door to greet my cousin.

"Hi Lily," he said, getting out of his car and giving me a hug.

"It's so good to see you. How are you? How are your parents?"

Lenny was on his way to California to study acupuncture. He was open-minded and intelligent, and I had always liked him. He came inside and we talked for a long time.

"I've found this cool little church," I told him. "Would you come to a service with me?"

He was up for just about anything, so he came along, just sat there quietly, taking everything in. After church we had a great day hanging out, but that afternoon he hit the road again. I didn't think too much about it until my mom called me at work about a week later.

"Aunt Esther called me," she said almost immediately, and I could tell she was upset. "We didn't raise you like this. If you're going to believe in this Jesus and completely throw your whole culture and background away, and betray your people, then we don't want you to come home again."

"Mom!" I said, trying to interrupt.

"You don't have a family," she continued, not letting me get another word in. "Your father would rather see you out in the street or buried in your grave than to be such a reproach as this to your family."

I started crying right there in Mulford's Greenhouse, trying to cover my eyes and not sniffle too loud, but I couldn't help it. This was not how I wanted them to find out — I wanted to tell them how my life had changed, how everything was so much better, how much joy and peace and hope my new way of life brought me.

But as my mother continued on her tirade, I couldn't help but think back over my life and theirs. My mind was a whirlwind. I thought of the years they had spent in a concentration camp, how hard my father had worked to give us a good life in America.

I thought of my father slipping money under my pillow when he'd leave to work all night in the bakery.

I thought of my mother lifting me up and twirling me around when I was a little girl, or how she came to all my shows and plays when I was in high school.

I thought of my father, now suffering terribly from his arthritis, hobbling down the city streets, clutching his bag of rolls.

This family that I loved, my mother and father who had survived so much, the people for whom I wanted to preserve my Judaism because of what they had gone through, were forsaking me because I accepted Jesus and wanted to follow His teachings. I felt alone, like an outcast, like I would never belong anywhere again. I wouldn't have hurt my family for one million dollars, yet here I was, in a situation where I was hurting them but couldn't change course.

I felt the crossroads in front of me. Did I believe enough to watch my family walk away from me? Couldn't I just tell my mom that I was confused? Could I leave this new faith?

I couldn't.

"Mother, I love you so much. I love Dad so much. But I don't want to lose what I've found. God is filling my heart — without Him I am too empty."

We didn't talk much longer. She hung up, and I wept.

In the next few days and weeks, the sadness was still there, but that solid peace kept coming back, a peace that I could not understand but that filled my whole being. Up until that conversation with my mother that day, I had always prayed using the words "Lord" or "God." But because of my Jewish heritage I still struggled to say the name Jesus. Yet, after confessing my newfound faith to my mother, I could go into church and say Jesus without any hesitation, as if something had been freed up inside of me. It was as if He was the only person I had left in the world.

Whenever I called my mother after that, she always led with the same question: "Are you still going to that church?"

And when I told her yes, she would grow cold and distant. But I still called and filled them in on my life, still told them I loved them so much. Eventually, a few months later, I visited them and everything went fine except when the conversation turned to my new life — then we would argue and everyone would cry or get upset.

It was okay, though, because I knew the only thing I could do was show them love and hope they would see the change in me.

CHAPTER EIGHT

Our musical career began unplanned, unheralded. At first we sang at our church, and Joe taught me all the old bluegrass favorites he grew up with. The new songs he wrote began taking on Christian themes, and sometimes he'd throw those in at church, too, playing his guitar at the services on Tuesday, Saturday, and Sunday nights.

Evenings at our church were informal gatherings with lots of different people getting up to lead songs as they felt moved, and we loved the chance to share our music. Soon visitors approached us after the service and asked if we'd come and sing at their church. Before we knew it we were traveling all over the area, singing at churches.

Our house also became a stopping point for local musicians, and it seemed someone was always playing music in the house. We asked one of them, a terrific mandolin player named Leroy Ramsey, to join us at some of our gigs, and he started traveling with us. We were inspired by southern gospel groups like the Singing Cookes and the Marshall Family, but Joe always led us toward the bluegrass sound.

But things were about to change.

~ ~ ~ ~ ~

The fall of 1971 marked the beginning of one of the most beautiful parts of my life: I would be a mother. I got pregnant. A part of me that I hadn't known about woke up; something deep inside of me stirred at the realization that a new life grew inside of me. I had experienced an awakening when I found Jesus, and the news that I was pregnant seemed a continuation of this new life experience.

The news excited Joe and I because by then our marriage was stable, we were involved in our church, and we both wanted a family. To be honest, I had never thought about being a mother, but I loved the idea of carrying Joe's child. Doctors didn't do regular ultrasounds then, so I couldn't find out if the little one was a boy or a girl, but I couldn't have cared less. I was just so happy.

I was also a bit on edge — coffee, which I loved, began making me sick. Soon everything made me sick. I was nauseous all the time, barely able to keep any food or drink down. But somehow I gained 30 pounds pretty fast and started having the oddest cravings, like wanting to eat paper and loving the smell of Ajax (I finally tasted it one day, put a little on my finger and licked it . . . which cured me pretty quick of that craving). My body was changing rapidly, and I wasn't sure how to feel about that.

The further along I got, the more I felt the pressure of one particular concern: how would my mother and father respond to this baby now that I was a Christian? Would they change their course and welcome us back? Or would even this little child face rejection by his or her Jewish grandparents?

Life went on, though. Joe and I worked a lot of hours and only played music a little on the weekends. We decided that if we wanted to make some money from our music we would need to cut an album to sell on our mini-tours to local churches.

So Joe, Leroy, and I rehearsed an album's worth of material and bought time in a studio in Hamilton at Pinetree Records. It was owned by an old preacher named Merle Jones. You might think that making an album would feel like old hat to Joe who had an album on Decca Records, or after my experience with Columbia Records, but to be honest, we were both thrilled and nervous and couldn't wait to have the final product.

But the recording process crept along at an unbearable pace: we recorded onto a two-track machine, everything live to tape. Many times we'd get to the end of the song and someone would forget the words or hit a bad note and we'd have to start from scratch. Sometimes we'd work on one song for hours.

Those days were long. It wasn't unusual for us to start recording at 10:00 a.m. and go until 2:00 the next morning. Throw in my pregnancy and the fact that both Joe and I were still working full-time, and some mornings I could barely pry myself out of bed.

When that process was finally finished we took some photos to a graphic artist and had 500 copies pressed up under the title "Live It Every Day." I think they cost us a dollar or two each, and we sold them out of the back of our car for five dollars.

It was an inauspicious entry into the world of southern-gospel-bluegrass music, but we were proud of what we had put together.

~ ~ ~ ~ ~

I don't know if I thought about it at the time, but I went through that whole pregnancy without my mom, and it makes me kind of sad now when I see what a wonderful experience it has been, living alongside my daughters as they bring their own children into the world. But even though it was just Joe and I, we really enjoyed that time. It was exciting, like a gateway into a new era of our life, and we entered it together.

On July 25, 1972, around three in the afternoon, I went into the hospital with pretty heavy contractions, but delivery didn't begin until after 11:00 p.m. I got a spinal block to ease the pain I was in, and before midnight I was holding a little boy in my arms. Joe and I hadn't picked out a name yet, so on the birth certificate he was simply listed as Male. Joe wanted to name the baby after him, James Joseph, but I wanted a more Jewish-sounding name, and there was already a Joe Jr. in the family.

I looked down at his little face, so perfect and wrinkled and alive, and we named him Benjamin Joseph. It was a similar name to one of my father's brothers, Berrell, and would be in keeping with the Jewish tradition of naming children after deceased relatives. I hoped Benjamin would be a bridge back to peace with my family.

Things didn't work out that way, though. In fact, it didn't take long for Ben's birth to bring about another blow-up between my parents and I. In Judaism, boys are circumcised when they are eight days old — it's a symbol of God's covenant with Abraham, spelled out in Genesis 17, and the ceremony is called a bris, which a rabbi performs in your home.

But Joe and his family didn't believe in conforming to the Jewish ceremonial traditions. A few days after Ben was born, it came up. I was in the hospital when I took mother's call.

"Lily! How are you? How is Benjamin?" my mother asked.

"We're both doing great, Mother. Everyone okay up there?"

"Yes, yes, fine."

Then her voice took on an inquisitive tone. "Your father is wondering about the bris?"

I guess I just didn't want to fight with them, so I tried to dodge the question.

"I don't know, Mom, Joe and I aren't sure what we're going to do."

I guarantee you that wasn't the answer she wanted to hear. "If you're not going to follow the Jewish tradition," she said, her voice picking up steam, "we don't even care about seeing him!"

I wept and wept in that hospital room — those family disagreements took such an emotional toll on me. I felt sad that my first child, their first American-born grandchild, could mean so little to them that the excitement surrounding his birth would be smashed by this rock of tradition. Sometimes I wondered if my decision to follow Jesus was worth all of the family heartache. But every time, when I remembered the foundation of peace and hope that came along with it, I knew it was.

A few days after I got back from the hospital I still felt pretty sad about the whole thing, so I went to church one night for some spiritual encouragement. I sat there, holding Ben close, happy to have him there with me, wishing my family would accept us. I couldn't believe, even though I had a son, no one from my own family was there with me to be proud of him or give him love.

In the middle of the service a woman walked right up to the front. Her tiny skirt barely covered anything, and she wore knee-high pantyhose. She began dancing around, bumping into people and shouting. I hadn't been a Christian very long, but the stories about Jesus encountering demon-possessed people came into my mind. I didn't understand it very well, but I wondered if there was some kind of spirit in that lady, making her act that way.

A group of women huddled around her and started praying, their voices rising up over her shouts. She started screaming, but didn't try to run, just stood there at the front of that packed little church shouting her lungs out. And there I sat in the back, holding on tight to Ben. Something was wrong.

Suddenly I remembered the story in the Bible where Jesus cast demons out of a man. When they left the man they looked for some other place to dwell, and eventually inhabited a herd of pigs. I got so scared that the spirit in that woman would leave her and enter into my baby — I don't know why I thought that might happen, but I just started praying so hard over him. Suddenly, the sweetest peace enveloped me, and I felt closer to God than I ever had before. Shielding baby Benjie, praying over him so intently; it was a moment so powerful that I didn't even understand it fully at the time.

When I looked up, the lady was lying quietly on the floor. The room was quiet, hushed. I looked down at Benjie and held him tightly, wondering what had come over me that made me pray like that. Such is the power of the Holy Spirit.

It wasn't until later that I realized he was eight days old when this happened, the normal age of circumcision for a Jewish boy, when the community comes together to celebrate the bris. It seemed a special blessing that I had been able to pray over him on that particular day, almost as if God was blessing him even though we didn't go through with the tradition.

~ ~ ~ ~ ~

I was in and out of a haze, sweating, then freezing cold, under the blankets, then kicking them off and moaning. I was lying in bed with Ben and somehow through the midst of sickness I knew that Ben was sick, too, terribly sick. Joe would check our temperature — "104," he mumbled after taking Ben's temperature, shaking the thermometer.

Still, we didn't go to the doctor. Joe's parents had never been to the doctor and never took medicine — they believed that going to a doctor exhibited a tremendous lack of faith in God, so we waited it out. But things just kept getting worse.

I remember crying through my fever, through the chills, praying that God wouldn't take Ben from me, begging God to heal him. We heard through the grapevine that it was the London flu, and people were dying from it.

Ben slept in my arms, flushed. He felt like a little hot water bottle — his skin was just burning up. I was in and out, and when I woke up at one point, still holding Ben, I saw Joe's parents there praying for us. I couldn't tell if I was dreaming or if they were really there. I found out that they were visiting for a few days.

Later, little Ben sat in my weak arms, and as I looked into his face I saw his eyes roll back. He started convulsing.

"Please, Joe," I whispered, not even knowing exactly what it was I was asking for. Joe called the hospital.

"Get him in a cold bath," the nurse said.

We filled our kitchen sink with water and lowered him in. He cried, but he was so weak that his screams didn't even get that loud. We fed him two bottles of cold water. Finally, his fever broke.

From that point on we kept liquid Tylenol hidden away so Joe's parents wouldn't see it. Soon even Joe went to the doctor when he needed to. This led to more fights with his parents, more disagreements. We decided at that point we were going to live our own Christian lives the way that seemed right to us, and not try to please everyone else.

There seemed to be such a gap between us and both sets of our parents, so many miles of misunderstanding. I guess it swept the country in those days, the differences between the generations. Our parents had fought the war to end all wars, experienced a shrinking world.

They didn't know what to do when their own children went to war, or became hippies, or marched for peace and integration. They didn't know what to do when the opportunity, for which they came to the United States, ended up changing their kids, and their grandkids, leading them off in different directions, threatening to dilute their culture and their heritage.

I think it was confusing for everyone, a difficult time to navigate.

~ ~ ~ ~ ~

When Ben was 18 months old, I became deathly ill again and had flu-like symptoms for three days in a row. It was bad. I spent most of my time in bed, or in the bathroom, and poor little Ben didn't know what was going on with me. Joe tried to take care of me as best he could, but he was working full time. Eventually I went to the doctor.

He did some blood work and discovered I was pregnant! Joe and I were excited — we had already decided we wanted to have more than one child. I couldn't believe our family was growing so quickly. Little Ben would have a brother or sister!

But I didn't seem to have normal morning sickness: my eyes and skin held a yellowish tint, my fever wasn't going anywhere and I still felt very weak.

"I think there's something else going on," the doctor said, insisting on more time to examine me.

After additional blood tests I was diagnosed with infectious hepatitis. It sounded scary to me, but I had no idea what it was.

"There's no cure," the doctor said quietly. "It pretty much has to run its course. But we are very concerned about your unborn baby. There are no tests that we can do this early on to see if the baby has contracted it, but your husband and son will need a vaccination. And we'll have to monitor you closely."

Now that I think back on those days, I realize that I must have gotten it from the first farm we lived on in Waynesville, Ohio, when I drank unclear water out of a cistern. The farmers let us live there for free as long as Joe did the chores: milked the cows, fed the pigs, that kind of stuff. There was also a septic tank there that sometimes overflowed, so it must have been from that or from our close contact with all the animals.

However I got it, I was very sick and didn't get much better during those first six months of pregnancy. Ben was only 18 months old. Because none of our parents lived close by, Joe and I hired help almost every day, and he missed a lot of work when the sitter couldn't come. Eventually one of his nieces came to help us take care of Ben, and I was in bed for nearly two months straight.

This whole time I worried so much about the child still inside of me. The doctor told me that the baby could be born with heart problems or possibly even brain damage due to the high levels of the disease in my system. I didn't know if we were having a boy or a girl, but I prayed hard for that little one every night.

Folks from our church came to visit with me a few times a week, and when I could muster the strength to make it into church, I would. At the end of the service I'd stand in the prayer line, feeling faint and nauseous, desperately pleading with God to touch that child and keep them from getting the disease.

I carried full term, and the last three months got a little better. I felt stronger, and I could even take care of Ben. Then, on July 22, 1974, Joe left for work, just like any other day, but I called him back home. The baby was on the way.

I felt so much fear about number two's arrival: would the birth be more challenging than my first one had been? What if the hepatitis caused complications we hadn't yet seen? I just wanted the whole thing to be over so that I could hold my precious little child and know that everything was okay.

It would end up being the easiest birth of my three children — much easier than Ben had been. This little one popped right out!

"It's a girl!" the nurse announced, and tears immediately filled my eyes.

"Is she okay?" I asked the doctor, watching as the nurses looked her over.

Sonya weighed 8 pounds 9 ounces and was as pink as could be. She was named after mom's sister Zlotta. I was still sick so I couldn't feed her. We started her on formula, but she got severe diarrhea — turns out she was allergic to the formula. We tried another brand of formula, but with the same results. For two weeks we were worried about whether or not she was getting the proper nutrition. The doctor suggested we try homogenized milk and give her vitamins in liquid form to supplement what she wasn't getting. Finally, that worked.

Even though those first few months were difficult, I was so excited that she was okay. We even kept her in the room with us for a few months.

All of my prayers were answered — she was healthy and showed none of the ill effects hepatitis could have inflicted on her. Joe and I settled into a new life with our two children. Every so often I looked around at that little family and couldn't believe how much God had blessed me. Beautiful and healthy, a little boy and a little girl.

~ ~ ~ ~ ~

When Sonya was about four months old I started getting sick again, the same symptoms from hepatitis — nausea, throwing up, fever. It was starting to feel like I was going to be sick for the rest of my life. I was sure hepatitis had returned, and I just couldn't imagine dealing with that again, plus taking care of my two little babies. Immediately I went to the doctor.

"You've got to do some blood work," I said, dreading what they would say. "I think it might be hepatitis again."

But I had no idea.

They ran a battery of tests, and when he came into the room to talk about the results, he had a smile on his face. "This might be good news, and it might be bad news," he said.

"What?" I asked. I felt confused.

"Well, first let me ask you, do you have a good washer and dryer?"

Now I was very confused.

"Why?" I asked.

"Because you're pregnant again."

I was in complete shock. My mouth dropped open and I didn't know what to say. Sonya was only four months old, Ben barely two years old. I was just getting back my strength from childbirth, recovering from my first bout with hepatitis and suddenly I was pregnant again. It took my breath away. I stopped at a Frisch's Big Boy and ordered a hamburger, onion rings, and a milkshake in the drive-thru. Then I sat there and cried all over my food. I didn't think my body or mind could take it.

Finally, I called Joe and gave him the news.

I carried our third child full term and had to wear tight surgical pantyhose (Joe had to help me put them on!) to fight off the varicose veins that formed due to having three babies so close together. The pregnancy wasn't easy because my body was tired. Chasing two little ones around the house while a third grew inside of me was no easy task. I hated wearing those hose, and my back seemed to grow weaker with each pregnancy.

Plus, I kept gaining more and more weight. I just didn't have the time in between kids to lose what I had put on. I already felt conscious of my scoliosis, so the extra weight didn't help my self-concept. I couldn't imagine how I was going to get through those nine months.

Labor was longer, too, but I was overjoyed when Rebecca Marcel entered the world August 2, 1975. She was named after my mom's brother Mendel.

Joe and I decided to call it quits with three kids. After three so close together, and my scoliosis acting up, and that fight with hepatitis, I just couldn't imagine getting pregnant again.

Joe picked me up at the hospital — one of his nieces came along to help us — and I remember scooping Sonya up in the front seat. She was one year old.

"Sonya," I said, "you are going to have to be the big sister and help me."

She just looked back into my eyes and smiled.

Life with three — I get sentimental thinking about it now, but at the time it was hard. Very hard. I took them everywhere with me, those three kids, all of them three years old and younger. Joe worked all the time, trying to support us, and we were going to church a lot on the weekends and singing. Becky was usually right there on my hip while we sang.

One night, while the kids were still very young, we sang at a country church in Kentucky. The windows were wide open in the church because it was so hot. One minute I told the kids to sit down, and the next minute they were gone! It wasn't long, though, before I spotted Ben sitting in the front seat.

But where were the girls?

Then I saw them. Sonya was riding on Becky's back down the middle aisle of the church, the biggest smile on her face. Those were the times we had.

~ ~ ~ ~ ~

During all those years, we traveled in an old van — Joe built a bunk in the back for the kids, and we stored all the equipment underneath it. We covered many miles in that thing, and the kids had a lot of dreams in that bunk. It was hard when they were little, but that was our life, and I wouldn't change it for the world.

One of the fun things about being a parent is seeing how different each of your children becomes. Ben always wanted to roughhouse, but Sonya was the opposite — sometimes she was so quiet I'd have to go look for her. Becky was the one pulling the pots and pans out and beating on them like drums.

When my father died in 1978, I had to leave the kids with my sister-in-law, Martha. Well, one night Becky was crying and Ben was upset because we hardly ever left them — they were so used to traveling with us wherever we went. So Sonya, five years old at the time, rocked Becky to sleep and held Ben. She always had that mothering spirit.

Then there was Joe — throw him into the mix with these three kids and sometimes it just got plain crazy. He loved showing them new instruments and singing with them and especially playing tricks on them. One time when we lived at the house in Morrow he discovered that he could hear the kids digging through the heat register for some change, even though they were in a different room. So he bent down close to the vent and growled like a monster.

I was in the kitchen washing dishes and heard all this commotion — I thought someone had gotten hurt. Those kids jumped over the couch and ran as fast as they could into the bathroom, trying to get away from whatever was in that vent as quickly as possible! By the time I got to the bathroom, Joe was doubled over laughing, and the kids had practically climbed up on top of him, they were so scared. He had to show them what he had done, just so they would believe him.

~ ~ ~ ~ ~

I pushed the grocery cart slowly through the store, every once in a while double-checking for the $20 bill I had in my pocket. It was all the money we had, and I had to make sure the grocery bill stayed under that amount. Joe had recently had his appendix taken out. He would be in the hospital for ten days and out of work for three months. It was almost Christmas.

I had all three of my children with me. Becky was a year old and in a baby carrier inside the cart. Sonya sat on top, in the cart's seat, playing with the food items I put inside. Ben climbed around underneath — I guess he would have been about four.

The list was too big for $20, and it seemed like everything was necessary. I had that empty feeling inside, and I was worried I wouldn't have enough money. At the very bottom of my list was a luxury item: Duncan Hines chocolate cake mix with a can of chocolate frosting.

"Could you subtotal everything else, first?" I asked the cashier, holding the mix back.

She totaled up all of the items.

"Nineteen dollars and seventy-five cents," she said.

Oh well, I thought. *It's not that we need cake.*

"Thanks. Could you have someone put this back on the shelf?"

She took the mix and put it under the counter. I gave her the $20 and she gave me my change, which I put very carefully in my pocket.

That night our whole family went to a revival meeting at a church about ten miles away. When we came back out to the car and opened the doors I couldn't believe my eyes — someone had bought us two full bags of groceries, and the Duncan Hines chocolate cake mix frosting was right on top. No one knew that I had to put that cake mix back.

God so often isn't only faithful with our needs, but also with our wants.

In 1984 I had the opportunity to fulfill a lifelong dream of mine: travel to Israel. For every Jewish person, this type of trip holds a very special significance. The only problem? I needed to come up with $700.

I remember the day I walked out the driveway to get the mail, wondering how in the world I would make $700. It seemed like an unbelievable amount of money, especially back then. I so badly wanted to make that trip, to see the land where my ancestors had lived, to walk the streets Jesus had walked, but it seemed like such a monumental amount of money. I started giving up on the idea of going.

I opened the mailbox and pulled a few envelopes out. One had my name handwritten on the outside with no return address. I opened it and found a small card. Inside the card were seven crisp $100 bills. I stood there at the end of the lane, leaned against the mailbox and cried my eyes out.

~ ~ ~ ~ ~

Life went on. Joe worked full time, and I became a full-time mom, surrounded by diapers and bottles and laughter and tears. In the midst of all this living, having children, and working, and trying to make enough money to get by, going to church and visiting with Joe's family, our music career (if you could call it that at the time) continued to creep forward. We put out a few albums and just kept traveling from church to church, singing our hearts out, selling albums from the back of our van. All three of the children got caught up in the music — I don't know if any of them had the chance not to.

"If you want to get kids to play an instrument, leave one lying around the house," Joe always said, and that's exactly what he did. There was always a banjo on the bed, a mandolin on the sofa, and a guitar in the corner of the room. The kids, as soon as they could crawl around and grab on to things, started fooling with them, plucking on the strings and smiling at the sounds. We didn't have a television until 1983, when Ben was 11, and the instruments were some of the best entertainment in the house.

From early on, we could tell they had talent. Ben played the bass by the time he was eight, Becky learned piano from her cousins, and Sonya was always plucking on Joe's mandolin. By the age of seven she could play really well. And, without any coaching, all three of them could harmonize. If Becky or Ben started singing lead, Sonya automatically fell into the tenor, and the other would find the third part without Joe or me showing them.

We encouraged them as much as we could, inviting them on stage with the band when we played at churches or in concerts. They had more names than we knew what to do with: "The Gospel Chipmunks" or "The Kosher Hillbillies" or "The Briarhopper Hebrews." They sang "Someone Will Love Me in Heaven" on our "Lord Light My Way" album when they were nine, seven, and six, and they did an entire album as "The Isaacs Trio" a year or so later.

I guess this was the first sign of the Isaacs.

~ ~ ~ ~ ~

One day we were on our way to a weekend of singing — it was just Joe and the three kids and I in the van. The kids were bored, and it was a long drive. Sonya found a matchbook, got curious, and wondered if she could start a tissue on fire. Obviously the tissue lit right up, she panicked, and dropped the match on to the box of tissues, which quickly caught fire.

Sonya screamed at about the same time that I smelled the smoke. Joe veered off the road and stopped. Ben, trying to get out of the way, tangled with some fishing gear still in the van from a previous trip and ended up with a fish hook in his foot.

Joe put the fire out and then nursed Ben's foot, removing the hook. What a hectic trip! Joe and I scolded the kids and before we knew it, we pulled back on the road again, the smell of smoke mingling with the silence of children who had just gotten into trouble.

It seemed there was always something going on with these kids. When Ben was around 12, Joe bought him a mini-motorcycle, and he was allowed to ride it in front of the house on the street. Suddenly one of the neighbor boys was knocking on the door to our house, screaming that Ben had wrecked.

Well, I grabbed the girls and drove to the end of the road and there was Ben, his leg gashed open. We had to run into the hospital where he ended up getting eight stitches.

These family emergencies seemed to be a weekly occurence. One day Ben grabbed Becky's baby doll and ran through the house with it. She chased him, fell and hit her mouth on the end table in our bedroom, and busted her lip open.

Another trip to the hospital.

Then there was the day our kids were playing basketball in the neighbor's yard. There was a fence separating their yard from the next one over, where a large dog constantly walked back and forth in a dog pen, staring at the kids while they ran free. Someone knocked the ball over the fence and into the pen. Becky convinced Sonya to climb into the dog's pen to get the ball — Becky said she would distract it. Sonya, being the bravest, climbed the fence and jumped down to get the ball. Unfortunately she landed on a piece of sheet metal and gashed her leg open.

When I looked out the window Becky was carrying Sonya on her back to the house. They were always taking care of each other. We drove to the emergency room and the doctor got ready to put stitches in her leg.

"Now," the doctor said, "if you close your eyes and count from one to ten, you won't feel a thing."

Sonya looked up at him and asked a question. "Would it be just the same if I prayed?"

CHAPTER NINE

I looked at the nameplate on the door at the hospital in Cincinnati: Dr. Alfred Khan III. I had been having terrible back pains for months, and a friend from church knew someone who had come to that particular doctor for advice. I took a deep breath and walked inside.

"I have to tell you, Mrs. Isaacs," he said after my first examination. "I can't believe you have let your back get this bad. The scoliosis you were born with is getting worse. The pain you are living with must be intense."

"It's terrible," I admitted. "But when I was eighteen the doctor released me to live my life normally. He said it wouldn't get any worse."

"Well," the doctor said, "it has gotten worse. The curvature of your spine is severe. The S-curve is such that, if you don't do something about it, your rib cage could eventually crush your heart and lungs."

"Why? What caused it to get this bad?"

"Carrying three babies probably had some effect. You said you spent years cleaning houses — that kind of work, bending over, moving furniture, running a vacuum for long hours, all of those things could aggravate your condition. I don't see that you have much choice. You need to have this surgery."

I thought back to when I had cleaned houses with my friends Brenda and Janice. We had worked two days a week and got through two houses each day, usually in ritzy neighborhoods near Dayton, Ohio. We each made about $20 per day, and nine times out of ten we'd spend the money at garage sales before we got home.

I smiled when I thought back to the crazy spots we got ourselves into, from being questioned by police to being held hostage in a small bathroom by a large dog. Those had been fun times. But it had been hard work for long hours with lots of lifting and bending over and not a lot of rest. I wondered how much of a factor cleaning those houses was in my current back situation.

"But, doctor," I argued, "I don't have time for surgery or rest! I'm 35 years old. I have three children and they are 11, 9, and 8. It's all I can do to keep up with them! I'm playing music with my husband all the time — we have concerts lined up. I can't be in bed for months at a time!"

"You don't have a choice," he said. "Those things will have to take care of themselves."

I didn't want to have the surgery done, but I just couldn't live with the pain any longer. Part of the decision-making process involved Joe and I going into the hospital and watching a detailed video about what they would do to me. My heart nearly stopped as I watched the surgeries. I found myself holding my breath as the surgeon made the incision. When I saw how much it involved, fear washed over me.

The thought of being in the hospital for a month overwhelmed me, and the two surgeries looked gruesome and painful. I also knew I'd have to leave my kids, something I never did. Who would watch them for that length of time? My family was all in New York City, and Joe's brothers and sisters all had big families of their own. But I knew I had no choice. I had to have the surgery.

We got through it with the help of two elderly women who lived down the street, sisters named Helen and Hazel. They offered to come watch the children during the day and on the few nights that Joe had to stay with me in the hospital. Sometimes, before the surgery, I felt so much anxiety about leaving the children that I couldn't quite catch my breath, but with Helen and Hazel there, I knew everything would be under control.

The first surgery took place on January 25, 1983. They removed nine discs from my spine. They took out a rib and a piece of my hip to freeze and use in the next operation. When the world slowly came back into focus it greeted me with the most excruciating pain I had ever felt. I was flat on my back in halo traction meant to stretch my spine for two full weeks. I couldn't even turn myself over.

A nurse came into my room and raised me to 45 degrees so that I could eat, and even through the medication streaks of pain shot through my body. Then they would slowly lower me back down. A few days after the surgery they put me in a wheelchair for a few hours a day, and the halo held my head in place.

I dreaded the next step but was so anxious to get it over with. Just as I started to recover, it was back into surgery for the second round — they fused the nine vertebrae using bone from my rib and hip in place of the discs they had removed. They braided two 14-inch stainless steel rods around my spine to give the backbone more strength. Six hours later, my back was straight.

I opened my eyes and stared at the ceiling. It felt like someone had put me down on red-hot bricks, which now burned through my skin and into my back. A breathing tube snaked down my throat. Pain and despair made me ache. I blinked and tried to look around the room without moving my head. I drifted back to sleep.

When I woke up there was no one around me. I was in the recovery room and I needed help, but I couldn't speak. And I couldn't move. All I could see was the clock on the wall in front of me, and I passed in and out of consciousness. Each time I came to, I wanted to yell, but I couldn't. Inside I wept, but I couldn't cry out loud. The clock just kept ticking, and the pain just kept getting worse and all that I wanted to do was feel the touch of someone's hand. But no one was there. Just the sound of the ticking clock.

Then I woke up again, and they must have let Joe in because he stood there beside me, his eyes full of concern. I tried to speak but the breathing tube choked back my words, and I was too tired to fight it. Then I was unconscious again. The only time I wasn't in excruciating pain was in my sleep.

"When will this pain go away?" I asked a nurse with my hoarse voice, as soon as I could speak.

"You'll feel better each day," she said, smoothing my blankets and writing some notes on a clipboard.

This was not encouraging.

I counted down the minutes between my shots of morphine, every four hours.

Visitors came and went in this strange dream called recovery. Joe was there most of the time. My brother came. Folks from church visited. But their faces were lost in a haze of pain and medication, and I couldn't stay awake long enough to remember exactly who I spoke with.

"So thirsty," I murmured to a nurse coming in to check on me.

She nodded, a look of sympathy on her face.

"You won't be allowed to drink again until your stomach makes some noise. You were under anesthesia long enough that your bowels shut down — drinking anything before your body is functioning properly would be very dangerous."

The IV provided fluid for my body, but my mouth and throat felt so dry. The nurses put Vaseline on my lips and put ice in a plastic glove to cool my mouth, but I ached with thirst. I dreamed about 7-Up, that cold, clear, bubbly liquid, and in my sleep I felt it trickling down my throat. But then I woke up and it was all Vaseline and ice bags. I was dying for a 7-Up.

Lying there on my back, I had a lot of time to think over my life. Sometimes I couldn't believe where I had ended up — somehow this Jewish girl from the Bronx had gone from singing folk music in New York City's Greenwich Village to having a family and singing a hybrid of southern gospel and bluegrass music in Ohio.

But it wasn't just my external circumstances that had changed — somehow, in that small country church, I had found God. Or He had found me. Either way, I wasn't the same Lily from the Bronx. Little did I know that, even with all of the different twists my life had taken up to that point, I could never have imagined what the next ten years would bring.

Every single morning in that hospital a nurse came into my room. Every single morning I asked her the same thing: "Can I have something to drink today?"

"Not yet. We'll have to wait for the doctor."

Then the doctor came in.

"Can I drink anything yet?"

The doctor examined me and I'd wait for the okay. "Maybe tomorrow, Mrs. Isaacs. But not today. Not yet."

A few days later I asked the same question. "Is today the day?"

She looked at my chart. "Well, Mrs. Isaacs, I think we might be able to get you a cup of tea."

I just about jumped out of bed with excitement. I took little tiny sips of that tea and made it last. The feeling of the liquid slowly running over my tongue and down into my throat was heavenly. Later we found out the doctor had not released me to drink yet, but I didn't care. It would have been worth any consequence.

Early the next day I was cleared by the doctor, and I drank my first 7-Up. Nothing has ever tasted as good.

As I became more and more aware of what was going on, and as my physical pain diminished, I became emotionally distressed during each of my examinations. They should have made me happy, as each one showed I was progressing nicely, but I couldn't help but feel painfully embarrassed by the fact that I hadn't shaved my legs for so long. Every time the nurses lifted my covers to see how the feeling in my legs was progressing, I turned red with shame and wanted to cry. Then they would examine my back and ribs and see that I also hadn't shaved under my arms.

I doubted the wisdom of the bartering I had done with God, promising not to shave if Joe came back on that night over ten years before. I knew I had made a vow, but I was doubting my commitment. I felt humiliated, but stayed true to my promise.

Anyway, soon it was time to learn to walk with my new back. It didn't bend very well, and there was metal all through it, but it was straight. I couldn't wait to heal completely, to walk upright. I couldn't wait to wear normal clothes again, and not the baggy ones I gravitated toward because they hid the curve in my spine.

One step at a time. One new exercise, and then another. I moved forward, and I thought I could see the light at the end of the tunnel of my recovery. But as I learned to walk, first with the help of others, then slowly by myself, another medical challenge was right around the corner, one that would threaten not only my physical well-being but my life.

~ ~ ~ ~ ~

One day, a few weeks after I got home, I was sitting in a chair while a friend of mine, Nina, cleaned the house. She came over a lot while the kids were at school and talked to me while she did the chores that I couldn't do while I was still recovering from back surgery.

"Lily," Nina said reluctantly, as if she didn't want to say what she was about to say. "Oh, never mind." She turned away and was about to switch on the vacuum.

"What is it?" I asked.

She looked at me, worry in her eyes. "I found a knot in my breast," she whispered. "I don't know what it is and I'm really scared."

It wasn't like Nina to be that way. She was normally very happy and carefree.

"I'm sure it's nothing, Nina," I said, trying to reassure her. "But if you're worried about it, maybe you should go see a doctor."

"I don't have insurance. What if they tell me I need surgery? It would ruin me, Lily. I just don't have the money."

"Let me see where it is," I asked, and she placed my finger on the bottom left side of her breast. I could definitely feel a knot. I tried not to show my alarm. Instinctively, I put my hand on my own breast, in the same spot. I had a knot there, too.

"See, I've got one, too. Don't worry about it," I told her. "It's probably something all women have, maybe a gland or something that's supposed to be there."

We didn't talk much about it after that. At first, since we both had the same knot in the same place, I think we both felt relieved. But as the day continued, and the more I thought about it on my own, the more concerned I got. I had always had so many other physical problems that self-examinations had been the last thing I had thought to do.

But what was that lump?

Later that night I tried to sleep but instead I tossed and turned, thinking about that lump in my breast. I had conversations in my mind, one moment reassuring myself that Nina had the same knot and it must be okay, but the next moment a feeling a panic rose inside of me that it might be something much, much worse.

Finally I rolled over and nudged Joe. "Joe, are you awake?"

"Hmmm, what, Lily?"

"Are you awake?"

"Yeah. Yeah. What is it?"

"Feel this," I said. "I've never noticed it before."

"I'm sure it's nothing," he said.

"Nina has one, too, in the same place."

"Well there you go, Lily. Probably just a woman thing. There's nothing to worry about. I'm sure you're just overreacting."

I pulled the covers up and tried to settle in and go back to sleep, but his words did not comfort me. I kept feeling the lump, each time hoping that it would be gone. But it wasn't. It wasn't going anywhere. All night I kept waking up and wondering, and I even dreamed about it.

The next morning, Friday morning, I decided the best thing to do to ease my mind was to call my gynecologist, Dr. Goodman. I made an appointment for Monday and spent all weekend in my back brace, sitting around the house, nervously checking to see if the lump was still there. On Monday, Joe took me to the doctor.

I gingerly got out of the car, my back brace holding me straight, and we made our way into the office. Dr. Goodman examined me and after many "hmmms" and wrinkled brows he went out of the room. He came back in with a slip of paper.

"It's a visible knot," he said, "and, besides that, I'm not sure what it is. This is the address for a surgeon who can do a needle biopsy."

Another doctor? I thought to myself. *Is all of this really necessary?* But we didn't have any choice, so we drove to the next doctor.

The surgeon who examined me there was a woman. She came in and helped me lay down because I was still in my back brace.

"I'm going to place a needle in the lump and try to take out some of the fluid," she explained. "If it's just a fluid-filled cyst, then we should be able to drain some of it out and there will be nothing else to worry about."

I lay quietly as she inserted the needle. It hurt so bad that I wanted to scream, but I just bit my lip.

Please, dear God, let there be some fluid.

But after two attempts, nothing. No fluid came out.

She recommended another surgeon who would be able to do a biopsy on the lump, but for that I'd have to go into the hospital. By this time I worried that the stitches from my back surgery would pull out — it seemed I was on and off examination tables all the time at this point. I decided to call Dr. Khan, the one who had performed my back surgery, to get his advice.

He was direct and unwavering. "Lily, you need to get this checked out. There's a great doctor in Cincinnati you should see. His name is Dr. Hasle, and he works at the same hospital that I do. This is probably nothing to worry about, but you need to make sure."

I was a basket case the entire drive to Cinncinati. This would be the third doctor that day! My mind just kept circling back to the word "cancer," and nothing I did made me feel any better. I could barely speak. Joe tried to comfort me, but I felt myself nearing panic.

When we got to Dr. Hasle's office, he really put me at ease. "More than likely," he said, "it's just a cyst. We'll do a biopsy to determine if it's cancerous, but they're usually benign, so please don't worry yourself about it. You'll most likely have plenty of time to recover from your back surgery and then we can remove it."

He was so nice, and had such a sense of peace about him, that for the first time in days I began to believe it would just be benign — just like Nina's turned out to be — and they could take it out after I was fully recovered from my back surgery. That sounded simple enough. We stopped at a Chinese restaurant on the way home, and I felt myself beginning to relax.

It's no big deal, I told myself. *Nothing will come of it.*

Back at the house, I decided it was time to start doing some small things on my own. On Friday evening I mustered up the energy to put together dinner, something I hadn't done since my surgery. But it had to be simple, so I made one of the kids' favorites: fish sticks and tater tots, something I could just throw on a tray and slide into the oven. The kids and Joe all helped. One of them took the box out of the freezer while another turned on the stove. We bustled around the kitchen, all five of us, and there was life there. And hope.

As the wonderful smell of dinner in the oven started spreading through the house, I found my spirits rising. Fish sticks and latkes came to mind — fish sticks had been my nickname in high school, and the tater tots reminded me of latkes (potato pancakes), one of my favorite dishes we ate during Hannukah when I was a kid. For a moment I sensed the way my entire life had come together and led to that moment. My past and my present blended in a beautiful image of life. I knew everything was going to be okay.

We were having a great time, all laughing together while we set the table. I think all of us felt that the worst was behind us — I was getting better and we could spend more time together as a family, just the five of us without people in and out helping us all the time.

At about 6:00 p.m., just as I pulled dinner out of the oven and put it on the stovetop to cool, the phone rang. "Hello?" I said.

"Lily, this is Dr. Hasle."

My heart sank. All of the good feelings I had built up during the evening just melted away at the sound of his voice. I knew something was wrong. "Your biopsy came back. I have to tell you this: there were malignant cells in the tumor. We're going to have to do surgery as soon as possible — can you come in first thing Monday morning?"

A tremor started somewhere inside my soul and made its way out. Soon I trembled like a tree in a storm. I felt delirious, like I might be dreaming, and Joe had to snatch the phone from my hand before it fell to the floor. Somewhere far away I heard Joe talking quietly with Dr. Hasle. They made an appointment for me for Monday, only a weekend away.

I sat down somewhere, and a slide show of my life ran through my mind in a matter of moments: playing as a child in that Bronx apartment, acting in those high school plays, my time with Maria in the Village, marrying Joe at the courthouse. Then I saw the birth of each of my children — my precious children!

Just as I thought about them, they gathered around me, small and concerned, knowing something was wrong. Their little hands were on my knees and my shoulders. They hugged me, their eyes wondering: why is Mommy crying?

How could I leave them? How could God ask me to leave them?

As the sun set that evening I felt like a final darkness was closing in on my life, as if there was no way that sun would ever rise again. I couldn't imagine going back under anesthesia, through another round of surgeries, another painful awakening, another painful recuperation. Cancer! It sounded like a curse word in my head, a death sentence, a word I couldn't even say without feeling anger and fear. Cancer!

I was only 35 years old. Why me? I had three sweet children I adored. They needed me. I had tried to be a good mother, a good wife, a good citizen. A good Christian. God, why would You let this happen to me? What if they opened me up and found cancer all through my body . . . who would look after Joe and the kids?

Because of the operation and the stiff back brace, I hadn't been on my knees for weeks. I knew now was the time to get there. I went into my bedroom and clumsily got down on my knees, but the brace made it too difficult, so I fell forward on my face and just lay there, my arms stretched out, my legs reaching back under the bed. I felt like I was nothing, just a small speck in the great universe.

I prayed on the floor of that room, laying on my face, for what felt like hours and hours.

For the first portion of that time my mind focused on one thing: survival. I wasn't afraid to die and I wasn't afraid to meet God, but I was afraid for my children and what would happen to them without their mother. I didn't want to lose my family.

But then, in the far reaches of my prayers, a subtle thought began taking shape. What if, for some reason, God needed to take me? Was I willing to go? My prayers shifted away from all-out survival mode and took on more of a submissive tone.

"Lord, You know that I want to serve You the rest of my life. But give me the strength to accept whatever plan You have. Whatever plan. If You will, God, spare me so that I can raise my children. But help me accept what You have in store."

That evening leading into night passed slowly, painfully. Joe and the kids couldn't do anything to help me, and none of us were hungry after that phone call, so the food stayed on the oven and got cold. I never did eat anything that night.

But while I prayed, the house filled up with church friends and Joe's family. They came and they prayed with us. We felt such intense support. God was there with us that night, and He came in the form of our church community.

As the weekend passed, slower than I wanted, quicker than I would have liked, a curious movement took place inside of me. I began to feel better, encouraged. I knew there were many people praying for me, and I felt more than ever that God's Spirit was inside of me, giving me strength. Ever since I committed my life to Jesus, I knew I had a connection with a supernatural God, something I never experienced as a kid. This connection felt stronger than ever, and it gave me a sense of hope that no matter what happened, everything would end well. I suddenly felt like God was my best friend, and He was protecting me.

~ ~ ~ ~ ~

"Lily?"

"Yes, this is Lily," I said into the phone.

"This is Dorothy," she said. "How are you doing?"

It was Dorothy Lamb, our pastor's wife. She was a rock in our church with the gift of prophecy. She was a wonderful woman.

"I'm doing okay," I said quietly. "I'm still worried, but it's not as bad as last night."

"Lily, I'm praying for you today. I'm going to take a drive out in the country and just pray for you all day until God tells me what is going on with this cancer."

Just knowing that filled me with a new sense of peace and hope. Later that day she called me back.

"Lily, I drove and drove today, just waiting for God to tell me something about you."

"Did He tell you anything?" I asked. I respected her a lot and believed if she was praying for me then nothing could go wrong.

"There is a Holy Seal."

"What?"

"That's it. God told me there is a Holy Seal. I'm going to keep praying for you, Lily."

After I hung up, I thought about what she had said. "A Holy Seal." I assumed that she meant the Spirit of God was going to comfort me that the Lord would be the seal that would be all around my situation and protect me, at least from fear, if not from the cancer itself.

On Sunday night we went to our church for services. I felt better all the time, believing that the diagnosis must be wrong, the cancer was benign, and everything would be okay. I sat up front and, as people sang and shared, God's peace surrounded me. I thought that might be the seal that Dorothy had told me about.

Then a friend of mine, Ruby Dalton (Dorothy's sister), got up from where she was sitting, walked over in front of me, and just started talking, real loud, so the entire group in the church could hear her.

"Sister Lily, I just have to tell you that God gave me a vision."

Everyone grew silent and listened to what she had to say.

"I saw you standing at a pulpit with all three of your children, and they were all taller than you."

I was so happy to hear it that I started weeping, just holding my hands over my face. I so badly wanted that to come to pass.

~ ~ ~ ~ ~

Monday finally came.

"Hi, Lily," Dr. Hasle said as he came into the room where Joe and I waited. "As I mentioned over the phone, the biopsy has shown a malignancy. But we're going to do a freeze biopsy anyway, and at that point we'll know more about it. It's a surgical procedure, and we'll have to put you under with anesthesia."

"Okay," I said nervously, holding Joe's hand.

"There's one other thing you'll have to think about, and decide on before the procedure begins."

"What's that?" Joe asked.

"Which direction do you want to go if this test confirms that the cells are malignant? You have two options. The first is a lumpectomy followed by chemotherapy. The other is a radical mastectomy."

"That means . . ." I said, but my voice trailed off.

"That's right," he said quietly. "Removing the entire breast."

"The odds of removing all the cancer by just removing the lump are not as good as if we remove the entire breast," he continued. "And then there's the long period of radiation and chemo you'll have to undergo."

Joe and I looked at each other.

"What do you think?" I asked him.

Joe looked at Dr. Hasle. "What do you recommend?"

"I would recommend the mastectomy. It's entirely possible that we could remove the lump, Lily could go through the chemo, and then if the cancer is still not gone she would have to have the mastectomy anyway. And by then the cancer could spread farther, especially if any of the lymph nodes show malignancy."

I didn't have to think very long. "I have three kids," I said quietly. "I want to live. If that means living with one breast, then that's that."

I looked at Joe again, and he nodded.

"Okay," the doctor said. "It might not come to that, but it's best to make that decision before surgery begins."

Even after being presented with the options, I still felt so much faith that the cyst was going to be benign. God could do that. He could make the previous tests invalid, right? We went back into the hospital

Tuesday night, and I didn't even pack anything extra — I just knew they'd go in Wednesday morning, remove a benign cyst, and send me on my way the same day. I felt so much hope.

Just after the surgery began, and while I was under anesthesia, Dr. Hasle went out to have a word with Joe.

"Hello, Mr. Isaacs."

"Doctor," Joe said, looking up at him expectantly.

"The tumor is malignant, and it's about the size of a fifty cent piece. It's probably been in there a couple of years, and it needs to come out right away."

"Okay," Joe said.

"Because your wife is only 35 years old we feel the best thing to do is a radical mastectomy. That way we don't take any chances of it spreading."

Joe reconfirmed our permission to have the mastectomy done, and the doctor turned to go back into surgery. But then he paused. "It's the oddest thing," he told Joe. "I don't know that I've ever seen a tumor like this one. There's a crust around it, like an eggshell, that's encasing it, which means it almost certainly hasn't spread. It's almost like it has a seal around it."

It was "The Holy Seal" Sister Dorothy had told me about.

~ ~ ~ ~ ~

Slowly I came up into the light of my recovery room. I felt dazed, not sure of where I was at first, but once I realized my surgery was over, the first thing I did was reach for my breast. I was still out of it but could only feel a very thick bandage under the covers and was vaguely reassured that they hadn't removed it.

The longer I lay there, though, the more I realized that what I felt was just a thick layer of dressing and gauze, and I couldn't be sure whether or not my breast was still there. I lay there quietly for a little while, wanting to know, not wanting to know. The faith I had felt before the surgery was on the verge of crumbling.

Finally a nurse came into the room. She bustled around, preparing things for me, checking my charts. Finally I mustered up the courage to ask her. "Did they have to take my breast?" I whispered.

Her eyes filled with pity, like a parent looking at their injured child, and before she even said it I knew. "Yes," she said, nodding her head sadly and hugging her clipboard. "Yes, they did."

This huge wall of faith and confidence that had slowly built up since my hours-long prayer vigil collapsed, and I cried. I kept crying all day through any conversations I had, through any meals I ate, and even, I think, while I slept. I just couldn't stop crying. I didn't even let them open the shades in my room — I didn't want to see myself, and I certainly didn't want anyone else to see me. I just wanted to sit there in the dark and be sad and somehow wish it were all a dream that hadn't happened.

Later in the day the doctor came in. "We got all the cancer," he said, but I just kept crying. My spirits were dashed, my faith confused. I felt like God had walked away from me and rejected me. In my naive thinking, I believed that real Christians didn't go through things like that.

Some friends of ours from a church in Kentucky came to visit me. They brought me two dozen roses, absolutely beautiful flowers, and the scent filled the room. They were bursting with life. But I didn't even want to look at them — I was crying, pouting, because I felt like God had dropped me. I felt relieved that the cancer was gone but devastated by the cost to get there. I couldn't face looking at myself in the mirror.

The next day they told me my lymph nodes were clear. The fact that the tumor had been sealed had kept it from spreading.

There had been a Holy Seal.

The cancer was gone.

Yet I still felt defeated and devastated.

~ ~ ~ ~ ~

My first glimpse of my new self didn't help how I felt. After they removed the bandages and the nurses left the room, I limped over and stood in front of the mirror. Pulling back my hospital gown hurt me, but not in a physical way. It was an emotional tearing that I felt.

There it was: a four-inch scar across my chest. My breast was gone, replaced by a jagged line of red, sensitive flesh. All I could do was weep at my disfigurement. I felt unattractive, as if half of my femininity had been removed in that surgery and this body they had left behind wasn't man or woman.

On Friday a stylishly dressed, beautiful woman floated into my room. She was in her forties, and something about her made my hospital room feel brighter, fresher.

"Hi," she said. "Lily? I'm here from the American Cancer Society. How are you doing?"

I told her I was doing okay, not great. I told her they got all the cancer, so that was a relief. I told her they had to take one of my breasts. My voice got caught in my throat, just talking about it, and instinctively I moved to hide myself.

"I had breast cancer," she said, putting her hand on my arm. "There is life after cancer, Lily. I had a mastectomy, too."

I couldn't believe it. Looking at her, you would have thought she was the most confident, beautiful, assertive woman there was. And she, like me, only had one breast. Unbelievable.

"You can still be a woman and go on with your life," she said, explaining to me all the different options when it came to wearing prosthetics, or having reconstructive surgery. "No one outside your family and friends ever has to know," she said.

She told me stories of going to work and forgetting to wear her prosthesis, and I laughed. Laughed! I hadn't done that for weeks, maybe months, but there was something in her voice, in her demeanor, that lifted my spirits.

Yet it was a temporary happiness.

"I have to get through this. This is just part of my journey," I told myself over and over again, but sometimes it just didn't make sense. I fought to stay strong — reading the Bible helped, focusing on what the Disciples had gone through. I gradually began to realize that being a Christian didn't mean I was exempt from all the things that we experience simply because we're human: sickness, trials, and, someday, death. But I could let these experiences make me stronger. It took me months to rebuild my faith, but with God's help I did.

Finding a comfort level with my new body took much longer. I had lived a life of self-consciousness because of scoliosis, always wearing baggy clothes to hide my curving back. Then, just when that was taken care of, I lost a breast, and my confidence went with it.

Doctors fitted me for a prosthesis and I wore it for five years. During that time I never even let Joe see me without it on — I felt so embarrassed of my naked body. The only time I took it off was to take a shower. I even slept in it.

"Why are you embarrassed around me? You know it's crazy. I'm your husband, and you're as beautiful as you ever were." He was so supportive all the time, but I still felt awkward around him, so on the fifth anniversary of being cancer free, I had breast-reconstruction surgery.

Those two surgeries were spaced out over six weeks. In the first stage, they implanted a balloon in my breast cavity and started filling it with saline. Each week they added a little more fluid, and it gradually stretched my skin. Then, after six weeks, the second surgery was done. That's when they inserted the actual implant.

I hated to go into surgery again, but it was worth it. I finally felt whole again.

So many things changed after my battle with cancer. One of them was my attitude toward storms. I had always been afraid, but after winning my fight with cancer I realized that there were too many things out of my control for me to worry about storms. For all of those years I had been petrified of storms, yet one had raged inside of my body and I never knew it! Suddenly, after cancer, storms didn't scare me anymore. In fact, I enjoy listening to the thunder and watching the lightning flash.

The other thing that changed was my attitude toward God, and all the bartering I had done with Him through the years. I realized that not shaving my legs had nothing to do with Joe coming back to me that night, and that it was silly for me to try to do all these things so that God would love me more, or accept me.

One day I took it up with Joe.

"I feel like I've been disfigured all my life because of my back problem," I said, "and now my breast is gone. It really bothers me that I don't shave my legs. I made a really silly vow to God and I feel like He's releasing me."

Joe just shook his head. "I didn't know you made that vow. Go ahead and shave — it's not a big deal."

It was a new start. When he said that I really examined my heart. All those years, all the embarrassment during exams and surgeries, and it really didn't matter. I do believe that God saw my willingness and my commitment to Him, and for me that justified everything I felt during those years.

CHAPTER TEN

My back surgery and fight with breast cancer took place in 1983. As I regained my strength and the family traveled again, it felt like a second life started for me. I was alive. My children were healthy and happy, and I would get to see them grow up.

For the next seven or eight years our music just kept growing. My health stabilized, and the kids did well with school. Our lives actually started to feel normal! We went from recording our own albums, to having a producer, to having a label. Our venues got bigger, not in leaps and bounds, but slowly, steadily. We were playing in larger churches, farther away from home, and selling more albums.

Soon the kids stepped up and our band was exactly what the name implied: the Isaacs. We've had the pleasure of working with some of the finest musicians and singers in the world during the span of our career, but at that particular time, around 1988, it was just the five of us: Becky played guitar and sang while Sonya played the mandolin and led many of the songs. Joe sang and played guitar and banjo, and was also our emcee. Ben played the bass, and I was a vocalist. We traveled together, lived together and played together — it was a lot of together! But we created our own sound, and the kids grew in their knowledge of music and performance.

Because we began traveling farther, and overnight, we felt the need to get something that we could sleep in and have some more space. We took a leap of faith and bought our first bus — we were comfortable doing that because Joe was such a good mechanic. We had a friend in Crossville, Tennessee, that had a 1960 GMC bus for sale. It was old but in decent shape, so we bought it for $8,500. We used the money we made on weekends to pay the loan on the bus.

Soon after we bought it, the transmission went out, and I have vivid memories of that old bus sprawled out in pieces on our driveway in Morrow — Joe tore the motor and transmission apart and spent many hours working on it. Ben, 15 or 16 at the time, helped out a lot. That's where he got his schooling on being a mechanic.

It was back-breaking work, and I felt sorry for Joe because he already had back trouble, but we couldn't afford to take it to a big garage, so Joe did the best he could to find parts and do the work. He and Ben put in a lot of hours. I don't know how they did it, but in about a month they had it running in perfect shape.

The inside of the bus was a little rough, so we bought an old couch and a chair, and Joe fixed the bunks the way we needed them. We ended up with six bunks, three high on each side. The back room was a wide-open space where we put a wire from one side to the other and hung all of our clothes. Joe glued a mirror on the wall so we could do our hair. That particular bus had no toilet, so Joe put a porta-potty in the back for emergencies.

We used a cooler to store our drinks and lunchmeat. The air conditioner only worked about half the time, so the windows usually stayed open. That was also the bus in which Ben learned to drive. When Joe slept, I sat on the buddy chair beside Ben while he drove. I was so worried that he would fall asleep. He kept telling me to go to bed, but I still sat there (usually falling asleep myself).

The first long trip we took in that bus after it was ready was to somewhere in Virginia. We were so excited that we had our bus! That night we pulled off at a rest area, opened the windows, and slept in it for the first time. We thought we had finally arrived.

For the next 25 years we went through a few more buses. Our next bus was a 1970 MCI, which again had to be completely redone (Joe and Ben were the masterminds in that again); then we bought a 1992 Prevost; then a 2002 Prevost. We never had a bathroom in our bus until we bought the 1992 Prevost. I have many memories of the porta-potties and empty jugs of water. How things change.

We went from a car to a station wagon, from the station wagon to a van, then pulled the trailer behind the van, and finally went through four buses, all in the last 35 years. It was a lot of blood, sweat, and tears, lots of hard work and long trips, to get from that first car to the bus we have now.

~ ~ ~ ~ ~

The first national recording company that paid attention to us was the Eddie Crook Company. We recorded three albums with Morningstar Records in Nashville. Then we moved on to Horizon Records.

In those days, we loaded up our family and all our equipment into the bus and drove to Asheville, North Carolina, to do our recordings with Horizon Records. We headed south through Cincinnati and over the river into Kentucky. Soon the road rose and fell, running along rolling hills covered in the greenest grass. Then we'd pass into Tennessee, and the mountains crept up around us.

It would take us about eight hours to get to Ashville, and it seemed like we were heading down that way more and more. As our band became known on a regional level, we started playing more shows in the south — Georgia, North Carolina, South Carolina, Florida, and Alabama. Nearly every weekend we traveled south, and when we'd pass that exit for Knoxville we'd be about halfway to wherever we were going.

We'd been in Ohio for a long time, and there were some divisive issues going on in our church, issues that led us to leave. Many of the ties we had to Ohio were dissolving. Becky was a junior in high school and dating John (he lived in Virginia); Sonya was a senior in high school; Ben was in his first year of college. We felt like we were ready for a change, and we wanted to move before the kids put down roots by getting married. It seemed like the right time.

So we made a family decision to leave Ohio. Poor Becky — she was in her junior year and would have to finish one year in a new school. But moving to Tennessee would mean she was a lot closer to John, so there was at least one positive for her. She still to this day says it was cruel to make her move during her senior year, and I kind of agree.

We befriended a family on one of our many trips south: the Overtons. They lived in LaFollette, Tennessee. They called us and said there was a beautiful place for sale in their town, on three acres of land. We stopped to look at it on one of our trips and to us it seemed huge! My girls had always shared a room, but here everyone would have their own space. There was even a long, flat lane where we could park the bus.

We traveled a lot on weekends and couldn't attend the auction of the house, so Mr. Overton agreed to represent us and put the bid in on the home. We had a certain limit on what we were able to spend, and we couldn't go any higher. Luckily, on the day of the auction it was storming, so not too many people showed up. Because Mr. Overton was a well-respected businessman, I think the other people figured they couldn't outbid him. We were in Alabama when we heard that our offer was accepted, and we were so excited about the opportunity. That spring we started moving little by little, with the goal of being down there for good in the summer after Sonya graduated.

~ ~ ~ ~ ~

"Mom, check out this song," Sonya said. We had recently bought the house in LaFollette, and she and Ben had been in the middle of one of those back-and-forth trips to Morrow to help finish the move.

> It hasn't been a bed of roses since I started on my way
> And Lord you know I'm not complaining
> There's just something I should say

For I've reached desperation and I've stumbled since my start
I've grown weary through the years
Now I'm crying bitter tears from the depths of my heart

As I sat there listening to two of my kids sing their hearts out to the tune of a song they had just written, I started crying. "My God," I said, "how did you know that was in my heart? That has to go on the album."

"From the Depths of My Heart" was a last-minute addition to our 1992 album, *Live In Atlanta*, and it became a #1 hit. It was #1 for three months in a row in 1992 in *Singing News Magazine*; it won Song of the Year from *Gospel Voice* magazine; and that year Sonya won the Horizon Award from the Singing News Awards.

As the kids became more accomplished musicians, they began experimenting with their own sounds and trying to play more contemporary stuff. This was great for them, and they started finding their own musical identity, writing a lot of original material and adding new chord progressions and harmonies that were not traditional bluegrass melodies. I loved the creativity they exhibited, and I was proud to see them develop.

It was an exciting time in the life of the Isaacs.

~ ~ ~ ~ ~

In 2001, thanks to our friends Bill and Gloria Gaither, I found myself back in New York City. The buildings rose up like mountains on either side of me. Blaring horns and screeching tires and slamming doors. Vendors shouted. The never-ending sound of a million shoes walking along the sidewalk, a million soles. I walked back inside, back into the place I had always dreamed of playing music: Carnegie Hall.

I remembered how it felt when Maria and I were in the city, together, but other than the small audience at Columbia Records, we had never played anywhere nearly as important. Our best had been reserved for the grassy lawns of the Village, or Gerdie's, or the next party. Yet here I was in New York City, nearly 40 years later, getting ready to play at Carnegie Hall.

At one point during that day, when the sound checks were over and a few of the sound guys wandered the hall preparing for the concert, I walked slowly up on to the stage and sat in one of the chairs. I stared up at the ornate ceiling, the balconies, the endless spread of theater chairs folded up, waiting for bodies to fill them. I thought of how far I had come, of how far my parents had traveled to get to that city.

And I wept.

My entire life moved through my mind like a movie: I envisioned my father, gone by that time, and my mother, still in the same apartment. I thought about Maria and Joe and all the other friends I had made in the city. I remembered the plays, the musicals, the gigs, the jobs, the schooling, and then eventually leaving for Ohio and my life with Joe. So many memories.

The Carnegie Hall show had been scheduled for quite some time, and in the interim 9/11 had taken place. The city was still reeling from that atrocity, and it felt quieter than I remembered it being. But it was a Gaither show, and Bill, the legendary songwriter and producer, decided that in light of those events we should do more of a patriotic tribute to the firefighters and policemen and emergency workers of the city. It would be an emotional night for everyone.

Bill also had one other idea for the concert.

"Lily," Bill asked, "do you think your mom would come out on stage if you asked her to, just so we could introduce her?"

I thought about that for a moment. "I'm not sure, but I'll ask her."

So I gave her a call. "Mom, I want you to take a cab to Carnegie Hall, you and Irving," I said. Irving was my stepfather. "I want you to come and visit with everyone. Just get dressed up, because I want you to meet everybody."

I didn't even tell her that Bill wanted her to come on stage, because I didn't want her to get nervous and not come. She had enough hurdles to cross when it came to my concerts without something else scaring her away.

So that day, after my time sitting on the stage and just thinking about my life, my mom and Irving came early and had dinner with the performers backstage. Everyone had heard about her story, so they were making a big deal about her being there, coming up and introducing themselves and asking her questions. And they were all so kind to her. Of course, she loved the attention.

Before the show started I decided to ask her. "Mom, when we're out there singing, would you care to come out and just let me introduce you to everyone there?"

"Yes, that will be fine."

"Okay, well, I'll have my friend come and get you while we're singing and he'll bring you out."

Ben, Sonya, and Becky sang "The Star-Spangled Banner" that night and their voices filled up that auditorium. I don't think I could have been more proud, and in the moments of silence between verses I scanned the crowd, watching those faces transfixed at the sound of my children's voices. Their eyes looked up, like people hungry for hope.

Then came the point when Bill Gaither set up my mother's appearance. "We've got a special guest here tonight. This is Lily's mother, Faye Fishman Blauschild."

I was standing there beside her as Bill introduced her to the crowd as an 82-year-old Holocaust survivor.

"Mom, is there anything you'd like to say to everyone?" I asked her, not really knowing what to expect. I kind of caught her off guard. But mom has always been a natural, the life of the party, and it didn't take her more than a moment to turn to the crowd and say in her thick Polish accent: "Well, I am proud to be an American now."

When she said that the crowd went wild. They gave my little "Yiddish Mama" the longest standing ovation of the night, and chills just covered my entire body. There were people from all branches of the military, the police department, firefighters, and emergency responders: all of them stood up with the rest of the crowd and clapped for her.

Tears welled up in my eyes — there was a woman who survived one of the worst times in the world, and she had never been recognized for anything, ever. She had come to this country with nothing but her husband, a tiny daughter, and the clothes on her back. She had passed under the shadow of the Statue of Liberty, stood in line at Ellis Island, and been given a new name.

Now, this city was honoring her.

She stood, beaming. It felt like the whole world said so much to her in that moment: how sorry they were that she had to experience the Holocaust, how happy they were that she could be there, how sad they were that she had lost so much, and how proud they were of the strength she had shown.

I, too, was proud, but all I could do was smile and cry and shake my head.

That night I walked her and Irving out to get a cab. The air was cool, and for some reason I remembered all the old Jewish customs we had celebrated when I was a kid. I remembered going with her and my father and my brother to see the rabbi, or walking through the park and throwing our sins into the stream. I remembered the red glass of shimmering wine, and my brother reciting out the questions.

I walked behind her, now taller than her, looking over her head. We hailed a cab and I opened the door, took her hand, and helped her inside. I said a few words to her and her driver, then closed the door and watched the yellow cab disappear into the streaming lights of Manhattan traffic. I stood there for a while after the car vanished, just taking in the city.

~ ~ ~ ~ ~

Our popularity continued to grow, and soon we had an international audience. The Gaithers also continued to invite us to more of their shows, so when they approached us about joining them at a concert in Israel, we couldn't say yes fast enough. We'd been to Israel several times during the years, but this would be different. We would be performing!

I have to say, the Gaithers have given us such an amazing platform. We are so grateful for the opportunity they gave us to share what we do with so many people. They first invited us to one of their shows in 1992, and since then we've been all over the United States and all over the world, singing alongside them. It's been a huge honor.

In the summer of 2004, we flew to Israel with the Gaithers for a concert in Jerusalem. During rehearsal I got the same feeling as I did at Carnegie Hall — this was my homeland, among the Jewish people. Stone walls, thousands of years old, rose up all around us, and a breeze blew in from the cobalt blue sky. If anything ever felt like heaven, this was it.

I have cousins who live in Israel so I invited them to come to the show — my mom's sister's kids, and I had only seen them a couple of times before.

"We're coming to perform at David's citadel in Jerusalem," I told them, "and I'd like you to come to the show."

Of course I was a little nervous about this, hoping they wouldn't up and leave in the middle of the show if our Christian message offended their Jewish sensibilities. But they were really excited about coming — some of my dad's family even said they would be there.

These family members all arrived early and came to the hotel where we were staying. We visited with them for a little, and it was fun telling each other stories about family members we had never heard of. But I was even more nervous after I saw them and became really scared they would leave since we were going to sing so many songs about Jesus.

We did a Hebrew song that night — "Hallelujah." The rehearsal was good, in spite of the jet lag and everything else, but when the show came it started getting dark, and the lights came up all around us. Israeli dancers moved on the rooftop. When we started singing "Hallelujah," and the audience stood up and swayed back and forth with the words, it was just amazing. I felt as though I was born for that moment in time.

This is my Jewish homeland, I thought, *and here I am with my children, my heritage, even some of my extended Jewish family, singing a Hebrew folk song that's going to be on television all around the world.*

The show went very late, until well after midnight, and my family stayed for the entire thing.

~ ~ ~ ~ ~

Mom came down and visited with me for Christmas in 2009. Becky and John still lived in the house beside us. Ben was happily married, and Sonya's wedding was only a few days behind us. It seemed like everyone in my family was happy and doing well. Moving on.

So for that week between Christmas and New Year's, Mom and I just hung out. It's the one time of year when we don't book concerts. The two of us drank coffee and ate a lot of our favorite nosh, dark chocolate. We talked for hours and I spent quality time taking care of her. She was 90 years old at the time, and not too much came easy for her anymore, whether it was preparing breakfast in the morning and getting ready for the day or falling asleep at night.

But I enjoyed just being with her. Just having her there with me in my big, empty house. We had our miniature spats, our disagreements, but she is my mother, and there is a bond between us that is hard to explain.

When her visit came to its end, I flew her back to New York City. For the hundredth time I looked down on the busy-ness and the buildings and the people going here and there like ants disturbed. The tiny matchbox cars. The drab coldness of a new year.

I got her back to her apartment building, and we took the elevator up to her floor, the old familiar landing, the old familiar door. *I used to sneak cigarettes in that stairwell*, I thought to myself, smiling. Gloria and I used to get into all kinds of trouble in this quiet apartment. I helped mom unpack and get settled, made sure the place warmed up for her, made sure she had food for the next few days.

The next day I went back to the airport by myself. I got in a plane and flew into the New Year — 2010.

~ ~ ~ ~ ~

Three months later. My brother and I sat in that very same apartment with my mother. Her caretaker had recently died after a fight with cancer, and we didn't think my mother could live there on her own anymore. So we sat on her plastic-covered sofa, and I marveled at how the apartment smelled the same way it always had.

"No, Mom," my brother said. "We're not trying to take away your independence. You would love it in a senior community. You could make new friends and be a part of a Jewish group again. You can't even leave your apartment anymore! And it's really not safe for you here, alone. What if someone breaks in? What if you hurt yourself and can't call for help?"

We gave her the choice of Tennessee or the West Coast, and she chose a community in San Francisco close to my brother. So in about a month my brother met me at her apartment again and we packed her up and he flew with her to California. All she took was her clothing and a few personal items. We knew we had to give up the apartment at that point, so I talked to the superintendent, and he said we could clean it out the following month.

Sonya, her husband, Jimmy, and I flew up one final time to clean out the apartment. Our friends, Bill and Debbie Becker, met us there. The five of us started packing everything into boxes for Goodwill. We gave away a lot of her furniture. We cleaned and dusted and vacuumed.

And memories bombarded me at every turn. We carried out the little kitchen chairs, the very same chairs Gloria and I had sat in while watching my mother dance around the room. They were the very same chairs Maria and I had sat in, plotting our musical careers. The very same chairs where I had sat, desperately waiting for a call from Joe when we had first met.

Then into the bedroom that Hymie and I had shared for so many years. I remembered laying there at night, pretending to sleep while my father looked in on us before going to work the night shift. His chin had always felt so sandpapery rough on my face when he gave me a goodbye kiss. If I closed my eyes, the traffic didn't sound all that different from my childhood.

We looked through my mother's papers and photos, and I stared at those memories. I had been so hurt by my parents' difficult relationship. Our existence as a family had felt so tenuous. I remembered how Dad would wake up during the day and go cough in the bathroom until I was sure his lungs were going to fall out. I thought about how he used to sit at the table and read his Yiddish paper.

In my mother's closet we discovered that she had so many shoes that she hadn't been able to take them all with her. I was shocked at how organized she was: her shoes were all in a rack and her clothes were separated by season. It reminded me of how fashionable she had been, how concerned about her looks. I smiled, thinking about how spirited she had always been. I imagined her in the relocation camps after the war, free and growing healthier every day. I imagined what she must have looked like when she married my dad.

In another closet we found 30 boxes of Kleenex piled up. Ten boxes of sugar. Innumerable containers of cotton balls. Tears trickled down my cheeks as I looked through these things she had stockpiled. Was she so lonely and restless that she needed a reason to get out of the house, even if it was just an hour trip to the store to buy a "much-needed" box of tissues? Or was it that 70 years and thousands of miles away from that barbed wire she would always be a Holocaust survivor, saving things for a day when she might need them?

We left a few large pieces of furniture that we couldn't take with us. The super said he would get them to the local thrift store for us. I kept three or four items, and our friends drove the rest of the boxes in a moving truck back to Tennessee.

It was a sad day. My mom was still living, but this move closed the door on a huge part of my life, a time I would never be able to visit again. I relived a lot of the loneliness I had felt as a child. For a moment, I was young Lily again, wishing my hair could cover my crooked back, excited about the next school musical, and wondering if my father would ever stop drinking.

I walked out through the door, carrying a few small keepsakes. I locked the door and handed the key to the super. I cried out loud that day, took a deep breath, and forced myself to walk. One step in front of the other.

I left that beautiful old apartment, dripping as it did with memories. I walked down the stairs and the echoes of my footsteps drifted up the stairwell behind me.

~ ~ ~ ~ ~

But I feel hope these days, and not the old despair that came with trying to be the buffer between so many people. I'm realizing now that God does not need me to take on the cares of the world — my own will suffice. Our band, our life together as a family, our future — it's all in His hands.

As the plane tilted back and rose up from among those buildings, I looked out the window and watched the city streets turn into rolling hills, then disappear under the clouds. I started thinking about how God knows the future, even when we can't bear to think about it. I pictured my parents traveling in cattle cars from Poland to Germany, on their way to be exterminated. Yet somehow they survived to tell their story.

Then my brother and I were born. And my life branched out and I got married and had three wonderful, talented children. Would anyone have believed this kind of a future was possible if they had seen my mother standing in a line of Jews walking toward a gas chamber just before her friend pulled her aside? Would anyone have thought a future was possible if they would have been there to watch my father bleeding on the ground in a concentration camp, the guard poised to strike again?

Yet there was always hope. Tyrants tried to destroy as many lives as possible. They tried to snuff out our existence, my existence, yet God's divine plan marched on. That's what I felt the most that day, flying home from New York. There is always hope.

CHAPTER ELEVEN

*L*ife goes on, you know? You settle into a routine and the days turn to weeks, which turn to months, which turn to years, and before you know it, a few decades have passed. It's amazing, and sometimes it's sad, but it can also be very healing, that passing of time.

Joe and I were divorced in 1998. I guess in some ways it's a similar feeling to closing the door on Mom's emptied apartment. You take the good memories, the cherished moments, and you leave the rest behind. Divorce is never easy, and after 28 years of marriage you realize how much you've shared in life. We have three amazing kids and six wonderful grandchildren together. I know I may never understand it all — but I know it was meant for us to be together for however long God's plan intended.

For the next 13 years I stayed in Lafollette, Tennessee, and found a new normalcy as a single woman again. Becky, John, and the kids lived right next to me, and I enjoyed the daily after-school visits from my grandkids Levi and Jakobi. Still, though, a part of my heart was missing. Sonya and Ben had moved to Nashville years prior and were raising families there that I didn't get to see as often as I wanted. Ben and Mindy's kids, Jacob, Cameron, and Kyra, were all very active in their schools and in extracurricular activities. I missed so many ephemeral events — ballgames, school plays, choir concerts, dance recitals, and so much more that a Grandma just needed to see but couldn't, living over three hours away.

Then in 2011, Sonya gave birth to her first baby, my sweet little grandson Ayden. He was growing up so quickly, and I missed him every day I didn't see him. I cherished our holiday times when we were all together and longed for us to live close to each other again. So much of our work was in Nashville — the recording studio, the Grand Ole Opry, industry awards shows, and business meetings, and even the holistic clinic Becky frequented for her autoimmune disease — all were there near their homes. So many days after mid-week Nashville runs, on top of weekend travels, I just wished that we could move there. But what good would it have been to leave one set of grandkids for another? My heart was torn. So, I prayed. A lot.

One day around Halloween in 2011, Becky and John came over for supper. John, who had been teaching at a school there for 6 years, had decided to leave due to some administrative changes. The last thing that I ever expected to come of his mouth that night did — "I think we should consider moving to Nashville." My heart was overjoyed! Could it be that at long last I would be in the same town with all my kids again? My wheels were spinning. I got a little nauseous thinking about the closets stuffed with 20 years of boxes that would have to be sorted through. I got a little sad thinking about the day we moved into that house, as an excited family of five, and now I, alone, would be moving out, and then I had to laugh a little thinking about my pattern of moving every 20 years or so. Let's see, the first 20 years in New York City, then 17 in Ohio, then 20 more in East Tennessee . . . I think 20 years in Nashville will make me the prime age for my final southern snowbird flight to Miami. You never know.

By February of 2012, our houses were on the market. It seemed like poor timing, putting two houses on the market in February. After all, who would buy a house in the winter? Didn't most people choose to move in the summertime?

Thankfully, it turns out people do move in late winter! During the second week of March, we got a call from the realtor. Two different families, unrelated, not knowing each other, had each made an offer on our houses. The first family that looked at my house bought it. I would move to Nashville the last weekend in May, and Becky and John were there by the second weekend in June.

When I signed the papers, in that moment I did think back with nostalgia on the many years spent in the house, yet I had no regrets. I went through so much there and it was time to go forward with this change, with a new phase in my life, with God leading the way as always. I was excited in one way but kind of scared, you know, that I wouldn't be doing everything the right way, but it gave me such a feeling of liberation, looking forward to new experiences and memories. I did dread the thought of all that packing! It seemed like such a feat to accomplish on an already busy schedule.

To make moving even more difficult, I had developed a quarter-sized ulcer on my ankle caused from varicose veins that I had had for years. I was in so much pain with my foot that I had to wear wraps and take pain medication just to function. I had already been to vascular surgeons and knew that if it didn't heal on its own it would require surgery down the line. I had to elevate my foot a lot, and wasn't able to do some of the most simple tasks. Maybe it's ironic how some pain distracts you from other pain. I had to let my family go through most of the boxes for me; some that would've hurt much deeper than any physical wound. Sometimes you don't have a choice but to move on and let the past be.

The kids all laughed about how I was wimping out on all the hard work, just sitting there being the bossy supervisor, so high on pain meds that I didn't remember the last thing I saw. They packed up my life and unpacked it in my new, much smaller home in Nashville. I'll admit it was nice having them do all my dirty work, but I still can't find half my house! Over the last two years, my health restored, I started tearing into those undisturbed boxes that made the trip with me. I just had so much stuff, over 60 years worth, and I wanted to take my time going through it all, item by item.

The first box I opened contained two sweaters I'd knitted while still at home with my parents. I remembered learning to knit, sitting in front of the TV on the couch waiting for Joe's phone calls. It seemed a little more productive than just twiddling my thumbs and it helped ease the anxiety of those forever long nights when he just couldn't call. *Wow!* I thought. *I kept these through all the moves and all the changes in my life.* Underneath the sweaters were three cassette tapes recorded in our little unfinished basement when we lived in Morrow. Sonya, no more than seven at the time, was the announcer and played the piano, while Ben, nine, and Becky, six, would join her in singing and interviewing. In perfect three-part harmony they recorded their very own radio show concert! One recording was a thank you gift for my mom, who had sent them the money for their piano. "The Star Spangled Banner" and "You Are My Sunshine" rang out at the top of their little lungs.

It's amazing to look back on their natural talent beginning at such young ages. At that time we were already singing locally on weekends in churches. My prayer was always that God would use us to be able to make a difference in the world with our music. Holding those cassette tapes, as I thought back on those early days, I had to pause to thank God for granting us the desires of our hearts. None of us could have ever dreamed this big.

In one box marked "kids' keepsakes" I found little hand-me-down dresses I'd made for the girls when times were hard, and a housecoat and rain jacket Ben wore when he was just a toddler. There were love letters, old Lincoln log toys, and their report cards, which I kept mainly for the purpose of saving my grandkids' hides if one of them ever got a bad grade. There were things the kids had made when they were young too — an essay Sonya had written called "Why I Love America" that won her a $100 savings bond; some beautiful sconces Becky had made in her all-boy-plus-one ninth-grade wood shop class; some well-designed drawings Ben had drafted in his favorite architectural class. It made me so proud looking back on their uniqueness and individual skills, and I wondered what they might have chosen as a career if they hadn't grown up on the road. I guess what they say about music is true — if it's in your blood you just can't be fulfilled doing anything else.

Opening the next box labeled "handle with care" was like opening a vault packed with painful emotions. There were my back x-rays taken when they discovered I had scoliosis, and the post-op x-rays showing the huge screws and pins going through my spine. There was that hot, itchy prosthesis I wore for so many years after my mastectomy. There was the Bible given to Joe and me when were first married, and the gently worn wedding album from that blissful day in that other life we were beginning together. What do you do with those kinds of memoirs? You don't need to display them anymore, but you just can't bear to throw them away. I suppose you do what I did. Just find another unvisited bottom drawer or unreachable top shelf to store them in until the next time you rediscover them while looking for your misplaced birth certificate.

I created a box for Joe that day, too; a box for things I knew he would want. There were some old records he had collected and some souvenirs from our travels abroad. There were some Polaroid pictures of him with the kids, old photos of his parents, and several we'd kept of his brother Delmer, who had been killed in that tragic car crash so many years before. I gave each one a good long look before putting them in Joe's pile. Would we have ever gone to church that first night if Delmer hadn't died? Was that the only way for us to embrace the fragility of life and surrender to our call of duty? I prefer to believe that this was one of those times when God made something beautiful out of something otherwise intended for evil. Whatever the reason, I just had to thank God again for Delmer, and that through his untimely death, for the first time ever, I found life.

Yes, life, but not without consequence. There underneath those items were some of my most cherished savings. Pictures from Europe of my sunken-faced father and my barely twenties mother taken shortly after their liberation from the Holocaust; pictures of me as a little girl, oblivious then to the challenges my parents had overcome, standing next to my curly haired little brother Hy, smiling. We were their hope and future, and I couldn't help thinking as tears rolled down my face, how old my young mother looked standing there with us in front of that Bronx apartment. Maybe it was then that I first felt the need to protect them all — the need to save and treasure everything of theirs that I could get my hands on.

In another box labeled "Breakable," I found a ziploc bag with the scarf I had knit for my father that he wore to work nearly every day. I pressed that scarf to my face and breathed in as deeply as I could — the strange but familiar scent of Camel cigarette smoke woven perfectly into the aroma of a fresh-baked loaf of bread. It was Daddy. It was a thread back in time that took me to that little apartment where the sound of his voice calling me "Mamila" or "little mother" reminded me of just how much I wanted to make his life better. I took one more deep smell and put it back in the baggie. I hope it always smells this good.

In another baggie was his teflin and talis, the ceremonial Jewish garments he wore to pray from time to time. Mom had given it to me after Dad passed away, and I'd kept it with the little prayer Bible he used at the synagogue. I wonder what he prayed for. He seemed so content with so little. Maybe he prayed to just stay that way. To them, the life we had was a dream compared to where they had come from. I thought of that when I opened the next little box taped shut with the Yiddish word "*Bahnkes*" written on it. Inside was what looked like a set of upside-down whiskey glasses, used in a European remedy known as fire cupping. I remembered years ago Dad told me this was how they used to treat body pain with heat. Before electric blankets, or heating pads, they would use a hot candle and heat the inside of these little glasses. When they were warm enough, they would lay five or six of them on the area of pain where the heat could be absorbed into the skin. Dad brought them over from Europe, and somehow they hadn't even gotten cracked. I love these little glasses, knowing that in a small way, even if only temporarily, they took away some of his pain. I only wish they could have done that for his mind.

Just one more unpacking project before taking a break. I was tired and emotionally drained and it was getting late. But it was like a movie that you can't stop watching, no matter how sad the plot at times. *Just let me go through this drawer before I go to bed*, I thought. It had been stuck for years, and rather than try to force it open, I just let it be. Now it was free and I could finally get inside. My discovery was the reason I believe with all my heart that I couldn't finish this book until now. There it was, my diary dated 1960-, buried under piles of old papers and documents. I couldn't believe it! I had forgotten all about it. I began looking through the entries, remembering each time I held the pen that allowed me to pour my feelings out onto every page. My teenage self had been so intense, so fiery. I found the page where I had asked my father to stop drinking. I found the page where I was so mad at my mom for wanting to leave. The raw, honest emotion in those moments blew me away. Being able to share those actual pages with you as I have in this book has been the icing on the cake for me. Reading it, I felt sorta like Ralphie in *The Christmas Story*; a little embarrassed, a little goofy, but mostly just thankful for the life I had to write about.

I lay in bed that night and for hours read those private, familiar pages. "Lenore," or "Lenny," as I affectionately called my diary, was my very best friend. The only one who really knew me . . . my thoughts, my insecurities, my dreams, my fears, my frustrations, all of me. I didn't know how to pray then. I didn't know who to talk to. My entries were so sporadic, spanning a three-year period as if the only time I needed Lenny was to share a highlight or a desperate moment in my life. I was trying to find myself. Perhaps in continuation of my parents' necessary history of changing our family name — Feigle to Faye, Usher to Oscar, Fiszman to Fishman — I was destined to evolve into who I am, too. I was born Lea. My citizenship papers called me Lillian. My school records were Lillie, and that's how Lenny knew me, too. My stage name was Lile´. Now I am just Lily.

For the first time ever, revisiting Lenny, I saw myself from the outside. I saw myself for who I truly am. I realized that I regretted not having asked my father more questions about his life. I realized that my anger toward my mother for so many years should have been compassion because she only wanted to live and have back the life she lost.

I realized that I've always tried to fix my world, and somehow broke myself in the process.

Now I know that changing your name, your address, your hair color, or your wardrobe doesn't change the fabric of who you are. Writing this book has been therapy for me, a spilling of my life into the open, a revealing of secrets, an admission of who I am. I feel like I know myself now, Lily Fishman Isaacs, in a way I never did before.

March 10, 2014

Dear Lenny,

I can't believe I've found you after all these years! A lot more than my handwriting has changed since I first opened you. Who would've thought when I bought you over 50 years ago that I would have so many unbelievable things to write about. My life has been like a rollercoaster; some highs, some lows, but a ride I wouldn't have wanted to miss. I hope you don't mind that I'm going to share our secrets with the whole world. Apparently there are people who think my life has been interesting enough that they encouraged me to write a book. So I did. If the things I've learned and lived through in my life can help someone else, then I'm willing to share it all.

When I found you again, I reread the pages that I had first written. I thought having a crooked back was the worst thing that could ever happen to anyone. Turns out it wasn't. Today is a special day for me. 31 years ago today, March 10, 1983, I was being wheeled down a hospital corridor to have surgery for breast cancer. I didn't know if I was going to live another day, let alone 30 more years. I am so grateful today and every day that God spared my life. I can't help but wonder what I'll be telling you next, or how many more diary entries I even have left. All I know is I am here now, and it's a good place to be. Thanks for being there for me Lenore. I promise I won't lose you again.

Love,
Lily

POSTSCRIPT

*I*t's an amazing story of how a Jewish girl from the Bronx, New York, became the matriarch of a bluegrass gospel family from Tennessee," Sonya, my middle daughter, says with a laugh as she introduces me nightly from the stage. And she's right. Look at me, an immigrant baby-boomer, a cancer-survivor, a 60-something divorcee, a Jewish believer. It is quite amazing. I get to do what I love the most with the ones I love the most, and every weekend when I get on that bus with my children and grandchildren I thank God for the light of truth that has led my path all these years. I thank God for blessing my family and me with the talent and platform to share my story and to tell others about the love of God and salvation through Jesus, Yeshua, my Messiah.

I thank God for my little Jewish Mamila. She is 94 years young and lives near my brother, Hy, in Novato, California. Although her physical health is holding up okay, she has been suffering from progressing dementia for several years. It's been hard to watch her decline mentally, but I'm glad there are some things she doesn't have to remember anymore. Hy and Sue visit Mom nearly every day at the assisted living home and take care of so many of her daily needs. Being so far away, I don't know what I would do without them. Hy has worked hard to establish his successful landscaping business, and he and Sue are wonderful parents to my niece and nephew, Alice and Nathan. I visit them as often as I can, and every time I have to leave to come home, my heart sinks, because I never know if it's the last time I'll see Mom again. I miss my West Coast family and wish we could all be together more.

Instead, here I am, 2,343 miles away, settling into my lovely new subdivision in middle Tennessee. I get to babysit Ayden at least one day a week while Sonya and her husband, Jimmy, write songs. There's no better feeling in the world than snuggling with my little "Munchkin" on the couch, watching *Power Rangers* and playing monster trucks. He likes to come to Meemaw's because he shares my affinity for chocolate and knows I'll sneak him an ice cream sandwich every time . . . shhhh . . . just our little secret. Jimmy has had a very successful country music writing career and has penned five #1 songs, including the song "I'm Gonna Love You Through It" that he, Sonya, and a friend, Ben Hayslip, wrote in 2011 about my experience with breast cancer. Country superstar Martina McBride recorded it, and even asked me to be in her music video. Team Martina, a foundation that was started because of the song, still helps cancer patients all over the world. I am honored that my 30-year-old story of struggle and survival has inspired such a beautiful song and is helping heal so many hearts today.

Becky is also an accomplished songwriter and she, Ben, and Sonya are called upon often to sing background vocals on various music stars' projects, including Reba, Dolly Parton, Vince Gill, Merle Haggard, and Trace Adkins, to name a few. I must say, though, I'm most proud of the parents they have become. I still get to see Jakobi and Levi almost every day despite the two-mile distance now from my house to theirs. It's hard to believe they're already teenagers, and Levi, who's a budding singer and musician, is going into college. Jakobi, the sweet, shy one in the family, is our athlete. Her name is a derivative of Jakabovitz, my mother's maiden name, and her life is a constant reminder that our heritage lives on. Becky's husband, John, travels with a successful bluegrass band called The Boxcars and also enjoys evangelizing in different states. When he's out of town, we have slumber parties, Becky, the kids, and I, and it's like it used to be in LaFollette again. We love to go shopping together, too, all of us girls, and I especially love it when my beautiful step-grandaughter, Madeleine, Jimmy's 15-year-old, joins us!

I get to see Ben, his wife, Mindy, and their kids mostly when we all meet for dinner or I have them over for a home-cooked meal. They only live about 20 minutes from me and stay busy shuttling all three of their teenagers to all the activities they are involved in. Ben spends hours each week in the studio and has become a successful record producer, producing popular artists like the Oak Ridge Boys, the Gaither Vocal Band, and many others. Mindy is a beautiful, sweet, strong woman who loves to make people hate her . . . she is a personal trainer, and physically puts us all to shame. Jacob, their oldest, is wise beyond his years and has excelled in boy scouts and ROTC. Cameron, the middle daughter, loves to sing and play guitar, and aspires to be an entertainer like her dad. Kyra, the youngest, has chosen dance as her art form, and she and Cameron both could be supermodels. I am as proud of my grandchildren as any grandma would be and am thankful to share the same town with them now.

When I'm not enjoying family downtime, I stay busy managing the Isaacs. I spend hours handling our financial affairs, working on scheduling, and talking to promoters to ensure successful concert events. I correspond with our booking agent daily and advance our dates each week before we leave town every weekend. I feel lucky because I'm the first to know when the really big career-changing things happen. And occasionally they do. I recall one particular fall Monday afternoon. I had just finished my favorite New Yorkish lunch of tuna bagels and kosher pickles and had just sat back down at my desk when my phone rang. "Hey, Jeff," I answered happily; not only is he our booking agent, but he has become one of my dearest friends.

"Hi Lily," he replied, "I just got a call from San Antonio, Texas. It was John Hagee's church calling to see if the Isaacs are available to come to Cornerstone's annual concert called 'A Night To Honor Israel' next month. Governor Mike Huckabee is the main speaker, and they'd like for you all to sing a few songs right before he speaks."

"Jeff, this is amazing! Are we free?" I asked anxiously.

"Weeelll," he explained, "not really, but we'll check to see if the church you're already booked at will reschedule. Cornerstone will arrange for seven of you to fly down that Sunday morning on a private jet if we can work it out."

It seemed like a long shot. I had heard about this special night in San Antonio. In addition to their thousands of church attendees, Pastor Hagee invites hundreds of people whose focus is to honor and help Israeli communities. He flies representatives in from dozens of Israeli organizations, hosts them for an incredible weekend, and on this special evening, divides millions of dollars among them to support their local businesses and charities. His efforts reflect his heart of love for the Jewish nation and his desire to rebuild their trust in the Christian community. We just had to go! "Lord," I prayed, "please let this happen. They are my people. I want to be there so badly — to sing to these men and women who represent the elite group dedicated to rebuilding our Jewish homeland Israel. Please, Jesus. Amen."

A few hours passed by, and finally Jeff was calling again. "Good news, Lily! The church we had scheduled was more than happy to move the date, so it looks like you're going to San Antonio next month!"

The weeks flew by, and before we knew it, we were crammed into that little seven-seater jet flying to Israel, I mean Texas. The night was even more amazing than I could've ever dreamed. When it was our turn to sing, Pastor Matt Hagee introduced us and shared that my parents were Holocaust survivors. There we stood, on the beautiful red-carpeted Cornerstone Church stage looking out over 5,000 people waving blue and white Star of David flags, smiling, waiting for the next opportunity to show their Israeli honorees how much they were loved. I couldn't hold back the tears. I thought back over all the persecution the Jewish people had been through, everything my parents had been through. I pictured my mother's friend pulling her from the line going into the gas chamber. I envisioned my father getting hit over the head with a brick, his life hanging in the balance. I imagined what it must have been like for them to be liberated. Over to the right of the stage was a section of very Orthodox Jews, wearing their plain black clothing and their yarmulkas. I thought over the years of my life, how all I ever wanted to do was live on a kibbutz in Israel and dedicate my life to my new homeland. And there I was now, singing in front of an Orthodox Jewish audience. I know they didn't believe in Jesus as Messiah, but I could feel a kindredship because of all our ancestors had been through. It felt as if I had come full circle.

Both of the songs we performed that night, "Shalom My Home," one my daughters had written, and the popular Israeli Hebrew song "Hallelujah," were the same songs we'd performed for the Gaither Jerusalem taping a few years before. I felt that same satisfying feeling, like I was right in the middle of God's will for my life. Like the day I was born, God looked into the future and saw me standing here singing.

I thought about another Hebrew song I often sing in concert taken from Psalms 133:1 that says perfectly, "Behold, how good and how pleasant it is for brethren to dwell together in unity!" To dwell together in unity means all people. When we gather together in unity we're immoveable, we're unshakeable. There were people from all walks of life, different denominations, and different religions, people from across the world watching this particular service in honor of Israel. I was hoping that we would make a lasting impression on our Jewish audience and maybe more doors would open where we could perhaps perform in similar situations like this.

We've been able to minister worldwide, but mostly to non-Jewish people. So my dream has always been to sing to the Jewish people. My own people. Singing those songs that night was so heartwarming to me, and I cherished the opportunity. I meant every word I sang, and I'm sure the emotion in my voice showed how proud and humbled I was to be standing there. We felt that we'd been received well and were relieved by the warm round of applause when we finished. I still can't believe that day actually happened. I am thankful for our legacy. And my children felt it too — they grew up with such a great respect for their heritage, and I am so grateful for that. We were all in that moment together, and it was more special than words can describe. Standing on that stage, I saw myself as a little girl again — there on our little apartment fire escape, with the world as my audience, singing my heart out. It's a long way from the corner of Waring Avenue and Bronx Park East to San Antonio, Texas. I closed my eyes, and for one brief instant I could see how everything in my life had led me to that moment.

Thank you, God. It's been a beautiful journey. What's next?

HEARTFELT THANKS TO . . .

Shawn Smucker: Thank you for helping me write my story. Thanks for all the hours of writing and re-writing all the chapters again and again. You have such a gift, and you somehow were able to capture my voice in such a special way throughout this book. I appreciate you and the many hours you've spent working with me. You are truly an artist!

Rob Simbeck: Rob, what can I say! You were the first person to actually listen to me; the first writer to capture my feelings and my story. Without your diligent research, I wouldn't know so many facts about my history. Thank you for believing in me and my story. We have shared so many hours together digging deep inside my soul, exposing the secrets of my heart . . . it was therapeutic for me and I love and appreciate you.

Bill and Gloria Gaither: Both of you have been a gift to my entire family. Gloria, thank you for encouraging me to write my life's story. I respect your creative writing ability more than you could ever know!

You have been a protective driving force throughout this whole experience. You've guided me through this emotional process and never gave up on me! You are a blessing to me, and I praise God for putting you in my life! Bill, you have been a mentor to my family and me. We have learned so much from being around you, both personally and professionally. It's hard to believe that we've all worked together for over 20 years now! Here's praying we have another 20 years together. You will outrun us all!!! I respect and honor you for being the man you are. I'm grateful for you.

Barry Jennings, Paul Sizelove, Bill Carter, and all the folks at Gaither Music Group: Thank you for believing in our family. We are blessed to be a part of such a great organization!

Tim Dudley and New Leaf Publishing: Thank you for believing in and publishing this book. All of you have been amazing to work with. I'm looking forward to the years ahead of us.

Andy Andrews, Joe Bonsall (this book wouldn't be possible without you!), Larry Gatlin, Terry Bradshaw, Rod Parsley, Ricky Skaggs, and Sharon White: Thank you for taking time out of your hectic schedules to review and endorse my book. I am honored to call all of you my friends.

Ed and Jeff Harper and the Harper Agency: Thanks for taking care of us for over 22 years and booking us all over the world! We appreciate you and value your friendship. Jeff . . . Thanks for being my BFF!!

Mike Vaden and Vicki Bracey: Thank you for helping me and my family in business!! Your professional guidance has saved me many times, and you've certainly taken a big burden off of me. More than that, thanks for being part of our family.

Auntie Anne and Jonas Beiler: Thanks, dear friends, this book would not have come into fruition without you. I love you and appreciate you.

Bill and Debbie Becker: My Old Groupies! LOL. I love you both! You're FAMILY!

Dave and Nancy Rogers: For being a blessing to us and our ministry.

Rick and Connie Coleman: My PEEPS and BFFs. Love you so much!

Roxanne Ricks: My beautiful friend. You're a blessing to all who know you.

Lisa Hildreth: Thank you for being with us from the very beginning! You are so much a part of who we are. Thanks for all the hard work. You're the best!

Pam and Deon Unthank and Absolutely Gospel Music: for all the P&R work and your dedication to gospel music.

Dr. Fred and Deanna Hurst: I don't know what I'd do without you, Doc! My dear friend. Love you both.

Tamara Mariea and Internal Balance: Thanks for keeping us healthy! This clinic has changed our lives. Tamara, you are a godly woman and an inspiration to all who know you.

SPECIAL THANKS TO THESE FRIENDS AND COLLEAGUES WHO ARE PRICELESS TO ME . . .

All our former Isaacs musicians & staff
Zak Shumate, Mark Capps, & Valencia Houston — our busmates
All the artists we share the stage with
Pastors Rod & Joni Parsley and World Harvest Church
Pastors Delmus and Rose Bruce and the Stanfield Church of God
Pastors Maury and Gail Davis and Cornerstone Nashville Church
Pastors Joseph and Yolanda Morgan and Celebration of Life Church
Pastors John, Matt, & Diana Hagee & Cornerstone Church
Pastors Tommy & Tara Bates & Community Family Church
Stubbs Mill Road Pentecostal Church
Brenda & Woody Horn and family
Emory, Dorothy, & Denver Lamb
Tom & Janice Roach

Diane, Bobby, & Rachel Bowman
Dee & Mary Hill
Governor Mike Huckabee
Judy Nelon Group
Jimmy & Amanda Sites
Mitchell Mosley
Julia Roy & boys
Andie Glass
Les Butler & Salem Publishing
Lang & Linda Davis
June McTaggart & family
Johnnie Yeary
Celeste Winstead
Gina Brisco
Deana Surles Warren
Rhonda Thompson
Jeff & Karen Foster
Tim & Nancy Dillman
Joey Bowman
Tom and Nancy Waller
Mary Ella and Gene Phelps
Kathy and Steve Hannah
Sharon Gregg
Gerald Russell
Peggy and Karen Haymon
Mike and Dawn Johnson
Shelly Jones
Lee Steffen
Pete Fisher & the Grand Ole Opry Staff
Roberta Croteau
Roger and Betty Holmes
Martina McBride & Team Martina
Gloria Feldman
Maria Ramas
Ronnie Nahoum

Danny Blauschild
Martha and Eugene Boggs
Alice Coffman
Morrow Elementary and Little Miami HS staff
Dr. Alfred Kahn
Dr. Robert Hasle
Dr. Wayne & Judy Rhear
Tim & Judy Moxley
Dr. Steve & Judy Lynn
Michael Bianchi & World Vision
Bruce Phillips
Tom McGalliard
Edie, Krystal, Brian, & Sophie Lawing
Tim Surrett & family
Homecoming Magazine
Singing News Magazine
CCM Powersource Magazine
The Gospel Voice

MEET THE
AUTHOR

Connect with Lily online:

THEISAACS.COM

FACEBOOK.COM/**THEISAACS**

TWITTER.COM/**ISAACSMUSIC**

To invite Lily and/or The Isaacs

to be part of your next event contact:

The Harper Agency- jeff@harperagency.com

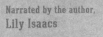